MAY 21

FIGHTING THE FIRST WAVE

Covid-19 is the biggest public health and economic disaster of our time. It has posed the same threat across the globe, yet countries have responded very differently and some have clearly fared much better than others. Peter Baldwin uncovers the reasons why in this definitive account of the global politics of pandemic. He shows that how nations responded depended above all on the political tools available – how firmly could the authorities order citizens' lives and how willingly would they be obeyed? In Asia, nations quarantined the infected and their contacts. In the Americas and Europe they shut down their economies, hoping to squelch the virus's spread. Others, above all Sweden, responded with a light touch, putting their faith in social consensus over coercion. Whether citizens would follow their leaders' requests and how soon they would tire of their demands were crucial to hopes of taming the pandemic.

Peter Baldwin is Professor of History at the University of California, Los Angeles and Global Distinguished Professor at New York University. His previous publications include *Disease and Democracy: The Industrialized World Faces AIDS, Contagion and the State in Europe, 1830–1930,* and *The Copyright Wars: Three Centuries of Trans-Atlantic Battle.* His latest book, *Command and Persuade: Crime, Law, and the State across History,* is forthcoming in the fall of 2021.

PETER BALDWIN

FIGHTING THE
FIRST WAVE

WHY THE CORONAVIRUS
WAS TACKLED SO DIFFERENTLY
ACROSS THE GLOBE

CAMBRIDGE
UNIVERSITY PRESS

CAMBRIDGE
UNIVERSITY PRESS

University Printing House, Cambridge CB2 8BS, United Kingdom

One Liberty Plaza, 20th Floor, New York, NY 10006, USA

477 Williamstown Road, Port Melbourne, VIC 3207, Australia

314–321, 3rd Floor, Plot 3, Splendor Forum, Jasola District Centre,
New Delhi – 110025, India

79 Anson Road, #06–04/06, Singapore 079906

Cambridge University Press is part of the University of Cambridge.

It furthers the University's mission by disseminating knowledge in the pursuit of
education, learning, and research at the highest international levels of excellence.

www.cambridge.org
Information on this title: www.cambridge.org/9781316518335
DOI: 10.1017/9781009000222

First published 2021

Printed in the United Kingdom by TJ Books Ltd, Padstow Cornwall

A catalogue record for this publication is available from the British Library.

ISBN 978-1-316-51833-5 Hardback

For Christopher and Ian,
frères et confrères

Contents

Introduction: One Threat, Many Responses . . . . *page* 1

1. Science, Politics, and History: Do They Explain the Variety of Approaches to Covid-19? 9

2. New Dogs, Old Tricks: Fighting Covid-19 with Ancient Preventive Tactics 31

3. The Politics of Prevention: How State and Citizen Interacted, Battling the Virus 53

4. What Was Done? Act One of the Pandemic 82

5. Why the Preventive Playing Field Was Not Level: Geography, Prosperity, Society 120

6. Where and Why Science Mattered: Traditional Chinese Medicine, Herd Immunity, Asymptomatic Carriers, Superspreading, and Masks 138

7. From State to Citizen: The Individualization of Public Health 170

8. Who Is Responsible for Our Health? How Prevention Was Enforced 197

9. Difficult Decisions in Hard Times: Trade-offs between Being Safe and Being Solvent 223

Conclusion: Public Health and Public Goods: The State
in a Post-pandemic World 259

Acknowledgments 289
Notes 291
Index 372

Introduction: One Threat, Many Responses

BY THE END OF 2020, THE CONTOURS OF THE CORONA-virus pandemic's first act were slowly coming into focus. Having passed through the first wave, some nations, such as South Korea, Singapore, New Zealand, China, and Australia, had arrived at the comparatively enviable position of battling second-order flare-ups. Many European nations, however, had let down their guard during the summer, permitting vacation travel. By the early fall, with the opening of schools, some of these spikes were turning into second waves – in Spain, Israel, France, and Britain. Though boosted by increased testing, infection rates were approaching and surpassing the first wave of the spring. Having dodged a bullet the first time around, Eastern Europe was now being hit hard.

The UK was scrambling to put out flare-ups in the northern provinces to sidestep another lockdown by clamping down in a more localized manner. New restrictions were imposed in October, hoping to avoid a "circuit breaker" lockdown. When that proved insufficient in November, non-essential businesses were closed again, people told to stay home. By September, Israel had closed down again to nip a second wave in the bud. Ireland shut down for six weeks starting in October, the Netherlands locked down partially. France and Germany imposed national shutdowns at the end of the year. A hundred thousand French police were mustered to squash New Year's celebrations. In the US, some states had tamed the first wave with firm measures, but in others, a premature opening up again, or little closure in the first place, had allowed cases and mortality to swell once more. Many states were reimposing lockdown. When schools and universities reopened in September, college towns became the new hot spots. By October, a third wave was rising, in effect the first or second waves in areas not yet hard hit.

Elsewhere, outside the developed world, the epidemic's first wave had finally peaked. Africa's infections had mercifully reached their preliminary highpoint in June, though by late December a second wave appeared to be swelling. By October, both South Asia and Latin America also seem to have gotten over their first humps.

Much about the virus remained unknown or still undetermined biologically and medically. How effective and enduring was the immune response? By November, the first vaccine successes were booked, sparking hope. Because we did not at first know if vaccines prevented transmission too, and not just symptoms, whether they would slow the pandemic's progress was unclear. The vaccinated might remain vectors. How quickly was the coronavirus mutating as it spread? Precisely how transmissible and how deadly was it? New, apparently more transmissible strains, sequenced at the end of 2020, were worrisome. But some aspects of the pandemic could now slowly be discerned. How had nations dealt with it as a public health emergency? Had some been more adept and more successful? Of course, subsequent waves and virus mutations may alter any judgments that can be leveled now. But, barring miscalculations and surprises, we can draw some tentative conclusions.

First, what we know about the virus medically has had surprisingly little influence on how nations decided to tackle the pandemic as a public health threat. The virus was rapidly identified and tests for it developed. That it spread primarily via respiratory droplets between humans, expelled as they coughed, sneezed, or breathed, quickly became apparent. Later, a more general aerosol transmission was identified as critical. Evident, too, and bad news, was its two-week incubation period, allowing it to spread undetected. Though crucial, it was less clear whether victims were infectious even before they developed, or without having had, symptoms. Still, there was sufficient information to plan the public health counterattack.

In the absence of a cure, vaccine, or other medical intervention, all the authorities could throw into the battle were the venerable contagious disease management techniques used against pandemics since Biblical times. These amounted to interrupting chains of transmission by identifying the sick and potentially infected, and isolating or otherwise rendering them harmless. Mercifully, the coronavirus seemed not to survive long outside its human hosts. That allowed objects, surfaces, and our everyday environment to be sterilized with fairly perfunctory disinfection using alcohol or soap.

The principle of breaking chains of transmission was simple, but not the practicalities of implementing it. Though the science of the disease was clear, what preventive measures followed on that was not. Most of the many and various tactics chosen had defensible scientific backing. Quite different preventive conclusions could legitimately flow from the same understanding of the disease. Politicians thus had a palette of preventive possibilities to choose from. While informed by science, their choices were far from determined by it.

Relations between politicians and the experts advising them were complicated. Those who spurned and mocked the scientific advice fared poorly. Presidents Donald Trump in the US and Jair Bolsonaro in Brazil presided over chaotic, almost deliberately inept, responses. Even Boris Johnson, another blustering populist, though less malevolent, paid a price for switching expert horses in midstream, flipping from a policy of moderate restriction to full-scale lockdown as the pandemic swept across the UK. Other leaders who followed what they understood as the scientific advice often did better, but not invariably. Whether it made sense to follow the experts depended on what they were counseling. Scientific advisors across the world delivered a far from unanimous message, pointing in many directions.

Sweden is a country we follow in detail because the unexpectedness of its response brought it to international attention. Its experts delivered unorthodox recommendations, advising the country's leaders to strike out on an uncharted course of only moderate clampdown against the epidemic. But when it came time to pay the political price, as Sweden's mortality rates rocketed past those of its Nordic peers, it was naturally the politicians who were called to account. At that point at the latest, it must have occurred to them that experts advise, but ultimately politicians decide.

That brings us to a second conclusion. Even though the threat was global and knowledge of the coronavirus was rapidly disseminated and shared, the preventive response was multifold. Faced with a common threat, the world's 200-odd countries implemented the principles of interrupting transmission each in their own manner. Keeping apart the ill and the well could be accomplished in many ways – from driving the sick out of the community at one extreme to having the well hide themselves away, *Decameron*-style, until it was safe to come out again. The coronavirus quickly spread to all the world's nations, except for a few Pacific island states. Even North Korea, which had long denied any cases, finally confessed to one in late July. Not every country set a clear course. Belarus dithered, Nicaragua sat on its hands. But most chose among one of three quite divergent strategies.

1. A targeted quarantine strategy tested the possibly ill, traced their contacts, and isolated both groups, thus sparing the bulk of the population further impositions. Hard-struck areas were cut off from their surroundings.
2. A hands-off mitigation strategy, in turn, let the epidemic spread through the population but slowed its progress by partial measures to interrupt transmission – social distancing and forbidding large assemblies, for example. The aim was to have the pandemic spread slowly so as not to overwhelm the health system, yet fast enough to arrive at broad herd immunity so that some semblance of normality could be re-achieved while waiting for a vaccine.
3. Finally, a suppression strategy recognized that for most nations, it was too late for targeted quarantine and too dangerous to flirt with herd immunity. Instead, it accepted the economic devastation of a wholesale lockdown, excepting a few crucial institutions and occupations.

That leads to a third concern: explaining the diversity of the global response to the pandemic. Given a common threat and a unified scientific understanding of the virus, why did the world react so variously? It is tempting to imagine that politics is the answer. Authoritarian nations, like China, could impose drastic measures without qualms about overriding individual liberties. Democracies, in contrast, could not act without ensuring majority buy-in. The tools available to each therefore likely varied dramatically. Despite the plausibility of this logic, nations' political identities seem, in fact, to have had only a passing relationship to the approach they chose or their success in tackling the pandemic. Autocracies and democracies could be found following each of the three strategies outlined above.

But politics were still pertinent. Responding to a pandemic is a quintessentially political dilemma. In the zero-sum situation where no medical solution allows an escape, some unfortunates must pay the price for sparing the majority. Barring recklessness or malice, few people are at fault for becoming infected by a transmissible disease that spreads through innocent interactions. Nature strikes us with Olympian impartiality. And yet, however unfair, the infected must be restricted, their activities curtailed so that others do not suffer similar fates. The sick must be isolated, along with their contacts, who can be numerous and may even be unaware of having been exposed to risk. Covid-19 is carried by many asymptomatic spreaders. People who seem healthy and are unconscious of the threat they nonetheless pose to others must also be rendered harmless.

Who was to be subject to which precautions were crucial decisions politicians faced. Many citizens – the number rapidly increasing as the pandemic steamrollered ahead – had to be brought under epidemiological control. Should they be quarantined? If so, could they stay at home or should they be removed to camps or infirmaries? If at home, whom could they interact with and what were they permitted to do? What could be demanded of those who were not infected? That they interrupt their lives, ceased work and schooling, stayed at home, did not go out, wore protective clothing, broke off relations with their social circles? When tracing their contacts, which secrets could legitimately be pried from them? If a treatment eventually emerged, could it be mandated? With a vaccine developed, could citizens be forced to submit? Could the authorities enter homes unbidden if required for prevention? Could they disinfect and, in the process, destroy property? These are examples of the normally inconceivable requirements that leaders suddenly had to impose on their followers. How much force could they use against those who resisted? What penalties could they inflict on the recalcitrant?

In epidemic times, individual and state stand antagonistically counterposed. The government acts for the public good in the most immediate sense – saving people from illness and possibly death by dealing with the infected. It has no choice but to violate the rights that ordinarily protect citizens from the full unleashing of its power. And like a lynch mob baying for blood, most of us, who still hope to remain among the spared majority, agree. Epidemics highlight the social contract's fine print. Any of us can find ourselves – for reasons we have no control over and in no sense deserve – considered a threat to others and forced to undergo what it takes to cease being a menace.

In a pandemic, the relationship between individuals and the state boils down to its essence. In every nation, the authorities have arrogated themselves emergency powers giving them very free rein in epidemics. In Germany, to take just one example, the contagious disease law permits far-ranging violations of civil rights, including, at the extreme, the state's authority to undertake medical tests short of those requiring anesthesia on blood or organ donors who prove to be contagiously ill. But every nation, however liberal and attentive to civil rights, has the power – that it considers entirely justified – to lock up those who threaten to spread disease. And in dozens of other ways, authorities can violate rights of movement, work, residence, and privacy.

Against states that were rendered quasi-omnipotent in the face of an epidemic emergency, citizens could consent or resist. Whether they complied depended on how much they trusted their authorities. Both sides of this relationship were on display during the pandemic. Some countries, such as Sweden and the UK, feared asking too much of their citizens. Populist leaders with hardscrabble followers, like Trump and Bolsonaro, expressly refused to enforce a lockdown that they judged them unable to comply with. But on the whole, the acquiescence on display was remarkable. By the late spring of 2020, a third of the world's population was effectively in house arrest. That would have been impossible without extensive buy-in from citizens who understood that the alternative was worse.

But how much slack did citizens cut their leaders? In some political systems, like authoritarian China, politicians could demand more and enforce stricter measures than elsewhere. But even democratic leaders had marshaled impressive powers. And ultimately, given the scale of action required by a global pandemic, sheer coercion was impossible anywhere, consensus was crucial.

Moreover, many of the behaviors demanded were ones that were best implemented voluntarily and required agreement. Yes, a government could forcibly isolate the sick if it was willing to build the facilities and expend the political capital needed to remove them there. And with enough police on the street, it could perhaps break up crowds violating distancing regulations and shut establishments that had remained open. But on the whole, asking people to self-isolate and keep their distance from others, not to mention washing hands at regular intervals and wearing masks, called for behaviors better accomplished when everyone understood their necessity and complied under their own steam.

The fundamental logic of abiding by the law is that it spares the compliant from further impositions. Assuming that the behavior demanded seems reasonable, citizens are freed of outside force insofar as they obey on their own. Freedom means being our own jailers. The state could force us to knuckle under, but everyone wins if we meet legitimate demands halfway and do not require enforcement. Law-abidingness is freedom from statutory imposition. That logic came out starkly during the pandemic. Friction was reduced where the state and citizens agreed on the measures required. Nations that were forced to compel the necessary conduct had to expend more resources and energy accomplishing the same tasks that elsewhere were undertaken willingly.

Where citizens thought they were getting a good deal, compliance remained high. But as the epidemic dragged on, and in those nations where leaders proved incapable of fulfilling their end of the bargain by assuring security and order, the social fabric frayed. Competence and compliance were closely connected. Where the state delivered, it continued to be trusted.

Those nations that initially seem to have been most successful were neither the authoritarian ones where the government could impose what needed to be done nor the democratic ones with broad buy-in from citizens. They were the ones with the ability to quickly choose a preventive course of action, imposing it effectively and consistently, with clear results delivered in return for sacrifices demanded. Largely independent of their specific political ideology, the most successful nations had the competence to make quick and effective decisions and the administrative capacity to carry them out. However, all the while, all countries had to manage the expectations, anxieties, and consent of their afflicted populations. Whether autocratic or democratic, no nation could address a problem that threatened every human on the planet without managing public opinion one way or the other.

CHAPTER 1

Science, Politics, and History

Do They Explain the Variety of Approaches to Covid-19?

WITH THE CORONAVIRUS, THE WORLD FACED A common problem. Yet it responded in many different ways. Why? That is the fundamental question the response to the epidemic has posed thus far. The scientific understanding of the disease might have varied, thus prompting diverse approaches to combating it. With some exceptions, addressed in Chapter 6, that has not been true. Despite a common etiological understanding of the virus and its spread, nations marshaled different preventive strategies. What about politics, then? Likely, democracies and autocracies would have approached it differently, on account of their being more or less able to enforce the painful measures to beat back a pandemic in the absence at first of any medical solution. Pandemics certainly posed a fundamentally political issue, requiring zero-sum trade-offs between potentially infected citizens whose convenience and economic well-being had to be sacrificed to spare others. Here too, obvious answers fail us. Nations' political complexions and the preventive strategies they applied did not line up in any evident correlations.

Carl von Clausewitz, the early-nineteenth-century Prussian general and philosopher, is best known for his aphorism that war is the continuation of politics by other means. War, in other words, is but another implement in the politician's toolbox – extreme, but sometimes necessary. A similar continuum connects politics and disease prevention. How we seek to spare ourselves the ravages of pandemics reflects the assumptions baked into our political culture and the systems that govern us. Pandemics are first-order political events. They differ from other threats, natural or human, in posing an immediate faceoff between the community's obligation to safeguard itself and individual citizens' claims not to be sacrificed in the process. In pandemics, citizen and community confront each other head-on. As members, each of us gains from measures to protect our community; as individuals, we may well end up being sacrificed for the common good.

This primordially political situation is itself likely to be colored by the structure of governance in question. How do different political systems handle pandemics? Do some cope better? Autocracies can command their subjects, exacting more obedience and sacrifices than liberal democracies. But, conversely, consensus and buy-in enhance a system's ability to act. Citizens of democratically legitimated regimes may agree to modify their daily routines, accepting sacrifices for the public good. They may be willing to submit to acts that would otherwise be hard to require or compel.

Montesquieu, the eighteenth-century political philosopher, thought that only despotic governments required severe punishments. In republics (he included monarchies too), citizens were impelled to behave as much by honor, virtue, and fear of disapproval as by force.[1] Subjects had to be coerced, but citizens motivated themselves to obey. The nature of law in representative systems also encouraged citizens to obey voluntarily. In republics, laws emerged from decisions that, ultimately, citizens themselves took. By following them, they conformed to what they had mandated their representatives to pass. Breaking the law therefore approximated the self-inflicted harm that Kant and Hegel discussed: thieves whose own right to property was undermined by their refusal to respect that of others, for example.[2] Legitimate law was self-imposed and obeying it was self-will.[3]

Yet, ultimately, even the most despotic regime relies on some consensus. Without a policeman standing behind each subject, people cannot be forced to do what they categorically reject.

Even Hitler and Stalin had to consider dissenting opinions. The Nazi euthanasia campaign against the disabled and mentally handicapped was called off after resistance, especially from the Catholic Church.[4] Protests in today's China may not portend the regime's downfall, nor even push it in more democratic directions, but they still require it to abide by informal rules acceptable to its citizens, not merely thrust demands on them.[5]

Authorities can punish people for disobeying – fining, jailing, or even executing them. Fines and prison are indirect techniques of compulsion. Someone willing to put up with them may decide to pay the price of disobedience. Fines can accumulate to the point where they cause bankruptcy, but that is their outer limit – as is a life sentence in jail. Indeed, the spectacle of multiple and concurrent life sentences highlights the inability of mere prison sometimes to render justice.

It is much more difficult to compel specific behaviors. Threatened with execution for his belief about planetary movements, Galileo saved himself by mouthing assent to heliocentrism, but it seems unlikely he changed his mind.[6] Where vaccination is mandatory, as in most developed nations, citizens have been subjected to the needle by force. Today, such direct methods have fallen out of use. Schools can refuse to enroll antivaccinators' children, and governments may perhaps fine or even jail the parents. Beyond that, they rarely go.

Even states willing to use force have only limited means of compelling behavior. They can directly deduct back taxes or unpaid child support and alimony from bank accounts or paychecks. Property can be encumbered with liens or repossessed to meet obligations. Police can confiscate drivers' licenses on the spot, putting those who continue on their way even more directly at odds with the law. Schools can be desegregated by semi-military force, clubs forced to admit women on pain of forfeiting their liquor licenses. The draft is obligatory, but a young man who refused it would be jailed or fined, not forcibly enlisted.[7] In theory, a conscientious objector could be compelled to serve in the military, but – other than setting an example for others – what would be the point? Deserters are often shot, which undermines the goal of mustering forces to defend the homeland in the first place, except by discouraging emulation. Compulsory labor is notoriously inefficient. No one makes an effort on chain gangs. Slacking and shirking are how subjects resist and undermine compulsion. Working-to-rule is the trade unionist version.

Emergencies and other states of exception raise the degree of intervention citizens will tolerate.[8] Cynics have argued that capitalism waltzes from one disaster to the next, deliberately exploiting crises to firm up its grip.[9] But even then, the state has not been issued a political blank check. The most autocratic regimes also rely on at least tacit cooperation from their subjects.

Democracies suffer from efficiency envy. They may have broad backing and stable support. But having to keep majorities onboard requires compromise, log-rolling, and trade-offs. That leads to short-term thinking and appeals to the lowest common denominator that undermine decisive action. Mussolini's on-time trains spurred admiration and envy in the 1920s.[10] China's ability to make massive infrastructure investments without the pork-barrel negotiations required in democracies and to pursue distant strategic goals without continually jollying public opinion along is today a source of wonderment to Western observers. Wanting to build a huge dam, the Chinese have the resources and the political clout to remove the peasants whose homes stand in the way.[11] Such considerations are amplified in emergencies. The nuts and bolts of democracy are little conducive to swift or incisive decision-making: consensus, checks and balances, due process, and voting. In emergencies, democratic procedures must paradoxically be temporarily sidestepped in order to preserve democracy.[12]

What are the implications as different political regimes face pandemics? Which systems have best been able to get their subjects to toe the preventive line? The Chinese government – seeking to paper over initial stumbles – trumpeted its successes with a global publicity campaign.[13] The nation's leader had decisively indicated the way. Its medical personnel had made countless sacrifices, building a Great Wall against the virus. And 1.4 billion Chinese themselves, with faith in the party, had – resilient and united – plunged into battle against the epidemic.[14] The Saudis, too, congratulated themselves on decisive, early interventions that contrasted their allegedly flexible, humanitarian approach both with the bumbling of next-door Iran and with the hesitations of European leadership.[15]

Or does consensual buy-in expand the state's repertoire of tactics and the leverage needed to guide its citizens' conduct? Does a free flow of information give more transparent nations a leg up? Standardizing for wealth, one study suggested that democracies have suffered lower mortality rates than non-democracies in pandemics over the past half-century. They also managed to reduce overall mobility, thus cutting transmission, during the coronavirus epidemic.[16] Among democracies, the ones led by women seem to have done exceptionally well.[17]

For the first half of 2020, the West admired the Asian nations that appeared better prepared and able to deal with the coronavirus. The West was simply not ready to tackle the epidemic with the speed and purpose seen in China, the WHO reported back in March.[18] But these effective nations ran a political gamut from autocratic China through technocratic Singapore to democratic South Korea and Taiwan. So factors beyond politics must also have been in play. These countries had also recently suffered epidemics – SARS and avian flu – and therefore sported an infrastructure of prevention poised to be remobilized. And possibly – despite their political differences – they shared cultural commonalities lacking in the West that enhanced their citizens' willingness to subordinate their interests to the social good.

A THOUSAND FLOWERS BLOOMING

How do we explain the gamut of reactions to a comprehensively global problem? Given a common dilemma, one might have expected a cohesive array of responses. In fact, how the world's nations dealt with Covid-19 spanned the spectrum: from precise testing, tracing, and isolating the ill and their contacts, through broad-gauge lockdowns of most citizens and economic sectors, to a moderate encouraging of social distancing and closing some institutions, and – finally – sometimes nothing much at all.

A politically polymorphous array of nations followed each of these various preventive strategies. Little unites them. The targeted quarantiners included China, Taiwan, South Korea, and Singapore, as well as New Zealand and Australia. Broad shutdowns were the tactic in Italy, France, Spain, eventually the UK, and most US states, and also in India. A hands-off approach was followed in the "ostrich alliance," nations led by strong leaders with their heads in the sand, Nicaragua, Belarus, Turkmenistan, and Brazil.[19] Yet irreproachably democratic countries were among them too – Iceland, the Netherlands, Uruguay, arguably Japan, and – most unexpectedly – Sweden.[20] Within the US, some states resisted lockdown strategies: both Dakotas, Iowa, Nebraska, Arkansas, among others.[21]

What strategy a nation took could not have been predicted by the nature of its political system. Nor did the world's surprisingly diverse preventive tactics seem to be determined in any straightforward sense by epidemiology. The science of the coronavirus was uniform the globe over. Indeed, as one of the epidemic's few silver linings, science's dissection of the virus underscored the noblest aspects of globalization. Scientific cooperation was immediate, prolific, and worldwide. An astounding amount of scientific information on the coronavirus poured forth almost instantly.

Pandemics had sparked an eruption of discovery before. When the cholera first struck Western Europe in 1832, thousands of books and articles appeared within the year. One contemporary diagnosed a "bibliocholera," a disease he considered as acutely contagious as its subject.[22] Today, economists gently mock the ferocious citation densities of the first generation of research, spreading as it traveled with the internet's speed and a transmissibility far surpassing that of the disease itself.[23] But the results spoke for themselves. Two decades ago, the SARS virus took several months to decode; the coronavirus required just weeks.

In earlier pandemics, information had been hamstered away for eventual publication in prestigious scientific journals, locked behind paywalls from all but well-heeled university and other institutional subscribers. The standard process of peer review delayed publication to ensure quality. For research on Ebola and Zika, even publications that had also been preprinted appeared in their official versions on average only three months later – a painful delay in epidemic times.[24] In the interim, however, preprint dissemination had become common. Like physics, mathematics, and computer science, some academic fields had long been issuing their most significant publications as preprints.[25] Peer review then arrived afterward, as early versions were commented on and revised or withdrawn. Biology and medicine now used the epidemic to take a step towards normalizing preprint publication for their fields. About half of the early work on Covid-19 appeared in this way.[26]

Epidemiological knowledge was now posted on the web, permitting efficient and timely use.[27] Preprint sites hosted data and research results almost immediately.[28] The downside – as for any not-yet-peer-reviewed information – was that wheat mingled with chaff. Several notable studies had to be retracted.[29] Preprint sites therefore began to extend screening beyond rudimentary issues like plagiarism to guard against other problems. Did articles advance misleading and possibly conspiratorial theories (similarities between HIV and SARS-CoV-2) or information that might harm the public health, such as unwarranted claims for cures?[30] And scientists proposed a rapid review system for preprints – in effect a turbocharging of the old system.[31]

Disputes over Covid-19's etiology were not an issue. In previous epidemics, plain ignorance and then differences of understanding had hampered preventive action. For cholera's first half-century, there was no agreed-upon etiology. Many considered it contagious, much like the plague. Others thought it a filth disease, caused by insalubrious surroundings. Depending on what seemed accurate, to prevent it meant either breaking chains of transmission or cleaning up urban decay. Only when Robert Koch identified the cholera vibrio in 1884 was the precise cause known. Even then, different approaches continued, all equally justified by appeals to the new knowledge – either cleaning up urban filth to hamper the spread of the vibrio or breaking chains of contact for the same purpose. Decades after Koch's discovery, German law courts were still hearing evidence whether diseases like typhoid were spread purely by microorganisms or whether contaminated soil too was a necessary precondition.[32]

Even as late as the 1980s, during the AIDS epidemic, disagreements framed in scientific terms had undermined unified responses to the disease. Science overwhelmingly agreed that the HIV was its cause. Yet disconcertingly many observers remained convinced that AIDS was generated not exclusively by a microorganism, but also by lifestyle or environmental factors. That spoke to the moralization that invariably accompanies diseases that are both sexually transmitted and associated with habits unlike most citizens'. How was it possible – so ran this logic – that an illness that especially afflicted homosexuals, drug users, and the promiscuous did not somehow stem from their conduct? Even prominent scientists signed on to such reasoning, discounting the HIV as the sole cause, as did some political leaders, most notably Thabo Mbeki, then president of South Africa.[33] Even gays succumbed to such reasoning in the years before the HIV emerged as the cause. The accouterments of anal fisting – Crisco, to lubricate, and amyl nitrate, to relax the sphincter – were considered possible causes, as was semen itself.[34]

Covid-19 suffered less epistemological static. Misinformation abounded, of course. Much was patent nonsense – the idea that the virus spread thanks to 5G networks.[35] Folk medicine offered useless treatments, which threatened to be harmful mainly if believers trusted them alone, ignoring the medical authorities.

"Immunity boosting" became a selling point even as experts cautioned that – if even possible – it would lead to inflammations and autoimmune diseases.[36] For the worried-well-off, Central Europe's weird and wondrous spa culture served up high-priced nostrums. Eating slowly, chewing properly and salivating, avoiding raw food in the evenings – all served to strengthen the immune system and prevent Covid-19, the quack Professor Doktors at Vivamayr in the Austrian Alps assured their clients.[37]

Some political leaders, too, decided to throw their weight behind pet cures of little use. Iran's supreme leader touted herbal remedies, as did Andry Rajoelina, president of Madagascar. Alpha Condé, president of Guinea, recommended hot water and inhalation of menthol, Mike Sonko, Nairobi's governor, Hennessy cognac.[38] Notoriously, President Trump extolled the alleged virtues of two anti-malarial drugs, hydroxychloroquine and chloroquine. He had been tipped off to them via a post by Tesla-manufacturer and Mars-enthusiast Elon Musk.[39] Brazil's president, Bolsonaro, jumped on the bandwagon too. French president Macron dignified Didier Raoult, an off-piste French clinician whose research had pointed to the supposed benefits of hydroxychloroquine, with a presidential visit to Marseilles.[40] The Japanese prime minister, Shinzo Abe, was not to be outdone with a campaign for avigan, an anti-viral with potentially severe side effects and an effectiveness for Covid-19 that has yet to be demonstrated.[41] From under every upended rock, cranks swarmed forth, as apparently they must whenever illness is the topic.[42] Most knotty, as we will see later, were the antivaxxers, who broached the threat that, even with a vaccine, they would shirk herd immunity.

But most other advice on the coronavirus at least posed no immediate dangers. The worried were counseled to drink water frequently, for example, thus washing the virus from the throat into the stomach where supposedly it did no harm.[43] Indonesians, who usually prize pale skin, began sunbathing en masse, hoping that sunlight killed the virus.[44] Later, when the virus really started to gnaw, sadder stories emerged – Bolivians consuming bleach in the absence of much else to turn to, Peruvians harming themselves with a cornucopia of homemade nostrums.[45]

More discouraging were the religious leaders whose claims that faith alone was sufficient protection deluded their followers into letting down their guard while crowding together. Tanzania's president kept his nation open, claiming that prayer was adequate protection.[46] So did Burundi's as well as Indonesia's health minister.[47] Mass religious ceremonies and pilgrimages turned into transmission hotspots in South Korea, Pakistan, and Iran.[48] Several American megachurches continued to hold services, and Jerry Falwell's Liberty University remained open for business.[49] California pastors insisted that churches be exempted from lockdown as essential businesses and vowed to hold in-person services for Pentecost Sunday in May.[50] Eventually allowed to reopen, when cases flared up again in July, churches were forbidden their most dangerous practice – singing.[51]

FROM KNOWLEDGE TO ACTION: DOES SCIENCE GUIDE POLITICS?

Except for some quackery, and what we deal with in Chapter 6, the etiological understanding of Covid-19 was largely uniform across the globe. A unified etiology did not, however, produce a consistent approach to prevention. But that did not prevent politicians from claiming a grounding in science. Regardless of their tactics, leaders insisted that they rested on the best available knowledge and that, as politicians, they were but the experts' handmaidens. That was nonsense. Whether invoking expertise or hiding behind it, and even – as Trump did occasionally – dismissing it altogether, politicians picked and chose among the possibilities science held out. Nor were they above pressuring the scientists to arrive at more palatable conclusions. US public health authorities partially authorized hydroxychloroquine and convalescent plasma after pressure from the White House.[52] We return to this issue when considering vaccines.

"Experts ought to be on tap, and not on top," said the Irish writer George William Russell. In Britain, rival groups of experts vied for the politicians' attention. The felicitously acronymed SAGE (Scientific Advisory Group for Emergencies) were the official advisors.[53] The Independent SAGE was formed to advocate instead for a firmer shutdown and a test-and-trace strategy.[54] About the etiology of Covid-19, there was little dispute. About preventive conclusions to draw, plenty. Experts disagreed among themselves, giving politicians cover for various approaches.[55] All nations setting out in their divergent directions were fully armed with what they considered a scientific imprimatur.

The Swedes claimed that their unusually relaxed approach was the outcome of allowing public health experts to make the decisions, untainted by political expediency.[56] Other nations, including their neighbors Denmark and Norway, were, they claimed, in thrall to populist ideology. But in Sweden, professionalism reigned supreme.[57] The choice in Norway and Denmark to lock down had been a political, not epidemiological, determination, the chief Swedish epidemiologist, Anders Tegnell, declared.[58] If only things had been that simple. In fact, Swedish experts disagreed among themselves, as elsewhere.[59] But one faction, the laissez-fairists, was in the saddle. Despite their credentials, once the epidemiologists began acting as the face of government policy, they ceased being experts to become hired guns. An epidemiologist in power is a politician, just as much as someone who may once have been an actor or a soldier.

Government by technocracy, rule by expertise, is nothing new or unusual. Some parts of modern states are meant to be officially neutral, not politicized in their day-to-day running. The judiciary and central banks are the usual examples.[60] Sometimes this has been generalized, with entire cabinets becoming technocracies. Epistocracy is a mode of governing that shifts politically unpalatable decisions to leaders who – pretending to act apolitically – make decisions that the public can accept as motivated by neutral expertise. But nations following this path usually did so only in emergencies and – had it even been possible – rarely sought to make a permanent transition to rule-by-expertise.

During the interwar years, governments of individuals, not representing a majority coalition, had been established to take hard decisions, like cutting unemployment benefits. Chancellor Heinrich Brüning's unparliamentary cabinets during the Weimar Republic's dying days had been necessary in the absence of viable majorities.[61] More recently, Italy and Greece had resorted to technocratic cabinets faced with their debt crises in 2011.[62] Such emergency, stop-gap ministries were not the usual company kept by a nation like Sweden as it claimed to be guided only by expertise.

Normally, politicians and experts play different roles. Experts offer advice, politicians take or leave it, making decisions informed not just by technical knowledge, but by its broader consequences. Just as librarians are happiest when all the books are unlent and securely in place on the shelves, so epidemiologists, if they stay in character, favor the safest approach – total lockdowns or other means of preventing all transmission. The minute they begin considering other issues – the collateral harm of postponing other medical treatments during a shutdown, the economic impact of mass quarantine – or more generally start weighing the consequences of different actions against each other, they are no longer acting strictly as epidemiologists.

Experts, who are often civil servants, are not punished at the ballot box for their choices. The ultimate responsibility for overall decision-making must rest with politicians. To leave decision-making to the experts is for politicians to abdicate their role. And to blame the experts for supplying misleading information, as some politicians tried, effectively suggested that the political leaders were slavishly following their advisors and not doing their job.[63] Those politicians who disparaged the experts could, of course, not then hope to hide behind their skirts when things went sour. They stood naked and exposed. But those who had claimed to be following the scientific advice, like British prime minister Boris Johnson, might later – some worried – try to set up the experts as fall guys.[64] Public Health England, the agency that had flubbed the national testing strategy, was forced to walk the plank in August.[65] Chickens were expected to roost eventually. France and Sweden announced government commissions of inquiry to investigate their coronavirus response.[66] One was called for in Spain, and one is likely in the UK too.[67] British civil servants expected to be hung out to dry.[68] Most embarassing among the officials' faux-pas, the Wayback Machine caught Dominic Cummings, Boris Johnson's Rasputin-lite special advisor, with his pants down, having retrofitted a tweet from 2019 with would-be prescient cautions about the pandemic soon to hit.[69]

The counterpart to Sweden's practice of letting experts lead the way came in neighboring Denmark. Outsiders often consider Scandinavia much of a muchness. But in this case, the Nordics headed in diametrically opposing directions. In early March, the Danish health authority, run by Søren Brostrøm, much like Tegnell in Sweden, advised the politicians against overly drastic measures, such as forbidding large assemblies or shutting stores and schools. The economic consequences, he argued, would be counterproductive.[70] In the middle of March, when the politicians closed the borders, Brostrøm was again opposed.[71]

The Social Democratic prime minister, Mette Frederiksen, however, feared the consequences of inaction. According to the existing contagious disease law, the politicians could act only on the health authorities' recommendations. To deal with the unexpected situation, where the experts were less cautious than the politicians, the prime minister introduced and passed emergency legislation on March 14 to alter the law. The government could now directly decree measures, no longer awaiting the health authorities' initiative. It used the opportunity to impose a drastic lockdown in the middle of March.[72] "It is better that we act today," she said at a press conference on March 11, "than regret ourselves tomorrow."[73] The new law gave the authorities temporary powers to compel inspection, isolation, vaccination, and treatment of victims, forbid public assemblies, blockade neighborhoods, shut down transportation, prohibit visits to hospitals and care homes, and close institutions.[74]

The British experience, in turn, demonstrated the perils of switching experts in midstream. Throughout January and February 2020, the newly elected Tory government, preoccupied by Brexit, did little. Only with the outbreak in the middle of February of cases and deaths in Iran and then especially Italy, where many Britons were vacationing during half-term holidays, did the gravity of the situation make an impression on the cabinet. On March 11, Italy announced a national lockdown, with Spain and France set to follow. Nonetheless, Boris Johnson resisted following suit. The nation was doing what it could to combat the epidemic, "based on the very latest scientific and medical advice," he announced on March 9.[75] On March 12, the government sought to justify its mitigation strategy of taking some measures but not locking down. Even as the rest of Europe was shutting down, the British authorities planned to allow the epidemic to sweep through the population to bring herd immunity.

Patrick Vallance, the chief scientific adviser, said that the government's aim was not to avoid everyone falling ill. "It's not possible to stop everyone getting it and it is also not desirable because you want some immunity in the population to protect ourselves in the future," he noted.[76] On the radio the following day, he elaborated: "Our aim is to try and reduce the peak, broaden the peak, not to suppress it completely. Also, because the vast majority of people get a mild illness, to build up some degree of herd immunity as well, so that more people are immune to this disease."[77] Though the government later denied that it had been pursuing herd immunity, the 500 scientists who now wrote to denounce this strategy certainly understood it as such.[78] The prime minister himself spelled out the consequences of pursuing herd immunity, warning that "many more families are going to lose loved ones before their time." Nonetheless, schools would not be closed, large gatherings would not be banned, and nor would contacts of the ill be traced and tested. Over-seventy-year-olds with grave medical conditions were merely cautioned against taking cruises, and those with coronavirus symptoms were advised to isolate themselves at home for a week.[79]

On March 13, SAGE told the authorities there was evidence to support implementing household isolation as soon as practically possible, in other words, to impose a suppression strategy. But it also noted that it was a "near certainty" that completely squelching a first wave would cause a second peak, once the initial efforts were relaxed.[80] The politicians were thus given a range of choices. Isolation should be done soonest. But suppression also meant deferring, not eliminating, much infection. Implicit in this warning was that the second peak would happen later, at a time when the government might have marshaled resources to tackle it.

A mitigation strategy meant isolating suspected cases at home, as well as the elderly and other vulnerable groups, but no further attempts to close down the economy, impose social distancing in public, or limit mobility. As it followed this approach, the British government claimed to be making decisions dictated by science. But that was a fig leaf. Politicians selected among the often conflicting recommendations issued by the experts. Three days later, the scientific advice firmed up, and so did the government's mind. Neil Ferguson's epidemiological team at Imperial College now forecast how many deaths mitigation would likely cause in the UK – a quarter of a million, more than half as many as had died in the Second World War. The health system would be overwhelmed at least eight-fold, especially intensive care units.[81]

These figures were no different from those of the government's own pandemic modeling committee two weeks earlier. But by this time, other nations had started shutting down, raising the stakes for those that refused such prudence. Analogous figures for France – 300,000 to half a million deaths – had been presented by the Imperial team to President Macron on March 12, four days before he imposed lockdown.[82] Having decreed shutdown on the

French as of March 16, Macron now threatened Johnson on the 20th with closing the border if the British did not follow suit.[83]

As they belatedly realized just how politically – not to mention morally – unacceptable deaths on this scale were, the Tories volte-faced. They pivoted in favor of a suppression strategy, now denying that herd immunity had ever been their aim.[84] On March 23, a new suppression strategy now imposed self-isolation on the entire population, except crucial occupations like health care, police, transport, and food and drug retail.[85] Schools and universities closed, along with theaters, restaurants, and sports arenas; gatherings were forbidden. Citizens were to stay at home except to shop for necessities and a daily hour of exercise. Suppression, the experts made clear, would need to continue until a vaccine was discovered and distributed.

The comparable calculations of likely Covid-19 deaths had similar political effects in the US.[86] Were merely a mitigation strategy to be imposed there, the Imperial College modeling predicted more than a million deaths, twice the casualties in the Second World War, and thirty times those of the Vietnam War. Simultaneously, the Trump administration responded through the CDC with a suppression plan, much like the new British strategy. Unlike the UK, which still imposed no travel restrictions, the Americans also closed the borders to foreigners from China and threatened to quarantine US nationals returning from Hubei province.[87]

In both instances, the politicians turned on a dime when new information revealed they were courting political disaster. Data did not determine politics, but updated input did encourage politicians to recalibrate their course. Elsewhere, too, politicians picked and chose among the advice they wanted to follow. In Sweden, public health authorities recommended against shutting secondary schools, but the government closed them for pupils over sixteen. In March, the Danish government asked its experts to develop a dire prognosis with high mortality projections even as the politicians were officially likening the Covid-19 epidemic to a severe flu.[88] Denmark locked down nonetheless.

In April, Denmark began unlocking only its kindergartens and primary schools against the experts' advice for a broader opening.[89] The Italian government ignored its experts' counsel that it target the north and instead shut down the entire nation.[90] When Iran loosened restrictions in April, requiring only what it called "smart distancing," it went against expert opinion.[91] Florida's medical examiner pleaded with politicians to shut beaches but was ignored.[92] The British government began relaxing lockdown in early June, earlier than its experts recommended.[93] As the authorities imposed quarantine on incoming travelers, they specifically did not ask the experts for advice, knowing they would disagree.[94] Plenty of German epidemiologists were willing to testify that their government's shutdown had been excessive.[95] Further examples could be multiplied at will.

WAITING FOR DR. FAUCI: EXPERTISE AND POLITICS

How politicians and experts interacted was ultimately the politicians' decision. Those nations that allowed experts the initiative did not uniformly do better than those where politicians kept the reins in hand. Even so, those who officially spurned expertise hardly benefited. The nations led by authoritarian populists suffered among the fastest-growing infection rates and the highest absolute and per capita mortalities.[96] Yet, there was no self-evident correlation between allowing expertise its due and mastering the epidemic. In early summer 2020, the US, UK, and Brazil suffered the highest absolute mortalities. In per capita terms, they were in the top fifteen. But so were Sweden, France, and the Netherlands, whose leaders had not disparaged experts.[97] Conversely, Belarus, whose leader had mocked the illness, continued to enjoy the low mortalities prevalent in Eastern Europe, below Norway and Finland.

Trump and Bolsonaro hogged the stage, showering their experts with disdain, and undermining their message with misleading remedies and nostrums. Bolsonaro lost two health ministers; one quit, the other he fired.[98] Boris Johnson typically appeared flanked by a rotating phalanx of top experts – Stephen Powis, Chris Whitty, Patrick Vallance, and Jenny Harries – but he did most of the talking. Spanish and Canadian leaders followed suit. In Austria, Japan, and New Zealand, the politicians also stayed front and center, with good to excellent results. President Macron of France listened to two scientific advisory committees, but followed Clemenceau's advice. Just as war was too important to leave to the military, so a pandemic could not be entrusted to the epidemiologists.[99]

In Greece and Ireland, in contrast, the experts were the public face of authority.[100] Sweden was in this respect, too, off the charts. The epidemiologists held court, becoming media darlings.[101] The prime minister, who fronted a weak and divided coalition government, preferred to hide behind the technocratic façade. Tegnell became a pop icon, with T-shirts and rival Facebook fan pages.[102] A cult of personality developed, with his daily press conferences assuming a ritual aura.[103] Victims tattooed his image.[104] In May, seven out of ten Swedes trusted him.[105] Journalists hailed him as incorporating the Swedish soul, which apparently meant forceful, blunt, unglamorous, and laconically humorous.[106]

It mattered less, however, whether experts or politicians stood at the front and more what they decided. The public often trusted the experts more than their leaders. Disparaging experts could come back to bite politicians who strayed off-piste. In May, Trump wanted to reopen schools. The teachers' unions pushed back, saying that only one official could reassure them that it was safe to go back. "I'm waiting for Dr. Fauci," Lily Eskelsen García, the National Education Association president, insisted. "I'm waiting not for a politician; I'm waiting for a medical, infectious-disease professional to say, 'Now we can do it, under these circumstances.'"[107]

HAND OF THE PAST

Neither political system nor science explained why nations differed so dramatically in fending off the pandemic. Nor did the heavy hand of the past matter much. Each country had accustomed ways it had dealt with previous epidemics. With the demise of the worst infectious diseases – plague, cholera, smallpox, yellow fever, polio – the legal infrastructure used against them had fallen into disuse. Public health regulations remained on the books just in case, giving the authorities tremendous powers of quarantine, notification, compulsory inspection and treatment, and contact tracing. These had long not been used, except during brief flare-ups of new epidemics, and then only rarely in the developed world.

During the SARS epidemic of the early 2000s, China had quarantined tens of thousands and threatened to execute anyone who deliberately spread disease. Singapore had passed travelers through thermal scanners to detect fevers. Vietnam imposed restrictions on travelers. The US authorities could hold suspected victims against their will. In New York, when they detained an arrival from Asia in 2009, he became one of the few non-tubercular persons in a quarter-century quarantined against his will.[108]

Acute contagious illnesses have declined. The disease landscape in the developed world is today dominated by chronic ailments and transmissible ones, where a purposive act – often sexual – is required to pass it on. As we will see, disease prevention has therefore now become a matter primarily of individual behavior, no longer state diktat. Potential victims are expected to make lifestyle adjustments to hold off chronic diseases and take their own precautions to prevent transmissible ones from spreading. But easily and involuntarily communicable diseases, like Covid-19, limited the scope for voluntary action. Victims were not in control of, and often not even aware of, their contagiousness. In contrast, sexually transmitted diseases, where purposive acts were the transmissive offenses, allowed voluntary restraint more scope.

The AIDS epidemic in the 1980s had been perhaps the last instance when first-world nations fought a toe-to-toe clash between preventive strategies relying either on the state's impositions or on voluntary behaviors adopted by citizens. Each country faced the epidemic with standard-issue contagious disease laws on the books. These typically allowed it to require notification of suspected cases, test those who appeared ill, oblige them to follow whatever medical regimen was available, trace their contacts, and detain those who refused to comply with directives intended to prevent transmissive behavior. The latter usually meant that they had to warn their sexual partners and not have sex except using barrier protection, mainly condoms.

Only a few nations put this inherited preventive armamentarium into effect. Cuba locked seropositives into sanatoria or camps, where the conditions were often so good that some people voluntarily sought infection to enter.[109] Mongolia followed a similar route, with compulsory screening and treatment and forcible abortions for seropositive pregnant women.[110] Some nations, like China, the Soviet Union, Iran, Iraq, Libya, and Saudi Arabia, screened resident aliens and returning nationals, and imposed travel restrictions on others.[111] In the developed world, however, such tactics were uncommon. Only a small and motley crew tried them, including some US states and Bavaria and Sweden.[112]

Most other countries pursued a more voluntarist strategy. The infected and those at risk of HIV infection were counseled on whatever medical treatments were available, advised to warn their contacts, and not have unprotected sex, but otherwise, they were left alone. AIDS was a disease fraught with stigma. Many of its victims were already persecuted before the epidemic and even more so afterward. The best way of persuading them not to hide and covertly transmit was to treat them gently, encouraging rather than commanding them. For perhaps the first time, a transmissible disease epidemic was dealt with by relying on individual behavior, voluntarily adopted and pursued, rather than on the state's ability to compel.

Similar disputes, as we will see, flared up with Covid-19 too. This time, however, the nature of the disease tilted things differently. Covid-19 was a contagious disease, spread involuntarily by sneezing, coughing, or even just breathing. Many, possibly half, of its victims had no symptoms, and hence were unable – with the best of intentions – even to know that they should take precautions to hinder transmission. Prevention therefore rested most securely on the authorities' judgment of how to act. Unlike sexually transmissible diseases, this was not an illness whose prevention could be left to the victims alone.

Moreover, the tactics used in the past against other epidemics did not seem to weigh heavily on any nation's public health authorities. Countries had changed direction radically in the past, as the government experimented with new tactics against novel diseases. Outside of Bavaria, Germany had defied its tradition of strict disease management when it grappled with AIDS, instead using voluntary methods, as had, to a lesser extent, the French.

With the coronavirus, a few nations did follow a course much like what they had previously pursued. The Netherlands had long been consistently voluntarist and remained so now. The Bavarians had been notoriously oldfashioned in their approach to AIDS and adopted similarly interventionist tactics this time. But others offered a surprise, perhaps even to themselves. The UK, traditionally laissez-faire, set off in the expected direction. The Tory government plowed a predictable furrow when the prime minister claimed that the freedom-loving British would not tolerate an across-the-board shutdown. On the same day – March 3 – his scientific team advised the nation not to shake hands, the prime minister boasted of doing so in hospitals with coronavirus patients.[113] But in late March, fearing the consequences of such insouciance, the government swung around to enforce a strict lockdown. Italy, homeland of the quarantine, defied what may well have been just lazy national stereotyping to impose one of Europe's strictest shutdowns.

Sweden, in turn, astonished everyone, but for the opposite reason. Having been strictly quarantinist against cholera in the nineteenth century, vaccinationist for smallpox, and ferociously regulationist on syphilis and then AIDS, the nation decided to change its spots amid the worst epidemic of the century. No broad-gauged shutdown was required, its epidemiologists advised the government. That was a tactic for nations where citizens did not trust each other or the authorities. A few common-sense precautions were eventually imposed, such as shutting down counter service at restaurants, closing universities, and forbidding large gatherings. But other than advising people to maintain their distance in public, little was demanded, and cafes, restaurants, and many stores remained open.

We have, then, a perplexing situation where, faced with a common threat, nations across the globe laid on a smorgasbord of different preventive tactics. This variation was not caused by politics in any straightforward sense, nor by differential knowledge of the disease. Not even past policies poured the mold for current tactics. Before we can ponder why such multiplicity emerged, we must look at what nations undertook.

CHAPTER 2

New Dogs, Old Tricks

Fighting Covid-19 with Ancient Preventive Tactics

E VEN WITHOUT A CURE OR MEDICAL FORM OF PREVEN-
tion against Covid-19, such as a vaccine, the toolbox of
measures against contagious disease was not empty. History provided examples aplenty of tactics used to face similar epidemics
before, many now marshaled once again to interrupt chains of
transmission. If anything, the lack at first of modern medical
solutions meant that politicians had only the venerable tools
used for millennia to work with.

Epidemic disease is as old as settled farm civilizations, as are
attempts to deal with it. In the literal sense of forty days of isolation,
quarantine was first imposed against the plague in Venice in the
fifteenth century. But the basic idea of sequestering and sometimes cleansing the sick is far older. The Old Testament prescribed
both disinfection and isolation, as well as more general sanitation-
ist measures like hand washing. Dig latrines outside war camps and
cover up excrement, it admonished.[1] Leprosy was considered in
detail to ensure that only those actually suffering from it were
treated accordingly. Pronounced unclean, they underwent severe
consequences: banished from society, required to identify themselves, and forced to dwell alone, their infected clothing burnt.[2]
Bodily discharges were treated as infectious. Contact with them,
the ill people from whom they came, and their possessions were to
be avoided. Thorough washing was the solution.

The ill were considered infectious for seven days after their symptoms abated. Both men and women were treated as unclean for sexual reasons – women during and after menstruation, men because of their nocturnal emissions.[3] Whether the Old Testament's dietary prescriptions were primarily ritualistic and religious or also inspired by health concerns has been long debated.[4] If punctiliously followed, its strictures on sexual conduct would have hampered venereal disease's spread – no adultery, nor seducing virgins, no bestiality, nor homosexuality, no incest, and no prostitution. But was that just a happy side effect of being moral or its own independent aim?

The medical approach to contagious disease has advanced since Biblical times. Yet, even today, absent a cure or medical means of prevention like vaccination, the only available weapons to combat epidemics are disinfection or cleansing, killing the culprit pathogen, and interrupting its routes of transmission. Such techniques have changed little over the millennia. We call them non-pharmaceutical interventions in homage to the primary role now assumed by medical prevention and cure. But for the first 8,000 years of humans dealing with transmissible disease, until sometime in the 1950s when the balance tipped in favor of medicine, these were the only available defensive weapons. As for avian flu and other recent pandemics, the same centuries-old techniques now did duty again against the coronavirus.[5]

WHAT CAN BE DONE?

Contagious disease can be fought in many ways. At one extreme, a cure handles the matter inefficiently by tackling it post facto, detouring the infected and sick through doctors' offices and hospitals. Even with a safe and effective therapy, the epidemic wastes time and resources. The individual victim suffers, and society has to pay for the necessary medical infrastructure. If it does not provide the redundancy needed to simultaneously handle regular care, the population suffers even more as other illnesses are neglected during a pandemic.

As millions of embroidered samplers attest, prevention is better than cure. A vaccine, artificially stimulating immunity, sidesteps disease's ravages altogether, but it presupposes a durable immune response. Many diseases have yet to find their vaccine: AIDS, MERS, SARS, and Ebola. Other preventive techniques, such as condoms against venereal disease, are a form of microquarantine, isolating the person, or at least the relevant appendages, from infection. Used to block the thyroid from absorbing radioactivity, iodine plays a similar role in protecting from harm.

Bereft of either cure or medical prevention, the epidemic rips through the population if nothing is done. If health care is inadequate, or treatment makes no difference, mortality remains at a maximum. But if medical interventions are helpful and if hospitals are well-staffed and adequately equipped, mortality will decline even in the absence of an outright cure or immunity. Whisked off to a top London teaching hospital when ill, Boris Johnson had teams of nurses who stayed with him through the nights in intensive care, plying him with oxygen.[6] Trump emerged from the hospital, still feckless about precautions, having received the best possible care, including experimental therapies available to no one else.[7] Not everyone gets that treatment, but those who do benefit.

In the worst case, no immunity follows and new epidemic waves repeatedly collect their tribute. Or the pathogen mutates and sweeps back again, despite an immune response. A too virulent pathogen kills its hosts before it can propagate. That is the parasite's paradox: while living off others, it cannot be too greedy. Better, from the virus's point of view, to moderate its effects and find an accommodation. Regular flus and colds are the outcome of that development.

Absent effective medical interventions, the only tactic against contagious disease is to interrupt chains of transmission through isolation, quarantine, or other behavioral modifications. According to a Danish joke, the word for sleeping bag in Norwegian is

"kroppskondom," a whole-body condom. The closest approxima-
tion to that are the hazmat suits that were occasionally issued to
frontline medical workers.[8] In July, a Canadian company marketed
an updated version of something analogous.[9] Such protective gear,
worn habitually, would turn us into epidemiological monads, blocking transmission at the individual level. Thus equipped, we could
venture out, living our lives semi-normally, so long as we avoided
physical contact with others. An external physical sheath would
achieve the same as the immunity conferred internally by a vaccine.

This was the logic heralded by John Snow once he had identified the waterborne conveyance of cholera in the London epidemic of 1853. Now everyone could avoid the disease by
foregoing infected water. "Every man may be his own quarantine
officer and go about during an epidemic among the sick almost as
if no epidemic were present."[10] That worked better for transmission by water than by air. But that, too, was solvable. At around the
time of Snow's pronouncement, a Scottish chemist named John
Stenhouse produced a charcoal respirator. With it, a "healthy
man ... may without fear visit the chambers of the sick, and the
sanitary officer without risk venture into the most dangerous
receptacles of filth."[11]

Such individual isolation was, in effect, the tactic that public
health has gradually come to decree for sexually transmitted diseases – a personally prophylactic approach requiring each person
to shield themselves from harm. The AIDS epidemic revealed the
frailties of traditional disease prevention. The inherited tactics had
been to test those most likely to be infected and trace and test their
contacts. Meanwhile, the infected were forbidden from having sex,
or at least were allowed to do so only while using precautions.
Followed to the letter, this would have solved the problem by
interrupting transmission.

But in the developed world, AIDS introduced a wrinkle by
primarily afflicting gays, ethnic minorities, and other marginalized
groups. Targeting them threatened to drive the already dispos-
sessed even further into the shadows. Inspecting sex workers for

syphilis during the nineteenth century had been one thing. For them, regulation could be justified as the price of doing business. Yet, attempting to impose similar techniques on gays and other sexual and ethnic minorities was likely to backfire. The disease might go underground, spreading even further. And in any case, gays had, in the meantime, mobilized to become a politically adroit pressure group, determined not to be made scapegoats.

A new solution was needed, partly to avoid discrimination, and partly because the old techniques had been hard to enforce. In any case, they required extensive surveillance. Universal safe sex was the answer, the insistence on fidelity or at least sexual parsimoniousness and – if not that – then universal use of condoms.[12] Condoms solved the problem (mishaps and slipshod usage excepted) at the cost of belatexing every sexual encounter for everyone. All were assumed to be potentially infectious and all were to share the burden of prevention. Only those who trusted their partners could shun barrier protection. No longer would only certain supposedly contagious groups be singled out. Prevention was universalized, democratized, and thereby de-stigmatized. Fortuitously, the same techniques also prevented not just AIDS, but all manner of sexually transmitted diseases.

Barring full-body condoms, or an equivalent method of individualized protection against infectious contact, all other solutions to epidemic diseases involve collective action to cut transmission. If the epidemic has not yet spread widely, it can be quarantined "in" or "out" – keeping the disease localized where it is or excluding it from still-healthy areas. Which of these tactics is most promising depends on how far the epidemic has spread. Quarantining out makes sense when the afflicted area or population is less than half the whole. If more, quarantining in may be preferable. The joke about an engineer, physicist, and mathematician seeking to construct the shortest fence around a flock of sheep grasps the logic. The engineer circles the sheep and throws up a fence around them. Having built a fence with an infinite diameter, the physicist shrinks it until it fits around the flock. Finally, the mathematician fences in his own person then defines himself as being outside. A real-life example of the mathematical approach came in the Siberian village of Shuluta, surrounded by trenches to prevent anyone from exiting once inhabitants became infected.[13]

Once an epidemic has taken hold throughout an area, territorial quarantine makes little sense. Instead, the ill and those who may be infected have to be isolated. With an accurate and quick test, identifying them is relatively straightforward. Without one, the evidently ill, those with symptoms, and their contacts are the targets. If the disease is carried and spread by the symptomless, too, as with Covid-19, matters become complicated. Silent carriers do not realize how they endanger others, and they cannot be detected without testing. Contact tracing is the means of finding the potentially infected but still asymptomatic carriers most efficiently. In the absence of a test, however, they have to be isolated until they develop symptoms or show that they are not infected by passing unscathed through the incubation period.

Like protective custody in jail, isolation can also be imposed on potentially vulnerable groups to spare them. Depending on administrative capacity, various approaches are available. A rudimentary way is what Bolsonaro, Brazil's president, called vertical isolation, quarantining everyone above a certain age.[14] The special hours that many countries instituted for the old to shop and visit parks were a variant on this. Turkey imposed this tactic more broadly, shutting in the old and the young, leaving everyone else free in their business.[15] Panama instituted a gendered version by allowing men and women to leave their homes on alternate days, with everyone at home on Sundays.[16]

With cheap and accurate testing, regular universal screening of entire populations becomes feasible, rather than aiming only at suspected contacts. How often depends on the incubation period. Those who turn out to be infected, and their contacts, can then be isolated. Universal screening requires vast numbers of tests. Targeted screening demands detailed information about people's movements, contacts, and behavior, raising privacy concerns. Both are complicated and costly to administer. Both require building a parallel quarantine universe to house and care for those needing isolation. But they have the great advantage of allowing targeting of the fewest people, doing the least damage to normality.

If neither targeted nor blanket screening is an option, that leaves only the bluntest and most destructive tool in the preventive armamentarium – universal quarantine or lockdown. If the authorities can identify neither – by symptoms and contact tracing – those most likely to be infected, nor – by testing – those sure to be ill, then that leaves only the choice of clamping down on everyone.

Besides imposing massively on daily freedoms and bringing much of the economy to a halt, asking all citizens to shelter in place raises practical issues – as it did in this pandemic. How did one define the groups that quarantined together? Who was to share epidemiological circumstances with whom? Families, roommates, dormitories, care homes – the groupings of modern society were linked by interdependencies: elderly parents visited in their retirement home or the granny flat above the garage; the roommate's boyfriend who lived elsewhere but often spent the night; the children who shuttled between divorced parents according to court-ordered custody schedules.[17] Not to mention conventional friendship and sociability. Such permeabilities undermined the hermetic sealing-off that prevention required.

However they were defined and enforced, who was to supply and maintain these self-isolated social groupings? Some fraction of the workforce, deemed crucial, would have to continue as usual in order to spare the rest. Food and pharmaceutical retail, transport, farming, logistics, health care, schooling, communication, policing: it turned out that much economic activity was on someone's list of key or core functions. Inexplicably, cargo sailors – without whom global logistics shut down – were not included. A quarter of a million of them languished at sea in June, having served out their contracts, while their replacements on land remained unemployed.[18] Meanwhile, 100,000 cruise ship personnel were stranded onboard, floating castaways with no country willing to receive them.[19]

Closing churches became a flashpoint where the lord's ministrations were considered crucial. Minnesota classified 78% of its labor force as essential.[20] Becoming acknowledged for their backbone role in feeding the nation, illegal aliens in California were suddenly issued letters from the Department of Homeland Security, attesting that they "were critical to the food supply chain."[21] But being crucial was not necessarily good news. Essential workers continued in their jobs at their accustomed pay, though now often exposed to more harm.

Meanwhile, their furloughed comrades got to stay at home. Some of them even made out better than normal. Workers in the US, especially the least paid, sometimes ended up with more in their wallets than while working thanks to generous new flat-rate unemployment benefits.[22] Conversely, in the UK, the stricter post-Brexit income qualifications for lower-skilled migrants taking effect in January 2021 meant that the care workers who were being hailed as heroes and classified as key workers in the winter of 2020 would likely soon be excluded from the country.[23]

Identifying workers able to work outside their homes raised further problems. If children were confined at home as schools closed, an entire cohort of parents was not available for work, however crucial their jobs. Nations where women remained housewives and those where several generations overlapped in households, with a broader array of childminding possibilities, might therefore prove more resilient, both practically and psychologically, than isolated nuclear two-earner families.

On the other hand, the fragility of modern economic and social interdependence was offset by novel communications technology. Lockdown would have been much more miserable in the analog era of expensive landlines and broadcast TV, not to mention radio and post. Ordering take-out by phone was doable, by mail, a disappointment. The internet made communicating with those outside the isolation bubble easy. Online learning may not have been as good as in the flesh, but it beat nothing. Netflix trumped the two or three broadcast TV channels most Europeans had to content themselves with as recently as the 1970s.

Much of the workforce avoided mustering up in person. White-collar employees, not to mention their bosses, discovered just how many tasks could be handled from home and how few meetings were crucial. Zoom usage increased twenty-fold in Britain.[24] And a significant class divide opened up between workers with no choice but to be physically present at the job and those who enjoyed the luxury of earning from home. The trope of dressing from the waist up became a standing joke, and pajama sales skyrocketed, including variants whose tops resembled office attire.[25] Even the Norwegian supreme court decided for pandemic casual, robes not required for virtual hearings.[26]

The universal lockdown that became the most widespread strategy in the West in early 2020 was economically destructive, but most nations lacked the administrative ability to pursue more targeted approaches. Either way, a rigorous quarantine, whether universal or targeted, could, in principle, have solved the problem. Had everyone been strictly isolated for the duration of the incubation period and the course of the illness, squelching all further transmission, in theory, the world would have been left in the same position as the day before patient zero was infected. Since the epidemic did not spread over the entire globe at the same instant, in practice, re-achieving that original null state would take as long as the disease's individual lifecycle plus the time the contagion required to spread into the last redoubt. Any territory that wished to reemerge in the meantime would have to forbid, or test and track, arrivals from still-infected places.

THE PROPHYLACTIC TOOLBOX

Universal lockdown was a drastic measure, imposed by states with no better solution to hand – either medical or some form of targeted quarantine that affected fewer people and damaged the economy less. As the authorities enforced such draconian impositions, they provoked the epidemic's primary flashpoints. Short of extravagant policing, the state has only limited abilities to implement such strictures directly. What other tools, then, were at its disposal?

Most obviously, the state legislates to forbid what it seeks to prevent and require what should happen. Drivers' licenses are mandatory, speeding banned; schooling is compulsory, truancy punished. Underaged sobriety is the law, so bars and liquor stores must require proof of age. Violators suffer fines or jail. Prison can both punish, in the sense of imposing a cost on culprits, and also incapacitate, preventing future forbidden acts. Sometimes the punishment itself incapacitates. Offenders are banished, or their living conditions are restricted. Political prisoners are exiled, pedophiles banned from residing near schools or playgrounds.

The state brandishes not just sticks, but also carrots, incentivizing desirable behavior. Prizes encourage learning and proficiency, scholarships promote literacy and knowledge. Consumers can be enticed to healthy eating by agricultural subsidies. Maternity leaves and child allowances promote fertility. Insurance discounts reward careful drivers. The Treasury is often as concerned with influencing behavior as raising money. Taxing married couples as a unit rewards families with only one working spouse by averaging income over two. Mortgage and property tax deductions promote homeownership. Sin taxes raise the cost of having illicit or unhealthy fun.

Finally, the state also socializes its citizens into correct conduct. Historically, molding behavior to community standards has been left to intermediary organizations – family, churches, schools, and voluntary organizations. But this task, too, has become ever more the state's. Rising nation-states in the nineteenth century sought an ethos to unite their members. Universal public schooling molded citizens, the draft, young men.[27]

Public health, too, has put such techniques to use. Vaccination has been compelled. In nineteenth-century England, officials removed children from their parents and subjected them to the needle.[28] Visiting Tanzania in 1931, Evelyn Waugh saw officials directly jabbing native travelers descending from the steamers.[29] The German contagious disease law allows authorities to violate bodily integrity to vaccinate, except for those with health or life at risk.[30] Zoning rules and building codes have improved living conditions, banishing most animals, requiring light and ventilation, and discouraging overcrowding. Food safety laws mandate requirements for slaughterhouses or restaurants – the temperature of refrigerators, cutting boards and utensils segregated by food groups, handwashing by employees after bathroom use, and the like. Violators risk being shut down.

Society and the state collaborate to encourage and sometimes require particular personal behaviors, which eventually are so generally socialized as to become second nature. Training our bladders and sphincters for relief only at certain intervals in specific places was the work of centuries. Goethe was surprised by the public defecation he observed while traveling in Italy during the 1780s. But the Spanish conquistadors in sixteenth-century Mexico remarked on the huts of reed or straw at the roadsides, built to allow excretion in private.[31] As recently as the 1950s, in agrarian societies, defecatory self-control was not crucial.[32] Today, India is campaigning for indoor toilets and discouraging outdoor defecation. Public urination laws – rarely needed for their intended purposes any longer – are instead used today to control vagrants and the homeless. Even so, the acceptability of toddlers relieving themselves in public still remains disputed.[33]

Now, human-style excretory restraint is being extended to our pets. In the 1990s, canine-less Berliners protested against dog owners' bad habits by leaving infants' soiled diapers on park lawns to deliver a taste of their own medicine. Today, walking a dog in most cities necessarily involves plastic bags. In South Korea, social media mobbed a woman who refused to clean up after her dog on the subway.[34]

We no longer spit in public, but that took long training, too. In the nineteenth century, spittle literally covered public spaces in the West. Once spitting became feared as spreading tuberculosis, the problem escalated from nuisance to threat. While municipal regulations outlawed the act, infrastructure was installed to permit safe execution of what was still regarded as a necessary biological function. Spittoons became ubiquitous.[35] During the Spanish flu epidemic in 1918, Philadelphia arrested those who spat in public, sixty in a single day.[36] China has undergone similar developments, mounting anti-spitting campaigns around the 2008 Olympics.[37] Indeed, this past echoed faintly when the mayor of Marcq-en-Barœul, a suburb of Lille in northern France, made spitting and uncovered sneezing punishable by fines in April 2020.[38] Today, we no longer regard spitting as an unavoidable reflexive behavior, like sneezing or coughing. Though we still salivate, we have learned no longer to spit.

Unlike spitting, sneezing and coughing are irrepressible but can be done in various ways. Unprotected sneezing and coughing is unpleasant and, in pandemics, dangerous. During the Spanish flu epidemic, New York City threatened open coughing or sneezing with fines of $500 – close to an average annual wage.[39] They were probably not levied often. But since these are involuntary behaviors, laws are not the best approach. Encouraging safe sneezing techniques – handkerchiefs, tissues, into elbows – is more effective.

The most useful tactics against transmissive behaviors vary, and much depends on the nature of the illness. Diseases whose transmission and vectors are amplified by insalubrious environmental conditions can be dealt with through zoning rules, urban planning, and civil engineering. The cholera vibrio was sidestepped by clean supplies of drinking water. Yellow fever diminished as mosquitos were prevented from breeding and stinging – by draining swamps, distributing bed nets, and releasing sterile mates. Keeping our distance from rodents and their fleas impeded the bubonic plague. Today, animals like prairie dogs and armadillos remain plague reservoirs, but we do not often meet them.[40]

Chronic, lifestyle diseases are least susceptible to statute and regulation. Diabetes, obesity, heart disease, and some cancers are partly caused by habits and behaviors, some of which are voluntary, others influenced by addiction. Getting patients to change lifestyles is often best tackled by some combination of regulation and socialization. Forbidding unwanted behaviors helps. Anti-smoking ordinances and taxing up the price of tobacco cuts use, as does constricting where and how we can consume alcohol.[41] Much debated is whether other drugs should be dealt with similarly, and not just through prohibitions. It is unlikely that a similar portfolio of measures would make inroads against obesity. A sugar tax, driving up the cost of sweet foods, combined with strict food labeling laws, has been successful in Latin America.[42] Banning large servings of soda, as Mayor Bloomberg tried in New York, was less so.

Habits are learned behavior, the healthy ones no less than the bad.[43] Society structures incentives and punishments, rewarding or clamping down on conduct and normalizing what might seem like individual decisions. With smoking advertised as glamorous, the adolescent finds resisting temptation hard. If rail-thin models are celebrated, girls may develop eating disorders as they emulate the unattainable.[44] Behavioral scientists have pondered the role of external incentives, like monetary payments, worrying whether such inducements undermine the internally motivated conduct that is both cheaper and psychologically more durable and desirable.[45]

Transmissible diseases require a purposive act to pass along, not just ordinary and unavoidable bodily activities like coughing, sneezing, or even just breathing. Many such illnesses are ones that we today consider sexually transmitted. But the very classification of some diseases as venereal is the outcome of major behavioral shifts. AIDS, for example, is not as such an STD. Sexual congress is only one means by which it is conveyed. Because it is transmitted via blood contact, it has also been passed through blood transfusions, especially among hemophiliacs, and among IV drug users sharing needles.

In the sixteenth and seventeenth centuries, syphilis was transmitted in the European countryside by intimate bodily contacts other than sex. Household utensils were shared, beds crowded, mothers licked away sties in children's eyes and snot from their runny noses, they prechewed infants' food and sucked crying baby boys' penises to calm them.[46] Syphilis transmitted by such daily interactions was known as insontium, of the innocent.[47] Passing the disease through chalices and other implements of eucharist in Christian churches also worried the nineteenth century.[48] AIDS, too, provoked similar anxieties.[49] Even today, non-venereal syphilis, spread mainly through direct contact with infectious skin lesions, is a common childhood ailment in some impoverished Middle Eastern, Asian, and African nations.[50]

So long as people's bodies came into contact in ways that today are largely banished, syphilis had routes other than the sexual to travel. Only when our changing behavioral norms made sex the sole form of bodily interaction to bring mucous membranes into proximity did syphilis become primarily sexually transmitted. Other diseases have also seen their routes of conveyance narrowed by our ever more punctilious habits. Leprosy spreads through extensive human-to-human contact, but not sex. It therefore began dying out with the spread of hygienic practices before specific treatments were available. Before vaccination eradicated it, polio had become transmitted in the West mainly mouth-to-mouth and no longer, as earlier, via contact through fecal matter.

Various preventive techniques have thus been tailored to different kinds of diseases. Not every weapon worked against each ailment. Yet, most every arrow in the quiver was tried against Covid-19. Some relied on the state's ability to compel, some on authority's attempts to persuade, others on each individual's responsibility for their actions. But before we see how that played out, a detour to the past is required.

DÉJÀ VU ALL OVER AGAIN: THE VENERABLE TECHNIQUES MUSTERED AGAINST COVID-19

Anyone who knows how past epidemics have been handled suffers a sense of déjà vu when following the Covid-19 discussions. The strategy of keeping human bodies apart is both rudimentary and unchanging.

Transmission between people was interrupted, and so were connections among nations and regions. Cutting off travel has long been the centerpiece of contagious disease prevention. Few attempts have rivaled the immense military barrier built by the Austrians in the early eighteenth century along the empire's southern border to keep out the plague: 1,000 kilometers long, it bested the intermittent US–Mexico border wall and rivaled the inner German demarcation line, though China's Great Wall still dwarfed it.[51] Things are less straightforward today. In the days of carriage, sail, and foot, the news of infection traveled slowly. But so did passengers, and there were fewer of them. Now people travel only marginally less rapidly than information, and everything has vastly multiplied. That has complicated matters. Even so, shutting down movement across borders and within nations was among the first measures against the coronavirus.

Travel out of Wuhan was cut in late January, but not until eleven million people had already left or passed through the prefecture during the first three weeks of the month.[52] The US shut its doors to foreign travelers from China in March and threatened to quarantine American citizens returning from Hubei.[53] The EU closed its borders for non-citizens in mid-March. Two island nations – New Zealand and Australia – made the most of their topographical advantages to shut down almost all entry and outgo. With some exceptions, travel restrictions focused on incoming foreigners rather than returning nationals, who naturally were equally likely to be infected.[54]

External quarantines were most common, but several nations imposed internal ones too against hard-hit regions – Hubei in China and Lombardy in Italy, among others. In Wuhan, high-speed trains simply sailed through the station without stopping, as they did later in Jilin.[55] Some US states, like Rhode Island, threatened to isolate newly arrived New Yorkers, and many others eventually imposed two-week self-isolation requirements on arrivals from elsewhere. In June, when some US states in the South and West suffered rising infection rates as they prematurely lifted restrictions, New York, New Jersey, and Connecticut once again imposed fourteen-day quarantines on arrivals.[56] By July, this had ballooned to thirty-one states.[57] Federal states in Germany imposed travel restrictions on each other, as did the Australian states.[58]

Pilgrims were a specialized subset of travelers of concern in the nineteenth century. The International Sanitary Conferences, held throughout the century to coordinate trans-border preventive measures, had been prompted by the dangers posed by Muslim pilgrims making Hajj and then returning to Europe or its colonies.[59] This time around, Iran shut down the holy city of Qom only in mid-March. In the meantime, it had become a hotbed of transmission among the Shia faithful. Rituals here involved kissing and licking the gates of the shrines.

In response to the threat from Iran in late February, Saudi Arabia shut down Umrah, the year-round pilgrimage, and access to Mecca and Medina.[60] The Hajj, scheduled to start in July, is in normal circumstances among humanity's largest gatherings, with over two million attendees. In June, it was radically scaled back to visitors only from the kingdom itself.[61] The Grand Magal was set to be held in October in Touba in Senegal, likely to attract as many as five million Sufi faithful.[62] Mercifully, the Kumbh Mela, a Hindu gathering, was not due again until 2025, when it would bring in 250 million people over 49 days, up to 50 million daily. And the Magh Mela, an annual event, had already passed in February, with up to 11 million assembling daily at the Ganges.[63]

We have mentioned the dangers of the eucharist and of churches that remained open. Many religious rituals involved kissing, touching, and sharing implements and symbols, putting faith and epidemiology in collision. A virtual eucharist was a contradiction in terms. Church services and religious ceremonies threatened to spread disease. Ultra-orthodox Jews in Israel (Bnei Brak), New York (Williamsburg), and Belgium (Antwerp) resisted calls to shun public ceremonies, provoking the authorities to shut them down.[64] Synagogues remained open in ultra-orthodox neighborhoods in Israel.[65] A Florida pastor was arrested for refusing to close his church.[66] In April, 100,000 followers defied lockdown to attend the funeral of Maulana Jubayer Ahmed Ansarin, a popular figure in a Bangladeshi Islamist party.[67] Brazilian churches remained open.

Many religious leaders, however, took the threat seriously. Religion went online. Virtual services were just a twist of technology, improving on other means of broadcasting the faith that had been in use for a century.[68] In most of Europe, churches were shut. In England, they were closed except for funerals and to provide social services.[69] Some Italian ones allowed individual prayer, but not services. Most US states shut churches, but a dozen did not, and in some, they were considered essential services.[70] Recalcitrants grabbed the headlines, but many of the faithful recognized the gravity of the situation and obeyed lockdown guidelines.[71] In Rwanda, congregants had to be registered and masked.[72] Holy water and singing came to an end in some churches.[73]

Saint Peter's was closed for Easter 2020, and the pope livestreamed. With individual confessions impossible, the church allowed bishops to offer group absolutions, with plenary indulgences for those who died unable to receive final rites.[74] Elsewhere, priests were less accommodating. When cholera raged in Russia in the 1830s, services had been held only in the open.[75] Tuscany, faced with cholera in 1835, introduced long spoons to avoid the perils of communion.[76] Now, such modifications met resistance. Ukrainian churches recommended disinfecting icons and crosses before kissing them or avoiding contact altogether. The Russians considered allowing worshippers to bring their own communion cups. But canceling services found little favor. Using common spoons to administer the sacraments had been a foundational cause of the schism between the Eastern and Western churches in the eleventh century. That was not about to change now.[77]

One enormous change this time around, compared with the past, was the unconcern with contagion via objects and, therefore, any fear of trade and commerce. Here, scientific advances imparted a distinct advantage. In the past, not knowing precisely what transmitted disease meant that both people and goods were equally suspect. Quarantining travelers in past centuries, even before the onset of mass tourism raised their numbers, was demanding enough. They had often sought to escape quarantine's inconvenience. So too today. Knowing they would be isolated, travelers to China dissembled about their symptoms.[78]

Goods, in contrast, had been a headache – especially before the era of standardized containers and consumer packaging. Staggering efforts had earlier been required to fumigate, disinfect, wash, cleanse, and air out luggage, ships, carriages, and later trains. Animals, too, whether as goods themselves or for draught purposes, underwent disinfection regimens and were often issued their own health certificates. Mail was punctured, fumigated, and soaked in disinfectant.[79]

Such worries have mainly vanished today. Global trade was not impeded and the only restriction of commerce came at the retail level for non-essential goods. People, however, remained worried about transmission via objects. Experts reassured them that it was unlikely and could, in any case, be diminished by simple precautions like hand washing or wiping down items with disinfectants.[80] The regimen of quarantine also became much simplified in light of better knowledge. Just as goods have today been spared the disinfecting purgation of an unidentified transmissive something, so too travelers, their clothing, and luggage no longer have to undergo the elaborate baths, washings, fumigations, and cleansings of the past.

BACK TO THE FUTURE

In the late nineteenth century, personal precautions against cholera were almost verbatim those now issued for coronavirus: do not touch your mouth or face, money is dirty and dangerous, paper napkins are preferable to cloth ones in restaurants. As today, detailed routines were earlier put in place to disinfect living quarters and the implements of daily life. Even the details of provisioning were similar. Germans were warned in 1831 against crowding in food shops.[81] Now, stores demarcated safe spacing of customers, allowing in only a few at a time. Personnel kept their distance when delivering online shopping parcels. In Wuhan, with housing complexes sealed, officials did the food shopping and distribution.[82] Apartment residents lowered buckets from windows to receive their purchases.[83]

Cash once again came to seem infectious and dirty. Oddly enough, as of March, the amount of currency circulating in the economy rose sharply even as shopping shifted online. Criminals, like drug dealers, may have found it harder to wash their illicit gains through the usual channels – restaurants and the like – and were sitting on a growing mountain of money.[84] The rest of us, however, shunned cash. The US government quarantined dollar bills repatriated from China.[85] Contactless credit cards were preferred to the oldfashioned variety requiring pin codes or – worse – signatures, and smartphone payments at a distance were now desirable. In Rwanda, congregants were forbidden to make church offerings in cash.[86]

German retailers are notoriously too miserly to absorb or pass on credit card fees and often charge a markup if customers insist on using one. When Chancellor Merkel went shopping during the epidemic, she sent a signal to her compatriots by paying by card – a behavior still so rare in Germany that the news noted it prominently.[87] That was the modern version of the elaborate procedures implemented in the 1830s to provision quarantined households. Would-be customers shouted their requests out a window. They deposited money on a table outside, the coins in a bowl of vinegar. Helpers retrieved the money with a long spoon, fumigating any bills, and then reenacted the whole procedure in reverse when returning with the goods.[88]

As today, social intercourse was restricted during the early cholera epidemics. People were advised to avoid crowds and limit their contacts with others. They were to wash their hands and face frequently, hold in their breath while near the ill, and wear protective outer garments of waxed cloth. Elaborate disinfections used chlorine, chloride of lime, or vinegar. Crowding in cafes and taverns was forbidden in Poland. Schools, inns, bars, and shops were closed in Austria and theaters in Berlin.[89]

Something as seemingly straightforward as determining the household unit to be isolated together was as fraught with misunderstanding then as now. Who were to be epidemiological buddies, likely sharing the same fate? Asian nations often isolated the ill and the potentially infected in infirmaries, sidestepping the issue altogether. But most Western countries instead imposed the non-hospitalized ill on their families, exposing them to infection.

Official guidelines now explained in detail how to prevent further transmission within households. The British government advised the infected to live in separate rooms with openable windows. Avoid sharing bathrooms, but clean them regularly if that is not possible, with the infected using the facilities last in a rota, and vulnerable people first, with separate towels for everyone.[90] The Germans recommended paper over cloth towels.[91] In potentially infected households, the British authorities counseled, do not share beds and use kitchens, one person at a time, with dishes washed and dried with separate towels, clothes not shaken out before being cleaned.[92]

German authorities suggested that the infected and others in the same household eat sequentially.[93] Here too, we had been before. European families self-isolating in Turkey against the plague in the early nineteenth century had walled off not only the domestic unit but each member within it. Meals were taken together, but with each person sitting at a distance from others, their personal space chalked out on the floor and onto the table.[94]

In the coronavirus epidemic, whom one could see and meet was strictly limited. In Britain, the unit of isolation was the household. Besides those contacts, one was allowed to provision – but not socialize with – the vulnerable – defined as those over seventy, younger with underlying health problems, and pregnant women. Taking exercise outside with one person from another household was also permitted as of mid-May.[95] Later, one could meet up to six others outside. Piers Morgan, a British broadcast personality, jokingly suggested using the official exemption for cleaners to hire his sons, thereby seeing them despite self-isolating.[96] The Germans required the isolated to list all their contacts and record their temperature and symptoms, reporting to the health authorities daily.[97]

The quarantines imposed on travelers and sometimes entire localities in the nineteenth century also had their counterparts today. The targeted quarantining undertaken in Asia had also been foreshadowed. As the cholera stayed on, an unwelcome repeat visitor in Europe during the latter half of the nineteenth century, experience allowed a more nuanced approach to prevention, even before Koch's discovery in 1884 of its actual cause.

As cholera returned continuously, its contagiousness became clear, imported to Europe from elsewhere, and then circulating within it. But it became equally evident that oldfashioned quarantines, interrupting all travel and communication, did as much harm as good. That was especially true with the massive increase of trade and travel over the century as steamships and trains spurred mobility. Instead, public health authorities, especially in Britain, began to impose targeted interruptions of transmission chains in a neo-quarantinist technique that foreshadowed similar measures taken now in Asia.

Rather than detaining all travelers from infected countries, the authorities now inspected them to identify the symptomatic. Likely carriers were isolated, sometimes against their will, and if need be in special institutions. The seemingly healthy were allowed to continue, leaving their contact details, and were then visited for several subsequent days by inspectors to see if they had fallen ill. Ships and trains were disinfected and then allowed to pass, rather than detaining them. The presence of disease had to be notified to the authorities, allowing them to isolate the ill. The infected who failed to turn themselves in were fined.[98] Like today, every imaginable public surface was repeatedly disinfected.

These new, more precisely targeted measures promised to sidestep the Hobson's choice between free trade and travel, on the one hand, and epidemiological security, on the other. Preventing epidemics did not now require shutting down all trade or society as a whole. Such neo-quarantinism was the ancestor of the test, trace, and isolate tactics now used in various Asian nations. Today, they have been gussied up with new technologies: fever-testing guns, internet-enabled thermometers, GPS- or Bluetooth-based tracking software on phones. But the fundamental premises were a century and a half old: impose isolation on only those most likely to be carriers.

CHAPTER 3

The Politics of Prevention

How State and Citizen Interacted, Battling the Virus

I N ANY SIMPLE SENSE, POLITICS COULD NOT HAVE CAUSED the remarkable variety of approaches to the pandemic. Both democracies and autocracies imposed targeted quarantining, whether Taiwan, South Korea, or China. The nations that prided themselves on the least draconian measures spanned the political spectrum, from democratic Sweden to dictatorial Belarus and populist Brazil. Those imposing lockdowns – the arguably least free approach – were among the most democratic: Italy, Spain, Denmark, the UK, and blue states within the US.

Conservatives in the US and Brazil protested against too stringent a lockdown and advocated a quick opening up once it was in place. So did the extreme right in Germany. But in Sweden, keeping things open had been the official policy of a Social Democratic coalition government. Here, it was the extreme rightwing, nativist Sweden Democrats who first publicly demanded a lockdown.[1] Similarly, the Dutch policy of pursuing a mitigation strategy, instead of full lockdown, was attacked by the two extreme rightwing parties, asking for more drastic restrictions.[2] In Italy, the president of hard-hit Lombardy, Attilio Fontana, member of the rightwing Northern League, battled Rome to get even stricter measures.[3] And in Bavaria, Markus Söder, head of the Christian Social Union, had been the first to close schools and issue stay-at-home orders.[4]

Meanwhile, the mitigation strategy of only moderate restrictions – aiming for herd immunity – that Sweden had become the poster boy for was damned from the far left as fascistic.[5] All the while, Nicaragua's leftwing Sandinista government extolled Sweden's hands-off approach as the inspiration for its own lack of interventions.[6] And "fascist" was the designation proferred for California's lockdown by Elon Musk, trans-planetary entrepreneur and compulsive tweeter, when his Tesla factory was shuttered.[7] In other words, a very mixed political salad. Politics do not seem to have explained in any straightforward sense the specific strategies employed against the pandemic.

But, of course, beyond the simple dichotomies between autocracies and democracies, politics did play a role in determining this diversity of approaches. Preventing and handling epidemics is a consummately political act, involving daily decisions that juggle the community's well-being against individuals' rights. Who took such decisions and on whose behalf? Whose interests were paramount, and were they measured in the short term or framed against a longer duration? Such were the relevant questions. Autocratic nations enjoyed certain advantages in being able to strong-arm subjects and enforce measures. Democratic ones were sometimes less decisive, often bordering on the chaotic, but could count on broad buy-in from citizens for efforts that met with popular approval.

First, a proviso. We are not holding a prophylactic beauty pageant. Implicit comparisons among nations' preventive strategies have been conducted all along. The US has been humiliated in contrast to China, its main rival, and even to its kid sister, the EU. Brazil has been written off as a no-go zone. Pakistan outperformed India. Both Britain and France have smarted at being bested by the Germans. Sweden's preening in the international limelight became puzzlement as its Sonderweg slammed into a dead end. But which tactics worked best will not be known for years.

As things looked ever worse in Sweden, the authorities pleaded for a long-term accounting – in four or five years. Only then, they insisted, would a final tally be possible.[8] Future historians will have to be the ultimate bookkeepers, totting up not just the infection or mortality rates as they stand now, in mid-epidemic, but in the long run. Suppression strategies may have squelched the first wave of the epidemic, but with most people remaining uninfected and therefore uninmmune, subsequent waves may prove even more harmful. Suppression may have to be reimposed repeatedly. With vaccines now successful, at least we will have been spared living with such measures on and off again for years.

Lockdowns also brought with them collateral damage that will have to be factored in. Missed schooling will dampen earnings and growth for decades to come.[9] Harms caused by self-isolation are part of the overall morbidity landscape: mental health disturbances, domestic violence and abuse, depression and suicide, hunger, or even – in developing nations – starvation.[10] So too are the indirect consequences of focusing the health care system on Covid-19. Children forewent vaccinations and school meals, sick people screenings and consultations. Illnesses that, as a result, were neither prevented nor cured will be added to the overall morbidity over the coming years. So will skipped or postponed procedures for already existing illnesses.

One of self-isolation's most striking outcomes was how the throughput of emergency rooms – heart attacks, strokes, detached retinas, and the like – evaporated. These absent patients may have added to immediate mortality rates, thereby lessening those of the future. Or they may have pushed ahead a wave of postponed mortality that will inevitably come crashing down. Like the proverbial pig moving through a python, the cohort of illness left untreated during the first wave of the epidemic will eventually demand attention. Or – an unlikely but not impossible suggestion – the developed world may discover that, having over-medicalized itself, these missed treatments did not have as severe an effect as feared.[11] Certain conditions that normally would have prompted emergency room visits, for example, may instead have been handled directly in one of the now-under-utilized non-Covid wards or via ambulatory care.[12]

Most such missed procedures would have been skipped anyway without lockdown, as the pandemic swamped the waiting rooms and hospitals with coronavirus patients. Not lockdown, but the epidemic, was ultimately responsible for most collateral damage. And lockdowns had beneficial effects too. Fewer of some violent crimes, auto crashes, and industrial accidents counterbalanced increased mortality from other causes, though some violent crime rates went up. Reported rapes in Delhi were down by 83%.[13] In South Africa, trauma cases admitted to hospitals plummeted by two-thirds after alcohol sales were banned.[14]

On the other hand, on May 31, Chicago registered eighteen killings, its highest single-day tally since 1961.[15] New York City saw twice the gun violence in this June than the same time last year.[16] Yet, on the whole, crime seemed to be down.[17] Less domestic violence was reported, but with perpetrators and victims locked together in isolation, it may still have occurred.[18] While other European nations moved abuse victims to hotels, in the UK, domestic homicides tripled in March.[19] Venereal disease transmission was also ambiguous. The immediately detected rates plunged for obvious reasons. But as contact tracers and testers who would normally have been working on STDs were redeployed against Covid-19, rates may have been rising without anyone knowing it.[20]

Which of the various tactics on offer – targeted quarantine, mitigation, or suppression – will prove to have saved most lives will not be known until such contradictory tendencies are summed. We have no idea yet what the ultimate conclusions will be. Worse, nor do the decision-makers, confident in the choices they have been taking. They have been acting, blind to the ultimate consequences of their selection, working on hunches and gut instincts, advised but not determined by expertise, and desperate to juggle the contradictory interests of health, prosperity, order, and normality. The retrospective Olympian view awaits future historians. Here we can do no more than try to understand the myopic fumblings of politicians faced with a foreseeable, yet unprecedented disaster of epic proportions.

DECISIVENESS: STATES CAN DO WHAT THEY NEED TO

First things first. No political system, regardless of complexion, found itself unable to take decisions in the face of dire circumstances. The Chinese authorities naturally had the legal instruments required to impose the measures they wanted. "We are not China," French President Macron assured his colleagues.[21] He meant that as something positive. Yet, even with their concern for individual liberties, the democracies too could override them as needed. Emergency measures, down to and including martial law, were arrows in the quiver of most systems. The South Koreans and the Taiwanese, for example, had in place provisions dating from the MERS and SARS epidemics, allowing them to override privacy protection laws for contact tracing.[22] By May 2020, half the world's governments had declared some form of state of emergency.[23]

Emergency powers invoked in the face of pandemics were not limitless, however. International law and conventions restricted the powers that sovereign nations could assume even faced with dire threats. The UN's International Covenant on Civil and Political Rights, taking effect in 1976, required that derogations from civil rights follow an official declaration of emergency and be necessary and proportionate. Nations were required to inform the international community through the UN Secretary General that they intended to sidestep certain rights.[24]

The Siracusa Principles, formulated in 1985 to flesh out the derogation provisions in the International Covenant, specifically aimed to impede misuse of emergencies to curb civil rights. They set out criteria to determine the lawfulness of emergency restrictions. Even when confronted with dire circumstances, public health measures had to meet specific conditions. They should rest on the law, be based on scientific evidence, aim for legitimate goals, be strictly necessary, be the least intrusive and restrictive means available, not be arbitrary or discriminatory, be limited in duration, and be subject to review.[25]

Faced with the pandemic, the UN urged its members not to use emergency powers needlessly or in a discriminatory manner, returning to normality as soon as feasible.[26] Responsible above all to their citizens, national governments unsurprisingly took steps they considered necessary, though mostly compliant with their international commitments. In February, early in the pandemic, well-meaning policy experts protested that travel restrictions aimed at the Chinese violated trans-national understandings.[27]

Such objections were brushed aside as nations rushed to slam their doors over the next several months. Nor was it clear whether such interventions were prohibited. The International Health Regulations, which were invoked against the restrictions on the Chinese just mentioned, specified that travelers should be treated with respect for their dignity, rights, and freedoms. Nonetheless, it also allowed countries to subject them to vaccinations or the least intrusive and invasive of other medical examinations necessary to determine whether they posed a public health threat.[28]

In late March, the Hungarian parliament granted its president powers to rule by decree, without time limit.[29] Sparking protests from other EU states, that was replaced in June by a declaration of medical crisis until mid-December, allowing the government to issue decrees but not change laws or restrict fundamental rights.[30] To lesser and more justifiable degrees, most other states limited their citizens' normal civil rights, whether to free movement and assembly or schooling. As of early April, some nations had registered derogations with the UN to the International Covenant on Civil and Political Rights: Guatemala, Latvia, Armenia, Peru, Ecuador, Estonia, and Romania. Among the democracies that had imposed some of the most drastic measures, such as Italy, France, and Spain, none had registered derogations. China was not a signatory.[31]

When the British government passed emergency legislation allowing police to patrol parks and roads, impose social distancing, forbid assemblies, and shut stores and restaurants, it did not thereby become more forceful or arrogate to itself new powers.[32] Like most democratic governments, it did, however, reveal the true scope of its authority by invoking emergency measures that lay latent in its mandate. American political culture is often portrayed as distrustful of centralized state authority. But in crises, like depressions and world wars, the executive has almost invariably succeeded in gathering the necessary weapons and then relinquishing them – though never entirely – once the occasion had passed.[33]

In the US, broadly defined police powers gave the national, state, and local authorities extensive abilities to intervene against epidemic disease. The constitution's commerce clause provided the federal government's authority. The Secretary of Health's powers were specified in code and delegated to the Centers for Disease Control and Prevention (CDC) in Atlanta.[34] The CDC was empowered to inspect and detain travelers from abroad and among the individual federal states if they were suspected disease carriers. Potentially infected travelers to the US received quarantine notices explaining that they would be housed with adequate food and water and subject to medical tests, though asked for consent first. Their circumstances could, on request, be reviewed during the fourteen-day quarantine. Penalties were fines or up to a year in jail.[35]

State and tribal law extended such powers to the local level.[36] Texas law, for example, gave the governor and health commissioner authority to impose restrictions on "an individual, animal, place, or object, as appropriate," including quarantining, detaining, isolating, and vaccinating.[37] Mayors could invoke disaster powers, as they did in Austin.[38] New Mexico appealed to its Riot Control Act in late April 2020, posting soldiers on highways to close access to Gallup, the nearest hub to the Navajo reservation, which was suffering an epidemic outbreak.[39]

Apart from emergency measures, most nations also had to hand wide-ranging epidemic disease laws. The Germans were praised for taming the epidemic by testing and tracing, while not imposing a full lockdown. In pursuit of that more limited goal, they commanded a formidable preventive machinery, anchored at both national and state level.[40] The German contagious disease law allowed them to restrict most fundamental civil rights in the fight against disease, whether bodily integrity, freedom of movement and assembly, mail secrecy, inviolability of the home, or the right to work.[41] Compared with the threat of deadly disease or the health system being overwhelmed, temporarily limiting civil rights was eminently defensible, as one local ordinance put it.[42]

The infected had to report changes of address, allow the health authorities entry to their homes, and provide all information requested. Blood or organ donors who suffered from contagious disease could be compelled to undergo any tests demanded of them, except ones requiring invasive procedures or anesthesia.[43] Contaminated objects could be destroyed. Patients who failed to follow instructions on isolating could be confined to an institution. Prison and fines were threatened.[44] Establishments could be shut, assemblies forbidden, freedom of movement restricted.[45]

Only the Swedes, seeking to explain their unusually lax approach to the coronavirus, claimed to have their hands tied by the legal system. Central government agencies, like the public health authorities, were independent entities entrusted with implementing in detail policies that had been adopted in broad strokes by the government. The domain experts were expected to take the day-to-day decisions.[46] Though setting the overall direction, ministers did not interfere with on-the-ground choices made by government agencies. Ministerial rule, interfering with the agencies, was not permitted.[47] Nor did the Swedish basic law allow the government on its own to declare a state of emergency during peacetime, thus preventing it from mandating lockdowns and other restrictive measures familiar from elsewhere in Europe.[48]

This was a curious approach. Being bereft of emergency powers is rarely considered an advantage worth boasting of by a sovereign power. Why give up a useful tool? And if the concern is with civil rights, why not hem in and specify the proper use of such mandates, rather than shun them altogether? Whether emergency powers are properly used is better answered by questions like, who can declare emergencies? Are such capabilities only temporary, and are the procedures for ending or prolonging them clear? Is the institution exercising such powers the same as the one declaring the emergency? Is judicial review provided for?[49]

In fact, the Swedish authorities' claim that they were constitutionally prevented from clamping down on citizens was something of a red herring. Their basic laws gave parliament considerable powers to act in emergencies.[50] Retrospective taxation was permitted in severe economic crises (ch. 2, §10). Property could be expropriated for reasons of public health (§15). The right to work could be limited if required by the public interest (§17). Authorities could restrict fundamental civil liberties, including freedom of movement, for purposes acceptable in a democratic society (§21). Freedom of expression and information could be limited to maintain public order and security, provisioning of the public, and generally for whatever pressing reasons the government had (§23). Freedom of assembly could cease if public order and security required it, expressly including preventing epidemics (§25).

Parliament could slow the passage of laws to take advantage of such powers, but a majority could impose them immediately (§22). Whatever the motives behind Sweden's constitutional silence on emergency powers, parliament had, in fact, retrospectively validated emergency actions taken by governments several times during the 1970s, faced with terrorist hostage situations.[51] The general principle was anticipatory statutorification, that Swedish law should anticipate emergencies and legislate for them. Hence, parliament passed a law on April 18, giving the government immediate powers to order anti-epidemic measures, short of a general curfew.[52]

Beyond the constitution, the contagious disease law also gave the authorities the necessary leeway to act decisively, even without declaring an emergency. Its provisions are detailed below.[53] The public order law gave the police powers to forbid assemblies to prevent epidemics (§15).[54]

WHAT STATES DEMANDED OF THEIR CITIZENS

The Swedish authorities' lack of powers was not nearly as big an obstacle to decisive action as their unwillingness to use them. All nations were technically capable of taking decisions. But some of them barely used their powers. Belarus's president, Alexander Lukashenko, offered up folk remedies – tractor-riding, ice sports, and vodka – but little else in the epidemic's early stages.[55] Nor did Nicaragua under Sandinista rule do much. If anything, the authorities spent their energies covering up the pandemic.[56] Mass gatherings were not prohibited, but were in fact organized by the government to convey an aura of normality.[57]

All governments – even autocracies – ultimately rely on some degree of public consent. But some are willing to twist their citizens' arms harder than others. We have noted how even democracies were well-equipped to treat the infected decisively if required to avoid epidemics. Most everywhere, scofflaws were fined and occasionally arrested for violating lockdown. But not every democracy considered itself equally able to make demands of its citizens. In Brazil, president Bolsonaro's resistance to a generalized shutdown owed much to concern for his supporters. Working in the informal economy, poorly housed, living from day-to-day earnings, these were not the people telecommuting from home offices or retreating to their country places. Pakistan did not clamp down as hard as India, claiming that its citizens' poverty forbade that.[58] Indefensible as the Nicaraguan government's inaction was, it was motivated by the impossibility of forcing its citizens, most of whom lived hand-to-mouth, to cease working.[59]

When, in late March, Prime Minister Modi decided to shut India down, he seems to have ignored how many millions lived precariously, unable to forego daily work or isolate themselves.

The immediate result was a pitiful rush of ten to eighty million street hawkers, laborers, and factory hands back to their villages – a vast migration even by Indian standards, sweeping infection with it.[60] Modi's eventual apology for the ensuing chaos was aimed at the poorest whose lives his orders had most disrupted. Similarly, middle-income nations such as Brazil, India, and Indonesia were among the first to begin opening up again in late May 2020, once the limits to the sacrifices they could demand of their citizens had become evident.[61] Even in the developed world, micro-exceptions were made. Parisian police did not hassle the homeless when first enforcing the lockdown in mid-March. "They have nowhere to go," one officer pointed out.[62]

Nor were wealthy nations spared such considerations. Across ᶢᵉ world, a loosening of lockdowns began in May 2020. Protests demanding a speedy opening up soon flared up in several US states, Europe, and elsewhere. True, the motives were both political and economic. A majority of Americans favored shutdowns, especially those who had been furloughed or laid off.[63] And Democrats were more likely to obey self-isolation rules than Republicans. Yet, those who hotly protested shutdowns were also often badly affected by them economically. As they faced off against counter-demonstrating health care workers in Colorado, one protester spoke for many by shouting, "You go to work. Why can't I go to work?"[64]

Who would be most affected by shutting down the economy? Who bore the brunt of the trade-offs between safety and prosperity? We return to that debate in Chapter 9, but in a more generalized sense, such concerns weighed on politicians deciding what tactics to choose in the spring of 2020. The Western nations had missed the chance to clamp down at the first arrival of Covid-19 in January. In any event, most were unequipped to test, trace, and isolate incoming vectors and their contacts. That left them only two alternatives.

They could let the epidemic burn itself out, overwhelming hospitals, mortuaries, and cemeteries. Or they could seek to flatten the epidemic curve. Lowering the immediate incidence of the outbreak by breaking chains of transmission promised to spare health care systems from disaster now, buying time while waiting for a medical solution. But it exacted a toll in other ways. Secondary waves might hit later. And in the short run, both upfront economic paralysis and the collateral damage attendant on keeping citizens isolated were costs. Where on the spectrum would politicians fall between accepting high mortality but relatively normal economic functioning, at one end, and lower mortality but economic havoc, on the other?

Different leaders judged their citizens variously, considering them more or less capable of some forms of pain and damage than others. China pressed ahead with drastic impositions, able and willing to take the political heat of whatever protests might ensue. And protest, Chinese citizens did. Unlike the autocracies we remember from the interwar and postwar period, Chinese citizens were left substantial leeway to make their misgivings known, despite official censorship. Though having had their wings clipped, social media hosted their expression. Chinese citizens may have been grateful to their government for being spared the worst, but they were also upset that it had hidden the epidemic at its onset and clamped down on the whistle-blowers who first raised the alarm.[65]

In turn, South Korea presumed that its citizens would tolerate drastic impositions on individual freedoms if the authorities managed to squash the epidemic. At the other extreme, Bolsonaro and Trump considered their electorates better able to weather the disease than a faltering economy. In their judgment, the cure was potentially worse than the illness.

In between these outliers, other leaders wavered. In February, the British government recognized the need to act. But it decided against universal lockdown, fearing that its citizens would not tolerate it. Oddly, these same leaders invoked the Second World War and the spirit of the Blitz as a mantra.[66] If that meant anything at all, it suggested an ability to rely on citizens' resolve to endure. But even so, endurance was precisely what they did not trust the

British to demonstrate, not even of a lockdown that was, of course, infinitely less horrific than the Blitz.[67] British politicians feared that if they asked the public for sacrifices too early, it would grow weary in the midst of the epidemic, giving up resolve just at its highpoint.

Until mid-March, the scientific advisors therefore did not consider stringent lockdowns. Britons, they feared, would simply not accept the kind of measures imposed in China.[68] Not until Imperial College's projections in mid-March of sky-high and thus politically unacceptable mortality rates laid out an even more unforgiving logic did the British government conclude that it had no choice but to ask citizens to tolerate full lockdown.

Along with Sweden, Holland was one of the few nations to stick with a mitigation strategy. Here, too, a similar logic held sway. In May, Prime Minister Mark Rutte argued that his citizens would soon tire of a lockdown and stop complying.[69] No point, therefore, in demanding such sacrifices in the first place. Sweden's leaders were also keenly attuned to what could be asked of their citizens. Their conclusions, like the Dutch, were the opposite of the British. Swedes would not tolerate lockdown and should not, they decided, be asked to bear it. Tegnell, the chief epidemiologist and de facto government spokesman on the matter, emphasized that a preventive strategy had to be sustainable and could not for long prescribe behavior citizens refused to follow.[70] Ann Linde, the foreign minister, argued that people could not be immured in their houses for months and expected to obey government lockdown rules.[71]

Sweden made much of the trust people had in their government and, conversely, the faith the authorities could put in its citizens. Swedish citizens were expected voluntarily to comply with what was demanded in epidemics, not needing to have it hammered fast with laws, regulations, and uniformed enforcement. For dramatic contrast, the Swedish media highlighted how police cudgels enforced lockdown elsewhere.[72] The Swedish authorities portrayed their strategy as asking citizens to freely accept what other nations had to rely on compulsion and force for. "Instead of draconian lockdown, social distancing became a matter of self-regulation. Citizens were instructed to use their judgment and take individual responsibility within a framework that rested on mutual trust rather than top-down control."[73] "No lockdown," said foreign minister Linde, "We rely very much on people taking responsibility themselves."[74] Swedes were trusted to self-regulate, agreed Mike Ryan of the WHO.[75]

The Swedish approach straddled a curious contradiction. The Swedes could not be locked down because depriving them of their freedoms was asking too much. But at the same time, the Swedes were trained and conditioned to do the right thing without being compelled. So which was it: could the government trust Swedes to act correctly, or could it not rely on them to endure lockdown? Or a bit of both?

DEMOCRACY VS. POPULISM: WHAT WOULD CITIZENS TOLERATE?

What could be asked of citizens faced with pandemics? How much sacrifice could authorities legitimately demand? What would people tolerate? Such questions went to the heart of each polity's social compact. In dire times, citizens had to be persuaded to buy into their government's dictates. At the same time, the authorities could require sacrifices. Both seemed legitimate claims.

We have touched on the role of experts in democracies. Experts had their own agendas, which did not always mesh with the politically possible. Faced with pandemics, public health officials and economists were likely to recommend contradictory policies. The former sought to break chains of transmission, the latter to prevent damage to trade and manufacturing. Such conflicting objectives could ultimately be squared only through medical solutions that permitted both at the same time. In the meantime, elected politicians had to weigh the opposing interests, as these zero-sum recommendations threatened harm to one side of the equation or the other.

When politicians claimed to be following expert advice, it usually meant that they were imposing lockdown or other means of interrupting transmission that public health authorities recommended. In the pandemic's first onslaught, economic interests paled before citizens' immediate security. Leaders who most overtly prioritized the interests of hardpressed social groups least able to endure lockdown were also the ones who most vocally rejected or disparaged scientific counsel – Trump and Bolsonaro.

The Swedes stood out for insisting that their laissez-faire mitigation strategy still had the full support of the public health establishment, even though it deviated from standard practice elsewhere in Europe. Their chosen advisors did, of course, support this approach. But medical authorities elsewhere in the world, and dissenting colleagues at home, were alarmed by Sweden's off-piste route. Many insisted that the politicians do their job of weighing epidemiological danger against economic devastation.[76] Even the usually consensual Swedish establishment began to fragment as mortality climbed. In late May, Sweden briefly rose to the unenviable position of the highest per capita death rates globally.[77] Carl Bildt, the former prime minister, feared that Sweden's smugness would stick in other nations' craws.[78] Tegnell's predecessor as chief epidemiologist, Annika Lind, also broke her silence to condemn his approach as "perhaps not the cleverest in all respects."[79] Swedish epidemiologists who considered the official course careless banded together, a thorn in Tegnell's side.[80]

Sweden implicitly assumed that, by following the experts' dispassionate advice, it was burnishing its democratic credentials. In contrast, other nations, which locked down, were being populist at best, responding to pressing fears and taking decisions that were perhaps of immediate benefit, but unwise in the longer run. Once again, a fundamental theoretical dispute at the heart of democratic governance emerged, stretching back at least to Rousseau. How much did the general will and the public good overlap with what the people desired? The implication was that Sweden's experts were attuned to the higher public good, while other nations, more populist, merely gave the people what they wanted – pandering to their fears, or perhaps their sentimental but economically illiterate determination to save as many lives as possible.

But ambiguity festered at the heart of the Swedish approach. The experts knew what was best, prescribing higher immediate mortality in hopes of sidestepping a needless economic shutdown and perhaps more deaths down the road. At the same time, for the average, not-at-risk Swede – the majority of voters – mitigation was also the most tolerable course, the one that demanded few sacrifices, still letting them go to work or school, walk in the park, shop, and drink beer outside pubs. As long as you were not old or frail, what was there not to like about Tegnell's Mephistophelean bargain? Swedish social scientists banged on about how no nation was more trusting.[81] But was trust really the operative concept here? After all, the authorities were asking citizens to do what they wanted to in the first place, not demanding sacrifices.

If the Swedish authorities' faith in their subjects was ambivalent, the British government's distrust, almost fear, of their citizens was explicit. Why did the British authorities place so little faith in their citizenry? Why did they believe themselves unable to make demands of it? Part of the answer may be the grip in which nudge theory held the British government. But it equally indicated a more fundamental problem – decision-makers' belief that they could not demand sacrifices in postmodern, hyper-individualist, hedonic cultures.

Nudge theory argued that the best way for government to get citizens to change behavior in desirable directions was through small, invisible incentives that encouraged laudable conduct. Rather than deliberately and consciously opting into organ donor programs, for example, the default position was to be enrolled, requiring those who objected to exempt themselves. Similar default assumptions were useful for pension savings plans.[82]

Such governance lite was attractive for regimes that expected to have only little leverage over their followers and even less ability to force them to comply. David Cameron's Tory government had been much taken by such ideas and, in 2010, established the world's first Nudge Unit in Number 10 (officially called the Behavioural Insights Team).[83] Columnists claimed that its influence had led Johnson's government to fear that the public would succumb to "behavioral fatigue" if it imposed lockdown too early.[84] The Nudge Unit itself denied having ever used the term "behavioral fatigue."[85] And members of the government's scientific advisory committee, SAGE, argued that it was an ill-defined concept with no basis in science.[86]

Be that as it may, SAGE's advice was larded with nudge-like observations that most charitably can be characterized as self-evident. Some evidence exists, the advisors noted, that quarantining is harder to comply with the longer it lasts. "The evidence is not strong but the effect is intuitive." Experience, they added, lest the logic escape their political masters, "suggests it is harder to comply with a challenging behaviour over a long period than over a short period."[87]

David Halpern, head of the Nudge Unit, also favored the herd immunity strategy first advocated by the advisors.[88] Indeed, so influential was nudge-like thinking rumored to be that Labour's shadow health secretary asked the government for reassurance that its response was not being formulated in over-reliance on behavioral science.[89] Six hundred behavioral scientists also queried the British government why it thought that citizens would quickly tire of lockdown rather than step up to the plate and radically change their routines to stop the epidemic.[90] The Swedish authorities too talked the nudge lingo.[91]

WHY THE SWEDISH SONDERWEG?

The Swedish anomaly was less distinct than sometimes claimed. The Swedes did impose some restrictions. And many Swedes voluntarily worked from home, avoided going into public, socially distanced themselves, and generally followed the pre-scripts that would have been enforced under a lockdown. That was its point, after all – to do voluntarily much the same as elsewhere required a government mandate. Nor was Sweden the only nation to take a hands-off approach. And those nations that had locked down began opening up again after the peak of the first wave in May 2020. Nonetheless, the distinction between Sweden and other countries was notable, and the nation reaped much attention, good and bad, for its approach.

The Swedes kept schools, restaurants and cafes, and ski resorts open. They did not install plexiglass partitions to protect cashiers at stores. Travelers from abroad were not asked to isolate unless they had obvious symptoms. Rejecting the idea that asymptomatic carriers were a significant transmission source, they saw no reason to require masks or equip caretakers in old age homes with protective gear.[92] Later on, they forbade large assemblies and closed high schools and universities. In April, they did finally prohibit visits to care homes.[93]

In the meantime, the Swedes recommended the kinds of measures that elsewhere were compulsory. Sports associations should try to avoid close contact among participants, should seek to postpone meets, should aim to limit audiences. Associations should try to put off meetings, stores to limit the number of customers at any one time. The infected should stay at home and avoid contact. Citizens were responsible for preventing transmission and should wash their hands, keep their distance, avoid public transport in rush hours and unnecessary travel, not attend parties, funerals, christenings, and the like. Other countries implemented special hours in stores and public spaces when the elderly could more safely shop or visit. The Swedes simply advised everyone over seventy to limit their contacts, not use public transport, not shop in pharmacies or food stores, and not go where people congregated.[94]

Why were the Swedes treading this unusual path? The Swedes themselves feigned surprise at the very question. Was a consensual, non-coercive approach not what the world expected of this happy nation where authority was respected, expertise ruled supreme, people did not need formal rules to do the right thing, and force was superfluous? Perhaps the problem – some suggested – was that, with nothing awful having happened for a long time (they had sidestepped even the Second World War by staying neutral), Swedes had grown unaccustomed to the idea that it ever could.[95]

One proposed reason for Sweden's Sonderweg that can be dismissed out of hand is that it represented the obvious choice dictated by the nation's history. The Swedes retrofitted their national self-image with a long tradition of consensual public health, of which their approach to Covid-19 was just the latest example.[96] Tegnell claimed that Sweden had a voluntary approach to preventing epidemics that relied on individual responsibility.[97] "You give [people] the option to do what is best in their lives," he claimed. "That works very well, according to our experience."[98] But that, to put it mildly, was not the typical Swedish method.

If anything, the Swedes' traditional approach to contagious disease was to clamp down exceptionally firmly.[99] The first cholera epidemics in Europe came late to the nation, two years after it had broken out in Russia in 1832. Swedish authorities had observed its progress across the continent, through Poland and Prussia, then via Bavaria westward on to Britain. That allowed them time to ponder the various attempts to bring it to heel, from strict quarantines to scrubbing it away through sanitation. Quarantines had done little good and much damage to those locked in. By the time cholera hit Britain, it had become conventional wisdom that the Russians' and Prussians' early attempts to keep it out by throwing up palisades and shutting down trade had done more harm than good.

Nonetheless, in the 1830s, the Swedes concluded that their nation was well-positioned to keep at bay a disease evidently imported from the outside. In practical terms, they were an island nation – surrounded by water on two sides, and by ice, mountains, and tundra on the others. At the time, unlike Britain, their economy was not heavily dependent on trade. For them, quarantine made sense. They shut down commerce, patrolled the coastlines, inspected and detained travelers, and generally imposed one of the strictest quarantines anywhere.

Sweden's approach to other transmissible diseases was similarly draconian. Prompted by yellow fever, the 1806 quarantine law was ferocious. Suspect ships were quarantined at Känsö, near Gothenburg. Captains of vessels that departed without permission could be executed if disease spread. Attendants in waxed protective clothing supplied the confined crew with food and necessities. Having been washed in vinegar, with their hair shorn, patients were taken onshore to the lazaretto by a lift, without being touched, and submerged in water fully clothed, their clothes then cut off them.[100]

For smallpox, the Swedes were keen vaccinators. Antivaccinators in other nations wrested concessions from the government. In England, entire cities, like Leicester, were taken over by resistors in the nineteenth century, battling authorities in the streets. In Sweden, such pushback was fainter. The 1853 law made vaccination mandatory, enforced by fines. Only in 1916 was an exemption allowed for parents who had conscientious objections to vaccinating their children.[101] The Swedish state came down even more harshly on venereal diseases. Other countries often regulated sex workers. They were tested and, if found syphilitic, forced to undergo whatever cure was available and prevented from plying their trade. Sweden extended this to the entire sexually active population. All infected citizens were obliged to be treated. Their contacts were traced and inspected. If the infected resisted being treated or reporting contacts and refused to abstain from sex, they could be jailed.[102]

Nearly two centuries later, Sweden tackled AIDS in much the same way. The tactics applied to syphilis in the nineteenth century now continued in the twentieth. AIDS was then an invariably fatal illness with a long asymptomatic incubation period during which patients could unwittingly infect others. Traditional public health tactics of cutting chains of transmission were considered the best answer in the early 1980s. HIV positives were mandatorily examined, their contacts were traced, and victims who refused to abstain from sex, or at least not to engage without condoms, could be quarantined. Those with positive test outcomes had their contacts informed. Gay bathhouses were closed.[103]

Even today, forty years later, Swedish public health authorities can – if they choose – impose draconian interventions against the coronavirus. The contagious disease law of 2004 gives them wide-ranging powers. Transmissible diseases must be reported. Those who suspect infection are required to take precautions to prevent transmission and warn their contacts. Physicians must report illness, including victims' names, identification numbers, and addresses, as well as their contacts. Victims must seek medical help and undergo testing. If they refuse, they are reported. Examinations can be compulsory. Contacts are traced and reported. Travelers from abroad or from infected areas at home can be inspected and quarantined. Infected areas can be isolated. The infected can be forbidden to work or attend school; they must inform their sexual partners and use prevention. Doctors must notify contacts of their risk if the patient refuses. Those who fail to behave so as to avoid transmission can be isolated.[104]

That law, not to mention Sweden's history, leaves even more mysterious the question, why the Swedes now struck out on their own. It may seem pointless to delve into the details of one small, distant nation's willfully peculiar path. Why not Belarus or Nicaragua? Sweden has long been a bellwether, often held up to exemplify what to seek or to avoid. The country has a firm grip on the global imaginarium. In the 1930s, Sweden was crowned exemplar of a middle way between socialism and capitalism – avoiding the rigors and reaping the benefits of both.[105]

More recently, Sweden has branched out to claim laurels in a variety of areas, fashioning itself as a moral superpower. It was the world's most gender-equal nation, a paragon of human rights, and a country whose political culture had been preternaturally resistant to the virus of ethnonationalism – at least until 1988, when it finally brought forth its own anti-foreigner party, the Sweden Democrats, who went on to become the third-largest three decades later.[106] The Swedes have also crowned themselves leaders of the fight against global warming.[107]

During this pandemic, the Swedes again grabbed the world's attention and enjoyed it. The government epidemiologists were relentlessly in the limelight. Their older colleagues came out of retirement to bestow interviews on seemingly any interested newspaper. As the biggest Nordic country, Sweden was accustomed to representing Scandinavia tout court. But in recent years, the sheen had dimmed. The Norwegians, with their oil and massive sovereign wealth fund, were downright glossy with prosperity. Swedish workers now made the unfamiliar pilgrimage across the western border, seeking well-paid work elsewhere.[108]

Even the Danes, often mocked in Sweden as practically Neapolitan in their southern habits and mores, brandished a currency that had long risen against the Swedish crown. It was customary Swedish practice to boost exports by strategically devaluing, but the Swedish krona's downward trajectory had now become disproportional to the Danes' secure Euro-linked currency.[109] Did the Swedes consider the epidemic a chance to reclaim their rightful place in the spotlight?

The Swedes were not, of course, alone in considering themselves exceptional. Trump's persistent booming away about how effectively the US had handled things suggested an even more delusionary mindset. So did Boris Johnson's initially breezy approach to what he seemed to regard as a minor distraction from the main show, Britain's latest triumph of standing alone, Brexit.[110] Indeed, the Brexit bluster about regaining sovereignty may have blinded the Tory government to the reality of fighting the pandemic. The belief marinading the Brexit campaign, that independence from the EU would unshackle the old lion, seems to have fostered a cabinet assumption that Britain could act more speedily and effectively alone than as an EU member. The reality, alas, was less flattering.

Of course, it made sense for the British to start some of the most promising vaccine trials since their biomedical research establishment was second only to the American. Setting off on their own to develop a tracing app was less convincing. The British government had repeatedly demonstrated its incapacity to manage big data software projects – most spectacularly when it took a £10 billion write-off by abandoning the NHS patient record system Lorenzo in 2013.[111] This time, a home-grown app that ignored the Apple/Google cooperation used by most other Western nations was trialed on the Isle of Wight in May. Predictably, it encountered teething problems and had its roll-out booted into the winter.[112] With the procurement of protective gear and ventilators, the situation was downright humiliating. Though technically still part of the EU and therefore welcome to participate in joint purchasing arrangements, the UK did not. The government claimed that the EU's invitation to join had been sent to an outdated email address.[113] Was anyone at home in Whitehall? End of the queue was, therefore, where the British found themselves in the sourcing scrum.

Still, the British were not alone in seeing Covid-19 as a chance to show the world they could do things better in their own way. So seduced were the Swedes by their exceptionalism that they began to define their national ethos as a kind of "public health nationalism."[114] It became yet another building block in the edifice of Swedish exceptionalism.[115] Even if controversially, Sweden was once again noticed by the rest of the world.[116] Other nations were starting to come around to the Swedish approach, crowed Tegnell in April.[117] "I'm proud that Sweden is allowing us to take responsibility ourselves instead of being under lockdown," one accountant interviewed on the street in Stockholm allowed herself to be quoted.[118]

Sweden did grab international headlines for its unusual path.[119] In part, the world was surprised that a nation otherwise

known for running a tight ship would toss aside the precaution-
ary principle and face down a global pandemic so laid back. In
Sweden, where usually everything is forbidden, the Danish paper
Jyllands Posten reported, now most everything is allowed.[120] At
first, the world paid attention because the Swedes insouciantly
portrayed their relaxed approach as their accustomed way of
doing things – consensually and non-coercively. For a while,
the media bought the schtick. Bemused foreign journalists in
Stockholm reported on blondes clustering in cafes while elsewhere, the cameras panned over ghost towns.[121] And sympa-
thetic foreigners piled on too. Sweden did not need to forbid
things, the head of the German–Swedish Chamber of Commerce
agreed, unlike in Germany.[122]

In late April, when protests against prolonged lockdowns began
in the US, Germany, Spain, and other nations, Tegnell chalked it
up as a vindication. Too drastic a shutdown could not hold, was his
verdict.[123] And Swedes took comfort from the admiration, or
possibly just a few polite phrases, from unlikely allies, such as the
Saudis, who had themselves imposed a harsh lockdown at
home.[124] Even controversy kept them in the public eye. They
tolerated it when distant Argentina, deciding to extend their
quarantine in early May, held up Sweden's high mortality rates as
an example not to emulate.[125]

More dismaying was the criticism from a nation that the Swedes
are ambivalent about, Germany – so proximate culturally and yet
so tainted politically by its past. The local reporter for ARD, one of
the leading German TV stations, caused a stir in Stockholm by
turning up at the daily press conferences to ask questions more
pointed and probing than customary for Swedish journalistic
habit. Christian Stichler reported that the Germans were mystified
by why Sweden – in other respects so Germanic – was relaxed about
Covid-19. Germans considered the Swedes naïve and blind, almost
suicidal, he warned.[126]

Nor, apparently, were the Swedes disconcerted by the unexpected company their new course put them in. Accustomed to

being the darling of the moderate left abroad, Sweden was now hailed by conservatives the world over for its libertarian willingness to stand up for individual rights against an overweening state. "The people themselves are primarily responsible for their safety," the Republican governor of South Dakota said in justifying her state's hands-off approach. "They are the ones that are entrusted with expansive freedoms."[127] Anonymized, it would have been hard to distinguish that sentiment from a Swedish Social Democrat's. That would have been true too of the comment by the center-right president of Uruguay, Luis Lacalle Pou, that his country's hands-off approach was based on "responsible liberty."[128] Conservatives everywhere praised the Swedish strategy as what they, too, were aiming for.[129] Since it promised an alternative to lockdown, herd immunity and Sweden's ambition to achieve it were part of the allure.[130] Sweden became the pet of conservatives globally, spanning the gamut in the US from the white-shoe Republicanism of the *National Review* to the brash populism of Fox News.[131] Not to mention of the libertarian fringe.[132]

Once the wheels began coming off the Swedish strategy in June, however, exceptionalism began to seem more like arrogance. In March, Johan Giesecke, the former chief epidemiologist who had been brought back as a consultant, claimed that "The reason Sweden's strategy distinguishes itself internationally is because everyone else is wrong."[133] That no longer resonated well. Some observers compared the assumption that Sweden could go its own epidemiological way to how it had reacted to immigration.[134] Its fellow Nordics had clamped down on immigration early, like Denmark, or had never permitted many immigrants in the first place, like Norway and Finland. They had long since spawned nativist parties. The Swedes considered themselves somehow immune to the hyper-nationalist virus. They admitted more foreign asylum seekers per capita than any other developed nation, resettling them in remote areas. Only when the influx finally took its political toll, with the nativist Sweden Democrats' rising power, did they jam on the brakes and make a U-turn.[135]

Besides the attractions of the limelight, other factors may have played a role. Was Swedish political culture even more consensus-seeking than elsewhere in Scandinavia? Could Swedish leaders count on broad support even while pursuing possibly unpopular policies?[136] Swedes trusted their government significantly more than the Norwegians did during the pandemic.[137] Political culture may have played a role. Two opposing forces fought for preeminence in Swedish attitudes – the sanctity of political authority and cultural individualism. Swedes were accustomed to being told what to do and, in many respects, their lives were minutely regulated. But at the same time, they resented this, feeling that, as autonomous individuals, they should be entrusted to make the right decisions on their own.

The hyper-individualism of Swedish political culture has long been noted, undermining the mistaken belief that theirs was a predominantly communitarian ethos. In international attitude surveys, Swedes are consistently the global outliers on measures of rationalism, anti-traditionalism, anti-communitarianism, and egalitarianism.[138] In the famous distinction formulated by the German sociologist Ferdinand Tönnies between community and society, they were more enamored of *Gesellschaft*, of rationalist, bureaucratic, scientific, individualist society, than anyone else in the world.

The secret of Swedish social policy was that the state has been the means for citizens to slough off their obligations to family, kin, and civil society, transferring them to the public so that they could live instead in independence from others. Swedes practice state individualism.[139] They happily pay eye-watering taxes to provide pensions and elder care, thus sparing themselves the obligation of caring for their parents themselves. Swedish women staff the country's excellent nurseries and daycares, being paid to nurture other people's children while their own are looked after by someone much like themselves. More people live alone in single-person households than in any other country. Swedes were, in effect, self-isolating long before the epidemic. As the joke had it, their success in beating the pandemic was due to Swedes abandoning the six-foot distancing rule and returning to their usual fifteen feet apart.[140]

Swedes achieve autonomy and freedom through and not in defiance of the state. In independence from civil society, they pursue what they consider the unchecked development of their personality. They are Pippi Longstockings, happy to have a father so long as he leaves his sack of gold coins behind and stays far away, sailing the seas. They delight in being unencumbered by domesticity and familial obligations. From this mindset, their approach to the pandemic flowed: individual autonomy meant each citizen was responsible first and foremost for themselves.[141] Where that left the old, frail, and others in need of collective protection remained unanswered.

DECLINE OF THE SWEDISH MODEL

Eventually, the Swedish approach started coming apart. By late May, the rest of Europe was opening up again. Sweden now stood isolated, having fallen between two stools. It had avoided neither the economic hardships of lockdown, nor the decimation of its elderly in the care homes. For a week in mid-May, it suffered the highest per-capita mortality rate in the world. But imposing a test and trace policy was no longer practicable since the virus had spread too widely.[142] And yet, Sweden had fallen short of its goal: herd immunity. The Swedes now began eyeing their neighbors' low death rates enviously. Gone were the facile prognostications that, in the long run, things would even out. The recent victories elsewhere in Scandinavia were tangible.[143] Medical experts came out anew for a course correction.[144] If the Germans had managed widespread testing, then surely the Swedes could too. Contact tracing should start up again.[145]

Its neighbors now began viewing Sweden suspiciously too. As Denmark, Norway, and Finland contemplated whether to allow in travelers, humiliatingly, they decided to keep the infected Swedes out.[146] Other nations opening up to European neighbors, such as Greece, Estonia, and Latvia, also put Sweden on their blacklist. The rebuff from the Scandinavian neighbors was especially stinging, flying in the face of decades of Nordic cooperation.[147] Scania, in southern Sweden, and Zealand, the Danish island that houses Copenhagen, had been amalgamating into one integrated economic unit for years now, underpinned by the bridge across the Sound. Many Danes lived in Sweden, with its cheaper cost of living, and commuted across to Copenhagen. All that now suffered.

The trust argument advanced by Swedish commentators, highlighting their approach's virtues, was turned on its head. Swedish government and citizenry had trusted each other too much, it was now suggested, no one daring to question whether the king was clothed. Media, politicians, experts, and the public were all locked into *åsiktskorridoren*, the "opinion corridor" that defined the narrow range of official policy, accepted views, and deferential media coverage.[148] High-trust societies may have been lulled into complacency, warned the *Economist*.[149] Too much trust in what was falsely presented as unanimous expert opinion – so the damning verdict of the German press – had led one of the world's wealthiest welfare states to protect its citizens worse than many developing nations.[150] Sweden was trying on a new status in the eyes of the world, announced the *New York Times* in a stinging reportage – that of a pariah state.[151]

Even Tegnell finally threw in the towel, or so it seemed. At the beginning of June, he admitted faults. Sweden should have implemented more preventive measures earlier, he now agreed.[152] But in a follow-up interview, he remained unrepentant, unable to identify anything, other than protecting the elderly better, that he would have radically changed.[153] And he still held out for a final accounting of mortality in the future and the possibility that Sweden, or at least Stockholm, would weather a second wave better thanks to herd immunity.[154]

On June 25, the WHO issued a list of eleven European nations where infection rates were still rising, including Moldavia,

Armenia, North Macedonia, Albania, Azerbaijan, Kyrgyzstan, and Sweden – together at last![155] Tegnell was apoplectic at being included in such company. Taking a page from Trump's playbook, he insisted that the only reason why infection rates appeared to be climbing in Sweden was that they had begun testing more.[156] Trump had advanced the same logic two days earlier, June 23, chalking up rising US rates to more testing.[157] While Trump was rightly mocked for his reasoning, Tegnell's currency apparently still traded at a lesser discount in the corridors of international public health. Sweden's name was retrofitted with an exculpatory asterisk on the website to explain that new confirmed cases in the nation had declined in the past two days. In early June, a choral meeting on the island of Vrångö, in the Gothenberg archipelago, led to a mass outbreak – a quarter of the island's population infected.[158] This came three months after a similar event in Washington state became one of the first superspreader events to be widely reported.[159] No lessons were learned there.

Public opinion in Sweden began drawing a predictable conclusion: enough with the illusion of rule by expertise! It was high time for the politicians to admit their mistakes and take charge.[160] The truce that had allowed Tegnell and his band of boffins to chart their own course was finished, and opposition politicians from the Sweden Democrats, Center Party, Moderates, and Christian Democrats now openly criticized the Social Democratic coalition government for its tactics.[161] Public faith in the authorities and their strategic choices plunged.[162]

CHAPTER 4

What Was Done?

Act One of the Pandemic

T
HE CORONAVIRUS EPIDEMIC PROMPTED GOVERNMENT
interventions across the globe on a scale unparalleled outside wartime. The shutdown was among history's largest exercises
of state power. Starting with Wuhan's closure on January 23, more
than a third of the world's population, two and a half billion souls,
was shut in at home over the following four months.[1] Governments
both closed down economies and then acted to keep their participants afloat. Interventions to stave off bankruptcy and unemployment were equally massive. Stimulus programs that dwarfed earlier
attempts sent oceans of deficit spending coursing through the
economic arteries. Scores of vaccine trials began, research papers
by the thousands were authored, entire industrial sectors retooled
to manufacture protective and medical equipment, emergency
hospitals were stamped out of the ground.

How and how well nations responded varied enormously and
had geopolitical implications. The Chinese were criticized for not
being forthcoming about the epidemic's start, for obfuscating the
role of wet markets and of their traditional medical practices in the
epidemic's origins, for throwing their weight around at the WHO,
for making strategic use of their prowess in producing and selling
protective equipment, and later, once they had gotten things under
control, for trumpeting their own horn.[2] But they were also widely
admired for their interventions' speed and decisiveness and how
they had localized the epidemic to one metropolitan area, avoiding

much seeding elsewhere. By late April, global public opinion rated China's response better than America's.[3]

In 2019, the Global Health Security Index had ranked the US as the best-prepared nation to deal with pandemics.[4] Three months into the new year, that reputation was in tatters. The federal government was widely seen as undermined by its president's divisive, self-regarding, and ill-informed leadership. Rather than spearheading the international response, as in past epidemics, it could barely cope with events at home. The CDC, weakened by budget cuts, was now sidelined, having fumbled mass testing.[5] The Trump administration's attacks on the civil service and bureaucracy, its hollowing out of the administrative state's ability to function unpartisanly, its nepotistic appointments of manifestly unqualified relatives to influential advisory positions, its inconsistent and often misleading use of scientific advice, and its undercutting of the state governors – all hobbled any effective national response to the epidemic.[6]

Trump's antagonistic approach to the rest of the world, his hawking of dis- or unproven remedies, and his preening insistence that all was well with the US response undercut not only his personal trustworthiness but the nation's credibility, leverage, and soft power. This was the first world crisis where the US had abdicated global leadership. By threatening to pull funding for the WHO, it actively undermined a coordinated international response.[7] European allies might have misgivings about China. But, increasingly unable to put their faith in the US, they resisted following Trump to take positions that goaded the Chinese. When, at WHO meetings in May, the US insisted on investigating the epidemic's origins, the resolution was watered down. American power was ebbing away.[8]

Between these two extremes, China's draconian but effective clamp-down and America's belated and fragmented approach, many other nations arrayed themselves. By the fall of 2020, America's performance had perhaps not been the world's absolute worst. With 4% of the world's population, it had suffered 20% of its mortality. Its excess mortality for the first half of 2020 was substantially above Europe's.[9] But per capita, it was "merely" at the bottom of the top ten of the worst-affected nations. Whatever the precise numbers, its performance had been nothing to crow about. Certainly, it was not what might have been expected from the still-wealthiest and most powerful country on earth. Differences in political regime between democracies and autocracies do not seem to have caused much of the variation among nations' preventive stances. So, why did some countries fare better?

As we have seen, absent medical solutions, only the time-tested methods of population management to cut transmission remained. In practical terms, that meant a combination of tactics: testing to identify and isolate the infected, tracing their contacts, supplying protective equipment, especially to frontline staff, imposing self-isolation on all citizens except crucial workers, limiting travel and mobility, forbidding public events and gatherings, closing all but essential retail outlets, imposing social distancing in public, and taking measures to isolate and protect the especially vulnerable. Any or all of these could be done more or less effectively, more or less thoroughly.

INSTITUTIONAL MEMORY

Since these tools were much the same armamentarium used for millennia to battle microscopic enemies, history mattered. Human societies and their governments had deep historical memories of plague fighting. But how far they tapped into them varied. Some nations had had more recent experiences than others, with still freshly seared institutional memories and hair-trigger policy reflexes. Many African countries that quickly imposed contact tracing and isolation had administrative muscle memory toned by their ongoing fight against AIDS. That worked in two ways: both a deliberate attempt to avoid past mistakes – dithering and quack medicinals – and also the ability to rev up an existing machinery of tracing and testing.[10]

Hanta, Marburg, Ebola, and other horrifying contagious diseases had also spurred institutional responses that were now picked up again. African nations may not have had Asia's technology and medical infrastructure, but in locking down neighborhoods, tracing contacts, and getting people to stay home and isolate, they were experienced and practiced. Since all nations began by tackling the epidemic with ancient tools no more sophisticated than managing human contacts, the lack of ventilators and other medical infrastructure was not at first a decisive handicap.

More to the point, the Asian nations with the most exemplary responses had also suffered deadly epidemics in recent memory: SARS, MERS, avian flu. Saudi Arabia, a quick responder this time around, had also been through an outbreak of MERS. Facing SARS in 2003, China had quarantined tens of thousands, locking down villages and city blocks. Those who fled quarantine or deliberately spread disease had been threatened with life imprisonment or execution.[11] Singapore had introduced mandatory health screening and passed travelers through thermal scanners to detect fevers.[12] Vietnam had taken similar precautions.[13]

Other nations, in contrast, suffered from institutional amnesia, though San Francisco may have initially handled things better than many other cities after its experience as an epicenter of the North American AIDS epidemic.[14] The Spanish flu in 1918 had been tackled with the same traditional tools of pandemic prevention as now. Schools, restaurants, churches, and theaters had been closed, public gatherings banned, masks worn. Medical historians pointed out two pertinent but contradictory lessons. In the US, the cities quickest to impose preventive measures had also cut deaths the most. But precautions had been leveled for just a few weeks, and often subsequent waves of infection rolled back repeatedly, usually higher where the previous one had been low.[15]

In the interim, the discovery and mass application of vaccines, sulfa drugs, and then antibiotics and anti-viral medicines to many transmissible diseases had fundamentally altered public health tactics against epidemics.[16] The developed nations had become victims of their own success. Enamored of biomedicine's quick technological fixes, public health authorities had gradually forgotten their craft's traditional tools. The standard textbook by Burnet and White, in the fourth edition from 1972, stated that – barring wars and catastrophes – the future of infectious disease was likely to be "very dull."[17] The ethical codes issued by the American and Canadian medical associations had once advised physicians that, confronting pestilence, their duty was to face the danger even at the risk of their lives. After the 1950s, such language evaporated, possibly in the belief that doctors no longer confronted astringent moral dilemmas.[18] Recent accounts of the measures taken against the Spanish flu in 1918 have suggested that such non-pharmaceutical interventions "be considered for inclusion as companion measures" to vaccines and medicines, as though they had been all-but-forgotten.[19]

AIDS had initially been tackled with traditional procedures in some nations, but medical solutions eventually defused the pressing need to rely on behavioral change and precautions. When cholera arose in Latin America in the early 2000s, passengers arriving in the US were quarantined and kept under medical surveillance. During the avian flu epidemics, travelers had been subject to classic restrictions. But these were small measures at the margin, not something affecting average citizens. For mass interventions, the administrative slate had been wiped clean. Outside of Asia and Africa, the tool cabinet was bare.

The neoliberal reforms of recent decades had also diminished Western governments' capacity across many competences.[20] Populist leaders, like Trump, had come to office suspicious of the established machinery, attacking even routine government administration as "deep state" entrenchment, and threatening all branches of government with budget cuts, except perhaps the military. Populist leaders had been elected by a citizenry whose faith in government had been eroding.

But public health had also been a victim of previous victories. The mistaken belief that pandemics were a problem of the past lulled authorities into a false sense of security. Even when being decisive, they had sometimes scored own goals. In 1976, mass vaccination against the swine flu had ended up solving a problem that never materialized, causing more harm than it prevented. The US vaccinated forty-five million, of whom some 450 developed Guillain-Barré syndrome.[21] The allure of mass vaccination suffered. In the fool's paradise that emerged, public health agencies had seen their budgets cut, their mandate trimmed. In general, public health spending had increased over the past several decades.[22] But in the US, after 2008, it had fallen by almost 10%.[23]

DEMOCRATIC FRAILTIES

Many democracies acquitted themselves well against the pandemic. New Zealand, Australia, Germany, South Korea, and Taiwan were exemplary in taking decisive measures early, following through, persuading citizens to make sacrifices, and carrying on despite it all. But other democracies suffered handicaps that hampered quick and decisive judgments and sustained follow-through.

The sheer basics threw up problems. How did one convene representative assemblies with social distancing rules in place? The House of Representatives in Washington temporarily instituted proxy voting for members not present. The Senate, with a Republican majority, conducted business in its usual in-person fashion.[24] The US Supreme Court successfully met via the web, with only minor blemishes to the majestic solemnity of its sessions, such as the sound of a flushing toilet in the background of one deliberation.[25] Parliament in London was at first dispersed, with debates conducted via video, thus deprived of its familiar locker-room atmosphere. That changed when the prime minister missed his noisy posse, smarting at the silence while he was forensically grilled by the new opposition leader, Keith Starmer, former chief prosecutor and a debator skilled in the art of rhetorical dissection.

To the dismay of elderly and frail MPs, parliament was recalled in June. Distancing rules permitted only fifty members simultaneously in the chamber. Since the venerably archaic voting procedures involved filing through doorways, safe voting meant MPs queuing kilometer-long to cast ballots, the "Rees-Mogg conga," named after its inventor, the now-unpopular Leader of the House of Commons.[26] After protests, the government caved, allowing the elderly and vulnerable to vote by proxy. To add to the general sense of confusion, when the prime minister himself succumbed to Covid-19 in April, Britain discovered that it had only a vague understanding of who would succeed him if he died.[27]

Due process limitations inherent in the democratic process also impeded decisive and long-term measures. US governors could implement emergency measures, but only temporarily. When state-level public health authorities issued or renewed shutdown orders, courts sometimes overturned them as overly broad.[28] Battles were fought before the bench over whether to shut churches. In various states, judges ruled that churches should be allowed to open, like other crucial businesses, using the usual techniques of social distancing and protective gear. In late May, the Supreme Court intervened, allowing governors to keep them closed.[29]

A South African court overturned government measures in June.[30] In Brazil, the government was court-ordered to continue publishing the mortality figures it had sought to bury.[31] In July, the Austrian constitutional court ruled that much of the now-otiose emergency lockdown legislation had violated the law.[32] In July, the Romanian constitutional court forbade patients being detained against their will. Thousands fled isolation, quarantine, and medical surveillance until the government could fast-track laws to give the authorities their powers back again.[33]

Democratic protests against lockdowns themselves created problems, spreading infection as demonstrators congregated without distancing or masks. So did protests that erupted for other, only tangentially related reasons, like the mass outbursts of public anguish and anger across the US at the death in Minneapolis at police hands of George Floyd. Democrats and Republicans each picked which mass violations of distancing regulations they preferred to condemn.[34] The president's rallies started up in late June, too, despite officials' concerns that they would transmit.[35]

Nor did leadership always set a good example. China summarily dispatched misbehaving officials. During the SARS epidemic, 1,000 officeholders, including the health minister and Beijing mayor, had been fired or penalized for slow responses.[36] This time, senior officials in Hubei were removed – or "reshuffled" in the official terminology – already when the death toll hit 1,000.[37] That was part of the problem in autocracies: who would be ready to deliver bad news with such drastic consequences? In Africa – as in Latin America – Covid-19 was initially a disease of elite big-city inhabitants with the wherewithal to travel.[38] That had been true for AIDS as well, as in Cuba.[39] As a result, many of Africa's first coronavirus victims were also government officials.[40]

Western democracies also saw leaders who ignored or flouted the same restrictions they demanded of their constituents. German chancellor Merkel rarely wore a mask, however sensible her leadership in other respects. Trump and Bolsonaro's refusal to mask-up was borderline pathological and part of a broader politicization of preventive apparel. Trump donned goggles briefly when visiting a mask factory in Arizona in May, but no mask in public until July, when he finally reversed himself momentarily to support their wearing.[41] In June, a judge ordered Bolsonaro to mask-up when out in Brasília, where masks had become compulsory in April.[42]

Trump paid for his insouciance when he fell ill in early October. Bolsonaro reaped the consequences of his in July when he tested positive. Boris Johnson nearly died after ostentatiously shaking hands in a hospital, and close colleagues fell ill too. Nicola

Zingaretti, president of the Italian region Lazio, shook hands demonstratively to inspire business confidence in late February and became infected.[43] The other way around, Vladimir Putin turned his residence into a hermetic bubble. World War II veterans who joined him at celebrations in June had been quarantined for two weeks beforehand.[44]

Many prominent politicians neglected the rules. Some were held to account. Having violated traveling orders by visiting her country home twice, the chief medical officer of Scotland resigned.[45] The Romanian prime minister, nabbed while out drinking unmasked, promptly paid the requisite fine.[46] The Austrian president, caught at a restaurant after curfew, apologized, as did the chancellor for having appeared unmasked in public.[47] The EU's trade chief resigned after attending a big dinner that should have been off-limits.[48] Having become infected at a party in Spain he should not have been at in the first place, Prince Joachim of Belgium was fined 10,400 Euro.[49] A Kenyan senator, found drinking in a Nairobi pub after curfew, was charged.[50] Others brazened it out. Boris Johnson's Svengali, Dominic Cummings, embroidered increasingly implausible stories to explain his peregrinations while ill to visit parents and local sights in Durham but retained his post.[51]

DIVIDED WE FALL: FEDERALISM'S STRENGTHS AND WEAKNESSES

The response to the pandemic also underlined that, despite premature obituaries, the nation-state remained in rude health. The international organizations did not impress. The CDC – in effect, an international institution, the global nodal point for information about epidemics – had been sidelined by the Trump administration and stumbled at the tasks left it, contact tracing and development of a test.[52] The WHO ensnarled itself in controversy over its allegedly cozy relationship with the Chinese, its early warnings, and the need to account for the pandemic's origins.[53] The EU had few powers to tackle public health problems, though it did issue travel prohibitions and responded vigorously to stimulate the economy. National governments remained the primary actors.

Federalism added a twist to their ability to respond. Many democracies were federal unions. That held especially for public health, where even some otherwise centralized nations, such as Sweden, Great Britain, and Italy, allowed their constituent elements leeway in these matters. Having to corral administrative subdivisions added another dimension to decision-making that did not promise speed or effectivity. Yet, it also allowed local experimentation and initiative, and possibly new solutions. In principle, centralized powers promised greater decisiveness and speed. But a mistake committed at the core threatened more havoc than one occurring somewhere in the branches of a dispersed network.

At least two policy areas were at stake. For the economic response, dealing with unemployment, central bank intervention, fiscal relief, and other financial tools to stabilize and promote aggregate demand and activity, decisions were usually taken at the national level. The US was federalized, with unemployment benefits determined and administered by individual states, thus varying widely. But Washington was decisive in other economic interventions. Generous top-up payments for the unemployed were implemented federally in the CARES Act, as was a program to subsidize businesses if they kept their personnel on the payroll. The Federal Reserve Board unleashed a firehose of dollars to support markets, promising in March to buy $750 billion in corporate bonds and half a trillion state and government debt.[54]

The Fed also played its role as the world's central bank, stabilizing the dollar by easing its swap line terms with foreign central banks. That allowed them to borrow on favorable conditions and not have to sell off dollar assets at fire-sale prices.[55] The American intervention in the economy was enormous, among the largest anywhere, some 12% of GDP.[56] Only the Japanese was bigger, 40% of GDP by May. That added to Japan's position as the world's most indebted nation.[57] In the short term, the

American stimulus achieved some results. While the US unemployment rate skyrocketed in April, poverty declined. Household incomes were 12% above their level a year earlier.[58] As the political parties squabbled about renewing the program before the November elections, that effect waned, and poverty rates rose again.[59] After long deliberation, the EU, too, rose to the occasion in July, agreeing to a three-quarter trillion Euro combination of loans and grants in its first-ever debt-financed stimulus package.[60]

Such heroic interventions assumed that the pandemic would pass within a few months, with economic activity and employment soon picking up again. For longer than that, they were unsustainable. As the pandemic's first act came to a close in the late summer, along with the first generation of stimulus programs, and fall brought second waves, the road forward was unclear.

Public health, however, was often a local responsibility. That usually made sense. Pandemics were an aggregate of local events, and the immediately affected areas often knew best what had to be done and how. Prevalence rates averaged over the nation, for example, were less useful bases for action than fluctuating local ones.[61] Central institutions did not always function well. That was true not only for the CDC. Public Health England, also tasked with testing, failed too, weakened by 40% budget cuts since its founding in 2013 and resistant to cooperation with other agencies and institutions.[62] Central authorities often hobbled the local.[63] In June, Leicester had to be locked down again as cases mushroomed. Local authorities knew only that hospitalizations and deaths were increasing but not test results, until London finally released the figures after weeks of pleading.[64]

But federalism was not destiny, and some decentralized approaches worked well. The German federal system handled testing well, unleashing its many private labs on the task.[65] Australia, a federation, established a war-style cabinet, with both national and territorial leaders, to ensure decisiveness and consistency.[66] Africa's nations banded together early to coordinate a pan-continental response.[67] Federalism was what people made of it. Unified efforts – at the EU level in Europe and the national in the US – would doubtless have been useful.[68] And the Chinese made much of their centralized, top-down approach's virtues.[69]

But in the absence of central coordination, some regions and federal states did rise to the occasion. Divided responsibilities could mean those agencies best able to act were also entrusted to do so, even while confused chains of command often left no one knowing their role or working at cross purposes. Multiplying the number of different policies in federal nations amplified the problem. One study tallied 1,200 separate anti-contagion policies in the US, compared with 214 in Italy and only 59 in South Korea.[70] Yet unity and efficiency were not synonymous. Iran had the lowest number of distinct policies in this list – twenty-three. It was hardly a model of unanimous decisiveness, riven as it was by internecine struggles among religious, secular, and military power centers.[71]

Both aspects of federalism were on display in the US, that half-continent masquerading as a nation. The Constitution delegated public health to the states, allowing for a variety of approaches. Like the Northeast and Pacific states, some, largely in Democratic hands, imposed quite strict lockdowns on par with the Europeans. In contrast, the Republican South and Midwest favored laxer measures, and mandates were also loosened up early, starting already in May.

Washington vacillated between hoping to foist decisions and responsibility off on the states and resenting it when they, seizing the initiative, both criticized the White House for absent leadership and imposed measures beyond what the administration wanted.[72] Trump claimed massive powers for himself, yet failed to use them to much effect. He did invoke the Defense Production Act to instruct companies to produce ventilators. The funding for vaccine development was enormous. And the CARES Act, passed in March, and HEROS Act, which passed the House in June, each multi-trillion-dollar boosts for citizens and companies, were, of course, federal programs.

But the president turned testing strategies and their implementation – which would have profited from central coordination – over to the states.[73] In the absence of federal leadership, even the underlying data – crucial to plumbing the epidemic's extent and location – was unreliable.[74] When and how to start opening up was also left to local initiative. As Michael Nutter, a former Democratic mayor of Philadelphia, said of Trump's strategy, "His idea of federalism is when it's all going well, it's us. When [it] hits the fan, it's you."[75]

Coordination between the states and Washington was sparse. The federal government failed to lead the way, set an example, or help the states align policies. Often, it got in the way. During the Ebola epidemic in 2014, Obama had appointed a tsar to coordinate efforts. Nothing like that appeared this time. To supply sufficient quantities of reagents, swabs, protective equipment, and ventilators, Washington often competed with the states, snatching away kit and driving up prices with rival offers.[76] One federal agency outbid Massachusetts for masks, seizing them once delivered to port. Maryland's Republican governor sent state troopers to secure half a million testing kits fresh from South Korea before the feds could get them.[77] A million masks were flown in from China on a plane belonging to a local basketball team in Massachusetts. They later turned out to be deficient.[78] Had the outcome not been so tragic, it would have been Keystone cops material.

Into the vacuum left by Washington stepped the governors. With some exceptions, like Florida's Ron DeSantis, most followed the CDC's guidelines, often doing even more. The states took different approaches largely according to their political complexion.[79] Yet, even some Republican governors were pragmatic and proactive – Larry Hogan in Maryland, Mike DeWine in Ohio, and Charlie Baker in Massachusetts. Governors in activist Democratic states rose to prominence, burnishing their political credentials and likely deepening the talent pool for coming presidential primaries: Andrew Cuomo, J. B. Pritzker, Gretchen Whitmer, Gavin Newsom.

Governors rose to the occasion, providing welcome relief from the chaos in Washington. In New York, Cuomo gave daily press conferences that offered a competent, reassuring counterpoint to the rambling, ad hoc, endless, amateurish, and ego-stroking sessions Trump presided over in Washington. Having long been regarded as the bully from Albany who tormented New York City's more progressive mayor, Bill de Blasio, Cuomo was now idolized by fan clubs of Cuomosexuals.[80] But that was only after a disastrous start, delayed compared with more rapidly responding states, including Washington and California, and marred by reckless decisions, such as forcing care homes to take back infected patients from hospitals.[81]

On the whole, the US's federalism was a handicap. Central powers could or did not impose much coordination or uniformity. Local powers, however capable, were not sovereigns and therefore unable to take decisive action within their own borders, such as testing and effectively quarantining arrivals.

Federalism was fractal. The same problems of divided powers and jurisdictions could bedevil relationships at the national, state, regional, and municipal levels. Feuding with Washington, Governor Cuomo also engaged in a series of petty disputes with New York City's mayor over school closings and mass transit.[82] De Blasio, for his part, disastrously dithered and delayed. He was swayed by hopes of herd immunity similar to those in the UK, seeking to avoid full-scale lockdown.[83] He finally imposed one only after aides threatened to quit.[84] In Texas and Florida, governors refused to impose state-wide bans, leaving such decisions to localities.[85] Democratic municipalities in Republican-led states sparred with their capitols over how quickly to open things up again in May 2020.[86] And die-hard conservative areas, such as West Texas, refused to submit to their governor's impositions, like mask-wearing, when cases re-erupted in July.[87] A federalist nadir was plumbed in July when Georgia's governor felt called on to sue Atlanta's mayor to prevent her from mandating masks.[88]

Local administrations did some of the best and most innovative work. Before his death in July, Seoul's mayor implemented most of the measures that garnered worldwide praise for South Korea. Latin American mayors stepped into a vacuum left by the national authorities.[89] In Italy, public health authorities in the Veneto successfully tried different approaches from hard-hit Lombardy: extensive testing and tracing, lots of home diagnosis with samples collected directly from patients' residences, and effective protection of frontline personnel.[90] Conversely, London's mayor failed for months to persuade Downing Street to mandate masks on public transport. Bereft of much clout, he could only remonstrate.[91]

Not just federal systems were plagued by localism, however. Geographical proximity delivered similar problems. US governors worried about a race to the bottom when they tried to enforce stricter measures than their neighbors, even though shopping, dining, hair styling, and other services, verboten at home, were available by a short drive to another state.[92] Some ended free movement across state lines. When Rhode Island police went door-to-door looking for newly arrived New Yorkers fleeing disaster at home in March, Governor Cuomo threatened to sue, and the policy was eventually rescinded.[93]

Native Americans who locked down their reservations to protect themselves were granted more leeway.[94] In mid-March, New York, Connecticut, and New Jersey coordinated their business closure policies precisely to avoid forum shopping by potential customers across state lines.[95] Thanks to its devolved governance, the United Kingdom was also fairly un-united once it began opening up again. Scotland and Wales refused to follow England's example of looser measures starting in early June and clamped down for longer.[96] Police here turned away English daytrippers for violating their no-travel rules.[97] The UK's four countries pulled even further apart as the pandemic progressed.[98]

Similar dilemmas plagued Europe. Locked-down Copenhageners crossed the bridge to Sweden to shop in Malmö.[99] Norway was more consistent, shutting the border with Sweden, thus bankrupting stores intended to lure Norwegians across with cheap EU prices.[100] Meanwhile, the EU's member nations repeatedly violated the

Schengen agreement's fundamental free-travel principle, slapping each other with travel bans. Adding injury to insult, once things began loosening up again in June, they picked and chose whom to readmit, angering the spurned: Italians in Austria, Swedes in Denmark and Norway, Cyprus, and Greece. Czechs and Slovaks, once a nation united, banned each other. Dependent on tourism, Italy opened up to most comers in early June. When Italians were shunned elsewhere, their politicians were angry at being treated like lepers.[101] Furious at what they regarded as the lax Dutch approach, Belgium clamped down on an ordinarily frictionless border crossing with the Netherlands.[102] During the opening up in June, they kept the borders closed for friends, but not family.[103]

Hurt national amour propre was aggravated as nations paired and tripled off in travel bubbles: the Baltics together, New Zealand and Australia.[104] Who trusted whom was laid painfully bare, a bit like the regional voting alliances revealed at every Eurovision song contest. Air bridges were used by some to allow travel between nations that regarded themselves as epidemiological peers. In June, the British and Swedes were hurt to find themselves outside of many such European arrangements. Smarting at a taste of their own medicine, the Americans too found themselves on the EU's unwanted list at the beginning of the summer.[105] Even the Mexican state of Sonora banned crossings from Arizona in response to the rising caseload north of the border in July.[106]

WHY TIMING WAS SO IMPORTANT

Time was of the essence with all pandemics. If the rate of transmission, the R_0 number, was above one, they grew exponentially, with subsequent cohorts of the infected geometrically larger than the preceding. One study estimated that, without interventions, Covid-19 infection rates at first grew on average by 43% daily, thus doubling the infected every two days.[107] Though Covid-19 could be nipped in the bud at the onset, the problem would have grown insurmountable just days later. Even a week's delay threatened catastrophe.

How quickly leaders reacted and imposed preventive measures was therefore crucial. Even the Chinese had faltered. Local officials at first hid the magnitude of the problem from Beijing.[108] Even after Beijing realized they faced an epidemic as severe as SARS, they sat on the news. During six days of silence, from January 14, Wuhan hosted an outdoor banquet for tens of thousands, and millions of travelers set off to celebrate the lunar new year. Perhaps 3,000 people were infected during this time, seeding the epidemic that followed.[109]

Similar procrastination elsewhere, as the pandemic unfolded and the lay of the land had become evident, was less forgivable. As Europe shut down during the first half of March, Britain dallied. On March 7, England played Wales in rugby, with 81,000 fans, including the prime minister, in the stands; Liverpool played Madrid five days later. The Cheltenham Festival – four days of horse racing and amusements – ended on March 13, with a quarter of a million visitors in attendance.[110] After Italy shut down on March 7, France twiddled its thumbs for ten days, pondering the fine points of holding municipal elections.[111] On March 7, the Danes had their elimination round for the Eurovision competition with no audience. The day after came the Swedish version, as planned, with an audience of 27,000.[112]

The epidemic spread along routes determined by economic and travel connections. Northern Italy became an early flashpoint likely because of its close economic ties with China – tens of thousands of semi-documented Chinese workers toiling in sweatshops to produce luxury goods that could be sold as "Made in Italy."[113] From Italy, Covid-19 journeyed to Germany, Scandinavia, and Britain, carried by skiers from Alpine resorts returning home from vacation. Despite close links to China, America's West Coast was initially less hard-hit than the East, where infection was seeded by travelers who had caught it in Europe. From New York City, where leaders were slow to recognize the threat and failed to bottle it up, the epidemic spread to the rest of the nation.[114]

Since the disease arrived at varying times in different nations, measuring whether countries were late to respond means evaluating the timing of their measures in relation to the outbreak on their territory. It is hard, however, to make much sense of the timing of precautions imposed. Correlating their introduction to the date of the 100th case reveals little about the anticipatory acumen of politicians. As might have been expected, the interval between the 100th case and imposing mitigation strategies was three days in South Korea but thirty-three in Iran. But Iran did no worse than Hong Kong. The time it took to impose full lockdown was six days in New Zealand and nine in Denmark. But Germany, which otherwise handled things well, took three weeks, three days longer than the UK and only a week less than Italy.[115]

Singapore banned visitors from Hubei already on January 29 and then everyone from China three days later. But it waited until mid-March to bar visitors from hard-hit European countries. By the end of March, 80% of Singapore's cases were coming from abroad. Even though the number of imported cases eventually fell to zero, it was too late.[116]

If measured in the time that precautions were imposed after the third death, however, some patterns emerge. The East European nations were quick off the mark, decreeing most measures already before that event. The UK, Italy, and France were laggards, waiting almost two weeks to shut down shops and movement. Spain, Belgium, and Greece were faster.[117] New York imposed its lockdown (March 22) a week later than the Bay Area and than Spain, harvesting 50% more cases two months down the road.[118] Among the measures that it did impose, Sweden did so consistently last among the Nordics.[119]

The early lockers-down spared uninfected parts of their countries. China managed to contain the epidemic largely to Hubei province. Italy isolated Lombardy on February 22, saving the south, at least from the first wave. But tarrying in the UK and spotty enforcement in the US allowed the epidemic to become generalized throughout. That impeded later hopes of contact tracing and a workable opening up.[120]

In practice, measures were imposed in response to different kinds of triggers. Politicians sometimes acted after becoming aware of high case numbers at home, often in a particular region, as happened in China, Iran, and France. They responded to epidemics threatening from neighbors like China, Iran, or South Africa. Occasionally, they acted only after delays required to deal with domestic political exigencies, as happened in Italy and the US. Sometimes politicians' hesitations seem to have been determined merely by their inattention. In Britain, a week of inertia separated firm recommendations from the scientific advisors to shut down in mid-March and government action.[121]

How carefully leaders had been paying attention at crucial moments and whether they responded in time became fuel for political attacks. Trump paid a price for not reading his briefing books, which had been warning him since January.[122] Those nations, such as Sweden, the US, and the UK, that clamped down only late ran the numbers afterward and realized how discouragingly many lives an earlier shutdown would have spared.[123] Imposing the lockdown a week earlier, Neil Ferguson told a parliamentary committee, would have halved the British death toll.[124] Over 20,000 Britons died after Boris Johnson dithered for a week.

Speed and timing also mattered in other respects. In the absence of widespread testing, being alert to symptoms was the only way for anyone to discern their status. Covid-19 produced many symptoms that varied widely among victims. As experience grew, more joined the list. The first ones, fever and cough, were only rough and ready approximations. Sore throat, runny nose, shortness of breath, headache, vomiting, diarrhea, blackened toes, and watery conjunctivitis-like eyes were often present too, eventually skin rashes as well.

In the UK, public health information focused only on the first two at all others' expense. In late April, anosmia was still considered merely an accompanying symptom to other, more serious ones.[125] When British authorities added the loss of taste and smell to the official list of symptoms on May 18, they trailed the French by a month.[126] In systems that lagged on testing and relied on self-diagnosis to prompt victims to self-isolate or seek medical help, the more symptoms to look for, the fewer would be the false negatives who were still out and about, transmitting disease.

ASIA TAKES THE LEAD

The Global Health Security Index is a list compiled by a panel of experts ranking the preparedness of nations in the face of biological threats. Its first report appeared in 2019. On the whole, it was unimpressed. No country was fully prepared, it concluded, and collectively, readiness was weak. With even these provisos, however, the experts deemed the two best nations to be the US and UK. South Korea was number nine, Germany stood at fourteen, and Brazil bested Singapore at twenty-two. New Zealand appeared only at thirty-five, beating out plucky Albania by a mere three spots.[127] Whatever the global boffins were measuring, it bore little relation to any actual response to the coronavirus.

The most successfully intervening nations picked a preventive course of action early and then operationalized, implemented, and stuck to it. Above all, they put into effect all its various elements at once and coordinated among them.[128] As noted, some successful states were authoritarian, others unimpeachably democratic. Being able to coerce and twist arms, without too much oversight from courts or concern for due process, simplified some things, but it was not crucial to being effective.

Many observers have pointed to Taiwan as exemplary of the best-organized response: a nation that implemented its first measures immediately upon discovering the threat, already on December 31, took scientific advice seriously, and did not hesitate to make demands of its citizens.[129] It is hard not to be impressed, indeed astounded, by the measures Taiwan imposed almost instantly: strict travel bans, minute tracking of arrivals through phone and personal contact, eye-watering fines and punishments for transgression, centralized production of protective equipment at twice the expected demand, with officially set prices to prevent profiteering, and a clamp-down on spreading misleading information.[130]

Among many impressive feats was contact tracing 3,000 passengers of the Diamond Princess. They had taken an onshore tour from Keelung harbor on January 31, five days before Covid-19 broke out on the ship. The authorities were able to identify the passengers' mobile phones and triangulate their locations during the day, whether they had taken buses, taxis, or bicycled and walked. Some 630,000 possible contacts were identified from this, locals who had been within 500 meters of a passenger for more than five minutes. They were sent text messages and advised to quarantine at home. National health insurance data were also used to identify those with symptoms who had not responded to the texts.[131] By late October, Taiwan had gone 200 days without a case of locally transmitted disease – as good a measure of success as is likely possible.[132]

China's reaction had been only slightly less impressive. True, questions remain. Did it seek to hide the epidemic early on? Was it entirely forthcoming once news began to spread? Did its persecution of the first whistle-blowers undermine its efforts, endangering not only its citizens but also nations elsewhere, deprived of alerts that would have triggered their responses?[133] Such queries all ignore the elephant in the room: why has China been the source of so many recent pandemics? However, justified as such questions are, they do not directly affect our concern here, the measures taken once the authorities had faced up to the outbreak's reality.

Along with China, the first-hit Asian nations imposed a strategy of targeted quarantine. China's response was geographically specific, managing to restrict the pandemic to Hubei province. But it also adopted measures aiming at those who were victims or their contacts, wherever they were found. Universal lockdowns of the sort later implemented in the West were born in desperation, implemented only once the disease had spread so widely that it could no longer be choked off with specific measures against the infected. Targeted quarantine, in contrast, aimed to excuse most citizens from mass isolation by imposing precautions only on the ill and their contacts. The few suffered to spare the many. Identifying those few took enormous resources and agile interventions. Yet such upfront costs paled compared with the burdens of belated across-the-board shutdowns.

Targeted quarantine modernized the revised neo-quarantinist system adopted in Europe and North America starting in the middle of the nineteenth century. Oldfashioned quarantine had been reformed once bacteriology had compelled recognition that some diseases spread via particular vectors, which it was possible to neutralize by specific interventions. Rather than confining all travelers in lazarettos, awaiting a possible outbreak of symptoms, the revision system tested for the presence of microorganisms and allowed apparently healthy passengers to proceed, keeping tabs on them during the incubation period.

In effect, it transformed all of society into a lazaretto without walls, while focusing attention on those most likely infected. Everyone suspected of infection was inspected, tested, traced, and surveilled. All others were free to go. This was the underlying logic of the system now rolled out in Asia, including New Zealand and Australia, during the coronavirus epidemic.

Chinese authorities shut down the entire country and isolated infected areas. In April, only some twenty international flights were landing daily. Wuhan was cut off, followed by Harbin.[134] During February and March, Wuhan residents could leave their homes only to shop for food and were temperature scanned at stores. In public, everyone had to wear masks. All residents reported the state of their health daily, with community workers going door to door to collect data and verify it.[135] The symptomatic and those identified as infected once testing was available were mandatorily quarantined. Their contacts were traced, and they, in turn, were isolated.

Since the Chinese sought to squelch the pandemic at its outset, they housed the infected and their contacts in infirmaries. Home quarantine led to intra-family infection and the ill could not be medically cared for. Isolating at home, as in the West, made sense only once the situation had gotten out of hand and quarantines had to be universal. Once at that stage, isolation could occur only at home, short of building an entire parallel quarantine universe.

Anyone who tested positive in China was required to enter an infirmary-style institution, the Fangcang shelter hospitals, which were often set up in gymnasiums and equipped with oxygen tanks and CT scanners.[136] In Wuhan, the authorities converted stadiums and similar structures into quarantine centers and built over a dozen temporary hospitals for the ill with mild symptoms.[137] Two new 1,000-bed hospitals went up at blinding speed – six and fifteen days, respectively.

The infected and their contacts had to isolate, and they were taken off with whatever force was required if they refused.[138] Numbers of those who were mandatorily quarantined are elusive, but in early February, Hubei province had 75,000 people under medical observation. The Fangcang hospitals had 13,000 beds and by March 10 had cared for some 12,000 patients.[139] In Harbin in April, during a secondary outbreak, a single case found in a housing complex condemned all its residents to a two-week quarantine, after which they were not allowed to leave the city.[140]

China tested massively, dwarfing efforts elsewhere. At the end of May, Wuhan screened the bulk of its ten million residents. Of six and a half million tests, it found only some 200 cases, mostly asymptomatic. On one day alone, May 22, 1.47 million tests were processed in Wuhan, compared with the 1.7 million tests New York State had managed during the twelve weeks after March 4. People were ushered to testing stations by officials. Those who refused were threatened with a downgrade of their phone app health code status, hampering their ability to travel and move about, shop, work, or go to school.[141]

Then in June, the Chinese did the whole thing over again, testing the entire population of Mudanjiang, on the Russian border, a mere 780,000 this time. And again in October, on the nine million inhabitants of Qingdao.[142] Internal quarantines excluded travelers from infected areas, such as Wuhan, unless recent test results showed they posed no danger. Protective gear was routinely worn in public.[143] Geolocation software pinpointed hotspots of infection, allowing others to avoid them.[144]

Elsewhere in Asia, the strategy was similar, with contact tracing and isolation the core tactics. For travelers from abroad, that was comparatively easy. They were a known quantity, obliged to pass through the needle's eye at the airport, and could be kept under surveillance. In Taiwan, they were taken to their destination in special taxis, disinfected after each ride, the drivers quarantined every month.[145] Phone apps required of inbound travelers were employed to geofence them electronically to their quarantine locations.[146] Two or three phone calls daily ensured that they remained there, reminding them to wear masks unless they were alone.

One person described his phone running out of battery early in the morning. Within minutes, four different units had been in contact, with the police soon knocking on his door.[147] Dire sanctions threatened if travelers went out: fines deep into five figures and three years in jail. Phones were to remain on, and inspectors visited if the signal vanished or if the device had not moved, suggesting it had been left behind. Quarantinees received $40 daily during their fortnight of isolation.[148] International travelers were screened and kept under telephone app-based observation quarantine for a fortnight in South Korea, first arrivals from China in early February, then travelers from elsewhere in the world as of March.[149]

Tracing citizens within the nation was trickier. Thousands of contact tracers spread out. In Wuhan alone, more than 1,800 teams of five or more people followed tens of thousands of contacts. By the end of May, they had traced almost three-quarters of a million.[150] Close contacts were isolated for fourteen days away from their homes, at home only if that was not feasible, and medically monitored twice daily.[151] Modern technology helped. Mobile phone apps facilitated contact tracing. Two widely used ones, AliPay and WeChat – which had largely replaced cash in China – helped enforce restrictions, allowing the authorities to track people's movements and stop the infected from traveling. These apps coded each person's health status, depending on their recent travel history, time spent in disease hotspots, and exposure to potential carriers. The resulting code – red, yellow, or green – determined whether guards at train stations and other checkpoints let them through.[152]

Getting into apartment blocs, workplaces, and stores required scanning a QR code, writing down name and identity number, temperature, and recent travel history.[153] Those without phones and codes, such as foreigners, had to register their presence for manual tracing. Early in the epidemic, before reliable testing, such coding could be no more than probabilities based on conjectures about exposure. Residents of affected cities duly complained about the arbitrariness of the electronic judgments. Facial recognition technology, already widely used in China, was tweaked to register temperatures of passersby and note the maskless.[154] The Taiwanese repurposed their national health data system, used to track procedures for billing. They merged it with immigration and customs information to identify people with suspicious symptoms who were risks because of their travel history.[155]

In South Korea, contact tracers used mobile phones and real-time bank and credit card data and CCTV feeds.[156] With the highest saturation of non-cash transactions globally, bank and credit card data gave a well-rounded picture of most adults' movements. The same held for South Korea's mobile phone penetration, one of the highest anywhere and equally useful to track the infected. Unlike in the US, but as in many European nations, mobile phones had to be registered in the owner's name.

CCTV coverage was also dense. Between these various technologies plus oldfashioned legwork, the authorities could identify, track, and isolate with some certainty.[157] The potentially infected's movements – stripped of identifying details – were also made public so that others could determine whether they had been put at risk. Phone alerts were sent to those identified as having been nearby.[158] South Korea also set up testing booths that delivered results in minutes. It could test 15,000 people daily and, in absolute numbers, was bested only by China.

Privacy concerns were not ignored. In May, a secondary outbreak in South Korea was traced to a cluster of gay bars in Itaewon in Seoul. Itaewon is Seoul's so-called International District, a kind of reverse Chinatown, popular with tourists seeking non-Korean food and gay bars. Because of the stigma attached to homosexuality, authorities tested anonymously, retaining only mobile phone numbers to convey results. Those who had overlapped with the infected in time and place were urged to screen.[159]

Impressive as these measures were, some Western nations were able to emulate them. New Zealand, Australia, and Germany took a similar tack. Both Pacific Anglophone island nations effectively shut down all incoming traffic, as we discuss below. Germany's system of contact tracing stood out among the Western democracies, which were otherwise unwilling and, in any case, technologically unable to be as draconian as the Asians. It mobilized an army of contact tracers, working primarily with oldfashioned analog technologies.[160] Once things opened up again, new rules helped track people's movements even in the initial absence of phone apps or other electronic tracking. Patrons at bars, restaurants, hair salons, and the like were expected to leave their contact details to be warned should an infected person also have visited.[161] Should similar requirements be imposed on sex workers' clients – the details perhaps left in sealed envelopes?[162] New Zealand, too, adopted oldfashioned analog contact tracing. Having noted the limited uptake of a phone app there, Australia also decided to stick with pen and paper when registering customers' details as things began opening up.[163]

THE WEST LIMPS AFTERWARDS

Elsewhere in the West, however, matters were less impressive. By the time Europe and the US began reacting, in March, it was too late to impose a strict test, trace, and isolate strategy. In mid-March, the French authorities acknowledged they had missed that boat.[164] The disease was now widespread, and even had the infrastructure for targeted quarantining been in place, it would have made little difference. Unable to nip the epidemic in the bud, the Western democracies faced the choice of letting it run its course – the herd immunity strategy – or imposing across-the-board lockdowns that, by freezing things in place, would cut chains of transmission. As death rates rapidly climbed, the only question that remained was whether to shut down sooner or later.

Travel restrictions were confused and ineffectual. Trump made much of his ban on flights from China in late January, but it was too little too late. In any case, it targeted only foreign nationals who had visited China recently, though it also imposed quarantine on Americans returning from infected regions there. Iran was hit with similar restrictions in late February.[165] Then, on March 11, Trump suspended travel between Europe and the US. Keen not to be marooned abroad, a crush of Americans, some infected, booked the last flights back. The airports turned into cattle pens as incomers queued densely for hours awaiting perfunctory screenings. Rather than clamp down on transmission, this botched ban delivered a massive infusion of infection. "We closed the front door with the China travel ban," said Governor Cuomo. But in delaying banning travel from Europe, "we left the back door wide open."[166]

A similar effect had already been seen in Italy where the announcement that Lombardy was to be quarantined leaked on

March 7, prompting a massive exodus southward.[167] On March 15, once it became clear that the government was about to impose travel restrictions, thousands of Parisians decamped for the provinces.[168] If one can draw one practical piece of advice for politicians from this epidemic, it would be never to announce a policy before implementing it.[169] The Scots took this on board in part when they forced the English to bring forward by twenty-four hours a decision to quarantine travelers from France, rather than give British vacationers two whole days to scramble back before the deadline.[170]

Besides chaos, there was lassitude. Even where imposed, restrictions on travel were indifferently enforced. In June, the British finally got around to imposing travel restrictions, just as other nations opened up again. But none of the information submitted by entrants at the border was verified, several destination addresses could be given, and the spot checks that were threatened appeared to lack bite.[171] Nonetheless, having been warned at a meeting on June 2 that 3.5 million jobs were on the line if the hospitality industry did not open for summer, Johnson voltefaced yet again and promised new easements.[172] In early July, a fifty-nation list of exempted countries was duly issued, allowing Brits plenty of leeway for their summer hols.[173] Three weeks later, Spanish infections having spiked in the meantime, that nation was slapped with a fourteen-day quarantine. Johnson's transport secretary, Grant Shapps, had taken his family off there and was now stranded.[174] In the US, the fourteen-day self-isolation required in some states of incoming travelers relied mostly on voluntary compliance – although the Vermont public health bureaucracy did pleasantly surprise one voyager by calling to follow up shortly after arrival.[175] Some states, Hawaii notably, enforced quarantines more stringently than elsewhere, with fines and even arrests.[176]

Lockdowns, too, were enforced with variable strictness in the West. Outside perhaps of Italy, Spain, and Greece, they were well-described as "giant garden parties."[177] What counted as necessary retail varied. South Africa banned alcohol and tobacco sales until that was struck down by court order in June. Alcohol sales were allowed in the UK and the US. Marijuana dispensaries also stayed open in California and other US states where they were legal. British homeowners itching to get on with a project while idled were embittered by closing hardware stores and garden centers. Observers probed the logic of being allowed to take walks in parks, but not to sunbathe.[178]

If challenged by police on the street, the French needed to carry a form they had printed out and filled in at home, explaining why they had to be out.[179] The British thought that was hilarious, but the logic was that, by making things complicated, gadding about would be kept to a minimum.[180] The Greeks had to produce a similar form from a website, in some cases from their employers, but could also text a government number for the same purpose. If all else failed, a statement of what they were up to in a signed personal declaration on a plain sheet of paper did the trick.[181] The French shut parks, beaches, and gardens.[182]

Everywhere people were allowed out to shop for food, but exercise was debatable. In France, it could take place within a kilometer of home, in Italy only within 200 meters, in Spain not at all until the end of May.[183] In France, you could take a walk (*se promener*), but not go for a stroll (*flâner*).[184] Taking exercise did not include jogging before 7.00 in the evening, ostensibly to spare shoppers lining up on narrow sidewalks outside stores.[185] Spanish authorities threatened a man with fines for bicycling to work since that counted as exercise – which was strictly forbidden, though walking a dog was OK – when he should have been taking public transport.[186] In Britain, the public was encouraged to take any means of transportation *other* than mass. Rituals were changed. In Britain, bizarrely, only Jews and Quakers had been allowed to wed outdoors. Now even Anglicans were permitted such eccentricities.[187]

As things opened up again in June, even more seemingly curious contradictions abounded. Pubs and bars opened long before schools. Hairdressers were allowed to see clients again, but not manicurists. Why were cramped airplanes OK, but theaters and cinemas not?[188] Why the Paris metro, but not the parks?[189] How did gyms manage to sneak in ahead of bars in the US?[190] Why could one meet one's significant other in a hotel room, but not at home?[191] Were sandwich shops stores, thus requiring masks, or restaurants, then not?[192] Yet the finer distinctions sometimes reflected a rational stocktaking of Covid-19's transmissive peculiarities. Pubs and cafes could open while nightclubs – more enclosed and heavier breathing – could not. Arcades were more likely to be well-ventilated, therefore allowed to open, but not casinos. Cinemas, theaters, and concert halls could open, but no live performances.[193]

And many of the regulations, while tedious, did reflect epidemiological realities. In England, though now permitted, wedding ceremonies were fenced about with restrictions: they were required to be short, and with no reception or party afterward, nor singing or raised voices, and no wind instruments, but recorded music instead. Hands were to be washed before any exchange of rings, and ablution rituals to take place before the ceremony. No kissing or touching of ritual objects, no devotional materials or items, no cash presents.[194] Danish wedding celebrations, Cinderella-like, had to end at midnight until June.[195] And rightly so: in Israel, 2,000 pent-up ceremonies in the ten days from June 15 to the 25th helped spark a second wave of infection.[196]

In most Western nations, attempts to emulate the Asians were pale indeed. German contact tracing was effective, but that was the exception. Wuhan hired and trained 9,000 contact tracers. America's CDC had about 600 and state and local health departments another 1,600, against an estimated need for perhaps 300,000.[197] By July, those numbers may have been as high as 68,000, but in the meantime, with the pandemic spreading, they remained woefully inadequate.[198] New York City's tracers were able to get responses from only about a third of their caseload when they started up in June.[199] With among the best-established programs in the country, Massachusetts could get answers from 60% and Louisiana, about half.[200]

The UK at first simply lacked the capacity to track at all. It had fewer than 300 staff for the task.[201] Its assumption that each instance would involve isolating 160 contacts meant that it could handle 5 cases weekly, at most 50.[202] A lack of testing capacity only worsened matters. Statistics were compiled by hand and fudged.[203] By June, however, the system was functioning better, though still bereft of any tracing app to help.[204] Yet, in July, stories persisted of contact tracers being able to reach only half their targets.[205] Even in tidy Zurich, tracing the visitors to a nightclub where one guest had infected twenty others proved difficult. A third of the email addresses registered for tracing proved to be fake.[206] Unsurprisingly, privacy advocates pounced on the use of individuals' data.[207] And more extremely, contact tracing was attacked as an unwarranted state imposition.[208]

PROTECTING THE VULNERABLE

If test and trace strategies were unworkable in most Western nations, the next best approach to avoiding the costs and misery of whole-scale lockdown was to identify those groups most in need of protection and isolate them. Protecting the most vulnerable was a corollary of the mitigation strategy. The idea was to allow the disease to sweep through the population to achieve widespread immunity while walling off the susceptible. Isolating the vulnerable was thus a form of reverse quarantine, seeking to block out the infection.

The scope of the problem varied with the size of the group that required protection. So, who were the susceptible in need of cocooning? Their identity was determined partly by the disease and partly by modern society's socio-pathologies. Depending on how they were defined, perhaps half of some populations might need protection. As that group increased, the difference between isolating only the susceptible and total lockdown naturally faded.

The Spanish flu had preferentially killed the young. In the Covid-19 pandemic, the elderly were among the first-noted vulnerable groups. Their presence varied across nations. In Saudi Arabia, 3% of the population was over sixty-five, in Japan, ten times that. Even among developed countries, the range was broad. The US (16%) clocked in at about half the Japanese ratio of almost 30%.[209]

The first Covid-19 mortalities also suggested that, as with SARS and MERS, men succumbed more often than women. From China, those figures were tempered by the observation that more men than women there smoked – half of men, only 2% of women.[210] Yet subsequent studies suggested – which is seemingly perverse for what at first appeared as a respiratory disease – that smokers' survival rates were better. That beneficial link quickly vanished, however, as smoking, including vaping, was confirmed as statistically associated with infection.[211] Men mounted lesser immune responses to the virus than women.[212] Baldness, linked to androgen levels, also seems to have been associated with susceptibility.[213] Further experience revealed that some underlying medical conditions rendered even the young liable. In order of importance, these were: heart and kidney disease, obesity, diabetes, asthma, hypertension, and immunosuppression.[214]

One of the pandemic's most discouraging revelations, laying bare a swath of modern society's pathologies, emerged in April and May, with the first reports that ethnic minorities in the West were especially vulnerable.[215] In the nineteenth century, it had been taken for granted that the poor and specific categories conceptually assimilated with them, like Jews, were likely to succumb. Filth, putrefaction, and crowded and unsanitary living conditions were considered predisposing and possibly causal for disease. The rise of bacteriology, however, encouraged the belief that microorganisms cause disease and that, by and large, they strike indifferently, regardless of social circumstances. Of course, we understand that lack of proper sewerage or clean water makes it hard for people to protect themselves in developing nations. But it came yet again as a rude shock to industrialized nations' self-conception that, even today, ethnic minorities and the poor were hardest hit.

Why were ethnic minorities especially afflicted? We can take no more than a first stab at what doubtless will be puzzled over for years to come. Many of the factors can be decomposed into class terms that overlap with ethnicity statistically and sociologically. Both in the US and in the UK, where the data emerged first, ethnic minorities worked disproportionately in manual, low-paid employment. They remained on the job during the epidemic, unlikely to be working from home. When Leicester suffered a flare-up of new cases in June, it became clear that many of its garment factories, staffed by immigrants from Bangladesh, had continued producing during the lockdown, toiling without distancing or protection to supply internet retail outlets.[216]

Minorities often lived in undesirable neighborhoods near airports, roads, and industries where pollution, traffic, noise, crime, and other factors ravaged their health.[217] Food deserts, such areas made it difficult to eat healthily even with the best of intentions and a steady paycheck. Minorities often lived in multigenerational or otherwise dense households. In the UK, for example, 2% of white British households had more residents than rooms, but 16% of Black African and 30% of Bangladeshi households did.[218] When sick, their access to medical care was also restricted, especially in the US, with no universal coverage. They made less use of preventive counseling and interventions. They were also more likely victims of diseases that left them vulnerable, suffering disproportionately from diabetes, asthma, cardiovascular disease, hypertension, and obesity.

Added to ethnic minorities and the elderly came younger members of the majority population with comorbidities. How many? One study estimated that 22% of the world's population had at least one underlying condition putting them at higher risk of severe illness if infected with Covid-19. That was an average, and riskiness varied widely. Apart from countries with the oldest populations, like Japan, Puerto Rico, and most of Europe, African nations with high HIV prevalence (Lesotho and eSwatini) were vulnerable. So were small island nations with high diabetes rates (Fiji and Mauritius).[219]

There were 2.2 million shielded residents in the UK, the clinically vulnerable who had been told to take special precautions.[220] The old and those with preexisting conditions, along with their carers who also needed isolation, made up perhaps 40% of the UK population.[221] About a third of the French were especially exposed.[222] Forty-five percent of Americans were considered at heightened risk because of underlying conditions, and that was not counting the old, much less their carers.[223]

Whatever the precise quantities, the figures were large. If, say, half the nation's population was at heightened risk, the point of cocooning the vulnerable dissipated. The larger the category of those needing to be sheltered, the less isolating them paid off and the more a general shutdown became necessary.

Nonetheless, those nations that were incapable of Asian-style targeted quarantining and that, in the winter of 2020, were still seeking to avoid the pain and havoc of a general lockdown, did make a stab at protecting the vulnerable first. Bolsonaro's idea of vertical distancing, sheltering especially the elderly, was professed in most nations. But the results were catastrophic. Had the cause not seemingly been sheer incompetence, the elderly's treatment during the pandemic would have amounted to senicide.

In all Western nations, the authorities claimed to be protecting the elderly in care homes. In none did they manage it. In almost all countries, the mortality rates in old age and nursing homes were appalling – often half or more of the total deaths. Of course, the very old were prone to succumb to any number of causes that might push them over the edge, whether Covid-19 or something else. But the excess mortality rates revealed that the elderly who would otherwise have survived were now dying as the pandemic ravaged their homes. In March and April 2020, England and Wales recorded 12,000 coronavirus deaths in care homes. But that was a grotesque undercount. Compared with the same period the previous year, excess mortality in these care homes was two-thirds higher, 20,000.[224]

Elsewhere the percentage of Covid-19 deaths in care homes was equally staggering. Data from late May ranged from a quarter of all pandemic-related deaths in Hungary to a shocking 82% in Canada.[225] Within the US, care home deaths measured in May varied from a low of 1% in Wisconsin to 80% in West Virginia and Minnesota.[226] Horrifying cases of mass death, with the bodies sometimes abandoned and still-living residents uncared for, occurred in Canada, the US, and Spain.[227] A more everyday cruelty followed when the policy of isolating care homes was finally implemented. In the UK, physicians, too, were now reluctant to visit.[228] The ill were left to suffer and often died alone, without medical care or even painkillers or sedation. Their families were often only in whatever contact a mobile phone held by a friendly nurse could offer.

Most nations failed abysmally in protecting the elderly. Many took largely symbolic steps. US stores reserved special shopping hours for the elderly.[229] In Greece and Bulgaria, "golden hours" were set aside for them in parks.[230] But these minor gestures paled compared with the mismanagement of the risks faced by the elderly. Governments were late to recognize the problem, did not supply care home staff with protective equipment, neglected to test them or residents, and were tardy in shutting down to visitors, leaving them exposed to infection.[231] That care home workers were among the worst paid, usually hourly temporary staff, motivated to work even if feeling ill, often recent immigrants, and frequently shuffled among homes in rapid succession, bearing infection with them – none of this helped.[232]

In Sweden, Tegnell sought to explain away the high mortality rates caused by his laissez-faire policies by admitting what seemingly counted for him as the lesser crime of having neglected the elderly. The average age of the dead in Sweden was higher than in Norway. Thus, the problem was not his mitigation strategy as such, but the more specific failure of allowing the virus into Swedish care homes.[233] In fact, the percentage of all coronavirus deaths which had occurred in Norwegian care homes was higher (though the number was much lower in absolute terms) than in Sweden.[234] Sweden was not distinct in terms of the percentage of overall deaths occurring in care homes. It had failed in that respect no more than most other nations.

The problem was that, with a broader spread of infection in general, more care home residents had been infected than otherwise.[235] Both unions and care home management at some Swedish institutions sought to water down requirements that were eventually imposed for protective gear.[236] As the urgency of the situation became clear, local authorities took their own initiatives, in effect breaking the law by forbidding visitors.[237] At the start of April, the national authorities finally got around to prohibiting visitors.[238] As with all policies announced prior to being implemented, this too prompted a last-minute rush by kind but foolish relatives to visit the care homes.[239]

In Sweden, high numbers of care home deaths may have been bolstered by the triage of elderly coronavirus patients in hospitals. They were not admitted to intensive care or even hospital wards but left in their homes to die.[240] In the UK, the problem was almost the reverse: the dumping of patients from hospitals into care homes. Like all nations, the UK sought to spare its health system from being overwhelmed by coronavirus patients. Yet, the NHS occupied so special a place in the nation's political affections that it may dysfunctionally have affected care homes. Care homes had been neglected, understaffed by underpaid employees, more of them run by for-profit corporations than was true even in the US.[241] "Protect the NHS" was one of the three mantras of the government's initial strategy, rolled out in late March, along with Stay at Home and Save Lives.[242]

To free up beds before the dreaded coronavirus onslaught, the NHS moved thousands of elderly patients from hospitals to care homes in the late winter.[243] From mid-March to mid-April, some 25,000 patients were sent from hospitals to care homes. In fact, this was 10,000 fewer than under normal circumstances in the previous year. But since the hospitals had, in the meantime, become sites of Covid-19 transmission while undertaking little testing, infected patients ended up being delivered to care homes. Only on April 15 did it become policy to test all patients being transferred.[244]

Horror stories of standoffs between care home staff and ambulance drivers with untested patients they intended to deliver back from the hospital circulated in the press.[245] Meanwhile, the English authorities also refused to shut down access to care homes to cut transmission.[246] With no rules against visiting, personnel often working across several homes, and with little protective gear, the bulwarks against epidemic spread were few.[247] Only on April 28 did care home staff become eligible for testing, but test numbers were capped even then.

The whole idea of shielding the vulnerable was itself vulnerable. The susceptible, the elderly above all, often lived in multigenerational or other sociable forms of housing and, in any case, relied on contact with many others for their daily needs. How could they be shielded without taking with them the significant fraction of the workforce that served them? Shielding also meant cutting many of the social contacts without which many elderly lived dreary lives.[248] As noted, the more who needed protection, the less a shielding strategy was distinct from full lockdown. In effect, shielding was an attempt to compensate for being unable to institute targeted quarantine while still wanting to avoid the worst consequences of complete lockdown.

Much better – had it been possible – to protect everyone equally. In the Asian nations, where everyone – vulnerable or not – was shielded by targeting the infected, the elderly did no worse than others. In Hong Kong, the infected from care homes were isolated in hospitals for three months, their close contacts in a quarantine center for a fortnight. The outcome was no reported deaths in care homes. In Singapore, the percentage of care home

Covid-19 deaths was 11% of the total.[249] In July, the penny began dropping even in the West. The best way to spare the old and infirm, five Swedish professors of medicine now argued in an editorial, was radically to diminish infection's prevalence in the population as a whole.[250]

CHAPTER 5

Why the Preventive Playing Field Was Not Level

Geography, Prosperity, Society

NATIONS WERE RESPONSIBLE FOR THEIR ATTEMPTS TO keep the pandemic at bay, but the playing field was rough and angled. Some were favored by geographical placement, far from the transmissive currents, others were well-equipped with medical and public health infrastructure. Some had institutions able to deal with the consequences for workers and businesses of interrupted economic activity. Not all enjoyed the political consensus or cultural cohesion required to demand the necessary sacrifices of citizens. Some countries had populations so young as to promise some respite, while elsewhere, widespread morbidities threatened a hard slog. Switzerland and Swaziland faced the onslaught from very different starting positions.

GEOEPIDEMIOLOGY

Epidemics are inseparable from geography. Starting at one point, they spread elsewhere. Their travel history and flow influence how those further along the pandemic path react. Some places – distant or secluded – are spared for the moment, able to marshal plans and resources. Topography also plays a role. The world is lumpy, not just a plane crossed uniformly by epidemic flows. Mountains and deserts impede travel and disease currents. In his classic study of the Mediterranean, Fernand Braudel argued that before the modern era, land separated while water united.[1] Sails were faster than carts. Today, air travel homogenizes. Densely populated and well-connected places are disproportionately endangered. The Covid-19 pandemic hit Africa late, leaving it at first seemingly spared. But those parts with the best air connections were the first seeded – South Africa, Egypt, Morocco.[2]

A learning curve also allows those nations first hit to serve as exemplars – good or bad – for later ones. England enjoyed the advantage of observing how quarantinist measures were of little avail as the cholera epidemics of the early 1830s moved westward across Europe. So did Sweden, but it drew conclusions quite different from England's laissez-faire approach. With the advantage of a later placement in the Spanish flu's movement in 1918, Western cities in the US tended to impose protective measures more quickly than in the East.[3]

These various factors – topography, distance, geography, and learning curve – we may sum up as geoepidemiology.[4] No law of geoepidemiology holds that remote, sparse, isolated places are spared, while dense, pulsating metropolises are doomed to become nests of infection. But its broad logic helps explain aspects of epidemic ebb and flow. Networks of transmission simply coalesce to higher density in some places. Yet, sometimes such sites can better cut themselves off or police access.

Covid-19's epidemic currents seem to have spared some parts of the world, not just because they shut down early. Take the figures from June 2020. By this point, the pandemic had spread from Asia to North America and Europe. It was in the process of ravaging South America without yet hitting its peak there, and its incursion across Africa had only just begun. But in the developed nations, the first wave had crested and infection rates were declining in most. What then explained why eastern Europe remained spared compared with its neighbors to the west? Was it the precise and well-administered measures imposed? The foresightedness and acumen of their leadership in wielding the right tools? The cunning, compliance, and surefootedness of their citizens in dodging infection?

In late June, hard-hit nations had per capita mortality rates in the mid-hundreds (UK 644 per million, Italy 575, Sweden 526, US 390). Germany, admired for its deft response, had 108. The eastern European nations were consistently below that. Hungary, a country that had ostentatiously cracked down, entrusting the president with extra-legal powers, was the worst-performing, but still had only sixty-one deaths per million. Estonia and Slovenia ranked in the low fifties, Poland, Czechia, and Serbia in the thirties, the other Baltics and Ukraine even lower.[5] Even Belarus, the nation whose president had thumbed his nose at the pandemic, leaving his citizens to fend for themselves, was in the low forties.

Greece's unexpectedly impressive performance during the first wave raises similar questions. Was it due to its exemplary handling of the epidemic, which doubtless was quick, thorough, and efficient? Or was it simply spared as big a problem as elsewhere by lying outside the main currents of infection's movement? And what about Maine and Vermont, also sparse, rural areas off the beaten track for most of the year which had imposed measures early?[6] Such issues will doubtless occupy future researchers.

Eastern Europe's placement slightly off the beaten path may have been part of its salvation during the first wave. Its airports were significantly less busy. Working down the lists size-wise during the last normal year for air traffic, Moscow (54 million seats in 2019) had slightly more than Heathrow (50 million). Still, Frankfurt had close to twice Prague's throughput, Paris more than twice Warsaw's, Amsterdam almost three times Budapest, Madrid thrice Bucharest, and so forth.[7] Immobility may also have played a role in lessening Pakistan's problem compared with India. India had 6 times Pakistan's population, but 16 times as many international travelers and 130 times the number of railway passengers annually.[8]

Similar questions, though likely different answers, surround the excellent performance of the Buddhist nations of Southeast Asia, Cambodia, Laos, Myanmar, Thailand, and Vietnam. Vietnam, ever distrustful of China, quickly shut its border, but not the others.

Indeed, Thailand was the top destination for travelers from Wuhan.[9] Low population densities in the countryside and an absence of closed windows and air-conditioning perhaps played a role.[10] As may have the Mekong delta habit of no-contact greetings.[11] Effective tracing programs may help explain the low Thai incidence.[12] More intriguing was the possibility that, having once been exposed to related viruses, endemic in wild animal populations, humans here had developed some cross-immunity to this coronavirus.[13] Similar in its as-yet unproven suggestiveness was the argument that residents of countries with poor hygiene might have their immune responses to Covid-19 boosted, thus suffering lower mortality than citizens of the developed world.[14]

THE ADVANTAGES OF INSULARITY

Whatever their placement in the epidemic currents, other areas were in a position to protect themselves. Take islands. On the whole, they were the easiest to defend against an epidemic incursion from elsewhere. In 1918, Australia had managed to quarantine out the Spanish flu until late December and was rewarded with mortality one-third that of the US, one-quarter of Italy's.[15] Being surrounded by water was no guarantee, of course, as Britain showed, together with Puerto Rico, Hawaii, Guam, and the Maldives.[16] Insularity was not destiny, and an initial advantage could be fumbled. Japan capitalized better on its equally favorable starting position. Although its politicians did not acquit themselves brilliantly, its overall pandemic performance was better than most.

But Taiwan, New Zealand, Australia, Iceland, Cuba, many in the Caribbean, even Mauritius and the Shetlands, all impressed, not to mention plucky little Corsica, which threatened to demand tests of all would-be vacationers.[17] So did South Korea, which, though technically peninsular, in effect was protected on all sides from unregulated incursion. Perhaps it makes sense to include North Korea here too. The Hermit Kingdom made a virtue of necessity. It clamped down on whatever cross-border trade with China took place and long claimed – who knows the truth – zero cases.[18] Probably the Gaza Strip should be counted here too, surrounded by water and hostile borders, able to quarantine and test arrivals and spared community spread, at least through August.[19]

The insular logic presents most starkly across the Pacific archipelago, where ten countries dodged infection.[20] These nations could protect themselves and were strongly motivated to do so. When the Solomon Islands finally had its first case in October – a student repatriated from the Philippines – it was big news.[21] Some had had good experiences during the Spanish flu. Shutting down all foreign shipping, American Samoa had avoided even a single case. In contrast, Samoa (then Western Samoa) under New Zealand's jurisdiction imposed no quarantines and suffered one of the highest mortality rates anywhere, losing 22% of its population.[22] In the Covid-19 pandemic, Fiji shut down travel from infected nations already in February. It banned cruise ships in mid-March, and on March 19, almost all international flights ceased.[23] Case numbers remained in the low double digits with no deaths.

Other islands followed suit. Some simply reemployed long-practiced measures. Cuba's approach to the AIDS epidemic provided a ready template: screening foreigners, testing locals, and strictly isolating the ill in camps with conditions that often improved on life at home.[24] Since Covid-19 was not a prolonged disease, the camps were superfluous this time, but foreigners were kept out and masks were mandatory in public.[25] With the highest doctor-to-patient ratio globally, Cuba sent tens of thousands of medical personnel door-to-door screening cases. The ill went to hospitals, suspected carriers to isolation centers for a fortnight.[26]

Islands knew all too well where the bulk of their infections first came from. In Australia, 70% of infected residents had picked it up abroad.[27] As a result, Australians were forbidden from traveling out, foreigners from visiting, and returning natives were quarantined when they were allowed in at all.[28] Despite reliance on tourism,

Iceland isolated all incoming travelers for two weeks. It tested 16% of its population, quarantining 19,000 infected and their contacts for a fortnight.[29] As we have seen, Taiwan imposed quarantine on all passengers from abroad.

DOMESTIC ISOLATION

A similar quarantinist logic held within nations, too. Rhode Island sought to clamp down on refugees from New York. The Navajo nation cut itself off entirely, as did the Sioux in South Dakota.[30] The Australian territory New South Wales shut the border with Victoria as the caseload flared there.[31] Conversely, the Greeks cauterized the foreign element within their territory on March 18 by isolating refugee camps on its islands. Locked down over-night, families could designate only one person to exit during the day, with police controlling their movements. Some camps were locked down entirely.[32]

When cases reignited in Leicester in June, police turned arrivals back and aimed to keep locals from leaving.[33] Rural areas in many nations – Maine, Cornwall, Brittany, the Norwegian hinterland – resented and, at times, rebuffed city dwellers descending on their weekend and vacation homes, threatening to bring infection and overload hardscrabble local infrastructure.[34] The Italian South begged its compatriots who had emigrated to the North for jobs not to return bearing illness once Lombardy locked down.[35]

Its location in the geoepidemiological logic could also influence a place's attitude on how and when to reopen. Low population density often meant little epidemic transmission, which sometimes encouraged an insouciant attitude. In the US, such areas were often home to Republican voters and a dislike of lockdowns.[36] Every nation had hard-hit and spared areas, with local attitudes varying accordingly. In Germany, the Ruhr was slammed, Berlin spared. In Sweden, Stockholm was the epicenter, Scania let off easy with one-seventh that rate in June – indeed, less infected than Copenhagen and Zealand, just a mile or two across the Sound.[37] Eastern France, near the German border, and Paris were the hardest hit.[38] Maps of its incidence revealed the dramatic spottiness of the European epidemic. A fraction of regions accounted for the vast bulk of deaths.[39] Areas that had been spared sometimes became fools' paradises, seeing no reason not to deconfine early.[40] For them, the pain of lockdown exceeded – for the moment at least – the cost of disease. Other places – such as New Zealand – were acutely aware of the efforts that had gone into protecting themselves and eased up only warily.[41]

The pandemic's territorial specificity, how it hit certain areas hard, also affected its overall impact. China managed to contain the disease to Hubei province, sparing the rest of the country. Many European nations at first suffered it in certain hotspots. However, those hardest hit in the aggregate had broader infections, like Britain, where it pummeled the entire country for longer. In the US, too, the coasts were at first the hardest-hit areas, but then, as other regions failed to erect or dropped their defenses, the illness went endemic there too. A widespread pandemic lasted longer, as in the UK and US, and was harder to tackle with localized test and trace methods once it had gone viral.[42]

Some nations were in a similar position as islands, able and motivated to shut out the epidemic. Saudi Arabia, a small country with a massive airline, locked down hermetically. Its native population was dwarfed by transient foreign workers, living in cramped quarters. The Saudis' extended families lived together in high-density households. It was the destination for vast religious pilgrimages and neighbor to thoroughly infested Iran. Disease threatened to spread, its leaders concluded. Within a month of the virus hitting Saudi Arabia, 150 members of the royal family had fallen ill, triggering an interest among the highest circles.[43]

Conversely, much of the discussion surrounding the Swedish case reflected a geoepidemiological intuition that the country simply should not have been among the hardest hit. Why was its situation so unlike that of its Scandinavian neighbors? To distract attention from the role of its laissez-faire policies in its high mortality, a cottage industry generating explanations for Sweden's exceptional situation arose, supposedly explaining why it was not actually like the other Nordics. Tegnell frequently compared Sweden's whole-country mortality rates with New York City's or Belgium's (population sizes roughly the same) as though that somehow got him off the hook.[44]

Other times, he claimed that Sweden was demographically more like the UK or the Netherlands than its Scandinavian neighbors in its "larger migrant populations and dense urban areas."[45] That made little sense either, given that in its fraction of foreign-born, Sweden lay closer to Iceland and Norway than it did to the UK and the Netherlands.[46] And that its main metropolitan area, Stockholm, was less densely populated than Oslo, not to mention 70% less so than London.[47]

In contrast, others pointed out that, given Sweden's sparse population, single-person households, lack of major cities, and position as the endstation of most travel itineraries, these were not the places it should have compared itself to in the first instance.[48] Total air passenger departures and arrivals at Sweden's major airport, Arlanda in Stockholm, in 2017 amounted to 26 million, a quarter of those in Atlanta that year.[49] Admittedly, Atlanta was a big airport, but Denver, serving a state with half of Sweden's population, had over twice the annual airline seats. Seattle and Charlotte, supplying states smaller than or the same size as Sweden, had close to twice the seats. Minneapolis, the main airport of a state that was home to half as many people, had per capita almost thrice the airplane seats annually.[50] Even compared with Copenhagen and Oslo, Arlanda was sleepy, with less traffic than either for a country twice as large. New York City had been seeded in March by multiple waves of arrivals from Europe and elsewhere in the US.[51] That was less probable in Stockholm, where Tegnell blamed one cohort of Swedish ski vacationers returning from Italy during one fateful week in early February.[52]

Tegnell thought that Stockholm had proportionately more ski vacationers arriving back from Italy than elsewhere.[53] Others have gone to almost comical lengths to emphasize the Swedish fondness for Alpine skiing – compared with fellow Nordics – that, they claim, was the nation's Achilles heel.[54] Even if it mattered, how likely was this? Per capita, skiers were thicker on the ground in Norway, by about 30%. Granted, Danish skiers were 36% fewer than in Sweden, but – as flatlanders – they had to go abroad to have their fun.[55]

By late March, one-third of Danish cases, but only one-sixth of Swedish ones, had been traced back to Ischgl, the Austrian ski resort that was ground-zero for the north European spread.[56] Approximately 560 Norwegian infections were linked to Ischgl (40% of the total in late March), about 1,000 in Sweden.[57] Given population sizes, this was proportionately the same level. Austrian resorts shut down on March 15. If skiing were to be the culprit, perhaps it made more sense to look to Sweden's domestic resorts, which stayed open for business for another three weeks, until April 6.[58]

Sweden was likely the only nation on earth where the chief epidemiologist could argue against requiring masks by insisting that there was simply no crowding – not even on public transportation – and that they were therefore unnecessary.[59] This geoepidemiological logic was also implicitly reflected – by cooking the books – in a study that modeled the effects of voluntary compliance. Rather than contrast Sweden's results geographically with its obvious comparators, its Nordic neighbors, it instead looked at speed and firmness of preventive measures. On this measure, Sweden's late and mild interventions placed it closer to the continental nations than its fellow Scandinavians. Not surprisingly, its results, seen thus, fell broadly into place, halfway between Italy, Spain, and the UK, on the one hand, and Denmark, Norway, and Finland on the other.[60]

Reflecting the geoepidemiological logic from the other end, some nations were so in the thick of things that trying to keep contagion out seemed pointless.[61] The Dutch were among the few countries that had pursued a consistent epidemic strategy across generations. Already in the nineteenth century, they had recognized the hopelessness of their predicament, situated at the nexus of travel and trade currents across the continent and closely connected by sea to Britain and elsewhere.[62] The Netherlands were the opposite of an island, and quarantine made little sense. So too, faced with Covid-19, they did not lock down. If anything, they were even more exposed now than earlier. Schiphol was the third-busiest airport in Europe, Rotterdam, the largest container harbor in the West (eleventh globally).[63] The Dutch depended on open connections both to the world and to the rest of Europe.[64]

WEALTHY NATIONS BUY SECURITY

Some nations enjoyed geographical advantages, others financial ones. Harshness is cheap, finesse costly. While much was said about trust and how those countries whose citizens took responsibility for themselves did not have to unleash the snarling dogs of government enforcement, the reality was that persuading was more complicated and expensive than clamping down. That is how it had been in the nineteenth century, too. Yes, quarantines and cordons, bristling with fortifications, weapons, and soldiers, did not come cheap. But they were a bargain compared with the armies of inspectors and other public health personnel needed to inspect civilians across the nation. Not to mention the vast infrastructure of socialization – daycare, schools, and the like – that it took to inculcate as second nature the responsible behavior public health authorities like.

In the nineteenth century, Europe had weighed the advantages of neo-quarantinism, sometimes called the English system: admit all travelers directly into the nation on arrival, rather than locking them up in quarantine, but keep tabs on them as they went about their business. Britain could afford – and was willing to pay the price of – freer movement and the trade and commerce it facilitated, compared with the lockdown of quarantine. But could others?[65]

Similar considerations left a mark now too. Third World nations were often the harshest interveners, sending in the police against transgressions. The logic was simple: the less the health system could handle the pandemic, the more it had to be prevented in the first place. Without the possibility of testing and tracing, lockdown was the only option. President Duterte of the Philippines threatened to shoot shutdown violators.[66] South African police smashed down doors, fired rubber bullets, and beat people.[67] Officials of the Indian state of Telangana threatened to have curfew violators shot on sight.[68]

Something similar held when we look away from the enforcement stick's blunt end to the harshness of strictures. One study concluded that poorer nations tended to enforce stricter measures relative to the severity of their outbreaks. Haiti imposed lockdown already upon confirming its first cases – though this may have been it hoping to take advantage of its island status to keep pestilence out.[69] Most developed nations outside of Asia took much longer than that.

A composite measure of government intervention revealed that, as of mid-May, the strictest enforcers were found in the global South, along South America's west coast, in Africa and the Middle East, and included India.[70] India was delighted to score the highest possible stringency rating already in March.[71] Vietnam's leaders estimated that the nation could handle 1,000 cases. Beyond that, they feared being inundated like Italy or Spain. Do not, they therefore instructed, allow case numbers to climb any further.[72] To save money, the Vietnamese avoided testing on the South Korean scale. Still, they did impose drastic quarantines, isolating over 50,000 suspected cases and contacts by late April in repurposed resorts and military camps.[73]

Strict lockdown may have been drastic, but it made sense in nations where even a mild epidemic threatened to overwhelm hospitals. Already in early January, with only two deaths reported in

Wuhan, Vietnam began implementing draconian measures. It grounded flights from China in early February. Each of the thousands of contacts in quarantine camps was tested, revealing asymptomatic carriers. While it did not lock down across the board until April, it isolated large areas where clusters of cases arose.[74] The party's network of local informants was put to use enforcing isolation measures.[75] Aware that its medical system was parlous and that most of its citizens worked in the informal sector, Peru took a two-pronged approach: a strict lockdown, combined with a strong stimulus, worth 12% of the GDP.[76]

African nations, too, often imposed severely restrictive measures. With few reported cases, airports and schools were shut. Uganda and South Africa imposed strict shutdowns, banning the sale of alcohol and tobacco.[77] South Africa forbade jogging and dog walking and sent caseworkers door to door.[78] Masks were required, on penalty of fines and jail.[79] Senegal closed its borders and outlawed large gatherings within days of its first case.[80] Malawi and Zimbabwe quarantined returning nationals who had been working in South Africa and Botswana. In some instances, they then had to be tracked down, having fled their detention centers.[81] Djibouti screened massively. Lockdowns and curfews were widespread.[82]

Dharavi was one of India's largest slums, almost a million people living in an area of Mumbai about two-thirds the size of New York's Central Park. It contained the spread by clamping down. Widespread testing identified the infected, who were taken from their cramped quarters to isolation stations – 10,000 in all by mid-June.[83] Kenyan authorities imposed a curfew on Kibera, an equally vast Nairobi slum.[84] As so often, Rwanda was best in class. It was one of the first nations on the continent to impose measures. Travel was interrupted, and the country shut down. Authorities tested randomly on the streets and at drive-through stations at the national stadium in Kigali. After flare-ups in June, it reimposed lockdown in certain areas.[85] Rusizi district was isolated and parts totally shut down. Only in July was some internal movement allowed again.[86]

THE SOCIAL BASES OF PREVENTION

How the authorities dealt with the epidemic was just one aspect of a broader framework of governance where each nation used different tools at its disposal. In some instances, there were happy synergies between disease prevention strategies in the narrow sense and broader aspects of a nation's demography, morbidity, and other characteristics – in others, dysfunctionalities.

How old and how sick was the host population? When, in the spring of 2020, observers sought to explain why Africa had not yet been hard struck, such considerations clamored for attention. Perhaps its rurality was a blessing, with transmission difficult if the nearest village was a day's walk. So might its youth be, since Covid-19 singled out the elderly.[87] Three percent of sub-Saharans were older than sixty-five, 23% of Italians. Even so, many Africans suffered from other illnesses that might leave them susceptible. And medical personnel and equipment, including protective gear, were scarce.[88] That Africa would somehow be spared the pandemic's ravages struck many as implausible.

Such foundational considerations figured among developed nations too. Italy's population was older, but America's, though younger, was sicker. How did that affect the disease's spread? Perhaps the elderly, aware of being vulnerable, were risk-averse? Maine and Vermont, with among the oldest populations, were also the least-hit. Did something similar hold for Japan?

How did people live and interact? Cultures differed in their associational patterns. Density and proximity varied enormously, from Sweden, with the highest proportion of single-person households globally, to a Mumbai slum or a favela in Rio. But even within the developed world, disparities were stark. Urban densities varied, even among agglomerations commonly considered metropolitan. Predictably, Dhaka was forty-six times as densely settled as Boston. More surprisingly, Genoa was close to four times as dense as Copenhagen.[89]

Swedes might live alone, but in Italy and among minorities in the US, multiple generations cohabited, with extended households acting as epidemiological amplifiers.[90] A third of adult children in Italy lived with their parents.[91] Though few in international comparison, three-generation households were more common in the US than in Italy or most other Western nations (excepting Greece, Israel, and Poland).[92] In Asia, where people crowded together too, the ill had been isolated outside their homes to avoid such dangers.

The sheer physicality of interactions also varied by culture. Earlier modeling of respiratory disease spread had confirmed folk sociology by revealing that Italians averaged twice as many daily bodily contacts as Germans.[93] Elbow bumps now replaced hugging and kissing. In Sweden, curmudgeons welcomed the decline of these more overt forms of greeting, which had spread even that far north during recent waves of global Mediterraneanization.[94]

Even taking such ancillary factors into account, the variation in how the pandemic spread remained a mystery. We have touched on the unexpectedly favorable outcomes in Eastern Europe, Greece, the Netherlands, and Southeast Asia's Buddhist triangle. Might such factors have played roles there? And why did America's Pacific coast initially fare better than the East? The West's closer connections to Asia might have pointed in the opposite direction. But, in fact, most disease seeding in the East came via Europe. California shut down earlier than New York, but was it quick enough to explain the outcome? Density of habitation may have played a role when comparing New York City with Los Angeles, but less so Boston with San Francisco. Greece did brilliantly, but why? Was it the ferocity of its clamp-down, despite countervailing factors such as its elderly population and multigenerational households?

And Japan did much better than its – on-paper – lackluster response suggested. Businesses remained open, citizens were free to roam, contact tracing apps and testing were rare, and its population was the world's oldest. Yet, schools closed early, mask-wearing was already customary, the Japanese were healthy, and oldfashioned analog contact tracing was put to good use. Though not isolated at home, nor told to distance themselves in public, the Japanese were counseled to avoid enclosed and crowded spaces and close contacts in general.[95] Whether their use of low-contact greetings – bowing rather than handshaking, kissing, or embracing – played a role remains speculation.[96]

The technology of shutdown may also have played a role in encouraging nations to take one preventive approach or another. One of the pandemic's surprises was how Japan, commonly assumed to be hypermodern, remained dependent on outmoded analog technologies that impeded working from home. Offices still relied on faxes, seals – hanko – were often needed to formalize documents, only a third of businesses were equipped for staff to work remotely, and face-to-face meetings remained the norm.[97] Applying for government subsidies to telework required companies to print hundreds of pages of forms, submitting them in person.[98]

Nor had nations all embraced the pleasures of internet commerce equally, which had an effect once shops closed. Where internet penetration was low, online shopping was naturally rare. But even in the developed world, far from everyone worshipped at the altar of Amazon. Internet shoppers varied from a low of 32% in Greece and 35% in Italy to 70% in the US. Even otherwise technologically sophisticated nations like Taiwan clocked in at only 43% and South Korea at 54%. Only 42% of the Japanese had bought something on the internet in 2017.[99] That now started to change.[100]

Unsurprisingly, overcrowding and lack of sanitation in emerging countries impeded rudimentary precautions like distancing and even hand washing. New soap technologies were invented for such places.[101] But similar problems afflicted impoverished areas of the West too – on reservations for Native Americans, among farmworkers in California, and in some southern states in the US.[102] A third of Navajo Nation homes did not have running water.[103] Similar conditions were common among Roma settlements in Europe.[104] Average citizens of developed nations were also remiss. Only 70% of airport visitors in the US washed their hands after using the toilet, leaving a third to spread microbes and possibly disease.[105]

Economic factors, too, were significant. How big was the informal sector? In India, Pakistan, the Philippines, and Brazil, the 75% who worked outside official employment, beyond the reach of social benefits, taxes, and labor regulation, diminished the government's leverage or ability to do much of anything. Lockdowns simply could not be followed. The world over, over 60% of working people toiled informally, some two billion souls – 85% in Africa, 68% in Asia, 40% in South America. Even excluding agriculture, half of all workers remained outside official employment.[106] An otherwise developed nation like Italy still had an informal sector that accounted for 14% of output. Many simply fell between the stools, bypassed by programs to maintain income during shutdown or even regular social benefits.[107] The US and European programs, aimed at regularly employed wage earners, failed to do much for the small self-employed. When Brazil introduced a program aimed at informal workers in April, many more applied than there was capacity.[108]

The differing presence of wage earners and the self-employed threw up similar problems in developed countries. The former were easier to help via unemployment benefits or support for companies. Some nations aided workers through unemployment benefit schemes. Workers had to be fired or furloughed, then apply for and collect jobless benefits. That was cumbersome and naturally drove up unemployment rates. Others, especially in Europe, relied on wage support schemes to help companies that agreed not to lay off during the epidemic.[109] In Japan, to fire workers was sufficiently complicated and disparaged that companies did so only reluctantly.[110] The US had a bit of both systems.[111] Unemployment benefits were topped up by generous federal subsidies that ended up giving many workers more during the epidemic than at work – one-fifth received twice lost wages.[112] And the Payroll Protection Plan extended loans to employers that became grants if they kept their payrolls intact. The Asian nations implemented policies more akin to the American than the European, with direct income support schemes.[113]

Using unemployment benefits had the advantage that, once the economy started up again, a fluid labor force could now go where most needed, rather than being locked into old jobs that might – whatever the formalities – no longer exist. Over 40% of jobs laid off during the pandemic, one study calculated, were gone for good.[114] Supporting existing employers assumed that the economy would come back in much the same shape as before lockdown – a prospect that seemed decreasingly likely as the epidemic dragged on. Would zombie companies be preserved in aspic?

Unlike previous collapses, however, the pandemic had shut down both the demand side and the supply side. Perhaps freezing the economy in place therefore made sense.[115] At the least, it meant that employees and employers did not have to find each other all over again. Nations with sickness pay programs could conveniently rejigger them to channel support to idled workers – one example of automatic stabilizers built into the welfare system. They also eliminated the temptation for workers to continue work even though suspecting they might be infected – as was an issue in the US.

Conversely, when it came time to return to work, employees in the best-feathered nests were least willing to reemerge. Teachers' unions in England saw no reason to restart the academic year just weeks before ending it for the summer.[116] Many French employees were content to postpone taking up tools again, even as President Macron begged them to return.[117] Thanks to the CARES Act top-up of unemployment benefits, even American workers found themselves sometimes better treated while furloughed than in work. They were not eager to see that end.[118]

Childcare also reared its head in determining which strategy suited best. Nations where stay-at-home mothers still bore the brunt of caring for the young and grandparents were also roped in faced different problems than where two-earner families relied on schools and daycare. Lockdown could more easily be dealt with in three-generation households, even as they increased infection rates. Crucial workers required parenting relief to continue their tasks. Schools remained open for key workers' children in Britain, and the Swedes motivated their refusal to shut grade schools with the need to keep pupils' parents working in the health care system.[119] But the French closed daycare and schools already in mid-March.[120] The Dutch provided daycare for key workers' offspring. Because childcare providers counted as crucial workers, their children had claims to daycare.[121]

Health care financing mattered as well. Those systems that relied heavily on fees found themselves in a position similar to retail and hospitality, bereft of clients and funds. Many hospitals were in dire straits in the US despite an influx of corona patients and a $175 billion government bailout.[122] Health care spending dropped during the winter and spring – by 13% on hospital visits, 33% on dentists.[123] Insofar as suppression measures succeeded and the hospitals were not overwhelmed, many grew eerily empty. Patients stayed away from procedures, tests, examinations, and treatment for anything other than the coronavirus. Even when almost overwhelmed, private health care was starving. In contrast, state-financed systems like the Canadian got their budget allotments whether hospital beds were occupied or not.[124] That might be inefficient in the long run, but it tided them over the immediate pitfalls.

With high numbers of uninsured, the question of who was to pay also raised its ugly head. Where fee for service was the primary mode of payment, potential coronavirus victims were motivated to shun testing and treatment, worsening the situation. Early measures therefore sought – not always successfully – to deliver free testing and treatment. The US faced such problems, but so did China, where authorities agreed to cover testing and treatment if patients' insurance did not.[125] Perverse incentives also abounded. Poor Medicaid patients in the US brought in less income for nursing homes than coronavirus patients on Medicare or private insurance. Nursing homes' most lucrative business, caring for post-surgery rehabilitation patients, dried up as elective procedures were postponed. As a result, ordinary Medicaid nursing home patients often found themselves discharged, with better-reimbursed replacements in their beds.[126]

CHAPTER 6

Where and Why Science Mattered

Traditional Chinese Medicine, Herd Immunity, Asymptomatic Carriers, Superspreading, and Masks

THE UNDERSTANDING OF COVID-19'S ETIOLOGY WAS broadly uniform worldwide. During past epidemics, ignorance of the precise means of transmission had allowed multiple and contradictory ideas of how best to tackle the problem. This time, the reasons why public health officials recommended their tactics were relatively straightforward. That advice was not always followed. Politicians often ignored it. And politics colored the choices and timing of scientific decisions. The major vaccine-producing nations jostled for recognition and preeminence, with the Russians and Chinese this time seeking membership in the club. Vaccine trials were rushed in hopes of political advantage, whether election victories for Trump or geopolitical preeminence more generally.

Certain preventive tactics depended on which direction etiological understanding of the coronavirus took. Immunity passports were pointless without an immune response, whether from natural infection or vaccination. With advances in knowing the virus, changes in tactics followed. As its aerosolized spread became recognized, masks gained favor as a means of prevention, and the dangers of small, contained spaces were laid bare. At first, it seemed as though the young were largely spared the illness and were perhaps even not vectors of transmission. Significant preventive decisions relied on that assumption. The Swedish logic of keeping schools open and fulfilling their childcare function so that parents could work rested on the premise that children not only were less afflicted but also spread the illness more seldom than adults. Conversely, the French closed daycare and schools already in mid-March on the assumption that children, though often asymptomatic, were carriers like everyone else.[1]

Some of the first studies, from Iceland and Italy, suggested that children were less infected and infectious.[2] But when larger and more thorough ones from South Korea appeared in July, that began to seem like a pipe dream. The cohort of ten- to nineteen-year-olds spread disease, just like adults.[3] Meanwhile, other studies showed that children's viral loads were at least as high as adults'.[4] And that even the youngest could be vectors.[5] Starting schools up again now promised to become even more vexed. As schools (and universities) reopened in the spring and late summer in South Korea, Israel, France, and the US, infections flared.[6] Yet other results suggested that elementary schools did not seem to be sources of spreading.[7] In other respects, too, knowledge of the virus and its development pushed prevention in different directions.

TRADITIONAL CHINESE MEDICINE

One notable twist to the story of a broadly shared etiological understanding of the coronavirus came with the Chinese use of their traditional medicine (TCM). The Chinese were keen to emphasize how they based their approach to Covid-19 on science and expertise. "China's response has been professional," they insisted, "because its response measures were based on timely analyses and assessments by scientists and public health experts, whose views and proposals were fully respected."[8] But in that quiver of expertise, one arrow was TCM.

Mao had treated TCM as yet another approach to treatment. He personally was skeptical, but thanks to their cheapness, availability, and popularity in the countryside, traditional remedies allowed servicing more ill.[9] The current regime had gone beyond that tactical alliance, regarding TCM as a valuable aspect of Chinese culture and a potentially useful supplement or alternative to conventional Western medicine.[10] During the SARS epidemic in 2002–3, half of all patients had been treated by TCM methods.[11] Just months before the current outbreak, the government had issued guidelines on coordinating the two therapeutic approaches, ensuring that the Chinese be treated equally to the Western.[12]

TCM practitioners were a small minority, 9% of all healthcare professionals in China. They welcomed official China's support. Amid the epidemic, they saw the opportunity to advocate for a more substantial role.[13] In the absence at first of effective Western treatments for Covid-19, here was their chance to strike, showing how TCM "became the last, and somewhat best, resort."[14] Wang Wei, vice-president of Beijing University of Chinese Medicine, pointed out how Western medicine had to waste precious time during an epidemic analyzing pathogens, conducting research on animals, and running clinical trials. TCM practitioners, in contrast, "can rapidly put forward a treatment plan based on a number of factors, such as the patient's clinical symptoms and other outward signs, the geographical and weather patterns."[15]

The results spoke for themselves. Wang Wei adduced the Lung Cleansing and Detoxifying Decoction, a mixture of ephedra, licorice root, and other ingredients, which had supposedly achieved a cure rate of 99.28% among 1,200 Covid-19 patients over ten provinces by mid-April.[16] Here was a chance to consolidate TCM's reputation, agreed Pan Leiting, cell biologist and professor at the School of Physics at Nankai University in Tianjin.[17] China also promoted TCM in countries, primarily African, where its Belt and Road Initiative had spread its influence.[18] Exporters of TCM detected market opportunities abroad during the pandemic, though conceding that, where their treatments were unauthorized for hospital use, their primary purpose could only be preventive.[19]

In harmony with its traditional practitioners, the Chinese authorities lost no time making TCM the all-but peer of its

Western counterpart. They hailed TCM as an equal partner in treating and curing Covid-19. The etiology and the pathogen of the pandemic had been analyzed and confirmed using TCM methodologies, they insisted, and a set of diagnostic and treatment protocols worked out. In the seventh version of the diagnosis and treatment protocol, issued in early March, TCM methods received almost as much space as the Western. Among the pertinent TCM diagnoses was Cold Dampness and Stagnation Lung Syndrome. To recognize it, physicians were advised to examine the patient's tongue, which would have a "thin fat tooth mark or is faint red, and the coating is white thick rot or white greasy and the pulse is moisten or slippery." The cure involved ephedra, gypsum, almond, betel coconut, and ginger.[20]

Western methods were granted one – significant – concession. TCM patent medicines and treatments were recommended for mild cases of Covid-19, to boost immunity among their contacts, and strengthen the constitution of those who had recovered. Such therapies included Jinhua Qinggan Granules, Lianhua Qingwen Capsules/Granules, Xuebijing Injections, Lung Cleansing and Detoxifying Preparations, and Dampness Resolving and Detoxifying Preparations. They had been used in over 90% of confirmed cases. But for cases with severe symptoms, TCM methods should be applied in conjunction with Western techniques.[21] Even so, critically ill patients on ventilators were prescribed various patent medicines, distinguishing between those who had abdominal distensions or constipation while being ventilated and those suffering from what was described as human–machine asynchronization.[22]

What effects TCM had on Covid-19 lies beyond this investigation. A preventive influence may have been detectable.[23] Immunosuppressant effects of some traditional remedies may have helped calm overreactive immune responses (cytokine storms).[24] Whatever such results, the role of TCM raised a dilemma. TCM had very likely figured as an element of what had caused the Covid-19 epidemic in the first place, the medicinal usage of animals best kept at arm's length. During the SARS epidemic in 2003, that virus had been detected among masked palm civets and a raccoon dog at a wet market in Shenzhen. Civets are prized in TCM and eaten to convey immunity to influenza.[25] TCM had both helped create and was now hawked as the cure for Covid-19.

HERD IMMUNITY

The mitigation strategy allowed the epidemic to run slowly through the population, not overwhelming the medical infrastructure, but delivering broad immunity so that life could soon return to normal – for those who survived. Mitigation relied on herd immunity as its fundamental premise. Without it, there was no logic in letting the disease spread.

Herd immunity at first attracted both British and Swedish decision-makers, covertly influencing their approach. The Dutch, too, pursued herd immunity, but their leaders seem at least to have admitted it.[26] Oddly, both Swedish and British officials denied it hotly. Herd immunity attracted those who hoped to put an end to lockdowns and other drastic interventions. The faster a critical mass of people gained immunity, the sooner restrictions could end. Herd immunity did a vaccine's work even before one had arrived.

Libertarians the world over hailed the Swedes for their hands-off approach, which implicitly meant support for the premise that herd immunity was possible. In late August, the Trump administration, seeking to undo some of the pandemic's economic damage and open schools, began toying with a herd immunity strategy on the Swedish model.[27] They installed a new advisor who had earlier written in favor of herd immunity, though he now cautiously denied any such intentions.[28] In September, Rand Paul, the libertarian senator, warmed to the cause, claiming that New York's current low infection rate sprang from herd immunity.[29]

In September, a similar debate reignited in the UK, with some scientists now advocating cocooning the most vulnerable to allow the bulk of the British a return to normal life, achieving widespread infection and immunity in the process.[30] The herd immunists now joined together in early October, issuing the Great Barrington Declaration. They argued for a form of focused protection of the vulnerable, leaving others free to go about their business. That herd immunity would be both the outcome and the mechanism of their salvation, they did not doubt.[31] Shortly thereafter, they were granted an audience with the Health and Human Services Secretary, representing a White House meanwhile ravaged by its own mini-pandemic following the president's infection.[32] By October, the White House was officially onboard.[33]

Herd immunity meant that once enough people had been infected, and therefore supposedly rendered immune, sustained transmission dropped, winding down the epidemic. Usually, herd immunity is acquired through vaccination. But, in principle, a disease burning its way through its host population might also leave the survivors immune. Not all viruses prompt immunity, however, and even when they do, it lasts for varying times. As the issue was discussed starting in the spring of 2020, no one knew whether Covid-19 conferred immunity or, if so, for how long. But they did know that humanity has not yet developed herd immunity to any coronavirus.[34]

A study from Kenya, for example, had shown that other coronaviruses, those that cause colds, reinfected the same patients repeatedly, with no effective immune response.[35] And they knew that cities that had suffered the highest mortality under the first wave of the Spanish flu in 1918 did not enjoy lesser death rates in the second wave. And that Australia, which had avoided an outbreak in 1918 – therefore with no herd immunity – still had a very low mortality once it arrived in early 1919.[36]

Herd immunity was the joker in the tactical pack of cards. The Asian nations imposed targeted, surgical interventions against the infected and their contacts, leaving most everyone else untouched. All other countries relied on some variant of mass quarantine, in what came to be known as the hammer and dance strategy.[37] Everyone was at first hammered in self-isolation. Then came the dance of reimposing local quarantines against secondary wave outbreaks and/or belatedly trying to test and trace the infected.

Very few nations neither hammered nor danced. Even Belarus – despite Lukashenko's bluster – soon imposed border controls and the like. And Swedish officials repeatedly insisted that their strategy, supposedly mischaracterized as hands-off, merely sought voluntarily to achieve the same purposes that elsewhere required enforcement. Mitigation and suppression were both variants on hammering and dancing, with the emphasis placed differently. Both aimed foremost to buy time. While mitigation hoped to slow the pandemic's sweep, suppression clamped down more firmly to produce even fewer cases. Spreading infections over longer periods, flattening the epidemic's infection curve, would spare health care systems a sudden, overwhelming onslaught of patients. If there were immunity and eventually a vaccine, populations would become protected and the epidemic would pass. But, barring a vaccine or treatment, neither tactic had an exit strategy – unless herd immunity was relied on.

After one cycle of incubation and disease, a complete suppression would, in theory, have left the population healthy, but also unimmune – except for those who had fallen ill. The mitigation strategy, in contrast, aimed to spare the hospital system by allowing the disease to spread slowly. Eventually, enough people would have succumbed to achieve herd immunity. The suppression strategy could work only if applied universally and globally, eradicating the virus among all humans simultaneously. Otherwise, with most people still not immune, partial shutdowns would need to continue against second and subsequent waves or at least some form of targeted quarantine.

Simultaneous and global suppression was unlikely, to put it mildly. But some nations came close to achieving this in their own territories. By the late spring 2020, some Asian countries, as well as New Zealand and Australia, and perhaps Germany, seemed to have managed successful suppression. The epidemic was sufficiently smothered that subsequent cases could be traced, tested, and isolated, leaving everyone else unbothered. Intermittent secondary infections flared up – in transient workers' dormitories in Singapore in May, in a food market in Beijing and nightclubs in Seoul in June, as well as in and around slaughterhouses in Germany. But they were sufficiently limited that testing and tracing still worked. The same held for the reimposition of isolation in Melbourne in July, including a hard lockdown with no exit possibilities for five public housing towers.[38] And for the flare-ups in the UK, in Leicester and other northern towns. General lockdowns did not yet have to be reimposed.

That differed from the premature easing up that the US undertook, leading to rising case numbers in June in Texas, Florida, California, and the need to reimpose aspects of the general lockdown.[39] Precisely in which category to classify the reimposition of lockdown that Catalonia adopted in Segria and Spain in Galicia in July is harder to determine.[40] As is the dilemma Israel faced in July when cases surged after an initially successful clampdown, with lockdowns reimposed that month.[41] After the hammer and dance came the whack-a-mole strategy that Boris Johnson announced, locking down flashpoints as they re-flared.[42]

Unless case numbers diminished enough for an effective test and trace strategy, however, herd immunity was the only other exit option. For nations like Sweden that had opted for mitigation instead of suppression, herd immunity was crucial. Without herd immunity as the achievable goal, why not clamp down more firmly, suppressing the epidemic fully? Why let more people die, as they would if lockdown were implemented only partially, if the aim were not to achieve broad infection-based immunity?

The calculus was openly utilitarian. Herd immunity as an exit strategy from quarantine meant letting more people die now so that fewer – or at least no more – would perish over the entire lifespan of the epidemic. As one Swedish medical professor put it, "Much better to have high mortality today if that brings us closer to herd immunity." His proviso, that, in the long run, overall mortality would be lower, could, of course, have been only a pious wish at the time he uttered it.[43] Giesecke, the former chief epidemiologist, argued in May 2020 that Sweden's strategy would stand vindicated once the other Nordic nations had arrived at the same per capita mortality by the end of a year.[44] At that point, in late May, Finland, with its 308 deaths compared with Sweden's 4,029, would have to make many mistakes over the coming nine months.

The pleading was special, the logic tortured. Yes, an unimmune population emerging from wholesale lockdown remained at risk. But having re-achieved the same position they enjoyed at the onset of the epidemic, those nations that had held the worst casualties at bay could now begin anew. Having largely extinguished the epidemic by May, New Zealand now tested, traced, and isolated the few who fell victim and kept it contained. Giesecke's prognosis that New Zealand would need to quarantine all incoming travelers during the coming decade while they awaited a vaccine was highly misleading.[45] Earlier in May, the Austrians had begun testing arriving passengers at the Vienna airport, subjecting them to a delay of three to six hours before allowing the uninfected to pass.[46] Iceland had a similar program.[47] And at this point in the epidemic, New Zealand's mortality was 100th of Sweden's.[48]

We have touched on how the Tory government began by pursuing herd immunity in the winter of 2020, believing that the British would not sit still for a broad lockdown. But once they realized just how many deaths a free-rein coronavirus epidemic would cause, the cabinet pulled that option off the table. The Swedes drew the opposite conclusion. The Swedish authorities also spurned the idea they were pursuing a herd immunity strategy.[49] Just as in Britain, the many deaths that followed were politically intolerable. Even if the long-run death rate might be less, the political cost of the upfront mortality was unwelcome. The foreign minister, Ann Linde, expressly and repeatedly denied that Sweden was seeking herd immunity.[50] The ambassador to Britain was trotted out to spout the official line of denial.[51]

Tegnell was harder to pin down. In mid-March, he admired the British for what was then still their herd immunity strategy, claiming that Sweden was pursuing a similar approach. "We are careful about using the word," he cautioned, "since it sounds a bit like we have given up." But that herd immunity meant six million Swedes becoming infected, was the calculation he was working with.[52] And in April, he both claimed that herd immunity was not the goal and welcomed it as the eventual outcome.[53] But the Swedish authorities' denials contrasted even more starkly with their actions. What Tegnell pursued was indistinguishable from herd immunity.[54] One of the first serious studies of the Swedish approach agreed that herd immunity was clearly what the public health authorities had been aiming for, however little they later wanted to admit it.[55]

In mid-April, Tegnell claimed that immunity had spread so widely in Stockholm that it was beginning to affect the epidemic's course.[56] He based his prognosis on mathematical modeling. It could hardly have been otherwise. At the time, antibody tests were barely reliable. Sweden was, in any case, undertaking no mass testing. And on the crucial question of whether the presence of antibodies indicated immunity, science was still mum. And yet, Tegnell categorically insisted that there was an immune response.[57]

In early April, results from antibody screening conducted on small sample populations worldwide began trickling in – Santa Clara, Los Angeles, Miami, Spain, France. They all indicated that many fewer people had been infected than necessary to achieve herd immunity. Most figures were single digits.[58] Only the ones from New York (14%) and New York City (21%) broke into double digits.[59] In May, hard-hit Spain had only 5% of its population infected (even in Madrid, only 11%).[60] In France, it was 4.7%, in the US, less than 10%.[61] Even the miniature Wuhan of Europe, the Austrian ski resort Ischgl, reached only 42% in June.[62] Iran reported 30% in July and Delhi 25%, Mumbai was 41%.[63]

That was still a far cry from the 60% to 80% required for effective herd immunity, and some Swedish commentators did bite the bullet by acknowledging this as bad news for their tactics.[64] Pune in India reported approximately 50% seropositivity in early August.[65] But otherwise, the only herd immunity on the horizon was found in testing at a storefront clinic in the fortuitously named Corona, a hard-hit working-class neighborhood in Queens. There 68% of results showed antibodies.[66] Manaus, in Brazil, may also have achieved something similar. As might communities of migrant workers in Qatar.[67]

Meanwhile, the WHO warned that no evidence yet showed whether the sick were developing immunity to future rounds of coronavirus.[68] It cautioned against relying on the concept of herd immunity, which, it pointed out, was intended to describe the results of widespread vaccination, not a silver lining to an epidemic's ravages.[69] Since viruses were often able to dodge the body's immune response, while vaccines targeted their weak spots, vaccine-derived immunity was often much more vigorous than that derived from a normal infection. Against the papillomavirus, for example, natural infection provoked only a weak immune response, while HPV vaccination triggered a strong one.[70]

In July, studies showed that antibodies dropped off steeply a couple of months after infection.[71] Other scientific opinion was even more robust. That the idea of herd immunity was ever on the table beggared belief, the editors of *New Scientist* thundered. Without knowing whether natural immunity even existed, relying on herd immunity as an exit strategy was "scientifically illiterate."[72] To achieve natural herd immunity would require Covid-19 to spread so far that likely thirty million would die worldwide, six million in China, a million in the US, and some 40,000 in Sweden.[73] Herd immunity was unethical, the WHO's Director-General warned.[74]

The perils of predicting based on modeling alone were also soon laid bare. In late April, a Swedish report suggested that 11% of Stockholmers had antibodies.[75] For each reported case, it extrapolated, about 1,000 symptomless ones existed. According to this calculation, by May 1, a third of all Stockholmers would have been infected. With some 6,000 infections reported in the Stockholm area, that implied six million asymptomatic cases – far more than the region's entire population.[76] When the arithmetic miscalculations were pointed out, the report was withdrawn and reissued with revised numbers that now proposed seventy-five asymptomatic cases for each confirmed one.[77]

That still suggested a peak of some 70,000 cases on April 8.[78] The revised report anticipated 26% of the Stockholm population would have been infected by May 1.[79] Then, in May, the results of antibody tests conducted in late April (week 18) became available. They showed that far fewer Swedes had been infected in early April (it takes a few weeks for antibodies to develop) than predicted; 7% of Stockholmers and 3% or 4% in the provinces.[80] The herd immunity approach had failed, for the moment at least. In mid-June, new surveys revealed 17% infection among Stockholmers – still far from the 60% required for herd immunity. This was of voluntary test-seekers too, which may have skewed the results.[81] No sign of herd immunity was the unsparing verdict of one account.[82]

Nonetheless, Tegnell was back, banging the drum of unmeasurable immunity: "We are really confident that our immunity is higher than any other Nordic country's," he announced in mid-June.[83] At the end of July, he remained at it, insisting that Sweden had a higher "basic immunity" than Norway and would do better in a second wave in the autumn.[84]

The whole circus repeated yet again in September, as Sweden enjoyed momentary low infection rates while the rest of Europe suffered from secondary waves driven by vacation travel. Finally, Sweden's strategy was bearing fruit, Tegnell insisted on French TV.[85] Did we miss the herd immunity boat, Danish and Russian observers now wondered?[86] Yet this time, once the Stockholm rates started upwards again in the fall, the bravado toned down, and Tegnell was prepared to impose new restrictions.[87] Despite protestations to the contrary, he had finally given up being exceptional and was adopting much the same hammering and dancing strategy as elsewhere in Europe. Contacts of the infected had to isolate at home, starting in early October, regardless of symptoms. Local lockdowns were now on the menu, with Uppsala the first municipality to impose one.[88] And the government proposed a new contagious disease law to limit public assemblies and other restrictions.[89] The politicians were taking back control and the Swedish Sonderweg had ended.

An exchange earlier in May had revealed the thought processes at the heart of the Swedish approach. A Belgian epidemiologist, Pierre van Damme, had warned Swedes against complacency. Tests elsewhere in Europe had revealed much lower rates of infection than they were anticipating. Even if some immunity were the outcome, it would vary within the nation, not conferring blanket protection. A Swedish professor, Jan Albert, replied, admitting that the results of antibody testing were not clear. "But we have to believe," he concluded, "that we will achieve herd immunity. We cannot keep society locked down as we have now for however long it takes to get a vaccine."[90] Herd immunity, in other words, was the get-out-of-jail card the Swedish authorities were counting on since they did not consider their citizens willing to tolerate extensive lockdown.

MASSAGING THE NUMBERS

Just how much was at stake in delivering herd immunity can be judged by how scientists and the authorities who relied on their expertise worked the evidence to fit the justification they sought.

Scientists were uncertain about immunity. Was it conferred by having had the disease? If so, for how long? Was immunity measurable by antibodies only? Or could immunity also be conveyed directly by immune cells or by a broader immune response, a "memory" of having encountered Covid-19, or even by other similar diseases, that promised protection against future infection? However much the Swedish authorities denied it, their hands-off approach was motivated by the promise of herd immunity.

Tegnell and others held out the likelihood of widespread immunity as the upside of the high mortality that his country was enduring. When the first antibody testing results arrived in May, the figures were low, even for hard-hit Stockholm, where only 7% of the population had antibodies. These unexpected results prompted the official epidemiologists to ponder other explanations for why herd immunity seemed slow to arrive. Tegnell massaged the numbers, claiming that the infection rates would soon be much higher, perhaps as much as 20%, since the tests now reported had measured infection two weeks prior to their release and therefore before herd immunity's build-up.[91]

Meanwhile, Petter Brodin, an epidemiologist who agreed with Tegnell's approach, shifted gears, moving the argument away entirely from antibodies which – annoyingly – were refusing to cooperate with official strategy. He tried to account for the unexpectedly low rates by arguing that it was possible to have immunity without antibodies. No one had changed their behavior in the last month and nothing suggested that the virus had mutated. Even so, the epidemic spread more slowly than anticipated. "For me," he concluded, "that must mean that there is a degree of immunity in the population."[92]

The presence of antibodies most commonly indicates immunity. Antibodies were measured and found to be less present than hoped. Therefore, Brodin rejiggered the argument not to require antibodies at all. The desired conclusion – widespread immunity – could be asserted even in the absence of evidence. QED. Tom Britton, the Swedish mathematical modeler, pursued a similar logic. Why were so few showing antibodies? Either the epidemiologists' predictions had been wrong, he conceded. Or, he continued, grasping at a slightly different straw of unfalsifiability, "a larger part of the population has been infected than developed antibodies."[93] In other words, many had been infected (and presumably gained immunity) even though few had antibodies.

This claim that immunity was present despite the absence of antibodies was not unique to Swedish experts seeking to justify their herd immunity strategy. Other scientists have also taken similar approaches to the missing-antibodies problem. Covid-19 was a mild disease, some argued, that had already spread widely by the late spring of 2020, leaving behind a largely immune population.

The degree of already existing herd immunity had simply not been recognized.

In May, Michael Levitt, Professor of Structural Biology at Stanford, claimed that the epidemic typically burned itself out, infection numbers declining at about the same point in each nation's pandemic trajectory, regardless of what measures had been marshaled against it, lockdown or not.[94] They diminished as Covid-19 reached what he considered saturation level, even though that was not reflected in antibody prevalence.[95] When challenged as to why testing revealed so few with antibodies even in highly infected areas, he claimed that antibody testing failed adequately to measure immunity and that evidence of T cell receptors' presence was now emerging.[96]

Sunetra Gupta, Professor of Theoretical Epidemiology at Oxford, argued a similar line. The low antibody results from studies in May did not dim her conviction that the actual level of immunity was high. Other non-antibody-related forms of immunity must be present, she insisted: genetic advantages or immunity derived from exposure to other coronaviruses, like the common cold.[97] Giesecke, the former chief epidemiologist in Sweden, embroidered on this approach. Herd immunity achieved by infection, he insisted, was preferable to that via vaccination. For almost all ailments, it gave a better and more complete immunity.[98]

Given that virtually no one in the developed world suffers the diseases we are vaccinated against, it is unclear how he could make this claim, much less praise the virtues of spreading deadly illnesses. And indeed, it did not take long for studies to reveal that even previously infected patients showed only weak and rapidly diminishing antibody responses. That established, said Akiko Iwasaki, a viral immunologist at Yale, that naturally derived immunity was suboptimal and that natural infection could not be relied on to achieve herd immunity.[99]

Humans can indeed have immunity to diseases against which they do not produce antibodies. Neutralizing antibodies are just one of the correlates that sometimes indicate immunity and can be measured to detect it. Immune cells themselves, like T cells, can fight off illnesses, and the immune system sometimes retains a "memory" of previous infections in B cells that ramp up antibody production when attacked again.[100] Cytokines, proteins released by immune cells that act as messengers, sometimes indicate immunity.[101] Evidence did emerge of some cross-reactive T cell response in unexposed subjects between common colds and this coronavirus.[102] And T cell memory of SARS infection appears to have lasted up to seventeen years.[103]

Early studies may also have underestimated the role of asymptomatic carriers. Later ones suggested that almost half of all Covid-19 cases could have been asymptomatic. Some of these asymptomatics may have been merely presymptomatic, but most appear to have been genuinely symptomless.[104] If these carriers then also proved able to transmit for long periods, it followed that Covid-19 might have spread silently, quicker, and more widely than realized.

Similarly, modeling studies showed that if there were broad cross-reactive immunity from other coronavirus exposure, then herd immunity might be achieved at lower levels of Covid-19 exposure.[105] But no one was yet testing for other non-antibody-related forms of immunity against the coronavirus in the general population and there was no evidence that it might be present. So counting on this, at a time when no other form of immunity had been measured, to explain the outcome these observers were banking on – herd immunity – can most charitably be described as magical thinking.

In late June, then, good news arrived for those looking for other forms of immunity. Studies at the Karolinska, Stockholm's medical university, showed that T cell immunity was more critical than realized. Studying asymptomatic contacts of the ill, and those with only mild Covid-19 symptoms, the researchers found T cell responses among twice as many as those who showed antibodies.[106] Promptly, in July, the Swedish authorities cashed in that theoretical possibility. They now retrofitted the observation that death rates were not climbing as fast as earlier with the causal presumption that immunity levels in Stockholm could be as high as 40%, well over twice the most expansive antibody results.[107] Like a dog with a bone, they would not let herd immunity go. When infection rates started rising again in October, more now in posh Stockholm neighborhoods than in the hardscrabble immigrant areas that had been hard-hit in the first wave, herd immunity was naturally the possible explanation trotted out.[108] Meanwhile, other studies threw cold water on the significance of cross-reactive immunity.[109]

While the news in June was welcome, it is worth repeating the obvious. Even tripling the numbers of those Stockholmers proven immune would still not come close to herd immunity levels. Nor was it clear yet whether T cells – much as was also possible with an eventual vaccine – had a sterilizing effect or not.[110] They might protect individuals from getting ill, but without stopping them from becoming infected, carrying the virus, and transmitting it.[111] In other words, T cell immunity might produce even more asymptomatic carriers.[112] If so, the advantages of herd immunity dimmed.

And, most importantly, whatever the truth of the matter, the Swedish authorities had taken their gamble on a song and a prayer. If politicians bet on a highly unlikely – though not impossible – outcome, they should stand accused – even if they won this one – of playing casino politics. On the day the study of expanded forms of immunity appeared, June 29, the Swedish per capita mortality rate was over eleven times the Norwegian. Compared with Norway, then, 4,800 Swedes would have died (out of a total death toll of 5,321 that day) on the off chance herd immunity might prove the right strategy.

Such attention to the vagaries of a few nations on the epidemiological fringe may seem excessive. But the British and Swedish authorities' reactions go to the heart of the political conundrum of contagion. Who trusts whom and to what end? The attentive reader will have spotted the fatal contradiction at the heart of the Swedish approach. The Swedes could have voluntary compliance, or they could have herd immunity. But to have both at the same time was impossible. Aiming for herd immunity meant assuming that voluntary compliance had broken down. In fact, the Swedish authorities did not trust their citizens to do the right thing. Their tactics presumed they would fail, in the process building up herd immunity. "In Sweden," the government announced, "the population trusts the authorities. That means that people follow their advice closely."[113] If so, where was herd immunity supposed to come from?

ASYMPTOMATIC CARRIERS

Asymptomatic carriers illustrated how indeterminate scientific knowledge could be in guiding preventive tactics. They were either people who did not yet have symptoms (presymptomatic) or never developed them at all (true asymptomatics). Asymptomatic carriers had been recognized as a problem already with Koch's discovery of the cholera bacillus in 1884. Identifying it provided an objective marker of the disease, independent of symptoms. Thus, it brought forth the asymptomatic carrier as a concept – someone who was indisputably infected but did not show it. Until then, the only way to identify the asymptomatic had been to quarantine everyone, waiting for some to develop symptoms. Even that revealed only the presymptomatic and only retrospectively – in other words, pointlessly. In theory, Koch's discoveries would have allowed bacteriological inspection of everyone's excrement to spot seemingly healthy shedders. The practical problems, however, were enormous and obvious. The immediate result of identifying the cholera vibrio was thus to expand the ranks of potentially dangerous people to include also symptomless contacts who might be carriers.[114]

With Covid-19, the equivalent to mass bacteriological examination of excrement for the cholera vibrio was universal testing for the virus. Mass testing was at first impossible, but eventually, the technical difficulties subsided to render it merely impracticable. By June, cheap home antigen testing kits with rapid feedback were being trialed. They were less accurate, but, if used frequently with quick results, they provided an initial sorting with subsequent testing able to eliminate false positives.[115] Some observers proposed regular universal testing as the best means to uncover and isolate cases.[116] Like contact tracing, universal testing promised to identify the infected who had to be quarantined, sparing the rest. It solved the fundamental problem of targeted measures: lack of information.[117]

Universal PCR testing for the coronavirus would have required 21 million tests daily for fortnightly testing of all Americans and 10 million in the UK for weekly testing. Others proposed testing all Americans every three days, 100 million tests daily, but of the cheaper antigen-based method.[118] That sounded like an insurmountable effort, but in return, it promised to spare the bulk of the population lockdown, while also avoiding the complicated technical infrastructure and personal intrusiveness demanded by contact tracing. In late June, the UK trialed a saliva-based test in Southhampton on several thousand residents.[119]

Universal testing also had the huge advantage of spotting asymptomatic carriers, invisible to traditional contact tracing, except occasionally by a process of elimination.[120] By pooling samples and retesting each only when a batch proved infected, already in June, screening cost perhaps three dollars per person. In Rwanda, further improvements on pooling had lowered expenses so that by August, the government was testing all air passengers.[121] Even better, a virtuous cycle ensued. The more testing and more infected people detected and eliminated from future testing, the fewer the positive batches, and the lower the costs.[122] Without factoring pooling in, 21 million tests daily in the US meant an annual expense of 23 billion dollars – a bargain compared with the several trillion-dollar price tag of the CARES and HEROS Acts and other economic interventions.

Estimates of the price of developing one new epidemic disease vaccine ran from $30 million to slightly over $1 billion, so universal testing was still expensive compared with that.[123] As of July, the US had spent $3.8 billion on vaccine development; by September, it was $10 billion.[124] But on the other hand, Covid-19 had reduced US GDP by 30%, some $18 billion a day. If even massive investment in research could bring forward the arrival of an effective vaccine by one day, it would have paid for itself.[125] Ten billion had been spent on vaccines globally by the summer of 2020. Multiply that by ten, some suggested, and it would still be a bargain compared with the seven trillion spent or pledged so far to preserve jobs and income.[126]

Asymptomatic carriers undermined certain preventive strategies. The sorts of measures first taken against the pandemic, such as public awareness campaigns, airport screenings, recommendations to stay at home for those who felt sick – these all missed the mark.[127] The asymptomatic unwittingly spread disease, without others being able to take precautions against them. Other epidemic diseases had been more forgiving in that respect. With MERS, SARS, and Ebola, victims were generally not transmissive until they had symptoms. At that point, they were aware of their status and able to take precautions. Being sick, they were less likely to move about as vectors in the first place. But with Covid-19, asymptomatic shedders, like Typhoid Mary in her day, were unaware of the threat they posed, therefore doubly dangerous. To make matters worse, asymptomatics might still suffer harm from Covid-19 – to their lungs or livers, for example – that they could not detect.[128]

How much asymptomatics transmitted the coronavirus was unclear. The WHO got into hot water in early June for suggesting that spread from true asymptomatics was rare. Criticized for muddying the message, it retracted its claims.[129] Other studies set asymptomatic transmission low but also credited presymptomatic communication with 40% or up to 60% of new cases.[130] Further studies indicated that asymptomatics could be as transmissive, with as great a viral load as the overtly ill.[131] Either way, so long as presymptomatic spread was high, the practical consequences remained the same: it undercut many otherwise effective strategies.

The existence of asymptomatic carriers meant that testing had to be quick and widespread, ideally universal, and not just target those who had symptoms or had been in contact with the infected.[132] The inevitable delays of traditional, manual contact tracing prevented it from dealing well with a fast-spreading disease like Covid-19. Only if it began at once, when there were only few cases, as in the Asian nations, was it effective. A contact tracing phone app that rapidly notified people exposed to the ill promised to help.[133] Hence, the Chinese sped up their testing. They demanded results within twelve hours and onsite inspections within twenty-four, hoping to nab the asymptomatic before they did much harm.[134]

Asymptomatic transmission also undercut strategies based on voluntary compliance with behavioral prescriptions. Recognizing this, the Chinese isolated asymptomatic carriers apart from their homes.[135] Though not imposing isolation as rigorously as the Chinese, the French too understood the dangers posed by asymptomatic carriers from the very start, in mid-March.[136] In contrast, the Swedish model of self-regulation stumbled. It did not matter how responsible, sensible, and compliant citizens were; if they did not know that they were carriers, they were helpless. The Swedes recommended that those who felt ill self-isolate. Asymptomatic carriers definitionally felt fine. Even if they had wanted to follow the rules, they could not. The only way of finding them was mass testing. Since asymptomatics undercut a voluntarist strategy, their significance had to be denied. And that is precisely what the Swedish authorities did.

Rejecting at first the idea that asymptomatic carriers were a major source of transmission, the Swedes saw no reason to require mask-wearing or to suit-up workers in care homes in protective gear.[137] Tegnell simply denied that asymptomatics were a serious problem. Their role in transmission was small compared with symptomatics, he was convinced, though how he could have known that in the absence of widespread testing is unclear.[138] Faced with the same evidence of extensive asymptomatic spread, other public health authorities drew precisely the opposite conclusion. Germany reasoned that the existence of asymptomatic carriers, especially children, who could least be expected to be aware of their condition, meant that isolating the ill and their contacts had to be all the more strictly implemented, lest the hospitals be overwhelmed.[139]

SUPERSPREADING

Superspreading was a phenomenon about which little is still known, but it had implications for preventive tactics. Some events, locations, and activities, and possibly people, appear to have superspread the virus. In retrospect, it became clear that hypertransmission had taken place at specific venues. A megachurch in Korea and another in France, a choral practice in Washington state, a corporate conference in Boston, slaughterhouses in Holland, Germany, Denmark, and the American Midwest, singalong bars in Seoul, and various weddings, funerals, and other family events had given the virus an opportunity to tear through the attendants.[140] That specific venues – crowded, enclosed, airless – would facilitate the spread of a respiratory, droplet-driven contagion was clear. Prisons and slaughterhouses were the most extreme examples.[141]

The Austrian ski resort Ischgl became ground zero for the European pandemic. Thousands of people infected there – presumably more during après-ski than out on the slopes – dispersed home in February. In Germany, distance from Ischgl was one of the most consistently predictive factors of local epidemic severity. A third of all Danish cases and a sixth of the Swedish could be traced back to skiers returning from Ischgl.[142] Specific activities in certain venues were also especially dangerous – like singing.

Less certain so far is whether particular people were also epidemiologically more efficient spreaders. Did some people simply shed more virus than usual? Or did they pose extra dangers because they were sociable, active, mobile, and continued being so as long as they remained asymptomatic?[143] Certain professions were more likely to interact with others. A bus driver was potentially more of an infective hub than a night watchman.[144] In Chicago, one gregarious fellow, going from a dinner to a funeral to a birthday party, infected sixteen others, three of whom died.[145] A combination of peak shedding by someone in an enclosed environment was likely to have caused the biggest events.[146]

The logic of superspreading was familiar and a feature of most contagious diseases. Among the most famous culprits was Typhoid Mary, a cook and asymptomatic shedder, who infected fifty-one people, most likely through her peach ice cream. Having broken her promise never again to work as a cook, she was confined for much of her later life until her death in 1938.[147] In the MERS epidemic in South Korea in 2015, three-quarters of all cases originated with three superspreaders.[148] In the nineteenth century, public health reformers had targeted specific, especially noxious locales for attention.

Precisely which they aimed at varied with their view of disease etiology, whether they were worried by filth or contagion. During the AIDS epidemic, gay bathhouses were shut for being nodes of hyper-charged transmission that sent the HIV leapfrogging far beyond their inner circle of regular customers, borne off by occasional visitors who carried it back into the broader community.[149] Conversely, needle exchanges had been advocated to counter the superspreading effects of shooting galleries where drug addicts shared infected equipment.

Different tactics were called for, depending on whether it was the person or the event and venue that determined the spread's amplitude. Banning gatherings over a specific size and in certain places was among the first measures implemented against Covid-19, targeting the latter causes. Meatpacking plants may have been superspreading venues because they were crowded and cold, allowing the virus easy and prolonged movement.[150] If the epidemic's dispersion factor (measured as k) was low, that meant that few vectors were responsible for many cases. A few people did appear to be responsible for most infections, while most infected did not spread Covid-19 at all.[151] The conventional percentages used, in the SARS epidemic, for example, were 20% of cases being responsible for 80% of infections.[152] One study of Georgia's coronavirus epidemic estimated 20% of victims to have been infected by 2% of cases.[153] In India, it was 8% accounting for 60% of transmission.[154]

If superspreading was a significant source of epidemic push, then identifying and acting on the individuals or the circumstances that transmitted promised better results than non-targeted interventions.[155] Unlike the spread of flu, which was more even, coronavirus appeared to disseminate in fits and starts. That allowed preventive efforts to focus on specific people and places – if they could be identified. If implemented early enough, testing and tracing could spare nations the need for broad shutdowns.[156]

Airports were superspreading venues, funneling millions en route to their far-flung destinations. Simple interventions, such as increased handwashing among passengers, promised to cut disease spread by up to a third.[157] Aerosol transmission was more compatible with superspreading than droplets, suggesting a critical role for masks and ventilation. If a vaccine arrived, giving it first to the biggest spreaders, not just the most exposed, promised disproportional results.[158]

The converse of superspreading came from those who argued that susceptibility and immunity were differentially distributed in the population. If superspreading was a supply-side argument, this focused on the demand. Perhaps more people than expected had immunity from sources other than exposure to the Covid-19 – from previous contact with cold viruses, say – that generated cross-immunity. If so, then the pandemic would encounter large swaths of sterile soil and its spread might be hampered even without widespread immunity caused directly by this coronavirus. Herd immunity would then be achieved at lower infection thresholds than anticipated, perhaps half the usual estimates of 60% to 80%.[159]

As superspreaders were taken out of circulation by the disease's ravages, dissemination would also slow or the epidemic diminish.[160] This was the logic of what epidemiologists called harvesting. In part, the most susceptible died first, leaving less tinder to catch fire in subsequent waves. In effect, Western nations' neglect of care homes put in practice an inadvertent harvesting of one of the most vulnerable groups.[161] On a larger scale, those with comorbidities would also succumb first, either dying or gaining some immunity. Only if there were no immune response, or a weak one, would the vulnerable remain as fuel for subsequent waves. Superspreaders could also be harvested. People whose sociability and mobility made them efficient disease conveyors were likely to be quickly eliminated as threats either by dying or by becoming immune. Unless, of course, they remained asymptomatic and persisted as a threat to others. It was the same logic that governed the Darwin Awards – the feckless go first.

MASKS

Masks were a final example of a preventive technique whose significance depended on our understanding of the coronavirus's etiology. In the West, masks provoked a surprising fuss, though the rest of the world may well have wondered why. In Asia, mask-wearing was as customary as hats had been in the West. Though Japan emulated them from the West early in the 1900s, they became second nature and common sense by mid-century.[162] Ninety-five percent of Thais now wore them always in public, the highest rate in Southeast Asia.[163] Public health agencies routinely recommended them during flu seasons. And their ubiquity was likely part of the Asians' admirable preventive outcomes.[164] In Indonesia, the authorities wondered whether the niqab, worn by women, accomplished much the same as masks.[165]

In the West, however, issues arose. Masks had been widely adopted during the Spanish flu epidemic in 1918, then dropped once the emergency had passed. Women in San Francisco had also tried to get away with veils instead.[166] Now they were up for debate again. Did a moral hazard attach to their use, with people feeling more secure than they should and therefore taking risks? That was an argument the Swedish public health authorities and the WHO in April advanced against mandating them.[167] The same logic had done duty against mandatory seatbelt use in its time.[168]

More critical was supply. Shortages of the most effective masks, N95s, plagued most nations. Best, therefore, that they be reserved for frontline medical workers. The authorities, including the WHO, initially counseled against wearing masks, fearing that the competition for them would otherwise create shortages or drive prices up, depriving those most in need. The French, for example, at first did not have enough. The authorities recommended against wearing them, telling citizens that social distancing and handwashing were more effective and that only sick people should wear them.[169] In mid-May, the government took over their distribution, reserving them for medical staff. But once it had acquired sufficient supplies from China, it urged people to wear them and required them on public transport.[170]

Eventually, a consensus emerged in the West that other masks, whether less secure medical ones or homemade cloth ones, were also useful. In June, modeling studies suggested that universal mask use, including by asymptomatics, effectively prevented transmission even without other forms of distancing or lockdown.[171] The mask requirement imposed in New York on April 17, one study found, did more to drop disease spread than social distancing.[172] The use of cloth masks now became widely recommended. The WHO also came out in June in favor of their widespread use.[173]

A series of regulations resulted in many nations, from requirements to use masks where distancing was impossible – in stores, on public transit – to recommendations to wear them everywhere in public. In early July, it became understood that Covid-19 was spread not just via droplets expelled when sneezing or coughing, but more generally through aerosol emanations merely when breathing and speaking. Masks therefore became even more critical, now recommended for use indoors and even if distancing were possible.[174] They gradually became like condoms during the AIDS epidemic – an unpleasant necessity that allowed some semblance of regular interactions, while sidestepping even worse measures.[175]

In the meantime, however, masks became politicized. Trump's all-but total refusal to wear them as well as Bolsonaro's and Johnson's spurning of them encouraged their followers to follow suit.[176] The Italian prime minister Giuseppe Conte did not wear one in public in May, but was shouted at for it.[177] Even in maskless Sweden, Facebook groups formed for and against.[178] The UK fought cultural wars over masks.[179] In the US, they became the semiotic opposite of a MAGA hat, Trump's Make America Great Again baseball caps.[180]

Masks joined motorcycle helmets, seatbelts, and condoms as protective gear that suggested users were unduly concerned with their own or others' well-being and, therefore, somehow wimpy and unmanly.[181] Best left to semioticians is why other protective gear has taken on the opposite political signification. In the US, hard hats are the mark of burly blue-collar construction workers, apt to horse-whistle at women and vote Republican. High-vis vests, the *gilets jaunes*, were donned as a badge of honor by the allegedly neglected lower middle classes of the French provinces in their neo-Poujadist revolt against the Parisian elites. And let us not forget the police, who have all but disappeared behind an imposing armor of protective equipment, more like RoboCop than the fatherly officer played by Andy Griffith.

In the US, those most likely to wear one whenever they went out were liberal females from the Northeast or West, Black or Hispanic, who were either Baby Boomers or GenZs.[182] Protesters in the Midwest demonstratively rejected masks.[183] In Boise, demonstrators burned free ones handed out after the mayor issued a city-wide mask mandate.[184] Republican Congressmen refused to wear them even as Nancy Pelosi tried to force them in June.[185]

Courts defanged local regulations requiring them, as did the Georgia governor.[186] More Democrats than Republicans reported wearing masks.[187] But even Republicans turned out to be blessed with a self-preservation instinct, and by July, representatives, senators, and governors from the GOP were masking up like the Lone Ranger.[188]

A turning tide is relentless. New York required masks as of April wherever distancing was impossible, on crowded sidewalks, in stores, and on public transport.[189] In June, California mandated them indoors and out when distancing was not possible in public.[190] By late July, over half of US states demanded them in public, and only two (Iowa and South Dakota) had no mask requirements at all.[191]

But even the Europeans hardly shone as exemplars. Alone in Europe, the Czech Republic and Slovakia required masks in public already in March. Compliance was excellent, with only a few smokers, drinkers, and some nudist sunbathers first cited for violations.[192] The Germans discussed whether saunas should require them, where usually nothing was worn.[193] On the other hand, traffic cameras would be unable to issue automatic speeding tickets if drivers could not be identified, and so masks that covered too much of the face were forbidden.[194]

Britain resisted mask-wearing. In April, officials recommended against them.[195] The UK's scientific advisers were still discussing the issue as a trade-off between public use of N95 masks and their supply for medical workers, taking no account of cloth ones instead.[196] The authorities continued to view cloth masks suspiciously, as ineffective and possibly more harm than good. Among the concerns was a peculiar fear that those who could not afford cloth masks might be harassed in public.[197] Finally, on April 21, SAGE recommended cloth masks in enclosed spaces where social distancing was impossible.[198] In London, subway riders were required to don them in mid-June, and did, with 80% compliance on the first day.[199] Only in late July did a general mandate finally come down to wear masks, but then limited to stores, not everywhere in public.[200] That provoked demonstrations in Hyde Park against unwarranted government overreach and an unexpectedly powerful anti-mask movement.[201]

Once again, the Swedes were outliers, but this time allied with their fellow Scandinavians. Oddly, the Swedes, whose leitmotivs were individual responsibility, trust, and solidarity, specifically recommended against mask use. The mantra of the mask was "my mask protects you, your mask protects me." It was not quite the Three Musketeers ("One for all and all for one."), but likely as close as we will get in our lifetimes. Not for the Nordics. Face masks were not needed in everyday life, public health authorities cautioned.[202] Handwashing and distance-keeping sufficed. Ignoring the asymptomatic, the chief epidemiologist and his predecessor argued that those who felt ill should not be out and about in any case. By their reasoning, those wearing masks signaled that they were out in public even though sick. Better to have a simple message and rely on social distancing.[203] The prime minister weighed in, too, arguing that it was preferable to keep the ill at home than require everyone to wear masks.[204] Physicians who insisted on wearing masks at work were reprimanded, their contracts sometimes not renewed.[205] Unsurprisingly, the public followed their leaders, and surveys revealed the Scandinavians as global laggards in mask-wearing.[206]

In May, the Swedish prime minister said that his public health authorities did not think that requiring masks was effective. These were the experts, he added, so we listen to them.[207] In June, the WHO changed its previous recommendations. In April, the organization had not recommended widespread mask use in fear that public demand would cause shortages for frontline staff.[208] But, as the evidence of masks' usefulness multiplied, it switched to advise all to wear cloth masks in public where distancing was difficult.[209]

In response, Tegnell was determined not to allow the WHO's change of heart to ramp up pressure to modify his nation's rejection of masks. He therefore parsed the WHO recommendations painstakingly, seeking a way out. The WHO, he insisted, was not recommending masks except where social distancing did not work. In sparsely populated Sweden, distancing was always possible. Requiring masks would, in any case, undermine their tactics of distancing in public and having the symptomatic remain at home. Their use suggested that it was OK to go out even if ill so long as masked. One always had to be very careful about the WHO's recommendations, he cautioned, and not just pluck out one or two aspects, but rather see them as a whole.[210] In sum, not only did the politicians pick and choose among the expert opinions they wanted to hear, so did the experts themselves.

Even as late as June, the Swedish rejection of masks remained connected to their disregard of asymptomatic carriers. Masks were especially useful for those who did not know their status as disease vectors, protecting others from them. That masks could prevent the asymptomatic from spreading was dismissed by the Swedes, however, as a trivial consideration.[211] In April, the Swedish papers noticed how many other nations had introduced mask requirements, wearily wondering whether Sweden was once again going to remain the odd one out?[212] In June, other experts pointed out the increasing evidence for masks' usefulness.[213] Yet Danish dailies still penned opinion pieces, indistinguishable in sentiment from fervent Republican governors in the US, that lambasted masks as a severe incursion on individual liberties and unnecessary in their nation that had successfully halted the pandemic.[214] By July, the vast majority of countries globally had some mask requirements. The Nordics remained among the few holdouts.[215] Yet, the vice was tightening.

In August, the Danes began to turn coats. Passengers on public transport in Aarhus, the second-largest city, now had to mask-up.[216] So too, care home personnel.[217] The Finns now recommended them where distancing was not possible.[218] Even some Swedes came in from the cold. The head of the main medical university, the Karolinska, insisted on masking by students and employees as the fall semester began.[219] Some stores in Stockholm began requiring them of personnel and customers.[220] Tom Britton, the mathematical modeler, now recommended masks, given the crowding indoors expected as the autumn set in.[221] But not Tegnell. The same day Britton changed his mind, he was holding forth in the largest German tabloid on the dangers of relying on masks.[222]

It seems a safe bet that, in this instance, we will all turn Japanese. For masks to have become fashion accessories is an encouraging trend.[223] Seat belts are likely to have traced the course that masks will follow. Once, they were a politically neuralgic issue, supposedly a sign of an overly protective nanny state, resisted by libertarians and small-state conservatives as a violation of their right to become crippled as they pleased. And yet, despite much political posturing in the 1980s when seatbelts were first mandated, their use has become universal and uncontroversial.

Even Steve McQueen, the ultimate tough guy, playing Bullitt in the 1968 movie of that name, fastened his seatbelt halfway through one of cinema's most spectacular car chases to indicate that now things were going to get serious. When Jon S. Corzine, former senator and then governor of New Jersey, was seriously injured in a car accident in 2007, the public was amazed to discover that he routinely refused to wear seatbelts. "It's almost bizarre," said one flabbergasted constituent. "I bet even the strangest of rappers and punk rockers wear seat belts."[224] If so, we are all punk rockers now. The vast majority of developed nations toe the line, with compliance rates for front-seat belt usage arrayed from 90% up to 99%.[225]

Despite a shared understanding of Covid-19's etiology, scientific disagreements did thus influence politics. On some issues, such as immunity, certain scientific theories encouraged some politicians to move in a particular direction. If they were counting on herd immunity, then they could continue to claim scientific backing even as the evidence for widespread antibody presence faded by harnessing other theories, such as non-antibody-based immunity, to their cause. But in either case, the fundamental point holds. Politicians could, and did, find the scientific backing they wanted for the tactics they were advocating anyway. They were rarely compelled, or even impelled, by scientific arguments into a direction they did not want to go. Even in the case of Britain's volteface in March, it was not that science won out. Rather, one strain of expertise – social and behavioral science, based on nudge theory – lost out to medical and epidemiological prognoses of dire harm.

CHAPTER 7

From State to Citizen

The Individualization of Public Health

WHY DID NATIONS TAKE SUCH VARIED APPROACHES when fighting the same pandemic? What assumptions did they make about how their citizens would behave? How did their political cultures color their reactions and presuppositions? Our outliers here are China and Sweden. One, an authoritarian system making significant demands of its citizens, the other a consensual democracy, relying on its citizens' self-motivated ability to make the right decisions.

China's rulers had more than a big stick in their armamentarium. They were a nation with a sense of ethnic and cultural cohesion surpassing anything found in the West. China does not recognize dual nationality, it treats even foreign nationals as subjects if they are ethnically Chinese, and, in effect, it allows no non-Han to be naturalized.[1] Acutely embarrassed by having been the pandemic's source, China was keen to make a favorable impression by fighting it vigorously. Portraying itself as squelching disease at home while helping the rest of the world accommodated China's sense of its growing global heft as well as its desire to be seen doing the right thing.

For foreign consumption, it claimed to have released information on the pandemic in a timely and transparent manner, with accurate updating of case and mortality figures. It emphasized how it had shared protective gear with other nations, aiding vulnerable trading partners in Africa and elsewhere. China's authorities portrayed their actions against the pandemic as a collective effort, with everyone sacrificing for the public weal, fusing what was right for China and for the world. Uniting solidaristically behind the Communist Party's strong leadership, they claimed to wage "an all-out people's war" on the virus. The most massive containment effort in history had been possible thanks to the "deep commitment of the Chinese people to collective action." China had elevated saving lives above any economic considerations, accepting the enormous cost of lockdown.[2]

The Swedish pandemic philosophy was a far cry from such calls for common sacrifices by a people united behind strong leadership. Having been socialized to know what they ought to do, Swedes supposedly needed no more than a bit of prompting and some recommendations from their leaders to behave as the circumstances required. Yet, since even Swedes are human, occasional slip-ups followed. Having violated distancing rules, for example, several bars in central Stockholm were shut in April.[3] Even so, trusting its citizens, the Swedish state assumed that counsel phrased as recommendations, not commands, would be followed.

Its reasoning mirrored the venerable theological dilemma first raised by Anselm. If God is omniscient and knows what you will do, are you acting freely when you do what is foreseen? Foreign minister Linde put it thus: "These are not voluntary measures. You are meant to follow them. We believe the best way for us is a combination of some binding regulations and clear advice to the public. As far as possible, we want to build on a strong, longstanding relationship of trust between authorities and the public."[4] If the public knew and did what was expected of it, compulsion was not required. But if not, what then? What if the Swedes had free will, but used it for purposes other than what the state foresaw? Did the authorities have a plan B?

Or was plan B what they were aiming for in the first place? We have noted the inherent contradiction at the heart of the Swedes' preventive tactics between expecting citizens to implement on their own the behavior that would forestall epidemics while, at the same time, aiming to allow the disease to spread slowly, generating herd immunity. Herd immunity would emerge only if Swedes, in fact, did not do what was expected of them. If so, were the Swedish tactics a cynical appeal to trust, while knowing full well that it would not work?

Swedes were not alone in relying on voluntary precautions. Other nations' citizens did so too, sometimes in the absence of official directive, sometimes in advance of it. In countries where the authorities did little, citizens acted on their own. Nicaragua's Sandinista government had been notably inactive. In mid-June, medical associations therefore called on Nicaraguans voluntarily to observe a "national quarantine."[5] Inhabitants of Brazil's favelas organized their own protection once it became evident that Bolsonaro's government was doing little.[6] Belarusians began distancing voluntarily, wearing face masks, after Lukashenko's inept response.[7] Noting their government's initial lethargy, Iranians voluntarily quarantined and demanded more state action.[8] Citizens' initiatives could emerge even without faith in the authorities, indeed precisely to compensate for its absence.

Rational citizens, threatened with a deadly epidemic, naturally sought to shield themselves. Such voluntary protective behavior often betrayed a lack of trust in the authorities. Was voluntary preventive action undertaken by citizens themselves evidence that they trusted their governments – or the opposite? When civil society acted on its own, did it indicate state failure or – as the Swedes imagined – a welcome symbiosis between the two?

China enforced measures against citizens who might have resisted them. Sweden, in contrast, counted on its citizens to do the right thing on their own and saw no reason to wield the truncheon. In between, most other nations relied on some combination of exhortation, advice, trust, and enforcement. Whether the authorities invoked voluntary compliance or used a firmer hand depended on the nature of the regime. But the characteristics of the disease also played a role.

A highly contagious illness spread through everyday contacts by people who could themselves be asymptomatic and therefore unwitting vectors was a nightmare that might require the authorities to lock up anyone even remotely likely to be infectious. Conversely, a disease spread only slowly and infrequently through purposeful acts by people with evident symptoms could perhaps be left to individuals themselves to avoid, both as vectors and victims. That Covid-19 fell closer to the former explains why fighting it posed such political dilemmas.

Whatever its weaknesses, the Swedish approach did represent a strain of development in the history of public health that is worth exploring as we situate this pandemic in a broader context. The Swedish tactics rested on voluntary compliance with behavioral recommendations rather than diktats issued by authority. However self-righteous and smug their approach struck outsiders, the Swedes do seem to have believed that it was the correct one for their political system and stage of social development. In April 2020, the authorities recommended against but did not prohibit travel over the Easter holidays. The result was 90% less traveling than in previous years.[9] By free will, most Swedes had chosen what the authorities knew to be the right course.

Their coronavirus strategy represented a radical shift compared with how the Swedes had traditionally dealt with contagious disease. But it fit snugly with other recent developments in the nation's approach to public health. Earlier laws had empowered the authorities to compel vaccination, but that was no longer true. Vaccination was now encouraged and promoted and often administered to children in schools. But, technically, it was not compulsory and parents could exempt their children. Take-up rates nonetheless remained high.[10]

Such an approach, the director-general of public health in Sweden, Johan Carlson, argued, rested on the presumption that humans were wise, took account of others, and arrived at informed conclusions.[11] As we have seen, their 2004 contagious disease law equipped the authorities with the requisite powers to clamp down on epidemics. But it also emphasized individual responsibility. Everyone should be alert and take precautions to help prevent the spread of disease, it decreed.[12] For this, information was crucial and the authorities must ensure that citizens knew how to protect themselves.[13]

We have looked at the statist individualism of Swedish political culture, the way Swedes sought autonomy through the state, freeing them from civil society and its reciprocal obligations of dependency and community. The Swedish approach to the coronavirus made individuals responsible for their own epidemiological fate. Collectively, such autonomous individual decisions were expected to sum to more than their parts, achieving the common good of dampening the epidemic. We have quoted John Snow on how his discovery of cholera's transmission via polluted water allowed each person to take individual precautions and go about in an epidemic, protected by being their own quarantine officer.[14] Unwittingly or not, one Swedish observer now echoed this. He described the nation's tactic of making individuals responsible for the collective good as relying on each citizen being "their own contagious disease physician."[15]

Were the Swedes correct in thinking that they had achieved the pinnacle of prevention, the most modern, enlightened, and democratic approach? Compared with carting the infected and their contacts off to quarantine, or entire nations shuttered at home, it certainly seemed an attractive option to rely on autonomous citizens taking the right decisions, distancing themselves and self-isolating when ill, but otherwise free to go about their business. Yet, measured in per capita mortality, that approach did not seem to work, at least not in the short run.

Could one rely on individuals to take the right decisions when dealing with epidemic diseases where each person was definitionally a threat to others and the collective? Or was the Swedish approach a category mistake? Looking to the history of public health, the Swedes were not wrong to think that it had been moving in an ever more voluntaristic direction. The techniques used to prevent disease had always been thoroughly steeped in political and ideological assumptions. Opinions on how pandemics were best tackled were a Rorschach test for broader social attitudes. It was no different this time around.

SICK PEOPLE, SICK SOCIETY?

Whether individuals could be held responsible for disease depended on the ailment in question. Some struck indiscriminately with no ethical implications, others were freighted with moral valuation. Venereal diseases, arising from oft-condemned behavior, staggered under their metaphorical load. Tuberculosis was once associated with creativity, cancer thought to arise from repressed emotions, and autism out of refrigerator mothering.[16] For obesity and diabetes, the temptation to assign individual blame has been overpowering. Each person's habits – overeating, underexercising, drug-taking – influenced our well-being.

But individuals were not solitary. Part of society, their habits and proclivities were influenced by kin and community. Even more broadly, social circumstances determined their health too – whether they were poor, where they lived, how they earned their keep, who their family and friends were. Health or sickness were the outcome not just of bad luck, individual choices, habits, or environment. Most broadly, the various levels of health determinants – individual, environmental, social – were connected. A pregnant woman took drugs and harmed her fetus. Was she to be punished as criminally liable or pitied as one of two victims of social malaise? Were obesity, diabetes, and heart disease the outcome of discrete decisions to overindulge or a syndrome reflecting a broader entanglement of social, biological, and cultural influences that individuals only partly commanded? Whether to see sickness as individually or collectively determined was a choice marinaded in political assumptions and moral judgments.

Contagious diseases were an individual problem, as they spread indiscriminately from one person to the next. But fighting them was necessarily a collective task. In turn, transmissible diseases were more of an individual issue since each victim could perhaps have avoided them by not participating in the acts that passed them along or by taking precautions. Finally, chronic diseases were even more an individual responsibility, insofar as lifestyle choices caused them. But again, each decision could also be seen as influenced by social determinants and never entirely under the individual's sovereign control.

What fundamentally caused sickness has been debated throughout history, down to the present, eliciting answers colored by political ideology and science. Was disease brought about by a specific cause, some sort of microorganism or another unseen trigger, that spread from person to person? Or was it the result of something more general, whether noxious environmental influences, pernicious habits and lifestyles, or congenital proclivities that disposed some people to succumb to what others shrugged off? The debate over whether disease sprang from a precise transmissible something or environmental causes has long been a leitmotiv in the history of medicine. Nary an illness has not produced at least two competing etiologies, even as recently as the AIDS epidemic.

Diseases spread by fecal–oral contact, like cholera and polio, were easily misunderstood as arising directly from filth until the precise vector of their transmission was revealed. Smallpox and typhoid fever were initially understood as springing as such from putrefaction. Illnesses that appeared to be spread could also be interpreted as caused by noxious environments. A miasma could be generated in certain filthy places, yet then travel, bringing what was, in essence, a filth disease with it and giving it an aura of transmissibility. Even the plague – the most evidently contagious disease – was thought by some nineteenth-century observers to spring from environmental causes.[17]

Thanks to Louis Pasteur and Robert Koch, the bacteriological revolution in the late nineteenth century shifted attention to the specific, microscopic causes of disease and away from a more generalized environmental approach. Bacteriology narrowed the broad focus of environmentalist public health. Improving living conditions had once been the goal. Cordons and quarantines were not the answer to cholera, the physicians of Riga blithely concluded in the summer of 1831, but good food, clean housing, and warm clothing.[18]

Once the main goal became to prevent the transmission of a microorganism, however, cleaning up the environment took a backseat. Filth was no longer the primary culprit, cleansing and sanitary improvements were not the only approach. The new bacteriologically inspired public health movement realized that, rather than improving the living conditions of millions, disinfecting the discharges of a few hundred thousand active tuberculosis patients was all that was needed.[19] Widespread testing to discover diphtheria cases was cheaper than disinfecting and quarantining the homes of all those suspected of being ill.[20] Rather than cleansing cities and building sewer systems to combat yellow fever, once it was recognized as the product of a germ, not filth, disinfection became the preferred solution.[21]

But that hardly meant the end of a broader, more environmental and social approach to disease. Armed with the weapons of bacteriology, public health authorities had thought they could now strike surgically to cut disease transmission. That promised a solution without imposing quarantines, with their attendant damage to trade, travel, and social intercourse. Nor did it require major urban sanitation campaigns, much less the widespread alleviation of poverty advocated by ardent environmentalists. But they were mistaken.

Environmental strategies may have suffered an epistemological setback, but their appeal to social reformers and the popular imagination remained. They refused to concede victory to bacteriology and the idea that specific microorganisms were both the necessary and the sufficient cause of epidemic disease. The most radical denied any role to microorganisms at all. At most, they were corollaries or effects of disease, not a cause. A more moderate position granted that they might be a necessary precondition but insisted that, alone without any further factors, they could not bring about epidemics.

What, then, caused disease? Two kinds of factors were in play. The immediate environment might favor or resist the spread of illness. That could mean anything from poor sanitation, overcrowding, pollution, and bad housing, to the lack of food stores, parks, and hospitals. Another possibility was that individuals might be more or less susceptible. Why that was so ranged from mostly biological issues (victims' immune systems or the effects of hunger and malnutrition) to matters that were more within the individual's control (habits and lifestyle). At the extreme, the distinction between the two collapsed. Seemingly personally determined behaviors, such as drug addiction or overeating, were not immune to societal influences, nor were they choices made wholly independently of the individual's socio-economic position.

At the most general level, the personal and the social joined. People's individual predispositions, proclivities, and choices could not be isolated from their social circumstances. Poverty meant that some rarely saw a physician, worked dangerous jobs, suffered high stress levels, or lived near polluting industries, airports, or highways. Inequality had much the same effect, but was often just a proxy for poverty. However, some argued that the sheer fact of inequality itself, independent of poverty, had a noxious impact.[22]

These different approaches influenced the choice of how best to mitigate or prevent disease. Were targeted interventions sufficient – vaccinating children, requiring handwashing and hairnets of restaurant workers, adding fluoride to the drinking water, circumcising male infants, forbidding smoking in public places? Or was a better approach to improve living and working conditions, providing the poor with the minimal accouterments of a healthful, airy, middle-class lifestyle?

That could be dealt with at various levels. Most fundamentally, modern sanitary infrastructure was the outcome of public health reformers' campaigns to improve cities' health. For the great nineteenth-century urban reformers, democracy and public health were connected. Without enhancing life for the poor, disease would still run rampant. Everyone stood to gain. Until the poor too enjoyed adequate circumstances, epidemic disease would fester, threatening all urban residents.[23] "Think of what our nation stands for," John Betjeman, the British poet laureate, exhorted in verse, "Democracy and proper drains."

Focused on sanitary infrastructure, public health could be democratic and reformist. Drains, ventilation, sunlight, open spaces: all improved everyone's life, especially the poorest, even as they did not radically change society. But public health could also be hectoring and moralistic. Focused on lifestyles and habits, it could be a tool of class control. It invoked science to insist that middle-class habits were healthy and therefore encouraged or even required other social groups to fall in line. Smoking, for example, follows a socio-economic gradient – more prevalent in poorer nations and among the lower classes in the developed world. Alcohol is similar – with significant carve-outs for some cultures that abstain for religious reasons. Campaigns against smoking and drinking – as against spitting in its day – thus imposed one class's habits on others, however healthy and well-intentioned the outcomes.

INDIVIDUAL RESPONSIBILITY

Thus, broad political and social ideologies interacted with narrow questions of disease etiology to color how epidemic illness was understood and dealt with. Was it an individual or a social problem, or some combination thereof? Modern public health has been riven by two distinct and sometimes contradictory tendencies. One, which we have just outlined, is the ongoing emphasis – despite the development of bacteriology – on environmental and social factors in disease spread. The other is the increasing focus on individual responsibility for illness and its prevention. This individualized approach grew in importance as representative government and then democracy brought forth and empowered citizens as the ultimate sovereigns.

Quarantining to cut transmission and sanitizing urban infra-structure both required massive state intervention and top-down impositions on citizens. Yet, as both democracy and the scientific knowledge of disease causation and prevention expanded, individuals were increasingly roped in as responsible for safeguarding their own well-being. Indeed, democracy rested on individual responsibility for health. Hygienic self-control was part of the democratic ethos. Citizens who wanted to govern themselves politically had to demonstrate that they could do so bodily as well. Sneezing and suffrage went hand in hand. The French revolutionaries insisted that citizens conduct themselves to be and remain healthy. The state's task was to care for its citizens, but they, in turn, owed the community the duty of self-care.[24] Democracies required healthy citizens.

The *levée en masse*, mass conscription to the French revolutionary armies that replaced the absolutist kings' mercenary or impressed troops, was part of this shift. Each male citizen owed the nation his martial efforts and the possible sacrifice of his life. Uniforms signaled the change. Mercenary troops were dressed in bright colors to prevent them from shirking their duties, retreating from the battlefield. Why die for the minimum wage? Soldiers in democracies' armies, in contrast, were uniformed in practical colors and sensible cuts. They fought to defend themselves and their nation, with drastic consequences if they deserted.

More mundanely, something similar was demanded of all citizens in their daily lives. Citizens were a valuable commodity and no one was allowed to damage or destroy it. Citizens who undermined their own well-being, like those who killed themselves, were, in effect, shirkers and malingerers who sabotaged the communal effort. Being consciously unhealthy was akin to a slow-motion suicide. Whatever the moral implications, in practical terms, the suicide and the unhealthy person were both spongers on society.

The state could legitimately demand its citizens' health, much as it could require that they not flee the battlefield. A deserter would be court-martialled and likely executed. From the state's vantage, there was no more despicable crime – so heinous, that it was better to forego altogether whatever value the deserter's person might still hold for the community to set an example for others. In ancient Greece and Rome, infants were protected by a similar logic. Aborting a healthy fetus was a crime against the state and society because it eliminated an economic and military resource.[25] In common law, maiming someone was illegal, not so much because it harmed the victim as because it deprived the king of an able-bodied subject to defend the realm. Self-maiming was felonious for much the same reason.[26] As was homicide.[27]

This was the logic generalized in democracies.[28] Whatever the case in autocracies, once citizens became their own masters, they paradoxically were no longer free to dispose of their own bodies. At the opposite extreme, slaves who do not own their bodies also have little stake in maintaining the productive asset that they happen to inhabit. Citizens of democracies, however, owed the community a price for their sovereignty. Free citizens could once sell themselves into debt slavery. But no longer. Nor could they needlessly allow their bodies to deteriorate. Today, we discuss this issue in the mundane terms of health insurance's moral hazards. Are bad habits encouraged when we know that we will be patched up at the community's expense? Should we therefore make those who take drugs, smoke, or overeat bear more of the cost of their care? Should we increase insurance premiums for extreme sports thrill-seekers?

Individuals who are full members of society and thus expect the community's help in need, in return owe the collectivity their best efforts. Such attitudes reached their extreme in the pseudo-populism of the totalitarian regimes. The Nazi slogan was, "Your health does not belong to you."[29] Eugenics voiced an analogous logic of subordinating the individual to the community's greater good, defined in terms of health. Today we remember the Nazi regime's ambitions to perfect the race by removing what it considered imperfect specimens. The Holocaust aimed to improve the Aryan Volk by eliminating Jews and others deemed undesirable, in effect, as a massive eliminationist public health campaign. The Warsaw ghetto was walled off on the pretext of quarantining it against disease. Even more grotesque, it was pretended that the death camp gassings were disinfectant delousing showers to prevent illness.[30] But a similar logic of claiming to protect the population was followed by democracies too in their eugenic campaigns, above all in Sweden and the US. Killings were not the outcome, but the mentally disabled and others were sterilized, allegedly to improve the national stock.[31]

Short of such horrific extremes, in practical terms, the lessons of bacteriology required that citizens of modern democracies change their conduct. Bacteriology did not inform just zoning, city planning, housing, vaccination, and other state public health measures. The individual citizen, too, was roped into the process of disinfecting, distancing, and otherwise cutting chains of transmission. Personal behavior around others became ever more attuned to preventing microbes from peregrinating. We have touched on how syphilis became an exclusively venereal disease as people learned to avoid intimate bodily contact except during sex. Other aspects of sex have also become less implicated in transmission, but precisely which direction such behavioral changes point is complicated.

On the one hand, in sex, we have less unmediated contact than once. Condoms are more widely used today than forty years ago. As other effective means of contraception were developed (the pill and IUDs), competition arose for one of condoms' functions. The AIDS epidemic, however, enhanced their role in preventing STDs, and sales shot up. Heterosexual women now make up 40% of the market, and condoms are advertised as a personal hygiene product.[32] Dental dams similarly interpose latex for women receiving oral sex. Female condoms, however, have not proven to be crowd-pleasers, less popular with both sexes than the traditional variety.[33] Standard male condoms have, in the meantime, become a more attractive product.

Barrier methods were much tinkered with during the 1980s in hopes of making them more welcomed into sex play: spray-on and peel-off versions, embedded dual-control vibrating chips, disease-preventing but not contraceptive condoms for Catholics, and packaging requiring four hands to open, thus encouraging consensual intercourse.[34] Yet, little was accomplished for the product commonly available in drug stores beyond some playing around with color, shape, and taste. Nonetheless, the modern condom is an improvement from the days when Madame de Sévigné complained that they were "as strong as gossamer, as sensual as armor." They are cheaper, thinner, come in different sizes, flavors, and colors, not to mention various accouterments – ribbing, lubrication, sperm reservoirs, and sense-deadening chemicals to bring male time-to-orgasm more in line with that of women.

Sex toys, vibrators, and other accessories have become steadily more popular. Their use now drives a massive industry, $23 billion in 2017, and projected to double by 2026.[35] Web-linked devices allowing partners to manipulate each other at a distance had been adopted long before the pandemic but now became a convenient accessory for lovers separated by social distancing. Sex-toy sites enjoyed sales spikes of 30% over 2019.[36] Like condoms, toys too tended in the same direction of more corporeal distancing.

Yet, the repertoire of sexual behavior has also expanded and often in ways that made disease more likely to spread. Modern cleanliness has encouraged formerly uncommon behaviors, such as oral sex. Insofar as that was less transmissive than genital sex, an epidemiological benefit was won. Fisting, however, was likely more transmissive. It was first widely practiced among gay leathermen in the 1960s but came in anal and vaginal variants.[37] Anal sex more generally was old as the hills but became more commonly practiced in tandem with ever more meticulous hygiene – both moist toilet paper, sold with this in mind, and bidet-style water-spraying toilets that spread from their Asian homelands to become more commonplace in the West too.[38]

Anal intercourse became a central aspect of male homosexual sex. Among the ancient Greeks, intercrural sex was preferred for male-on-male contact and anal penetration was rare. Those considered homosexual in Mediterranean, Latin, and African cultures tended to play the receptive role in penetrative sex, with the active partner not counted as gay and often living an otherwise conventional heterosexual life. Modern Western gay behavior, in contrast, took role switching as one of its central tenets, with receptive anal sex practiced by most homosexual men.[39] Receptive anal sex – pegging – has also spread among straight couples, with strap-ons no longer a toy for lesbians alone.[40] That was one reason why AIDS spread so quickly among gays. Had they continued to divide the roles in sex between active and passive, chains of transmission would have died out more often with infection of the exclusively passive partner. But with role switching, both parties remained active transmitters.[41]

Despite ever more punctilious hygiene, some modern sexual practices have thus raised their own epidemiological problems. The normalization of oral sex may have diminished transmission insofar as it substituted for genital contact, but also promoted the spread of antibiotic-resistant syphilis. Rimming, which first became common among gay men in the 1970s, in effect, made a practice of the first behavior we try to discourage in infants, oral–anal contact. Intestinal diseases like amebiasis and giardiasis are typically found in unsewered parts of the developing world. When they began appearing among HIV-infected gay men, epidemiologists surmised oral–anal contact as the likely cause.[42] And all this is before we take even more outré behaviors into account, like felching.

For chronic disease and transmissible illnesses, especially sexual, public health became ever more based on individual responsibility. Traditional public health imposed strictures on subjects, quarantining, inspecting, and vaccinating them, tracing their contacts, and otherwise mandating behavior necessary to break transmission. For citizens of democracies, however, that made less sense. The growth of epidemiological knowledge, combined with assumptions of democratic responsibility, shifted the burden of prevention to the individual. For venereal diseases, the transition was most dramatic. The old approach had inspected, compulsorily treated, traced, and isolated the diseased – in some countries, sex workers alone, in others, all citizens collectively.

But in the modern era, everyone was held responsible for their own well-being. This change was worked out between victims and public health authorities during the AIDS epidemic. Most nations now ceased imposing the inherited collectivist methods of disease prevention that subordinated victims to the common good. Instead, they shifted to an approach that made the ill masters of their own well-being – offering but not mandating treatment and counseling but not requiring them to behave non-transmissively.[43] Universal safe sex became the norm. It imposed a behavioral mandate on all, gays and straights, men and women, to interpose latex in every interaction they were uncertain about. As Snow had foreseen, every person did, in fact, become their own quarantine officer.

Similar behavioral changes have taken place outside sex too. We have ever less physical contact with each other. What we now consider civilized behavior is conduct we have learned and adopted as normal to prevent more than a minimum of physical interaction. In the sixteenth century, Westerners learned what had long been common in Asia and slowly started to eat from individual plates, using utensils that were ours alone, no longer sharing implements or scarfing down food from communal bowls.[44] During nineteenth-century plague outbreaks in the Middle East, it was common to cease handshaking.[45] Shaking hands is ancient, depicted in Assyrian statuary. But earlier, it was more a ritual, used to seal agreements or, later, to indicate equality between participants.

Its spread in the West came in the seventeenth century. Quakers used it in preference to bowing or tipping a hat.[46] From there, it has gone global in the twentieth. Whatever its origins, it lessened the contact surface compared with anything more effusive, just as elbow bumping, the post-coronavirus norm, has done again. Cruise ship captains, commanders of floating Petri dishes, made it a policy not to shake hands, hoping to avoid norovirus transmission.[47]

In the late nineteenth century, men were encouraged to shave or trim their beards and women to wear skirts too short to touch the ground. Thanks to central heating, clothing became lighter, more easily cleanable. Bodily cleanliness and bathing were once avoided as debilitating and dangerous. Today we are so squeakily clean that it is potentially harmful. Thanks to banishing microbes from our homes, children's immune systems are so under-stimulated that asthma and allergies flourish.

Polio has afflicted humans for millennia, but only in the late nineteenth century did major outbreaks hit the West. It is often transmitted by a virus ingested via fecal matter, but with proper sanitation, a more common means has been from mouth to mouth. Polio epidemics began at about the time as sanitary infra-structure lessened the likelihood of encountering the virus in early childhood, leaving human immune systems less able to fight off infection. The triumph of public cleanliness, eliminating endemic polio, thus facilitated its epidemic spread and required a solution via vaccine instead.

Diminishing our interface with microorganisms, our contact with animals has also become strictly regulated. Globally speaking, that is not true. Covid-19, like many previous epidemics, is zoonotic. Even if they now spread among humans, six out of ten infectious diseases have originated with animals and three out of four of the most recent emerging ones.[48] Humankind's ever-larger footprint has pushed us into territories previously untouched and thus more contact with wild animals. But in the developed world, proximity to animals has diminished. Achieving that took time. Nineteenth-century cities, if anything, brought us into closer contact with animals. The phrase "like a bull in a china shop" was once meant literally.[49]

But gradually, with the declining use of animals except as food, they were pushed beyond the city walls. All but the most conven-tional pets have been banished. And the dogs, cats, and hamsters that remain are inspected, vaccinated, registered, chipped, clipped, and leashed. The law, in all its majesty, even specifies how to dispose of their excrement. Already in the 1890s, a quarter of all fines imposed by French auxiliary police were for public excretion – human and canine.[50]

Quite aside from the rise of vegetarianism and veganism, nor do we eat animals in ways once common. Even carnivores have had their diets restricted. Wild animal consumption has become highly regulated, often banned. Much of what pretends to be game, such as New Zealand venison, is farmed. Wild salmon is expensive and rare. Lobsters, crab, and shellfish are among the last wild animals commonly consumed. Bushmeat is common in Africa, and its illegal import to places like the UK an ongoing concern. Wet markets in China have become a paramount issue in past and present epidemics. The Chinese consume a Noah's ark of wild species – for prestige and supposed medicinal reasons. Besides driving species like pangolins to the brink of extinction, such habits and the associated threat of microorganisms migrating between species are now seared in global awareness.

THE PATHOLOGIES OF EVERYDAY LIFE

In such ways, our everyday lives have become roped into the broader project of preventing epidemic disease propagation. We live distanced and hygienic lives that minimize risks, even though we still permit ourselves a few indulgent behaviors that – in a less well-sewered, -sanitized, and -medicalized world – would be highly dangerous. Disease prevention has become integral to our daily routines. The responsibility for avoiding transmission is baked into our habits, proclivities, indeed our psychology.

We have been distancing ourselves for centuries. In 1788, Adolph Knigge, the writer whose name is now synonymous in German with etiquette, recommended dispensing hugs and handshakes more parsimoniously, lest overuse diminish their value. The same held for matrimonial obligations: best to keep spouses on a short leash, ensuring gratitude for favors bestowed.[51] In the early twentieth century, anti-VD campaigners hoped that children would feel the same distaste that kept them from touching public toilets or kissing strangers so that they were also revolted by the idea of intercourse with a prostitute.[52] To avoid penetration and infection during the AIDS epidemic, lovers resorted to outercourse.

Even as we pride ourselves on being sexually unfettered compared with our supposedly prudish Victorian forebears, our actual levels of mucous membrane, wet-interface contact have likely diminished. We are ever less sloppy. Pornography siphons off more libidinal energy. Sex dolls and robots – an industry gearing up for massive growth – threaten to diminish the longing for wetware erotic partners.[53] In response to Covid-19's social distancing regulations, film and TV have already substituted mannequins for actors in love scenes.[54] Cybersex is as riskless as it gets. Public health authorities remind us of the neglected pleasures and epidemiological safety of masturbation (*"You* are your safest sex partner").[55]

The swamps of promiscuity are being drained. The AIDS epidemic revealed how dangerous indiscriminate copulation could be. Bathhouses were shut, condoms promoted, harmful habits discouraged. Governments everywhere now regulate and often outlaw the oldest profession. We are all becoming sexually domesticated – even powerful men. The #MeToo movement has challenged one of the most fundamental assumptions of privilege: that power's rewards include sexual access. Long-tolerated behaviors by alpha males around subordinate women have become sanctioned.

Some cultures – the ancient Greeks and Romans – were long monogamous, but most not. Historically, it has been the norm that men who could afford it maintained multiple wives, others, none. But polygynous cultures have been vanishing. China and India, together well over a third of humanity, outlawed polygamy in the mid 1950s.[56] Only slightly more than a quarter of the world's nations today permit it.

Compared with our indiscriminately belching, farting, excreting, snorting, sniffing, spitting, copulating, and much, much hairier predecessors, in our deportment, we have become practically Vulcan – Mr. Spock's hyper-rational *Star Trek* clan. Cher, the main character in *Clueless*, the film that sets Jane Austen's *Emma* in 1990s

Beverly Hills, explains why when she accounts for having kept her virginity: "I'm just not interested in doing it until I find the perfect person. I mean, you see how picky I am about my shoes ..., and those only go on my feet."

In ways we hardly register, everyday behavior has adjusted to our knowledge of how disease travels. Our habits are more circumspect, distanced, and bodily abstemious than earlier, recognizing the lessons of bacteriology. Our housekeeping practices – dusted, vacuumed, washed, sanitized, dry-cleaned, foil-wrapped, refrigerated – make our homes more like hospitals than the living quarters occupied even by the well-off a century ago.[57] As does modern interior design, especially in its Scandinavian variants, compared to the Victorians' overstuffed dust- and germ traps. We clean our clothes continuously, changing them daily; we scrub, shampoo, deodorize, moisturize, and depilate our bodies. Horror would be our reaction if a time machine brought us face to face with actual Victorians in all their smelly, hairy, greasy glory – not to mention Vikings.

But not all our behavior helps defeat disease. Besides the risky sexual practices that remain, modern life has other inbuilt pathologies that expose us more to illness than in the past. Precisely because we have so sanitized our lives in some ways, we permit ourselves to live dangerously in others. Our promiscuous travel habits, for example, ensure that the highways of transmission are well-paved. Travel and even tourism are not just pastimes, like golf or checkers, something to amuse ourselves in an idle hour. It is a primal urge, an imperative of our curiosity, a species characteristic from our deep nomadic past. But not all movement is travel. Nor do its pressing motives make it less epidemiologically toxic.

Over four billion airplane trips were taken in 2019 – equivalent statistically to one half of the world's population visiting the other half. To gauge how crucial mass movement has become, consider this: had this pandemic been Covid-76, had it struck before Deng Xiaoping's reforms, liberalizing China and opening it up, we probably would never even have heard about it.[58] Today, major nations find it almost impossible to exclude passenger-borne pathogens from abroad. On April 22, not a single person entered New Zealand.[59] That is an unprecedented feat, especially for a country heavily dependent on tourism. Much more characteristic are the three billion trips taken by the Chinese over forty days starting in late January to celebrate the lunar new year. In normal times, it is the single largest human peregrination.[60]

Our cleanliness also affects our under-utilized immune systems. The "hygiene hypothesis" suggests that children may now suffer more asthma and allergies, and possibly autoimmune diseases, because they only infrequently encounter pathogens to stimulate their defenses. While domestic hygiene may play a role, so does our decreasing exposure to microorganisms attendant on modern life more generally – clean water and food, urbanization, vaccines and antibiotics.[61] Cesarean births, with no vaginal biome transfer, may also be a culprit, as they have increased to almost half of deliveries in China and the US.[62]

Of course, over-cleanliness, if that is a problem, afflicts the industrialized world primarily. If anything, the situation has deteriorated in developing nations where massive population movements from countryside to cities have spawned vast dense slums with only rudimentary sanitation. In the developing world, half the urban population are slum dwellers, in mega-agglomerations like Orangi Town, part of Karachi, Dharavi in Mumbai, and Kibera in Nairobi.[63]

With their gustatorially promiscuous consumption of most anything on four legs and much with none, Chinese dietary and medicinal habits will doubtless now be closely scrutinized. But also threatening is the massive misuse of antibiotics both for human health and for food production in the West. Overuse of antibiotics by physicians seeking to ward off the worried well is well-documented. Less known is the underside of antibiotic globalization. In developing-world shanty towns, patients bereft of reliable, regular medical attention often buy and take individual doses of antibiotics, ceasing when symptoms abate, and not finishing a whole course, thereby encouraging mutation of resistant strains.[64]

Similar consequences follow the growing use of antibiotics in agriculture. Livestock is massively dosed, to increase weight and fend off diseases that rage in its cramped quarters. But even orange farmers spray their crops with human antibiotics to fight citrus greening (huanglongbing). Both animal and plant applications use many times more antibiotics than humans. Thai farmers have been using antibiotics since at least 2012.[65] Florida farmers were allowed to follow suit starting in 2016. There, farmers requested permission to apply four times as much oxytetracycline and thirty-six times as much streptomycin as used by all Americans annually.[66] Such applications do not even solve the problem, only slowing the disease, but they hasten the moment when these drugs will become useless.

Already we live with the first consequences. Drug-resistant strains of tuberculosis and syphilis threaten public health. In the US, MRSA today kills 6 per 100,000, some 20,000 deaths annually.[67] That is well over three times the death rate for AIDS, hepatitis, or flus.[68] In other words, barring significant investment and dramatic breakthroughs, the antibiotic age that the middle-aged among us enjoyed for most of our lives is drawing to a close. Thanks to reckless and shortsighted misuse of medicines that we at first gratefully called wonder drugs but then treated like a rental car, our children will not enjoy our insouciance in the face of microorganisms.

Spas and health cures will make a comeback, focusing on the non-medicinal boosting of immunity. Perhaps Davos will return to what it was in 1924 when Thomas Mann set his novel *The Magic Mountain* there – a health sanatorium, no longer a global gabfest. That could be a silver lining. But we can also expect chronic invalids and people living with constant pain. And the average age at death will likely nosedive.

At issue is not just antibiotics, but the overcrowding that requires them in the first place. Animals for human consumption are so penned together that diseases run rampant. Factory farms become massive Petri dishes where viruses combine in lethal new admixtures. Mix in some visiting wild animals and the possibilities multiply. In 2000, an H6N2 influenza began circulating among poultry in Southern California. Sequencing the virus's genome, scientists discovered that it was derived from North American and Eurasian waterfowl lineages. Two separate genetic hemispheres had been bridged, a nasty downside of avian globalization.[69]

Democratic safeguards, too, make it harder to clamp down on disease transmission with the same resolution that once provoked little opposition. Regulating sex workers today would likely be more difficult than in the nineteenth century. Registering, inspecting, and treating sex workers when ill: something like the old regulationist system continues in many European nations, such as Germany and the Netherlands. But elsewhere, the trend has been prohibitionist, seeking to stamp out sex work altogether.

Where women's rights are taken most seriously, it has become politically impossible officially to tolerate sex work. And that is ignoring its gay analogs, which – bowing to an implicit sexual double standard – are largely ignored by authority. Sweden moved from a strict regulationist system, applied to the entire population, in the nineteenth century, to prohibit the purchase of sex, not its sale, in 1999. The aim of targeting the demand side was to end, not regulate, the sex trade. As official oversight of venereal disease's most efficient spreaders was abandoned, sex workers became like any other patients. Society now had to rely on their judgment and initiative to deal with infection.

CHRONIC DISEASE

Political battles over disease prevention became less pitched in the last half of the twentieth century, as antibiotics and other medicines triumphed over contagious illnesses. The problem was resolved, it seemed, by a technical fix, sparing us ideological disputes over how best to handle it. Two developments threaten to upend such easy solutions: the misuse and blunting of our pharmaceutical weapons against contagious disease and the proliferation of new emerging illnesses, stamped out of the ground as we encroach onto nature's last redoubts. Neither has yet left a mark on the popular understanding of the dilemma we face. On the contrary: our approach to disease remains colored by the last major tectonic shift in the epidemiological landscape, from epidemic to chronic illness.

As modern medicine and public health had an impact, contagious diseases became less dangerous, while the share of mortality due to long-term chronic ailments rose. Not that this has been a one-way street. Even before Covid-19, new emerging infectious diseases reminded us that epidemics are not just a historical curiosity. Avian flu, SARS, and MERS – all caused mercifully small short-term mortality spikes. But AIDS has killed over thirty million people globally during the last forty years. Resurgent antibiotic-resistant tuberculosis and syphilis are unwelcome visitors from the past.

Nonetheless, the big picture was of dramatic decline. In the US, deaths from contagious disease slumped 13-fold from almost 800 per 100,000 in 1900 to 59 in 1996.[70] The developing world, too, has started to share in the misfortunes of modernity and now also faces chronic diseases. Over the last thirty years, the share of chronic ailments in the total disease burden has risen globally from 40% to 60%.[71] People die less commonly in outbreaks of plague, typhoid, diphtheria, cholera, or yellow fever. They are now laid low by chronic diseases that often arise from bad habits or particular aspects of modern life. Cancer, heart disease, diabetes, and obesity are partly caused by sedentary caloric surfeit and the pleasures of tobacco and alcohol. Compared with epidemic ravages, these are nice problems to have. But that does not diminish their threat.

Chronic diseases threw up different problems than the contagious or transmissible. Most obviously, their victims did not pose immediate threats to their neighbors. Chronic disease raised issues of redistribution, not transmission. When someone succumbed to cancer, heart disease, obesity, or other illnesses that may have arisen from voluntary behaviors, the implications for others were limited to how much they had to bear of the costs.

Dealing with chronic diseases required different tactics. The state could encourage, but found it hard to mandate, healthy lifestyles.

It could tax and raise the price – thereby cutting consumption – of tobacco, sugar, or fat. It could ban smoking in public or trans-fats in commercial foods. Zoning, land use, and tax laws could stimulate family farms, farmers' markets, local greengrocers, and other avenues of healthy eating. The Nazis encouraged fruit and vegetable consumption. They tried to limit fats and took aim at whipped cream. So successful were they in promoting whole grain bread that nearly a quarter of all German bakeries sold it by 1943, compared with 1% in 1939.[72] Health insurance could reward certain behaviors, weight loss, exercise, or abstinence. Health authorities could encourage mothers to breastfeed.

In the autumn of 1918, handshaking was outlawed in Prescott, Arizona during the Spanish flu epidemic.[73] It seems likely that our own adoption of elbow bumping against Covid-19 will achieve broader and more lasting behavioral change than that little spasm of legislative delusion. On the whole, it makes little sense to command muesli for breakfast and salads for lunch, twenty minutes daily jogging, and no martinis. Only when it comes to substances and habits that the state wants to extinguish outright does it issue direct imperatives. Drugs were an obvious example. Even here, the harm done by driving use underground was sometimes outweighed by legalized and regularized consumption, as with marihuana. The sale, manufacture, consumption, and advertisement of alcohol and tobacco have, of course, been regulated in countless ways.

Modern public health rests less on the state's command of our conduct than on citizens' own self-willed and -imposed behaviors and habits. For chronic disease, that is most evident. As individual actors, we can do little about environmental threats other than move where conditions are better, stay inside when it's smoggy, filter tap water, and the like. These are ultimately public goods. However, chronic diseases depend on our habits, whether we smoke, drink, take drugs, overeat, exercise, and generally live healthily.

For venereal diseases, that is also mostly true. Whether we are promiscuous or indulge in other risks decides our infection rates. Not the state's impositions, but our behavior determines our health. Rather than the pest house, the quarantine station, mobile fumigation squads, and the other paraphernalia and impositions of public health's old regime, we now have James Fixx and Dr. Atkins, twelve-step programs and health clubs, designated drivers, and condoms.

To change behavior, public health has broadly shifted from relying on outward impositions enforced by the state to inward self-restraint. That holds especially for chronic and transmissible disease, less for immediately contagious ones. Nonetheless, the general tendency rules. The new social outcasts are those who spurn self-imposed restraint: smokers, drinkers, drug-takers, the sexually promiscuous, and extreme eaters of any stripe, in quantity or quality. The overly carnivorous are cautioned, but so are the exclusively vegan, accused of endangering their children. Gone are the days when we considered it medicine's task to allow us as much pleasurable self-indulgence as possible, patching us up once excess took its toll.

Now we have entered an implicit behavioral pact with our doctors, a lifelong agreement that, as the ultimate authors of our health destinies, we must agree to their countless precepts.[74] We could describe this as drinking the Kool-Aid, had not Kool-Aid long been banished from our diets. Those who long for the old regime of strict external control, with room for indulging pleasurable bad habits, attack this ethos of behavioral auto-limitation as "health fascism."[75] But apart from obesity, most middle-class people have given in to teetotalling totalitarianism.

One of the few examples of push-back against the tendency for health to override other concerns is the body shaming movement. On the one hand, the obese are subject to ostracization, ultimatums from insurance companies to lose weight or forfeit discounts, and other pressure to conform. Parents of morbidly obese children have lost custody.[76] Countering that, movements against body shaming have redefined obesity either as a choice, no more to be stigmatized than so many others, or as a fate not chosen and therefore something to which no blame attaches.[77] Either way, it is unclear that it will be treated like other blameworthy lifestyle choices; indeed, it may succeed in becoming valorized.

CHAPTER 8

Who Is Responsible for Our Health?

How Prevention Was Enforced

P UBLIC HEALTH HAD BECOME INCREASINGLY INDIVIDU-
alized. As the state sought to mold ever more behaviors,
getting citizens to improve their health, it had to rely on their
cooperation, not just order them around. Citizens were increasingly entrusted with the decisions that affected their well-being.
And yet, the state did not retire its big stick of enforcement. For
some aspects of public health, like pandemics, it was still needed.

In effect, public health has bifurcated. Chronic and transmissible illnesses have been increasingly dealt with by voluntaristic
individual behavioral changes, ones that best suit their etiology
and incidence patterns. But epidemic disease has not disappeared,
even as it has become less prominent in the overall morbidity
landscape. Indeed, as humans press deeper into nature, live
more densely, farm more intensively, and travel more widely, it
has resurged. Epidemic disease threw down the gantlet to the
belief that public health could rely ever more on autonomous
individuals voluntarily adjusting their behavior.

Even today, combating pandemics requires collective actions
that impinge on individual liberties. Sometimes freedom from
disease is best achieved through curtailing other liberties. As
treatments have improved, why not deliver them to all who
could benefit? But that means finding them. Physicians have
therefore sought to trace contacts, hoping to treat them.
Authorities have curbed rights as part of a positive-sum game,

not just trampled them on behalf of the community's demands. As AIDS treatments became more effective, it made sense to find, test, and treat infected people. Public health authorities sought a mandate to test routinely, without specific permission, informing and offering treatment to those who proved to be infected. In the days before a useful treatment, victims may have seen little point in being aware of their disease status. But now everyone ought to know. Indeed, social justice spoke for identifying and treating. Blacks in the US died more often of AIDS than whites in part because they knew of their status only later, forgoing earlier treatment.[1]

The Covid-19 pandemic put paid to the idea that there were behavioral solutions that avoided significant costs to economic well-being and citizens' liberties. In theory, given a literate, well-schooled, disciplined, and obedient population, the measures that other nations imposed by state diktat could be voluntarily adopted by willing citizens. If everyone self-isolated, worked from home, did not travel, wore protective gear when proximity was unavoidable, and so forth, then laws and regulations specifying such measures could be dispensed with.

Thanks to their trusting relations between state and citizenry, the Swedes thought they had cracked the pandemic dilemma, able to avoid having authority clamp down. The measures they promulgated were significantly less stringent than in Asia, of course, but also than in Italy, Spain, and France, and even in Germany and the UK, where matters had been laxer.[2] Theory predicted that, having internalized the necessary behavioral rules, the Swedes' conduct would be indistinguishable from those nations where laws were still required.

To some extent, it was. Swedish electricity consumption did not drop, while in Belgium, it fell dramatically compared with 2019.[3] But, as noted, traveling did decline voluntarily during the Easter holidays of 2020. To judge by economic activity during the spring, Swedes were also broadly as reclusive as the locked-in Danes.[4] Even if citizens independently adjusted their behavior, however, the fly in voluntarism's ointment was the asymptomatic carriers. They unwittingly threatened others and could not possibly – barring regular universal testing – know better.

A wholly voluntarist solution seemed impossible. Not even the Swedes tried that. Other nations' approaches relied on differing degrees of instructing citizens what to do and expecting them to know and follow such recommendations and mandates. The state's strength, ability, and willingness to compel was one aspect. At the same time, its speaking partner, civil society, was equally important. The more the state could rely on citizens to do under their own steam what otherwise had to be compelled, the less it had to fire the big guns of enforcement. One might call this trust, as did the Swedes. But, as seen, citizens acted spontaneously to protect themselves, even where they did not trust their state. Compliance is likely a more useful concept than trust – compliance with what common sense and self-preservation dictated, but especially with the state's requirements.

Compliance varied both among nations and over the course of the pandemic. At least three sorts of interactions between state and civil society can be mapped. Both in the autocracies and in the democracies of Asia, citizens did what the authorities required, with little overt resistance or objection. In most Western and other democracies, the vast majority of citizens complied with a less demanding palette of preventive measures – motivated either by government mandate, their faith in the authorities, or commonsense instincts of self-preservation. Finally, some nations' leaders, who did not think they could require drastic measures of their most hardpressed followers, either did not impose many or, like Bolsonaro and Trump, undercut the ones introduced by their administrations.

In addition to different complexions of interaction between state and civil society, citizens' reactions fluctuated as the epidemic followed its course. Lockdowns that had at first been tolerated, even welcomed, began to lose their charm as spring dragged into summer. Even citizens who had initially complied found their patience flagging.

Public opinion followed this broad outline. Surveys revealed widespread satisfaction with government interventions at first. If anything, public sentiment favored more action. In April, most Europeans agreed that measures had done more good for public health than harm to the economy.[5] Nor did it much matter what the authorities had done, so long as they had been decisive. Strict interveners were popular, so were lax ones. In April, 71% of Swedes said they trusted their hands-off authorities.[6] At the same time, 84% of New Zealanders approved of the opposite approach.[7] A global public that had soured on government now rallied behind it, with trust soaring to an all-time high of 65% approval in May.[8] Large majorities in the US agreed with lockdown policies and thought the balance of firm initiatives had been right or, if anything, not enough.[9] Even Trump enjoyed a bump in his approval ratings in March and April as Americans rallied around the flag.[10]

The French and the Japanese were outliers. Both administrations had been competent, though lackluster, responders, but they were punished by publics that turned on their politicians. Macron's support slipped, with over 60% unconvinced in May that he could control the epidemic.[11] If the Italians had been pleasantly surprised by how well-functioning their state proved to be, the French were disappointed in theirs – especially their health care system, widely regarded as a global paradigm, but now seen as an indifferent performer.[12] Slow off the mark, the Japanese government hemorrhaged popularity. Failing to declare an emergency until late, it suffered shortages of protective gear and testing. Its measures were insufficient to reassure a citizenry that longed for more decisive actions.[13]

TRUST, OBEDIENCE, OR COMPLIANCE?

China issued orders, Sweden expected voluntary compliance. Other nations arrayed themselves between these extremes. Democratic citizens, the ultimate sovereigns, could be expected to assume responsibility for their own well-being. The state's task was less to order them about than to make sure they were well-informed and able to act in their own defense. At the margins, dealing with the asocial, the ignorant, or the incapable, the state needed to step in. But what about in between? What could the authorities do with citizens who refused to isolate, insisted on taking walks, or visiting family, or who later rejected masks when they became mandated?

A full-blown pandemic was unprecedented, and most nations fumbled their way forward, learning as they went. We can follow the chain of experience and reasoning as one country, France, moved from an initial assumption that citizens would take the right decisions, through disappointment that they did not, to recognizing that firmer measures were needed. France discovered, in other words, not only that it was not China, as Macron had boasted, but also that it was not Sweden.

On March 12, as President Macron was briefed by his scientific council on the anticipated mortality figures calculated by the Imperial College team in London, the experts pondered what it would take to get French citizens on board. The measures imposed in China had been strict, the minutes noted. Perhaps less drastic ones would suffice in a population that agreed to comply with social distancing regulations. Everything depended on whether people obeyed. Popular support was crucial. Implementing overly strict measures even before the danger seemed daunting meant forfeiting public trust.[14]

That Thursday evening, Macron addressed the nation, announcing several measures: that daycare, schools, and universities would be closed as of Monday, that the elderly and vulnerable should isolate themselves, that those who could should work at home, keeping their distance from others, and that all should avoid congregating in public. Public transport would not be shut, but the president appealed to his citizens' sense of responsibility, asking them to restrict their movements.[15]

Over that weekend, Parisians gathered in large throngs outside in public spaces throughout the city. The authorities despaired of reining in the pandemic with the limited measures taken so far. Meeting on Saturday, March 14, the scientific advisors agreed that the public's behavior had fallen short and pondered further steps.[16] That day, stricter regulations were imposed, shutting restaurants, bars, and theaters as of midnight. Too many people, the prime minister admonished, had still been going out to cafes and restaurants.[17]

On Monday, the scientific advisors once again emphasized the role of individual responsibility in preventing the pandemic. But since the appeal to social distancing in public had clearly fallen on deaf ears, new measures were needed.[18] Voluntary self-control had not been forthcoming, the authorities concluded. Since the French were not being compliant, the inevitable next step was an Italian-style blanket lockdown, with exit only for particular purposes, and social distancing in public.[19]

With case numbers having doubled in the past seventy-two hours, on Monday, March 16, President Macron again addressed the nation, now evoking wartime conditions.[20] Further measures were needed, most dramatically a blanket prohibition on going out except for essential purposes. Hopes that a voluntary approach would suffice were dashed. The French had had their chance and blown it. When lockdown was imposed across the nation on March 17, the interior minister promised 100,000 extra security personnel for enforcement, on top of the existing quarter of a million.[21] Yet, no military were to be deployed, they were quick to emphasize.[22] Over the next three weeks, French police issued over 400,000 fines for violating confinement rules.[23] By May, it was over a million, most for failing to carry the official certificate attesting to why the trip in question was necessary.[24]

A similar sense of disappointment was palpable among the German authorities at their citizens' rambunctious partying during the days before the federal states began imposing lockdowns, led by Bavaria on March 20.[25] In the first week or so of lockdown there, police conducted some 25,000 checks, alerting 500 people to change their behavior.[26] In Spain, from mid-March to early

April, over 3,000 people were arrested and 340,000 fines imposed for breaking lockdown.[27] By May, Spanish police had issued 800,000 fines, making almost 7,000 arrests.[28] Even in mild-mannered New Zealand, officers were kept busy. A bit under 6,000 breaches of regulations were registered, of which slightly more than 600 were prosecuted, the rest mostly given warnings.[29]

As always, compliance was a pas de deux between state and civil society. Where citizens obeyed, police truncheons could remain sheathed. On the whole, the public complied – at least during lockdown's early weeks. The authorities reprimanded and fined joggers, hikers, and day-trippers, and people caught visiting elderly parents. Police in Marseille took their soundings in the Porte d'Aix, a lively immigrant neighborhood, and professed satisfaction at how well it had shut down.[30]

CARROTS AND STICKS

In the nineteenth century, those who violated quarantine, slipping out or surreptitiously crossing cordons, had been severely punished, sometimes with execution. Death was off the menu today, but lockdowns were enforced with sometimes surprising rigor. South African police beat citizens who did not follow regulations, kicking doors in. In New York City, police dispersed illegal outdoor gatherings with violence and arrests, especially – critics charged – against minorities.[31] Chinese police were filmed beating a man selling vegetables on the street.[32]

Other tactics were less extreme. High tech made an appearance, with drones admonishing hikers in Britain and robot dogs cautioning strollers in Singapore parks against proximity.[33] So did low tech, as when the Swedish authorities dumped a ton of chicken manure in a public park to discourage Walpurgis night festivities.[34] The English police dyed the waters of a popular lagoon black to deter swimming.[35] Jail sentences of up to three years, seven in aggravated cases, were possible in China.[36] Fines of various levels tended to be the norm elsewhere. But even those could, on occasion, be eye-watering. An illicit party in Australia, busted when the munchies prompted a run on KFC in the wee hours, was punished by a fine of $18,000.[37] A Maryland man ended in jail for repeatedly hosting large parties.[38]

The targeted quarantining implemented in China and other Asian nations required strict enforcement. Identifying the potentially infected, testing them, possibly quarantining them, and finding their contacts to repeat the same procedure: each step was crucial. Any missed vector potentially breached a regimen whose justification rested on extinguishing the source of infection at the earliest possible link. No surprise, then, that citizens felt the heavy hand of enforcement. A widely circulated video from China showed a man being stopped at a border crossing, temperature checked, asked to step from his car, resisting, and being grabbed by several officers, one of whom brought an oversized fishing net down over his head. Though staged, it spoke volumes.[39]

The logic of the system required severe punishments. Targeted quarantine rested on quickly finding and isolating the infected. Missing or overlooking a single vector threatened the entire enterprise. Since transmission was exponential, time was of the essence. Anyone who avoided restrictions not only endangered others but also subjected them, as contacts, to the full weight of preventive measures. Thus, in Qinghai province, a man taking the train from Wuhan to Xining falsely claimed to have been at home for the past forty days. When he tested positive, the 900 people he had been in contact with had to be quarantined. He was sentenced to a year in prison.[40]

How contacts were defined mattered. The more expansive, as this example shows, the more others suffered the consequences. The Chinese took a broad view of who counted as close contacts of someone infected. On planes, everyone seated three rows ahead or behind belonged to the unfortunates, along with all personnel servicing that area. On closed and air-conditioned trains, so did all passengers and crew in the same carriage.[41] In comparison, the Germans, who were – by Western standards – strict tracers, started more leniently. In the first instance, category one contacts included those on public transport sitting within two rows of the infected and others who had spent at least fifteen minutes nearby. Only after that did it expand to all who had been in the same room.[42]

But even in the West and other democracies where broad lockdowns – and not targeted quarantining as in the East – were the strategy, enforcement could be impressive. British police could arrest scofflaws or fine them. Maximum fines in mid-May were £3,200 for a fifth offense. Those who did not pay could be taken to court and fined unlimited sums.[43] In addition to such penalties, constables could physically return home those who contravened regulations by being out and about or congregating in groups, using reasonable force if necessary.[44] Later, faced with resurgent infection, punishments escalated to £10,000 for breaches of self-isolation.[45] Fines in Greece could be €5000, in Germany theoretically as high as €25,000.[46] In Delhi, those who violated curfew had their electricity and water shut off, as did party givers in Los Angeles.[47]

British police also seem to have been officiously zealous in enforcing details. Shoppers were admonished for buying non-essential items and would-be exercisers for straying too far from home.[48] In Sweden, things went the other way – punishing those who self-isolated. Homeschooling was forbidden, and grade-schoolers were required to attend classes. Parents who kept them home during the epidemic were threatened with being reported to social services.[49] New York police fined those who assembled in public and broke up private parties.[50] In Kentucky, the potentially infected who refused to remain at home had ankle monitors fitted to monitor their movements.[51]

In the US, an armed public made policing more ticklish than otherwise. In Michigan, armed helpmates guarded a barbershop that had reopened despite lockdown.[52] But Texas police arrested a bar owner and his armed accomplices who sought to open against the rules.[53] And when Texas bars were shut down again in June, Alcoholic Beverage Commission agents visited 1,500 Texas establishments, shutting down over fifty.[54] Though contact tracing was lax and inefficient in most Western nations, at times authorities lost patience. When attendees at an illegal party in the New York suburbs refused to cooperate with contact tracers, they were subpoenaed with fines of $2,000 per day.[55]

The public, too, piled into the policing scrum. Frustration with confinement encouraged citizens in a foul mood to turn each other in. In China, WeChat and Weibo opened hotlines to facilitate neighbors reporting the ill, and some cities offered rewards for turning them in. Those who did not respect social distancing regulations were also fair game for vigilantes. Violators – a mahjong party, for example – were videoed promising not to re-offend and to monitor other transgressors.[56] New Zealand set up a website for the purpose.[57] The British kept an eye on each other.[58] *Private Eye*, the satirical bi-weekly, mocked their fondness for snitching. Citizens rang the police, it reported, "to complain that the people at number 94 had a friend round for tea yesterday or that they can smell a barbecue coming from the south-west and the local authority should send in the tanks."[59]

A notable case concerned Neil Ferguson, the epidemiologist whose team at Imperial College had produced the stark mortality predictions in March 2020 that prompted the UK and US to switch course. Having succumbed to and recovered from the disease, he twice entertained a female friend at home. He resigned, even though he was only an expert, advising the government for no pay, not an elected politician, and though technically it was his friend who had breached regulations by crossing town.

The story broke in the *Daily Telegraph*.[60] But in classic British tabloid style, the competing venues, smarting at having been scooped, ran with it for days. The *Daily Mail* conducted an analysis – by tabloid standards quite forensic – of how he had been exposed, betrayed probably by neighbors, whether his, his ex-wife's, or his current girlfriend's. It was possibly a deliberate diversion, the government hoping to distract from the then-breaking scandal of unreported deaths in care homes.[61] In May, Dominic Cummings was outed for having traveled with wife and child to his parents' home in Durham while sick. Since he was unpopular among civil servants and Tory MPs, the tabloids had fodder for their speculations about who might have squealed.[62]

Naïve users of social media also found themselves hoisted by their own petards. A visitor from New York to Hawaii was arrested after he posted selfies on the beach when he was supposed to be hunkered down in self-isolation.[63] Stephen Kinnock, Welsh MP, was admonished by police having posted a selfie while visiting his father Neil, former Labour leader, on his birthday.[64]

ENFORCING MASKS

Masks provided a good example of the authorities' dilemma. How was their use to be ensured? In Asia, they had long become a habit. In any case, the sense of shame that bore the brunt of much everyday enforcement in these nations did its work here too. Groupthink spoke for masks as a collective endeavor. But in the culturally more individualized Western democracies, especially where mask-wearing had become politicized, how was it to be mandated? The police could not be summoned for every infraction. Those nations that did not require citizens to carry identification – mainly the Anglo-Saxons – were easily stymied even if they had wanted to enforce. Mask-wearing was much like littering, a behavior against which statute could be leveled, but that ultimately required a change of mind.

Like condoms, masks were another instance of public health doing better by persuading than mandating. All the more inexplicable why the Swedes shunned them. "Our authorities and our health system are doing everything they can," the government announced about its coronavirus strategy, though clearly, that was untrue. "But each person in Sweden must meet their responsibility."[65] One would have thought masks fit snugly with this ideology of individual accountability.

Violations of mandated mask usage in public were easy to spot and therefore, in principle, easily enforced. But short of tying up the police with endless petty offenses, or unleashing an army of snoops and snitches, making their wearing a habit was probably a better solution. As the West encountered what was likely to become a new sartorial custom, everyday conflicts threw grit into the social machinery. Anti-maskers with a point to argue stirred up trouble by refusing to mask-up where required, whether subways or stores. Those too lazy to assert a rights violation instead used the fake pretext that disability legislation exempted the handicapped.[66]

In theory, fines were the punishment for not wearing them. Yet, who delivered the culprits to their just desserts? French mayors found themselves legally hobbled in their hopes of requiring masks.[67] A Florida sheriff forbade his officers from wearing masks or enforcing ordinances.[68] As a condition of opening up again in July, Maine's governor required large stores to be the business end of enforcement.[69] Texas had done the same in June.[70] But in reality, what storeowner, smarting from months of lost sales, was going to pick fights with customers? And, in any case, the last-mile enforcing fell to minimum-wage floor personnel – unlikely to take up cudgels for their employers.[71]

That was true even of national chains, like Starbucks and Walmart, which required their customers to mask-up in July regardless of local ordinances.[72] In fact, the big chains wimped out, unwilling to refuse service to non-compliant customers.[73] The CDC advised employees not to argue with maskless customers.[74] The killing in May of a security guard enforcing masking in Flint, Michigan, home of the filmmaker Michael Moore and thus a location pregnant with significance, cannot have sparked enthusiasm for enforcement.[75] In July, a French bus driver was beaten to death by passengers who refused his request for masks.[76] In the UK, enforcement was left to the police, who were to remove refusniks if summoned by retailers, using fines and "reasonable force" if necessary.[77]

On the other hand, some authorities did rise to the occasion. In California, several localities rescinded mask ordinances in June after protests.[78] But, as the local situation deteriorated, Los Angeles Mayor Eric Garcetti took a stand: "Everyone should be wearing your face covering. I'm not asking you; I'm telling you," he announced on July 1. West Hollywood and Santa Monica stood ready to levy fines on maskophobes, $300 for a first offense, $500 for a third.[79] Even the Texas governor clamped down, with a state-wide mask mandate in early July, with fines up to $250.[80]

As conditions spiraled out of control in Texas, the authorities found that, faced with widespread non-compliance, the state's big stick was their only remaining tool. Hidalgo County authorities issued stay-in-place orders on July 20, with masks required in indoor public spaces and outdoors wherever distancing was impossible. Fines of $250 were the immediate sanction, and jail was expressly ruled out, except if police enforced trespassing laws for store or property owners. But the authorities also tweeted a threat of criminal prosecution for failure to comply.[81] Indonesian local officials who sentenced mask violaters to dig graves for coronavirus victims demonstrated a sepulchral administrative imagination.[82]

VOTING WITH THEIR FEET: HOW CITIZENS COMPLIED

Disappointed by its citizens' unconcern with the pandemic's seriousness, the French government decided that a mandatory lockdown was the only option. But once the authorities in most democracies decided to impose suppressive measures like self-isolation, closures, and social distancing, the public broadly complied. Given a choice between security and liberty, most citizens were happy to sacrifice some rights for a promise of bringing the epidemic under control. Even the freedom-loving Swiss in their mountain redoubt longed for strong leadership to face down the epidemic.[83]

Not only did people accept lockdown, they often willingly did what the authorities only later got around to mandating. Voluntary compliance was baked into the Swedish tactics – whether we call it trust or obedience. Whatever their motives, the Swedes adopted largely the same behavior as was required of their neighbors across the borders in Denmark and Norway. Shops, bars, and restaurants remained open and the international media was awash in stock photos of blondes quaffing beer al fresco in Stockholm. The reality was less frothy. Swedes curtailed their shopping, traveling, and visiting almost as much as the Danes, who were hunkered down in government-ordered lockdown. Measured by mobile phone data in mid-April, retail and recreation in Sweden were down 41%, transit use by a third, while – in compensation – visits to parks were up, 80% more than usual.[84] Aggregate spending in Sweden dropped by a quarter during the early months of the epidemic, only a tad less than Denmark.[85]

Although the rhetoric of nudging and the Blitz rested on opposite presumptions, the British government attempted to use both. As it turned out, the authorities had misjudged their citizens. The British proved more than willing to endure lockdown. While the government waited until March 23 to order isolation, people had begun shutting down by themselves earlier. Restaurant bookings had fallen 82% already by March 17.[86] Peak infection arrived on April 8, just two weeks after the official command to isolate, which suggested that voluntary distancing had started reducing transmission even earlier.[87]

Some chafed under the restrictions. But overall, the British endured the shutdown with the same patience and good humor as elsewhere. Internet polling revealed that the British were as dutiful as others in staying home and shunning proximity to their fellow citizens.[88] The government anticipated that perhaps a fifth of schoolchildren, facing straightened circumstances at home or having parents who needed childcare as crucial workers, would continue to attend school, even as they closed for most students. In fact, only 2% showed up, though that may have been due as much to bad planning as to any willing acceptance of self-isolation.[89]

In the Czech Republic, in late May, when face masks were no longer required in public, most people continued wearing them.[90] In the US, lockdowns were most stringent in the coastal states and, more generally, where the epidemic initially struck hardest and where Democrats dominated the electorate. In those West Coast, Northeast, and mid-Atlantic states that mandated lockdown, people stayed put more than in the Midwest and South. In Connecticut, average mobility declined to half its normal level in late March and stayed there until late April. In Wyoming and South Dakota, it never reduced that far.[91]

One exception to tolerating lockdown was Michigan, where governor Gretchen Whitmer found herself attacked both from the White House and by protesters in Lansing. Michigan's measures were among the strictest, including a broad stay-at-home order, prohibition of public assemblies, and closure of non-crucial businesses. Of particular annoyance was cordoning off non-essential items in stores that otherwise remained open, such as carpeting, furniture, and paint.[92] Decisive governors, Republican and Democratic, were lauded, the federal leadership in Washington was not.[93] Those who neglected firm early measures were punished by public opinion, such as Florida's Ron DeSantis, who had failed to close beaches during spring break.[94]

The dirty little secret of the epidemic was revealed when, in May, it was time to begin undoing the lockdown and steer towards normality again – the deconfinement, as the French called it. Happy as the public had been to feel the government protecting it when lockdown was first decreed, so conversely, the deconfinement was perilous for most authorities. Lockdown had been universal and across-the-board. Deconfinement, in contrast, allowed exceptions and inconsistencies.[95] Reopening allowed more mistakes than had closing.

Once things began unfurling again in June, the mood changed. The problem now was not a populace bristling at being kept isolated against its will. On the contrary, many were more afraid of illness than shutdown. How to lure them back into a regularized world of jobs, transit, shopping, dining, and all the other risks? Between furlough pay, beefed-up unemployment benefits, and the third of the workforce able to labor from home, many had little urgent economic incentive to return to their workplaces. Add to that the many elderly and vulnerable, and few were tempted by the pleasures of the old normal.

The anxious confronted the impatient. Many, especially the middle-aged and elderly, hesitated to resume normality. Others, often young, crowded beaches, bars, and amusements once that became legal again. Neglecting the extent to which the shutdown had spared them pain, many now took the reopening as evidence that lockdown had been unnecessary in the first place.[96] Others, in contrast, preferred to stay in the cocoon.

School teachers and professors resisted reopening schools and universities even as students and pupils, not to mention their parents, were keen to resume their lives.[97] Schools in England were supposed to open June 1 for some grades. In many areas, none did. Overall, only 12% admitted additional pupils.[98] When schoolteachers effectively went on strike, the government caved, canceling plans to reopen schools before September, "at the earliest."[99] In the US, schoolteachers' unions dug in against the Trump administration's intention to open schools in August and September. Safety was understandably among their concerns, but not only. The United Teachers Los Angeles, the union of the nation's second-largest school district, with 600,000 pupils, piled up a daunting set of demands to be realized before schools opened again.

They understood well that the federal government needed schools to open physically to get business going again. Yet, the workers most exposed to risk were minorities and others badly treated by the economy. Whites and well-off communities, who had suffered little, wanted a rapid reopening. Precisely how the UTLA intended to square this circle was nebulous. Its core constituency was those both most dependent on their work and most endangered by it. Clear, however, was the ambitiousness of the conditions that the union held out as its opening gambit for negotiations to reopen schools.

Paid sick leave for parents, enabling them to keep ill children at home, and massively increased government funding to pay for distancing infrastructure were the start of demands made of the "politicians and the billionaires they serve." To that came Medicare for all, new wealth and commercial property taxes, a millionaires' tax, defunding of the police, new housing initiatives, a moratorium on charter schools, and financial support for undocumented pupils and their families. As the union concluded, "Normal Wasn't Working for Us Before. We Can't Go Back."[100]

University professors, often elderly, risk-averse, and accustomed to getting their way, were an equally formidable obstacle. Unlike schools, their business was a lucrative money-spinner for many economies. Scaring off international students who paid undiscounted tuitions threatened havoc with those university budgets dependent on fees.[101] How many Asian students wanted to come back to the chaotically infected Anglophone nations where many of them studied? And what if travel restrictions prevented even the willing from returning?

In the UK, the institutions most dependent on international students were often the most prestigious. Absent foreign immatriculation, they were likely to poach enrollees from lesser-ranked colleges, sparking a competitive cascade.[102] The Trump administration's attempt to force American universities to reopen by threatening to rescind foreign student visas was a mortal danger. When the universities rolled out the heavy legal guns, Washington caved.[103] Juggling the various demands of budgets, staff, and students made restarting universities – even in some hybrid of online and in-person classes – a microcosm of society at large.

An intriguing start into the brave new world we will all soon inhabit came with first stabs at universal testing. Testing could be either accurate or frequent, one characteristic compensating to some extent for the other's absence. Modeling studies revealed that, with a lab-rat population of resident undergraduates, testing them twice weekly with inexpensive and quick-result procedures, while isolating the infected, would provide reasonable and affordable protection for the cohort as a whole.[104] Yale and Cornell screened its resident students twice weekly in the fall.[105] Other hard-hit occupations headed in the same direction. Some professional sports created their own bubbles, testing all participants daily; airlines screened passengers on certain routes.[106] Nations outside Asia too began testing all citizens – Slovakia and then Austria in November.

While some groups dug in to defend their positions, for others, deconfinement brought a return to an undesired normality. The homeless, sometimes housed in hotels during the epidemic, ended back on the streets.[107] Vagrants who had not found refuge had suffered the closure of libraries and public restrooms.[108] That at least promised to change now. Physicians were now expected to return to their offices, waiters, their restaurants, and workers, their assembly lines. But to many, workplaces – however distanced and disinfected – still seemed dangerous.[109] For others, the deconfinement brought an unwelcome new normal. Swedes turned on their government when it became clear in June that, as vacationers, they were welcome nowhere.[110]

In late April, polls showed that in Brazil, the US, UK, and Sweden, significant numbers thought the authorities had not done enough to combat the epidemic.[111] Despite some protesters, both in the UK and in the US, majorities opposed a broad opening up of the economy again in early May. Few were eager to go shopping or out to dine, even fewer to go to the movies.[112] A majority was keener to protect against the epidemic than to open up business.[113] The French, too, preferred to stay home rather than go back to work. The head of the employers union begged the president in June to tell the French "that it is time to return to work."[114]

In Britain, public opinion was divided. Half were convinced that the government, having only belatedly locked down, was now, in May, loosening up too soon. Those opposed tended to be older and male – the most vulnerable.[115] In early May, fewer than one in five wanted to start loosening things. There was even less support for opening pubs and restaurants.[116] Winding down protective measures against popular will put the government in a tricky position, likely to be blamed for second spikes or other mishaps.[117] On the day, August 3, when offices were supposed to open up again in England, only one in twenty civil servants were at their desks.[118]

When he introduced lockdown in March, Boris Johnson had expected an uphill battle against ingrained instincts of British liberty and freedom. With that laddish bonhomie that his hospitalization had not yet dampened, he lamented depriving his subjects of "the ancient, inalienable right of free-born people of the United Kingdom to go to the pub."[119] As it turned out, he had misjudged his electorate. As always, *Private Eye* kept its finger on the national pulse. Despite their self-image, it mocked, Brits turned out not to be very interested in liberty, but "actually, they don't mind staying at home and doing exactly what they're told, provided there's a good reason for it." Thank heavens, it sarcastically concluded, that the government could be trusted not to "take advantage of this newfound national characteristic when this is all over."[120]

Johnson now found himself on the ropes. He floated unpromising trial balloons, such as asking seventy-year-olds to remain isolated for months to come (especially ill-received in the octogenarian House of Lords). He proved unable to persuade the teachers' unions to reopen schools, and he reversed himself on whether to continue providing school meals for poor children. He imposed an unpopular quarantine on incoming travelers just in time to ruin vacation plans as the rest of Europe began traveling. Here, too, he reversed himself yet again a few weeks later, another whiplash maneuver in his rule-by-focus-group. In June, the government's approval ratings were the worst of any, bar the Mexican.[121] Trump's opinion polls, too, plumbed new depths in June as he undermined governors who sought to delay the deconfinement. His response to George Floyd's killing by Minneapolis police was especially inept, a characteristic combination of tone-deaf indifference and threats of military force worthy of a banana-republic caudillo.[122]

If some voters feared returning to normality, others rushed to embrace it. The deconfinement also turned into a frat party. Some of the excess was just pent-up cabin fever and animal spirits. Vast bacchanalias erupted at the Lake of the Ozarks in Missouri and along Atlantic and Gulf beaches in the US.[123] London's Soho was crammed with jubilant drinkers in early July, while Bristol hosted raves and Liverpool two-day moshpits for football fans.[124] The Scots seem to have held their liquor better.[125] Lagos emerged from lockdown to find market throngs threatening to reignite the pandemic.[126] Lager louts defying police in Liverpool or Staffordshire were merely an annoyance.[127] More charming was the studied chaos of the Columbian city, Barranquilla, famed for its carnivalesque dissolution.[128] But in the cold light of morning, both were the outcome of social indiscipline that boded ill in pandemic times. Twenty-one US states saw increased coronavirus cases in June, twenty-one European countries.[129]

Whether this was just an outpouring of high spirits or also laced with darker currents was hard to know. Resistance to lockdowns became more politicized during the deconfinement than in the first flush of shutdown. As the initial threat seemingly passed, opportunities arose to push for a speedier opening-up and vent grievances. Protests against lockdown erupted in the American Mid-West in April and May. Demonstrators drove in caravans and rallied mask-less at statehouses, some even armed.[130] They demanded being allowed to work again and an end to civil liberties restrictions.[131] Republican states were most likely to see unrest, spurred on by the president, whose tweets advocated violating the rules promulgated by his administration.[132]

In June, those US states which deconfined earliest were dominated by Republicans, while Democratic ones were more cautious. The South and South-West, at first spared while the East had suffered, now opened up before having controlled the epidemic. Predictably, infections surged. By early July, Texas and Florida hospitals hovered on the brink of being overrun, much like New York City in March.[133]

Political opposites went toe-to-toe elsewhere too. Americans' distrust of centralized authority is a commonplace, but other nations suffered similar attitudes. Expecting more friction, the French police had been pleasantly surprised at how compliant citizens had been, filling out forms explaining the purpose of their journeys, for example.[134] Neoliberal provocateurs, like Bernard-Henri Lévy, were dismayed by citizens' docility, knuckling under to fear of the virus and the state impositions that promised to shelter them.[135]

Europe, too, saw protests against lockdown, usually joined by populist and rightwing parties, the AfD in Germany, for example.[136] In Germany, attendance in May numbered in the thousands and sometimes turned violent, with men, armed with stones and iron bars, attacking police enforcing social distancing rules.[137] Bigger ones followed in August, when the Reichstag was stormed.[138] Even Russia, where protests were routinely suppressed, had its share.[139] In Italy, MPs from the far-right Northern League occupied parliament to protest lockdown.[140] In Belgrade, right-wingers attacked the parliament building in July.[141] Britain had no powerful anti-lockdown movement, nor a political party to join forces with, though Nigel Farage aimed to turn his Brexit party into one.[142] Attendance at protests here was at first numbered in the dozens.[143] But on the other hand, the aging rocker Van Morrison lent his fading charms to the corona dissidents.[144]

VACCINATION

Vaccination, too, raised issues of compliance. We have been lucky enough to get a vaccine, and even several, which began being rolled out in December. Even as they are administered, some will spurn this blessing out of misguided fear of occult political intrusions or a belief that nature frowns when humans seek to avoid being lunch for microbes. Unfortunately for the rest of us, herd immunity is a public good. Unlike wearing condoms, vaccination does not protect us individually. No vaccine is 100% reliable. Nor can everyone be vaccinated. Victims of autoimmune disease or cancer patients rely on the rest of us not infecting them. Besides making each individual largely immune, vaccination thus also lessens the statistical likelihood of anyone encountering the pertinent microorganism, thereby – in the aggregate – delivering full protection. Given that not everyone can be vaccinated, a refusal rate over 10% is estimated to compromise herd immunity.[145]

Opponents of vaccination are as old as the technique itself. They were spurred to organize themselves when the state decided to make the practice compulsory and widespread. The English city Leicester appeared on the Covid-19 map when neighborhoods were closed down again in July, flare-ups having appeared in its garment industry. But Leicester was already etched in the history of public health. In the nineteenth century, antivaccinators there staged mass demonstrations and pitched street battles against the state's hopes of ending smallpox with the needle.[146]

In those days, objections were not incomprehensible. The early techniques of inoculation and arm-to-arm vaccination often spread other diseases. With poor sanitation, garden-variety infections were rife. More philosophical objections were also heard, both religious and political. Some regarded vaccination as an abomination, violating the Biblical injunction against mixing human and animal. Others saw civil liberties threatened, rejecting the government's claim to force individuals to any sacrifice for the public good.

As smallpox vaccination solved its teething problems, the medical concerns largely evaporated. It was broadly accepted, joined by new jabs against cholera, typhoid, yellow fever, tuberculosis, diphtheria, measles, polio, pneumonia, shingles, and HPV. But, like transmissible disease prevention more generally, vaccination became a victim of its own success. Collective memories faded of smallpox's hideous scarring or the ravages of mumps, rubella, whooping cough, polio, or measles. Living in a fool's paradise of herd immunity supplied by others' submission to the needle, antivaccinators underestimated the risks to their children.

Some argued that the triple jab of MMR overwhelmed infants' immune systems and somehow caused autism. Such concerns were based on faulty and misleading evidence. Others, then as now, saw vaccination primarily as a political question, whether the state could require the common good of herd immunity. Religious objections persisted among orthodox Jews, Hindus, and Jehova's Witnesses.[147] In 2019, the Russian Orthodox church rejected vaccinating school children, since parents alone were responsible for their well-being.[148]

As vaccination rates have dropped across the developed world in recent decades, authorities were compelled to tighten up enforcement – not allowing schoolchildren to matriculate and increasing the range of required vaccinations. It was an uphill battle. The WHO included "vaccine hesitancy" among its top ten global health threats in 2019, alongside air pollution, climate change, antimicrobial resistance, and an influenza pandemic.[149] On social media, antivaccine sites still had fewer followers, but they were numerous and better connected to still-undecided sites.[150]

Three-quarters of North Americans and Northern Europeans considered vaccines safe, but those numbers dropped precipitously in Western Europe (59%) and Eastern Europe (40%). Fully one-third of Frenchmen thought them unsafe, the highest percentage globally.[151] Declining vaccination rates helped explain outbreaks of measles in Europe in 2019. Cases that year were twice those two years earlier and the highest of the century.[152] In France, measles cases more than quadrupled from 2017 to 2018.[153]

From a movement of the poor, antivaccination became a resentment of the better-off.[154] Posh neighborhoods were home to the shock troops of well-educated, finely bred, holistic-minded antivaccinating parents who set their faith in organic food and childhood yoga to tame nature's evils. People who faced real problems had less time for it. Vaccination rates were higher in Mississippi than in California, higher in New York City's public than private schools.[155] While barely 60% of Western Europeans agreed that vaccines were safe, 95% of South Asians and 92% of East Africans did.[156]

Yet, as antivaccination spread more widely, it moved beyond the well-to-do. Though minority communities would likely benefit most from a coronavirus vaccine, those who had been under- and poorly served by the health system were often skeptical of its promises. When medical researchers went to Africa or Latin America searching for places where the epidemic was still active enough to test vaccines, they were easy targets for accusations of racism or colonialism.[157] The Tuskegee experiments in the 1930s, where Blacks had suffered untreated syphilis, left a legacy of suspicion among minorities in the US.[158] Should formerly mistreated groups (also among the most susceptible to Covid-19) be prioritized for the new vaccine?[159]

In France, 26% of respondents polled during the lockdown said they would not be vaccinated against Covid-19. Resistance was high among young women (36%), the old (22%), and low-income groups (37%), even though they were most exposed. Far-left and far-right political supporters were most likely to be against.[160] Twenty percent of Americans polled in May said they would not get a vaccine.[161] In June, 70% said they would.[162] And 85% of Australians said they would too.[163]

When the medical establishment rushed to discover, manufacture, and distribute a vaccine, it therefore met more skepticism than would have been likely a few decades earlier, before antivaccinationism had taken off. True, some antivaxxers dropped their guard when it came to a possible coronavirus vaccine.[164] In the past, epidemics have boosted vaccine take-up. Demand for flu vaccines had quintupled in the face of Covid-19.[165] But public health suffered from the widespread distrust that had also chipped away at faith in government more generally. Antivaccination was public health populism. And, of course, like all other non-Covid procedures, vaccinations had dropped off a cliff during the pandemic.[166] While most citizens fervently wished for an effective vaccine, others swore they would never contribute to herd immunity by submitting.

The usual civil liberties arguments made the rounds. The always-potent fear of privacy violations reared its head in the belief that recipients would have microchips injected along with the vaccine.[167] Celebrity attracted attention as usual. Robert Kennedy Jr., son of the assassinated US attorney general, was prominent in the cause.[168] Novak Djokovic, the highest-ranking male tennis player, claimed he would refuse a future anti-coronavirus shot even if required to play tournaments. In late June, he and his wife tested positive after an exhibition event in Croatia.[169] And predictably, Andrew Wakefield, the disgraced British physician who had been defrocked for a fraudulent study linking MMR vaccination to autism, was back for another bite of the apple.[170]

Oddly, the antivaxxers did not seem to ponder the likely unpopularity of their position, were they to be blamed for future lockdowns. Nor, in the late summer of 2020, when the first systematic evidence began to emerge of cross-reactive immunity to Covid-19 from other vaccinations, did it yet occur to them that they would have difficulty discounting that advantage.[171]

Knowing that citizens could no longer – as had been possible in the nineteenth century – just be dragged off for vaccination, fined repeatedly, or jailed, public health authorities sought to understand and accommodate resistors in hopes of persuading them to relent. Some surveys showed that antivaccinators were most concerned with side effects and being infected with the disease itself.[172] The media extensively covered how vaccines were being expedited through the usual research process, with abbreviated protocols and massive production chains geared up even before vaccines had been approved.

The US administration's Operation Warp Speed threw billions at vaccine development with the implicit hope of scoring political points by having one ready before the November election.[173] The Chinese made their vaccines available to the employees of state-owned businesses even before the usual phase-three trials had determined their safety.[174] The Russians, too, jumped the gun, releasing their evocatively named Sputnik V vaccine before mass testing, in effect turning the general public into guinea pigs.[175] Both nations apparently cut corners on testing and enlisted subjects as volunteers who were in no position to give consent – soldiers, government bureaucrats, employees of the vaccine companies.[176]

Emphasizing this all-out effort inadvertently raised new questions of safety and side effects. Such concerns suggested room for official reassurance of vaccination's safety and effectiveness. Public health authorities sought to anticipate objections by recommending widespread information campaigns targeted at the hesitant and other ways of actively engaging the public. With a $10 billion spend on vaccine development in the US alone, it made sense to unleash the behavioral sciences to ponder how to make the medicine most palatable.[177] However successful vaccination might turn out to be, the days when the authorities could just mandate interventions were gone. Civil society had to be treated as a partner, not just the object of the state's ministrations.

CHAPTER 9

Difficult Decisions in Hard Times

Trade-offs between Being Safe and Being Solvent

PANDEMICS PRESENT ZERO-SUM DILEMMAS. SOME GAIN, others lose. Just as individuals are sacrificed for the community, quarantined for the public good, so a palette of other trade-offs is factored between winners and losers. Few can escape the effects of a global pandemic altogether, but many were harder hit than others. As was often pointed out, all were weathering the same storm, but not in the same boat.

Within the law's confines, each of us took individual decisions during the pandemic that reflected our risk tolerance and circumstances. The Swedish approach allowed broad leeway for personal choice. But even many Chinese citizens daily judged whether to venture out to shop or report for work. Elsewhere, the state demanded a drumbeat of decisions from citizens: whom to isolate with and where; whether to work from home, if even possible; if not, how to get to work and secure protective gear; how to care for dependents living elsewhere and at home; how often and where to shop for necessities; how to manage the arrival of deliveries; whether to schedule and keep appointments with physicians; whether to venture out for recreation, exercise, and whatever distanced sociability remained legal. Each instance required a weighing of needs against risks. Every puncturing of the domestic veil of prophylaxis brought welcome contact with the outside world while threatening to admit the virus.

Whether to consult physicians for matters unrelated to the coronavirus was a primal decision. Could it wait? If so, when would it be safe again to attend? Anyone with an unexpected pain, bleeding, or lump faced such questions. Those in the midst of ongoing treatments did so urgently. Could procedures, tests, and surgeries be postponed without consequences? For how long? Such questions were pressing for cancer, where the benefits of early diagnosis and treatment had long been emphasized.[1] The NHS in Britain counted postponed cancer treatments and procedures in the millions.[2] Still, immuno-suppressed cancer patients, especially susceptible to Covid-19, had to be careful.

Telemedicine allowed us to sidestep some of these risks and was welcomed.[3] In Sweden, virtual doctor's appointments almost doubled.[4] In rural Maine, residents were permitted access to tele-medical consultations reimbursed by the local version of Medicaid.[5] As with telemeetings, online medical appointments were often better than expected for many complaints, but far from perfect for all. Virtual medicine was about as satisfactory as virtual sex, virtual dentistry rather less. Few saw their doctor in person if they could avoid it.

Unless, that is, they spotted an opportunity to get a bit of work done at an unanticipated moment when no excuses had to be made for the collateral effects. Cosmetic surgeons in Japan, South Korea, the US, and Australia were in high demand as clients discovered they could hide their bruising and discoloring at home or behind masks.[6] But regular doctor visits evaporated. Parents skipped the children's routine vaccinations, exposing them to future illness.[7] In France, GP appointments were down 40%, specialists, 70%.[8]

What about medical emergencies during lockdown? Victims of car crashes, falls from high places, and stabbings were dispatched to emergency rooms much as always. So too, overdoses in the US, already high, continued climbing during the pandemic.[9] But suf-ferers of heart attacks, strokes, and detached retinas had more control over their response. One of the pandemic's most uncanny and unexpected outcomes was the steep drop in patients with acute problems seeking urgent care. Visits were down almost half across emergency rooms in the US and UK.[10]

Fewer car accidents during lockdown eased up on the supply side. Increased handwashing may have cut gastrointestinal emergencies. And the same measures used against Covid-19 also lessened the incidence of common flus.[11] Premature births were down for reasons yet to be explained.[12] But strokes and heart attacks were unlikely to enjoy a pandemic-related slump. During the pandemic's first weeks in Paris, more heart attacks than normal occurred outside hospitals, and more of those making it to the hospital died.[13] The same was true in northern Italy, though there, the supposition was not that victims were staying away, but that Covid-19 was causing more heart attacks.[14]

Having postponed elective procedures, cleared out patients who could be discharged, and built temporary excess capacity, many hospitals were left with the wards intended for non-corona problems under-occupied. Doctors had been reassigned and patients feared being infected if they came in for other issues. So worried were physicians about their absent patients that their organizations began encouraging people to come in immediately if they felt ill.[15] Whatever the opposite of the worried well should be called (suspicious sick, anxious afflicted?), they were now the problem.

No one knows the precise cost of postponed or skipped procedures. Barring miracles, some neglected treatments would have to be caught up later when the underlying problem had worsened. A wave of future cases has potentially been pushed ahead, eventually to crest and break over health systems that will have been strained by the pandemic. During the month from June 15 to July 12 (weeks 25–28), in England and Wales, 3,033 excess deaths (compared with previous years) occurred at home, while 3,132 fewer deaths were registered in hospitals.[16] These were presumably the people who remained too scared to ring for an ambulance when in need.

Cancer patients went untreated, absent sufficient plasma for transfusions.[17] Corona-infected patients could not donate organs and fewer car accidents also reduced donor numbers. Transplant operations declined.[18] The WHO warned that in Africa, skipped vaccinations might lead to 140 deaths for every coronavirus death averted by lockdown. If tuberculosis, AIDS, and malaria treatments were postponed because of the pandemic, lockdown might ultimately cause more deaths than lives saved by shutting down.[19] Interrupting regular health care in developing nations was anticipated to affect child and maternal mortality severely.[20]

Skipped or postponed procedures are usually considered a downside of lockdown, part of its collateral damage. That may be true and it is possible that less of a dip occurred in the Asian nations' targeted quarantines. But it is equally plausible that the epidemic as such – both the fear of becoming infected in hospitals and the filling of wards with coronavirus victims – not the lockdown, was what scared potential patients from emergency rooms and doctors' offices. Uninsured patients in the US who used emergency rooms as ambulatory care clinics had some discretion over whether to attend during the epidemic and may have driven declines in visitors.[21] In the US, emergency room visits were down, while admissions to hospital wards from the ERs at first remained stable.[22] That suggested a possible decline in discretionary cases. In theory, the Asians with their targeted quarantines that affected mainly the infected, leaving others untouched, should have been visiting emergency rooms more normally – at least where hospitals were not overrun, as they had been in Wuhan.

Whether that was true is hard to determine. One faint hint comes from Taiwan. In a large Taipei hospital, despite the low prevalence of Covid-19 in the population, emergency room visits dropped by a third from February through May, though visits by the sickest (triage level 1) remained steady. The decline was thus less than in the US and UK. Out-of-hospital heart attacks in Taipei remained constant during the pandemic, but in-hospital cardiac arrests increased. Did this indicate a continued influx of patients with severe conditions, much as before the epidemic? Or was it because physicians and nurses attended instead to coronavirus victims?[23]

Whatever the case in Asia, if the Swedes' voluntary approach was working, they should also – in theory – have been attending emergency rooms much as always. They went about their regular business, protected only by social distancing, and continuing to patronize restaurants, cafes, and shops. Such behavior should have applied equally to hospitals and doctors' offices. But in fact, the Swedes were also nervous about hospitals. Those arriving with heart attacks were down 25% to 50%.[24] And newly diagnosed cancer cases dropped by a third as patients stayed away.[25]

Other than in acute emergencies, whether to seek medical aid remained our decision. Other choices, too, were entrusted to individual citizens. But some of us had more options than others. No need to dwell on the obvious. Social distancing involves space, and space is expensive. Some peasants in remote villages might be spared the fate of their cousins, cheek-by-jowl in the mega-slums of the developing world, but on the whole, the well-off had more space. For some, social distancing was easy – even painless – while others suffered.

The lucky did not have to weigh choices at all. The better-off took the exit option that was open to them. As cities turned into mass quarantine camps, the weekend-house classes decamped for the countryside. Paris's better neighborhoods emptied in advance of travel restrictions.[26] With occupation rates decreasing by 40%, Manhattan's upper east and west sides were deserted, the Hamptons were now crowded.[27] Florida, New Jersey, and California were favorite destinations for New York's elite headed further afield.[28] Wealthy Londoners not already in possession of a country house rented.[29] Behind them, the well-heeled left empty, spacious apartments and townhouses while a few blocks away, those who remained were shoe-horned into tiny metropolitan flats. In contrast, the Norwegians prohibited city dwellers from visiting their country homes, with ten-day jail sentences or fines as punishment.[30]

The affluent turned lockdown into an unexpected and often welcome break from it all. Those who could work from home, and be paid for it, had little reason to complain. The time once spent commuting and meeting, but now theirs, added to lockdown's advantages. The one wrinkle was caring for children during office hours, a potential productivity-killer.[31] The best-equipped looped nannies into the family bubble. In most other cases, even when both partners were telecommuting, mothers often faced the unforgiving economic imperative of earning less than husbands, therefore being the ones whose careers took a hit.[32]

Exuberant toddlers bursting into home offices during Zoom meetings became a cultural meme. With restaurants shut and take-out distant or suspect, the domestic arts enjoyed a renaissance. Runs on flour and yeast emptied grocery shelves. Sourdough grew fashionable, and a tsunami of carbohydrates washed over the baking classes.[33] Netflix became an addiction, and everyone, an amateur film critic.

HOW INDIVIDUAL CHOICES WERE MADE: THE CLASS DIVIDE

Such were the decisions that the well-off could take on their own. Other choices were made for us. What priorities were granted privacy and civil rights? Each of us daily confronts such issues. But in the aggregate, decisions regarding whether to emphasize or discount rights during pandemics could not be individual ones, any more than vaccination's herd immunity could be each person's choice. The Asian nations made no bones about tracing and tracking the potentially infected, marshaling inspections, investigations, and surveillance, including of phones.

The more information entrusted to the authorities, the more effective they could be. From the vantage of political ideology, little distinguished those who refused to wear masks as a violation of their right to disseminate viruses with every breath from those who denied the government knowledge of their phones' whereabouts. In both, individuals privileged themselves over others.

Many authorities had difficulty overriding such gut reactions. Some nations were more willing to compel. South Koreans allowed the state to use an unprecedented compilation of data sources to track citizens' movements.[34] And some authorities more readily imposed the strictures necessary to bring about compliance – like Taiwan's five-figure fines.

Epidemics lay bare society's scaffolding. Political instincts are put to the test, administrative capacities tried. But most starkly, inequalities are revealed and aggravated. During the cholera epidemics of the 1830s, it was a commonplace that quarantine was the tactic favored by the well-off, who were rarely removed from their homes, could isolate in comfort, and had the resources to ride out the storm. The poor, in contrast, worked daily for their bread. If they had to choose between an epidemic with trade flowing freely, on the one hand, or a trade embargo that also squelched the disease, one observer bet that the poor would prefer to brave illness rather than weather an economic shutdown.[35]

Harsh quarantinist measures imposed mainly on the poor provoked protests and riots across eastern and central Europe in the early nineteenth century. In Königsberg, home of Immanuel Kant, the poor refused to believe that the cholera was contagious. Preventive measures, they were convinced, were a means of harassing them. Cordoning off the city meant higher prices, and quarantining the infected left them unemployed, destitute, and hungry.[36] The same arguments did duty, almost verbatim, this time around too. Lockdown affected citizens differently, depending on social class.

During the coronavirus pandemic, a fundamental class divide opened up between the work-at-homers and those whose physical presence was required. A joke cut to the bone: "Our cleaning lady just called and told us she will be working from home and will send us instructions on what to do." During the earlier cholera epidemics, the need to differentiate among isolated workers had been clear. Those whose labor was crucial could be forced to leave quarantine, disinfected upon exiting. And some socially elevated professionals were allowed to violate quarantine, contacting the ill to fulfill their duties: doctors, priests, sanitary inspectors, and lawyers.[37]

So too now. Some high-earners could not avoid the front lines, above all the physicians staffing the emergency rooms and hospital wards. Some white-collar employees were at risk, too, like the Swedish translators and interpreters who worked with hard-hit immigrant groups and were thrice as likely as average to fall ill.[38] And some professions were by nature especially exposed to a virus expelled orally – dentists, of course, and speech therapists.[39]

How many could or did work from home was not entirely clear. Studies of the US labor force suggested that somewhere between a quarter and a third of all professions could be accomplished remotely.[40] Others reported that, in fact, a third of American employees shifted to at-home work during the pandemic, joining the 15% already there, for a total of half the workforce. Work-at-homers varied by place and group, including especially the young in labor markets with many white-collar and professional occupations (the US Northeast was highest, the South lowest).[41]

In the UK, at-home workers doubled during the first months of 2020, from a quarter to a bit shy of half the labor force.[42] About a third began working from home in Europe, ranging from 60% in Finland to a quarter in Greece.[43] In Japan, hidebound office routines – faxes, seals, and in-person meetings – hampered remote working.[44] The IMF estimated that 15% of the workforce in developed nations could not work from home and risked being laid off. Not surprisingly, they were mostly young, male, unskilled, undereducated, and low-paid.[45]

Many still had to show up: low-paid employees in retail and the online warehouses, the cleaners who allowed others to remain healthy. To these came the undocumented aliens in the fields, who were now at least recognized as crucial. Further up the social scale were nurses, police, mass transit, delivery personnel, and others whose labor allowed the at-homers to isolate. Those not active in crucial sectors were often surprised by just how many worked to permit them their efforts at creating surplus-value. Many a humanities BA had cause to reflect on the complexity and fragility of modern society's supply chains. Philosophers and litterateurs became aware "not only of the existence, but also the eminent dignity" of the "invisible people" who made their lives possible.[46]

Those whose jobs required their presence had no choice. Not surprisingly, they were most exposed to infection and death. In the UK, men in the caring, leisure, and other service occupations were well over twice as likely to die of coronavirus as those in professional and technical operations.[47] In Sweden, taxi drivers were almost five times more likely to fall ill than other professions, followed by pizza makers and bus drivers.[48] Texas construction workers had quintuple the hospitalization risk.[49] In the UK, drivers of taxis, trucks, and buses, and nursing assistants were two and a half times more likely to die in early 2020 than in previous years.[50] Security guards had the highest virus-related death rate.[51] Slaughterhouses, where workers crowded together, shouting to be heard over the noise, and the cold prolonged the virus's lifespan, were deathtraps for their employees – often immigrants, paid little and treated worse.[52]

Children of the away-workers whose schools closed were less supervised than their better-heeled peers. State schools implemented online instruction less than the private ones. In the UK, locked-down children did an average of only two and a half hours of schoolwork daily. One-fifth did none at all.[53] Only about a third handed in their last remote assignments before the summer vacation.[54] British children from well-off families had better experiences with online learning, spending 30% more time on educational activities than the poor.[55] As things opened up, private schools in the US and UK were more likely to receive pupils than state schools.[56] Nor did every child have a laptop and broadband. Almost half of Chileans had no internet at home.[57] In New York City, one-third of households were without.[58]

Nationally in the US, the figures were better, with 15% of households with school-age children bereft of wired broadband.[59] With public libraries closed, they no longer offered a refuge. Even internet cafes were shut.

The deconfinement, starting in May, reinforced the demarcation between at-homers and on-the-jobbers. Not just crucial workers were now expected to muster up. As the hospitality industry slowly came back to life, as offices, workshops, and factories reopened, more people were expelled back into a new working landscape of facemasks, plexiglass partitions, and social distancing.[60] Those who could postpone that reckoning with reality did. As seen, the teaching profession dug in its heels against returning to classrooms, even though, to judge from the Swedish figures, where primary schools had remained open, teachers were less likely than average to be infected.[61]

But exposure on the job was just one element explaining whom the pandemic hit hardest in the developed world. Women staffed many frontline jobs but were not the most at risk. In Italy, two-thirds of health workers, 80% of supermarket cashiers, 90% of home care workers, and over 80% of teachers were female.[62] Not just crucial workers, but also the poor more generally and ethnic minorities were disproportionately victims.[63] In Mumbai, slum dwellers were thrice as likely to be infected as residents of nicer neighborhoods.[64] In the US, Blacks and Latinx were three times as prone to infection as whites and twice as likely to die.[65] South Asians in the UK suffered 20% more mortality than whites, one-fifth of that excess due to diabetes.[66] The outcomes for other ethnic minorities were more dire, similar to the American. Black Caribbeans suffered hospital death rates thrice that of whites, Black Africans almost four times, Pakistanis close to three, and Bangladeshis twice.[67] In Sweden, Somalis were six-fold overrepresented among cases and in Norway ten times.[68]

Precarious jobs explain only some of their excess affliction. The poor and minorities were also more reliant on public transport with its attendant risks.[69] Their access to health care was iffy, their living conditions were dense and substandard, and they often lived far from amenities and shops. Multigenerational families crowded into small apartments were typical. It does not surprise that this was true in the US and the UK, with their wide inequality spans, looser social nets – NHS excepted – and multiracial demographics. But similar trends held elsewhere too. In Stockholm, Covid-19 cases were far more prevalent in poor and immigrant areas than in posh ones.[70] In Oslo, where the epidemic had first struck tony neighborhoods as the skiing classes returned from their Alpine vacations in February, it quickly refocused on poor and immigrant areas.[71]

Comorbidities were also a factor. African-Americans suffered more than their share of obesity, heart disease, hypertension, and diabetes.[72] Adjusting for age, the health of immigrants to Sweden gradually worsened the longer they spent in their new home. Rates of diabetes, obesity, and high blood pressure increased compared with new arrivals, even as their dental health improved.[73] In Denmark, refugees assigned to live in disadvantaged neighborhoods disproportionately developed cardiovascular problems.[74] Studies in the UK, however, suggested that despite minorities' higher mortality rates, comorbidities – other than diabetes – may not have played a significant role.[75] Others argued that metabolic syndrome, with diabetes as one aspect, likely worsened outcomes.[76] That comorbidities may have played little role was worrisome since it left open the question, why the all-too-real mortality disparities that minorities suffered?

Access to health care was worse for minorities. That was obvious in the US. But even in Europe, despite national health insurance, immigrants and minorities struggled with less and worse care than natives.[77] Minorities in the US were often mistrustful of the medical establishment, one outcome of the Tuskegee experiments we have noted. Antivaccinationism found a hearing among some minorities, especially Blacks, but also orthodox Jews.[78] Even though they depended more on their work than others, the poor and minorities also worried more about the risks of returning their children to school.[79] Black school staff in the UK, in particular, resisted reopening classrooms.[80]

The pandemic's social inequity was exposed most harshly where the state did least. Public health is like the police. The worst-off are often poorly treated by them, but they are also the ones who need them most, with the fewest other means of protection.[81] Public health is a public good. Either all have it or none do. If the state does not intervene and vigorously enforce measures, society fragments into its constituent elements. We have seen this pitiless logic in care homes. The most vulnerable, who were supposed to have been cocooned, were not spared even as much as the average. The elderly, necessarily reliant on others' help, died as caretakers were neither tested nor equipped with protective kit. As we have seen in Hong Kong, only where infections had been universally driven down for everyone did the elderly not suffer worse than others.

But the logic of the trade-off between private security and public risk was broader. The best-off were the ones who could most absent themselves from society, who continued their lives largely uninterrupted, distancing without sacrifice and sheltering far from the pandemic's fury. The only way of countering disparities between them and the hard-hit was to generalize protection, demanding a communal effort and reaping a collective benefit.

The more sacrifices were made universal, the fewer they excluded, the more they protected. As vaccines are rolled out, herd immunity will require participation by the majority. That can, in theory, be achieved voluntarily. If not, compulsion will be unavoidable. Those nations that mandated masks eliminated the individual quandary of whether to make a statement by wearing one or not.[82] Once they were required, the psychological hurdle of each individual deciding whether to don them vanished. What had been a personal choice – dictated by risk tolerance, ideology, or aesthetics – now became a citizen's duty.

Pandemics revealed that there are no purely individual means of protecting ourselves. Ultimately, John Snow's claim was misleading, that his discovery of how cholera spread through drinking water meant that everyone could now shield themselves individually, becoming their own quarantine officer. Short of level-A hazmat suits, few purely personal precautions could be taken against contagious disease. The condom came close to being the best example and even that was iffy. Yes, men could don one for each sex act and, yes, their partners could spurn any suitor who refused one. Even so, they were not foolproof – neither against malfunction nor against transmission-despite-latex. The chances of them being effective improved, the smaller the likelihood of our partners' infection. Individual precautions worked best – sometimes only – in the context of collective measures.

The same held for other preventive techniques. Taken together, distancing, handwashing, and masks promised to hamper circulation of the coronavirus.[83] Of these, only handwashing was entirely individual. Each of us could wash our hands, thoroughly or not, and the protection we gained depended on our acts. Even so, the more others washed theirs too, the less the virus was likely to appear on ours. Mask-wearing was even more embedded in a broader field of prevention. Unlike hazmat suits, masks were intended to protect others more than the wearer. That remained true even though some evidence emerged during the late summer that masks also protected their wearer, lowering the viral load they were exposed to and possibly moderating their symptoms if infected.[84] Their usefulness therefore depended on everyone donning one. Were we the only ones wearing them, they were pointless.

Distancing was even more evidently a collective enterprise. Yes, individuals could self-isolate at home. So long as they stayed there, they were safe. But they still relied on the machinery of modern society, provisioning their needs while in purdah. And distancing in public was a *pas des plusieurs*, each dancer dependent on all others. Each of us could keep our distance, but over others, we had little control. Short of throwing tantrums or relying on officially enforced mandates, we could not prevent people from squeezing into elevators or crowding up behind us in line at the check-out register.

Even vaccination was ultimately a group effort. A perfect vaccine would, in theory, be like a hazmat suit, protecting even amid contagion. But no vaccine promised absolute safety, any more than hazmat suits were guaranteed not to spring leaks. Herd immunity was crucial not only for those who could not vaccinate but also for the rest of us, who were safer, the fewer our chances of actually encountering a microbe. Public health rested on collective efforts. Some could weather epidemics better than others in well-upholstered cocoons. But ultimately, no one was wholly spared.

WHEN OTHERS CHOOSE FOR US: TRIAGE

At the extreme, we have no volition and others choose for us when we arrive desperately sick in emergency rooms, one of many on gurneys in need of the same scarce resources: expertise, attention, treatment. So far, most nations with sophisticated medical infrastructure have avoided their hospitals being wholly overrun with desperately sick patients. Wuhan and Lombardy saw the worst scenes of hospitals on the brink. New York City and cities in Florida and Texas came close. The situation in South America and South Africa has been more dire. But all nations drew up plans for allocating resources and triaging patients even though they turned out to be unnecessary. How did one decide which patients received what treatment? When a vaccine emerges, we will grapple with similar dilemmas of allocation.

With too few intensive care beds and ventilators, who got them? Tragically, this question moved from theoretical speculations among ethicists to wrenching choices forced on doctors in the north Italian hospitals that were first deluged with patients gasping for air. As with antibiotics, in this respect, too, modern medicine has become a victim of its own success. Ethical issues have mushroomed as expensive technologies have allowed physicians to perform life-sustaining miracles for patients who earlier would have died. The law of diminishing returns has been the common thread among one array of dilemmas. Though medicine can keep us alive in a technical sense, are the results worth it?

Doctors, able and wanting to prolong life, have increasingly faced patients and their families, unpersuaded that a few more weeks or months of life hooked into machines made sense. Do Not Resuscitate (DNR) orders, intended to spare patients heroic but futile attempts to keep them alive, have pushed back against physicians' pretensions to omnicompetence. With end-of-life interventions, more may be less.[85] Such considerations may now be affecting practice in intensive care units. Life-prolonging interventions have declined in European hospitals over the past two decades.[86] Half a century ago, it was considered an act of killing to withdraw a ventilator. Today, taking patients off respiration is the most common proximate cause of death for intensive care patients in the US, and withdrawal of support at the request of patients or surrogates is considered an ethical and legal obligation.[87]

More pertinent to the pandemic, however, have been the ethical issues of triage, whom to save at whose expense. Physicians in developed nations allocate scarce resources only rarely. They face the logic of triage infrequently, with organ transplants, or in allocating dialysis machines. The British National Institute for Health and Care Excellence (NICE) pronounces on the cost-effectiveness of medicines and treatments, thus rationing NHS patients' care. But otherwise, first-world physicians practice triage only exceptionally, during disasters.

Trolleyology is a means for ethicists to probe our moral intuitions, seeking to determine how utilitarian a calculus we are willing to employ. Participants are asked to compare situations where one person is killed by throwing a switch to divert a runaway trolley, saving several. Typically, respondents are willing to throw the switch but refuse a more active role in sacrificing innocents, even to save others. A basic utilitarianism recognizes that we should save lives, even at a cost to others. Yet, offering up innocents remains morally distasteful, even if the outcome spares more lives. Consulting our ethical instincts, we turn out to be at best contingent utilitarians.

Actual-world versions of such trade-offs have forced decision-makers to make life-and-death choices. Dengue fever can be vaccinated against, sparing thousands. But for children who have not yet encountered the disease, the vaccine can also cause severe illness. When 800,000 were immunized in the Philippines in 2016, enough children sickened that a strong public backlash against this utilitarian good forced discontinuation of the program.[88] Similar dilemmas will have to be negotiated if self-driving cars become commonplace. Whom will the algorithm sacrifice – passenger or pedestrian? Whatever the morality, will anyone buy or use a vehicle known to be programmed to commit suicide?[89]

The need to allocate resources during the Covid-19 pandemic was forced on doctors in the most overrun hospitals. The immediate issues were intensive care beds and ventilators. Where the epidemic swamped hospitals, overburdened and exhausted physicians had to choose whom to treat and ventilate. To help them grapple with on-the-spot decisions, professional associations formulated guidelines that allow insight into the thinking of those who decide over us when we are patients. Whom to ventilate, whom to pass over, and – most wrenching – whom to take off the machines – these were the immediate decisions demanded. Other hospital systems, spared for the moment, prepared for such eventualities by seeking to make the trade-offs explicit.

Nations took more or less utilitarian approaches – some unabashed, some hesitant. Ethically speaking, quite different priorities could be equally justified. The most lives could be saved or perhaps the most years of life. The youngest could be given priority – or the sickest and otherwise most likely to die. Special attention could be given to those with the highest instrumental value – medical care personnel able to save others or who had done so in the past. Resources could also be distributed on a first-come, first-served basis or randomly – either as a general principle or to select among cases with equal utilitarian value.[90]

The WHO's ethical guidelines for allocating resources during an influenza pandemic acknowledged differences of opinion. Some voices supported a "fair innings" approach that would prioritize the young with a moral claim to an average lifespan. While accepting the possibility that discrimination might occur by age, the WHO was careful to rule out a role for other criteria – gender, ethnicity, religion, or class.[91] A utilitarian allocation of resources also threatened to exacerbate already-existing inequalities. Taking comorbidities into account in deciding whom to treat might penalize social groups that already had the highest risk profiles and least access to health care.[92]

The Swedes were unhesitantly utilitarian. Human rights forbade rationing by social position or importance, or merely by chronological age. Intensive care should therefore be prioritized for those with the lowest biological age – chronological age discounted for underlying medical conditions. Those with a chance of surviving at least another year took precedence. Patients whose condition worsened could be removed from intensive care.[93]

The Karolinska hospital in Stockholm outlined an explicit hierarchy of triage. Patients with a biological age of eighty or over, seventy and above with failure of two organs, or older than sixty with three organ failures: none were to be admitted to intensive care.[94] Patients who, in normal circumstances, would have received intensive care, like sixty- and seventy-year-olds with mild symptoms, no longer did. Patients with a biological age of seventy or older with more than one underlying condition were not admitted. This included dialysis patients in their forties or fifties, otherwise active and gainfully employed, who were on the kidney transplant waiting lists.

The median age for intensive care patients, sixty-four before the pandemic, now dropped to fifty-eight.[95] Older Swedish patients with Covid-19 were more likely to die than be admitted to intensive care. In other words, they were triaged and kept out.[96] Ailing elderly patients who typically would have been treated were now assumed to be coronavirus victims and deprioritized. Physicians were free to deny care to the fragile and demented.[97] One feverish ninety-year-old was shunted aside until his wife insisted on a urine test, which revealed an infection, quickly cured with antibiotics. Usually, every second intensive care patient in Stockholm was elderly. But on April 21, coronavirus patients over seventy had declined to 11%.[98]

Some Swedish ethicists pushed for an even more unabashed utilitarianism. One argued for using chronological, not just biological, age as a criterion to distribute resources, prioritizing the young.[99] This frank utilitarianism raised others' hackles. Such an approach would violate the understanding that care was to be distributed equally, not conditional on functional capacity. Dismissing any attempt to consider life quality meant that, all else being equal, even though chronological age was not to be determinative, the young would automatically take precedence over the old.[100]

The UK took a similarly utilitarian approach. The British Medical Association issued guidelines outlining how, given more suitable claimants for resources, some patients might have to be denied care and others, already receiving it, have it withdrawn. Priority went to those most likely to survive. Age alone, however, would not automatically put a patient last in line. Comorbidities too needed to be factored in. Nonetheless, the elderly might well suffer once decisions also considered whether they had the "capacity to benefit quickly." Such indirect age discrimination was lawful under the NHS's mandate to use limited resources to their best effect.[101]

Other nations also applied similar principles. The Austrians were convinced utilitarians.[102] The Swiss forbade taking age directly into account, but were unfussed by considering it indirectly. Calculating whether patients were likely to profit from intensive care, the elderly's comorbidities meant that they would often be deemed unsuited. "In connection with COVID-19, age is a risk factor for mortality and must therefore be taken into account."[103]

New York State's guidelines for respirator allocation were similar. Even advanced age should not disqualify as such, since that was discriminatory. But age factored in indirectly with the increasing comorbidities suffered by the elderly.[104] The Belgians agreed that resources should be trained where most useful, suggesting advance determination of which care home residents were too frail to hospitalize.[105] Brussels hospitals turned away the corona sick from care homes even when the intensive care wards were only half full.[106]

The Belgians and Swiss also agreed that coronavirus patients should not be given extracorporeal membrane oxygenation (ECMO), a lung and heart bypass for patients not responding to mechanical ventilation. Nor should CPR be attempted on such patients out-of-hospital, given the danger to the resuscitator and the unlikelihood of a good outcome. WHO guidelines recommended using ECMO for patients with acute respiratory distress syndrome.[107] Other nations were agnostic about ECMO, treating it as a possible tool while recognizing its cost and complication.[108] The US National Institutes of Health considered the data insufficient to recommend for or against its routine use.[109] The NHS considered its possible use for coronavirus patients, but with clear clinical criteria, including scoring below a certain frailty level.[110]

Yet, not every nation was wholly unperturbed by utilitarianism. The Italians were deeply ambivalent. In the West, they were the first to face ethical decisions in their most unavoidable form. In mid-March, ten patients vied for each intensive care bed in Lombardy. In some hospitals, the age limit for automatic deconsideration for ventilation was lowered from eighty to seventy-five.[111] In such dire circumstances, a group of physicians sought to provide guidelines for allocating shortages. Their principles were utilitarian.

First come, first served meant rationing by random principles – where the epidemic struck earliest or who lived nearest the hospital – and unwanted outcomes as people certain to die occupied beds better given to others. Instead, these doctors explicitly advocated reserving intensive care for those with the best chances. Distributive justice and efficient outcomes were to be considered – how many years of life were likely to be saved – and not merely the patient's need or clinical condition. Nor did they shy back from imposing a simple age limit for admission to intensive care, the chronological criterion rejected both by the Swedes and by the British. Access to intensive care also had to be revocable. Non-responsive patients could have their beds given to someone else.[112]

The publication was welcomed for seeking to spare frontline physicians wrenching decisions without guidance.[113] But it also sparked intense debate in Italy, with many doctors rejecting what they regarded as its exaggerated utilitarianism. Utilitarian principles already applied to scarce resources like organ transplants, but they contradicted the underlying egalitarian ethos of Italy's health system.[114] In April, the National Bioethics Committee, the Italian government's ethical advisory board, argued that clinical conditions were the only legitimate triage criteria. Other aspects of a patient's identity could not be considered – gender, ethnicity, and class, of course, but also age.[115]

The French, too, were not die-hard utilitarians. They were vague on the precise trade-offs. But they decided that priority could not be given to those whose lives promised most utility.[116] And yet, they were also willing to admit that, with limited resources, egalitarianism might not work. It could make more sense to aim to preserve as many lives as possible – in other words, a utilitarian calculus.[117]

The elderly often felt singled out by utilitarian attempts to target resources at those who could pay back society's investment with the most QUALYs – med-speak for healthy years of life. The communitarian philosopher Amitai Etzioni bravely argued that he, though ninety-one, should be ventilated preferentially to his sixty-two-year-old colleague institutionalized with Alzheimers.[118] Beyond the pandemic's immediate victims, those most directly harmed were the patients who, when it hit, were in the midst of treatments for other illnesses that now were interrupted, delayed, or ended as resources went elsewhere. The Belgians insisted that the same triage principles applied to Covid-19 patients should hold for victims of other ailments during times of shortages, as did the Italian guidelines mentioned above.[119] In contrast, the Swiss sought to ensure that the criteria for hospitalizing non-coronavirus patients remained as always.[120]

Insofar as particular social groups, usually the poor and ethnic minorities, were disproportionately afflicted with comorbidities, did triage affect them especially? Such concerns were raised in Massachusetts. The governor issued utilitarian directives. Resources should go to where they would have most effect, maximizing life-years saved.[121] In response, an open letter from 500 health care professionals argued that comorbidities hit ethnic minorities most, who would therefore score worse on evaluations deciding whom to prioritize.[122]

The disabled, too, feared being disadvantaged. In Washington state, their advocates filed suit to ensure they would be treated like others. The state's recommendation that a patient's "baseline functional status" be considered when distributing medical care worried them. Would cystic fibrosis victims, for example, meet such criteria?[123] Alabama's emergency operations plan suggested that the severely mentally disabled might not qualify for ventilator support.[124] To soothe worries, the US Department of Health issued a reminder that decisions to treat should not consider any qualities of a potential patient other than the purely medical. The equal dignity of each was to be protected against "ruthless utilitarianism."[125]

In Britain, NICE guidelines (mandatory for NHS clinicians) specified triage for the frail. Physicians were to "sensitively discuss" with those scoring as very frail whether they would like DNR instructions and whether they understood the risks of intensive interventions.[126] Given the imprecision of the frailty concept, the disabled objected. Those entirely dependent on others for personal care – regardless of why – counted as severely frail. The autistic and other disabled – whatever their age or predicted lifespans – would likely score in that category, thus being disqualified for certain medical treatments. After legal objections, NICE amended its recommendations to exclude the young and those with long-term stable disabilities, learning issues, autism, or cerebral palsy.[127]

Only the Germans struck out on their own, resisting utilitarianism more than elsewhere. The German Ethics Council, the government's advisory board, inscribed on its banner a Kantian absolute value of the individual and shied away from utilitarianism. Physicians facing shortages would doubtless have to decide whom to prioritize, it admitted. But the state could not officially give guidance on which lives were most worth saving. The Basic Law ruled out any form of discrimination. Every life enjoyed the same protection. The state could not be party to any differentiation, classifying lives whether by age, social role, value, or predicted duration. "The state must not rate human life, and consequently must not prescribe which lives are to be saved first in situations of conflict."[128]

Apportioning limited resources on a first-come, first-served basis led to wrenching outcomes as needy patients were left untreated. Decisions among lives were even more morally fraught. If all ventilators were occupied, some by patients with little chance of survival, and a new patient with urgent needs and better prospects appeared, could one legitimately reassign the machine? The German state understood that such decisions would be required and taken. But it insisted that it was not "objectively legal" to withdraw care from one patient who needed it to save another instead. To remove medical care from a patient who needed it, a German ethicist argued, was legally speaking a killing.[129]

Whatever the official theory, however, German physicians in the trenches took an approach more like their colleagues elsewhere. In emergencies, a group of professional associations argued, resources should not be used where the prognosis was hopeless. The patient's chronological age or other social characteristics could not be taken into account. For constitutional reasons, they noted, lives could not be weighed against each other. And in Germany, breaking off intensive care might run up against legal hindrances. But otherwise, they recommended taking comorbidities into account, much like their colleagues in other nations.[130]

Why the Germans followed their own Sonderweg is understandable. The Nazi euthanasia program, starting in 1939, had selected out the sick, frail, and mentally disturbed for killing, considering them lives unworthy of life. To avoid any hint of a similar treating of some humans as more valuable than others, the Germans now sought to bypass such dilemmas altogether.

Producing away shortages is the best way to avoid triage. The Germans laid in the capacity required to sidestep ethical quagmires. They already had more intensive care beds per capita than any nation other than Turkey.[131] Useful data on ventilators is harder to come by, but with somewhere between 25,000 and 40,000 machines, the Germans seem to have been better provisioned than almost anyone else.[132] Most importantly, because they implemented an effective strategy to suppress coronavirus infections, these ample equipment levels were never tested. Here technology trumped triage.

SAFE OR SOLVENT? THE PRICE OF SECURITY

Faced with cholera in the 1830s, European governments had debated whether the cost of quarantine exceeded that of medical care for the ill, foregone production, maintenance for survivors of the dead, and other costs of not taking precautions.[133] In the Covid-19 pandemic, the trade-off between earnings and security reappeared. At the most general level, the choice was supposedly between stopping the spread and shutting down the economy. Time and again, the dichotomy was posed between jobs and disease, the slippery exchange between prosperity and security.

Bolsonaro and Trump were the two leaders most willing publicly to accept the heightened mortality that came with letting down their nations' guards. Trump found himself unexpectedly supported by otherwise unimpeachably left-of-center university professors applying a utilitarian logic to the lockdown's economic devastation.[134] The Swedes made a similar calculation, but more covertly. The cure, they all agreed, could not be worse than the sickness.[135]

As the British government debated whether to mitigate or wholly suppress the pandemic in early March 2020, economic considerations were weighty. Why shut down the economy if it merely postponed illness to a second wave?[136] When it discussed how early to open up again, such considerations reemerged. Was it still risky to reopen in June, or was restarting the economy now imperative? As England took its first steps, Wales and Scotland hesitated, postponing similar measures by weeks. "What the government will not say," Roula Kalaf, editor of the *Financial Times*, tweeted on May 31, "we're not at the stage where we should ease the lockdown but we're doing it anyway to save the economy."[137]

Similar debates fueled discussions in the US, where the South and West reopened before having really shut down at all or managing to get a grip on the pandemic. In July, some states then had to clamp down once more. They suffered the humiliation of having jumped the gun, as well as skyrocketing caseloads, rising mortality, and the economic costs of still further restrictions. Better, it seemed, to have gotten it right the first time around.

Middle-income nations faced this choice between security and prosperity more starkly than the better-off. Needing to restore livelihoods and exports, Brazil, India, Indonesia, Russia, and Mexico were among the first to reopen in mid- to late May, even though infections were still increasing.[138] South Africa at first introduced strict shutdowns and extensive testing. But much had to be abandoned, given the unforgiving economic consequences – GDP projected to fall more than in a century.[139] Malawi had shut down already in March, but small traders protested, refusing to comply.[140] The country was then forced to open up again temporarily in April after the Malawi Human Rights Defenders Coalition successfully petitioned the high court, arguing that the government had insufficiently considered the economic effects of lockdown on the poorest.[141] When Modi loosened up his massive shutdown in India, it was welcomed not only by business interests but by social activists too.[142]

By contrast, the Chinese pointedly emphasized the economic hardships they had assumed to beat back the epidemic. Lives, they insisted, had been more important than growth.[143] An editorial in *The Lancet* in April recognized the enormous social and economic costs shouldered by China for its success.[144] But the contrasts were not as stark as these snapshots suggest. Most countries, not just China, decided in favor of safety and lives, not the economy.[145]

Of course, some companies profited from providing what was required in lockdown – online commerce, protective gear, internet meeting software. Food stores boomed, restaurants went bust; air transport thrived, airlines tanked; theaters were boarded up, Netflix sizzled; retail rebounded, services faltered. But on the whole, economic interests were not determinant. No nation kept the economy chugging as usual. Nor could they have. The economic activity sought by employers, workers, and consumers was contradicted by the security demanded by voters, parents, and potential victims.

Very few people clamored to be allowed to return to work amid a pandemic. In one survey, almost three-quarters of the British wanted the government to prevent disease spread even at the cost of recession, depression, and job loss; 60% of Japanese and Americans agreed. Other nations were less sure, with barely half of Germans and Swedes concurring.[146] When asked what effect government precautions were having, majorities in more than half of EU nations agreed that the health benefits outweighed the economic damage. Dissent came mainly in eastern Europe, though joined by Dutch, Italians, and Belgians.[147]

Though seemingly intuitive, the dichotomy between security and solvency was misleading. The costs of targeted quarantine were great enough and those of full-scale lockdown painfully higher. The benefits of protective strategies were harder to spot, but very real. One study estimated that the interventions undertaken in six nations with a combined population of almost two billion had averted half a billion infections.[148] Across eleven European countries, some three million deaths had been avoided.[149] In hotspots like Wuhan, Italy, France, and New York City, lockdowns had reduced infection rates by between half and three-quarters.[150] The cardinal rule in all such evaluations of the relative costs of locking down was that the comparison could not be with a normally functioning economy, but with the consequences of not shutting down – in other words, with a full-blown pandemic against which nothing had been done.[151]

Unlike other recessions and depressions, this downturn was government-mandated. The economy was shut down, it did not spontaneously collapse. Ultimately, of course, it was the pandemic that closed the economy, not the government. The authorities' precautions may have amplified what would have happened in any case as citizens rushed to protect themselves. Yet, if preventive measures worked, they promised to spare economies even greater shocks. Had the virus been allowed to take its course, the economy would equally have imploded and the devastation would likely have been even worse.

The economic effect of the coronavirus pandemic was, in other words, a real recession, caused by a shock delivered by the world to the system. Unlike recessions caused by bad policy (interest rates set too high) or a crisis in the financial system (credit bubbles), a real economy crisis had the virtue of likely passing along with the external shock. Government policies could exacerbate the real shock or soften it. The issue for the post-coronavirus economy was whether (and, if so, how quickly) demand and activity would pick up again.

Would the shutdown have fundamentally altered the underlying economy? Would the hit to household income dry up consumption? Whatever the damage done economically, the likelihood that things would bounce back to where they had been, much less where they would have been in the absence of a pandemic, was small. The data from previous crises suggested that the road back would be long and steep. Past economic shocks provided little evidence of catch-up growth.[152] Banking crises had taken six to seven years before earlier levels were reattained.[153]

From such debates sprang discussions of what letter the recovery's graph would most resemble, V, U, or L.[154] Most past pandemics had caused a V-shaped shock and recovery – the Spanish flu, 1958 Asian flu, 1968 Hong Kong flu, and SARS. The Spanish flu could reasonably be taken as – one hopes – the outer limit of an epidemic disaster in the modern world. It had killed slightly more than 2% of the global population, the equivalent of 150 million today. Recent pandemics had not caused major long-term economic disruptions. The Spanish flu had been worse, however. That it coincided with the end of World War I made it hard to estimate its discrete impact.

Teasing apart their effects, economists had calculated that the war decreased real per capita GDP by 8.4%, the influenza by 6.2%. The GDP decline attributed to the Spanish flu was thus comparable to the effects of the 2008 Great Recession. But a comparison with 1918 assumed that the coronavirus pandemic would have as significant an impact as the Spanish flu, which seemed unlikely.[155] In Sweden, which had not participated in World War I, the effects had been more clearly discernable, but unexpectedly insignificant in economic terms. Though it had killed 1% of the population, especially the young and economically active, it had no upward effect on wages, though oddly – given a presumed shortage of labor – an increase of poorhouse inhabitants.[156]

Other studies of the Spanish flu in the US suggested that, because it killed workers in their prime, both wages and per capita growth rates were higher after the pandemic than they would have been otherwise.[157] Those American cities that imposed mitigation measures enjoyed the best economic performance in the long run. They lessened the pandemic's direct effect by flattening the mortality curve, thus saving thousands of lives. Secondarily, of course, they also dampened economic activity by suppressing interactions and mobility. But did that go beyond what would have occurred anyway, as the pandemic scared people into hiding? In 1918, cities that imposed drastic measures and those with less strict ones suffered comparable economic disruptions. The firmer shutdowns do not seem to have made a bad situation worse. The same held in the medium term. If anything, strict-measure cities fared better in the years after 1918 than those that had clamped down less on the epidemic.[158]

The expected trade-off between security and prosperity did not seem to hold in 2020 either. The current pandemic's main issue was whether government lockdowns, which were much stricter than anything imposed in 1918, would exacerbate the damage wrought in any case by the epidemic.[159] The pandemic itself, rather than the measures marshaled against it, was the primary cause of decline. Even greater mass death, as would have happened without interventions, was politically intolerable. And in any case, citizens would and did take their own steps to protect themselves, shutting down society voluntarily and not reemerging until they were convinced it was safe.

Just as the Swedes voluntarily restricted their mobility, so Americans in states without a lockdown during the spring also stayed at home more than usual.[160] And where they were ordered into their homes, they had already retreated ahead of the mandate.[161] But such effects could be amplified or diminished by the government's response. The evidence from 1918 suggested that quick and drastic interventions had not added to existing problems and may even have had positive economic outcomes in the medium term.

The current data, however imperfect, suggested a similar effect now too. Those nations in Europe that had imposed lockdown measures earliest had been able to be least drastic and suffered less of a drop in economic activity, at least as measured by electricity consumption and mobility.[162] Government precautions had caused only slightly more than 10% of the economic slowdown that would have happened anyway, was the conclusion of one US study.[163]

Only by lessening the threat of infection could the economy be started or continued. A suppression strategy, hammering down economic activity immediately, held out the promise of restarting it that much sooner, once the epidemic had been tamed. That effect held doubly if the time gained was used to implement a test and trace system to allow future surgical interventions rather than a reimposed lockdown. "Anything that slows the rate of the virus is the best thing you can do for the economy, even if by conventional measures it's bad for the economy," said Austan Goolsbee, a University of Chicago economist.[164] A leader at the unimpeachably free-market Cato Institute chimed in: government-mandated lockdown itself added only marginally to the economic effects of the voluntary distancing people were undertaking anyway. The problem was the virus, not lockdown.[165]

Business leaders at the coalface mostly agreed. There were exceptions, of course. Tesla, the electric car manufacturer and employer of 10,000 workers in the Bay Area, defied local authorities to remain open during shutdown. Its petition to be counted as essential work was denied, but, sued by the company, the authorities relented.[166] Unlike other Silicon Valley firms, who voiced no objections to lockdown, car manufacturers could not work from home. And local officials were hamstrung between safety and the worry that Elon Musk might make good on his threat to move production out of state.

But most businesses understood that security and profitability were intertwined. In the nineteenth century, some fervent free traders had rejected quarantine as hampering commerce and prosperity. Yet, most recognized it as a necessary cost of doing business in epidemic circumstances.[167] So too with the coronavirus. The only way of restarting the economy was to restart travel, said Tori Barnes, vice president at the US Travel Association. "The only way we're going to do that is through health and safety."[168]

Businesses seeking to reopen were stymied by those who scorned the rules. Blackmarket competitors undermined things for everyone, like the sweatshops of Leicester that had continued running throughout the lockdown and then caused a second wave of infection. Boisterous partygoers spurred renewed lockdowns in the US in July, disappointing businesses' hopes of finally reopening. Unclarity about the rules – on masks, for example – or how to police them meant a few spoiled things for the many. Business leaders in the US pleaded with the White House for consistent, enforceable rules on masks.[169]

The authorities weighed the countervailing interests of prevention and prosperity. Getting the balance right was tricky. Few managed it, and rarely for long. Texas had one of the shortest shutdowns and began opening up again already on May 1. It turned out to be premature. Less than two months later, it had to re-shut when infections surged.[170] There was nothing to argue about: no economic renewal was on the horizon until the pandemic had been beaten. Customers would stay away until they felt secure.

On a micro level, one issue was whether distancing should remain at six feet or could be safely halved. Much rested on it. Restaurants could squeeze in more customers, theaters, more patrons, and schools, more pupils. With one meter rather than two, three times as many pubs in England could hope to be profitable.[171]

One of the world's largest industries, tourism, illustrated the dilemmas. Ten percent of global GDP and jobs were tourism-related, but this varied among nations. The most prized tropical islands – Seychelles, Maldives, Bahamas – derived half their GDP from tourism. But even developed countries relied on it for a fraction of GDP in the low double digits – 11% for the UK, 13% in Italy.[172] To be safe, tourist-dependent nations had to forego a leading source of revenue, but they could never hope to earn again unless they did.

Cuba delayed imposing precautions for fear of endangering its primary source of foreign currency. But eventually, reality bit and it shut down hermetically, becoming a poster boy for dealing with the pandemic.[173] Conversely, having shut down, Greece opened up again prematurely, hungry for the tourist's disposable Euro. It ended up reaping more infection and little profit.[174]

Maine took quite decisive precautions, requiring masks, distancing, and visitors to quarantine for two weeks or test within three days of arrival. It enjoyed one of the lowest infection rates in the nation. It had decimated its early tourist season in anticipation of being able to demonstrate a safety record that would lure late-summer guests. "You can't have economic health without public health," as Janet Mills, its governor, put it.[175] By August, it had been so successful that a local free-market economic institute could insist that the lockdown had overshot its mark and was now imposing more costs than benefits.[176] That was probably an exaggeration. Having been very low during the spring, tourism picked up starting in July, though still down overall compared with the previous year.[177] In contrast, South Carolina's Myrtle Beach opened up for visitors in May, requiring no masks. It paid for letting down its guard by becoming a pandemic hot spot.[178]

Spain's attempt to welcome tourists back failed immediately when drunken, maskless Brits terrified the recently recovered Spaniards with loutish revelry.[179] Mallorca promptly shut its bars again.[180] Sri Lanka, in contrast, ran a tight ship, allowing in only tourists who could show negative test results before departure, with further testing on arrival and the fourth and tenth days of their stay.[181] Others were strategic. New Zealand famously shut down, at one point almost hermetically, but then made an exception to allow James Cameron and crew back in to resume filming another locally based blockbuster.[182] Other nations tailored their appeal to online employees prepared to move, attracted by the idea of working from paradise.[183]

One certain conclusion seems that targeted quarantines, imposing drastic measures where most effective, sparing the rest, did less damage than across-the-board lockdowns that became necessary in those laggard nations unprepared to do early and precise interventions.[184] Those places that got the epidemic under control first could best hope to return to economic normality.[185]

China's economy started growing again in the spring. Up 3.2% from April to June 2020, it was by far the best-performing big economy. By the third quarter, it was almost at its previous year's levels. Much of this relied on government infrastructure spending, and the economy was ill-balanced. Manufacturing increased, but consumer demand remained down, as was spending on restaurants, hotels, and non-essentials.[186] But other nations would have been grateful for such problems. In Taiwan's economy, bolstered by supplying the kit for 5G rollouts, the pandemic's effect was also barely discernable in the economic statistics.[187]

The Swedes hoped that their strategy would at least spare the economy even if the death rates remained startlingly high. Sweden was an exporting nation and did not want to shut down economically.[188] In March, Jacob Wallenberg, scion of the family estimated to control a third of the local economy, warned against the longer-term economic and social effects of a lockdown – unemployment, violence, and social unrest.[189] Swedish CEOs called already in March for lifting restrictions on movement simultaneously across Europe so as not to disrupt trans-continental supply chains.[190]

Any final accounting will have to await longer-term data. Mobility did decline here, but not as much as elsewhere. Tourism and hospitality, those especially hard-hit sectors, were not large fractions of the Swedish economy. More Swedes could and did work from home than in other countries. The banks were in good shape and the government was comparatively debt-free, thus in a position to stimulate the economy.[191] Bars, restaurants, and retail likely did better than their peers in shut-down nations. The service sector tanked less than the industrial, relative to its EU comparators.[192] On the whole, there were reasons to expect the Swedish economy to weather the crisis better than most.

On the other hand, Sweden's economy was open, exporting, and therefore at the mercy of decisions taken elsewhere. Like a Boston team turn (driver in the left lane turns right, forcing everyone else to follow suit), the Swedish economy went with its partners. To continue with the transport similes, as the speed of a convoy is that of the slowest ship, so Sweden's performance depended on what happened elsewhere. In June, experts warned that Sweden would fare worse than its more locked-down neighbors. Its exports were more reliant on economic cycles than Denmark's, primarily pharmaceuticals, windmills, and food. Swedish factories, such as Volvo, shut down in the absence of imported parts. We had no idea it would be so bad, said Volvo's head of communications.[193]

While the lockdown had been milder in Sweden, the high level of infection meant that, when the neighbors began opening up in June, Sweden remained more closed and its travelers were shunned. Foreign investment in a nation seen as less capable of dealing with the epidemic might also dip.[194] If economic protectionism were one of the pandemic's outcomes in the longer term, exporting economies would suffer. The OECD and European Commission projected GDP declines almost the same for hands-off Sweden and locked-down Denmark.[195]

The first real numbers were ambiguous. For the first quarter of 2020, while other nations took severe hits to their GDP, Sweden was one of the few to post at least a minuscule increase – along with Bulgaria, Romania, and Ireland.[196] So, what did that indicate? Germany had locked down despite being even more adept at exporting than Sweden.[197] Its second-quarter GDP decline was harrowing, slightly above 10%.[198] The Swedish figures turned out better, a drop of 8.6%, compared with 9.5% for the US – a difference, but hardly night and day.[199] Those exporting powerhouses whose bidding – cynics accused – Tegnell was doing – Ericsson, Electrolux – beat their quarterly earnings expectations in July, even if that just meant not declining as far as anticipated.[200] SEB reported better than expected second quarter results, which meant operating profits falling 25% from a year earlier. Its rival, Handelsbanken, lost only about 100 million crowns, not the one billion feared.[201] Compared with their German competitors, they were on top.[202] Nor had Sweden, as an international brand, seemingly suffered from its aberrant preventive path.[203]

Unemployment in June was almost 10%, compared with just under 5% in Norway and slightly over 5% in Denmark.[204] Whatever the numbers for 2020 and subsequent years turn out to be, someone will have to do the grisly calculations to figure what Sweden's economic performance should have been to justify the dismaying mortality differences between it and its plausible comparators, Denmark, Norway, and Finland. If that was the bargain, the devil had taken a cut.

THE GRAND SCHEME OF THINGS

No definitive conclusions can be drawn at such close quarters, other than that the pandemic has required innumerable trade-offs, from the national to the personal. Those nations unable to implement early targeted quarantines had little choice but to lock down across the board. The shutdowns were accomplished more or less thoroughly and the reopenings quickly or cautiously. Having shouldered the cost – economic and political – of successfully isolating the disease to Hubei province, the Chinese economy was up and running again by the summer. Having failed to squash the pandemic, America was facing subsequent waves of infection. Tourist destinations spent the summer hammering and dancing.

Each of us weighed similar considerations individually. The rowdy frat boy, partying on the beach without masking or distancing, was an epidemiological narcissist, pursuing immediate pleasures, not the common good. But, consider the school teacher, carefully isolating at home, hesitant to eat out even once allowed, resisting a return to work before the arrival of a vaccine, and indifferent to economic incentives thanks to her security of employment. Though compliant, she was equally anti-social in undermining hopes of returning to normality.

In the short term, many of us cowered in self-isolation, fearful of infection, and willing to pay the cost – which fell much more heavily on some shoulders than others. In the longer term, our sense of whether lockdown was worth it may change. Will the lives spared from the coronavirus outweigh those lost to other causes, and the damage done more generally to society? A full-scale pandemic without any precautions would have been devastating. But precautions would have been taken spontaneously, even without government intervention. Will the mandated lockdowns turn out to have been as bad, better, or even worse?

Among the factors to be weighed in this long-term accounting against the lives that lockdown saved: the excess mortality due to other causes in care homes and the psychological burdens of cutting off contact for the elderly; the deaths from ailments left undiagnosed and untreated; the illnesses and deaths of children who skipped vaccinations; the emotional traumas of confinement; pupils' and students' loss of schooling; unemployment and economic deprivation on a gargantuan scale and its social consequences in suicides and drug overdoses; and higher levels of some types of crimes. Wholly unexpected effects of lockdown will no doubt eventually be revealed. During prohibition, patents dropped by almost a fifth in some previously wet counties, thanks to shutting down contacts and exchanging ideas.[205] What else will fall victim to this pandemic?

It will take a careful economic and moral accounting to sum all the contradictory inputs. Thanks to shutting Wuhan down, declining air pollution may have saved twenty times as many people as had died of coronavirus.[206] But these figures were from early March and dealt with China, where pollution was fearsome and death rates comparatively low. Fewer than the usual 20,000 Indians who die in car crashes every month might perish thanks to lock-down. But more than the usual 30,000 who were lost to tuberculosis might die if not treated.[207] There were fewer traffic accidents, but more speeding tickets.[208] Overall, travel was down in Wuhan, but car trips doubled.[209] Commercial aviation tanked, but private jet flights quickly bottomed out, as the wealthy cocooned.[210]

Localized production in the future might cut transport emissions but decrease manufacturing efficiency. As Mexico banned alcohol sales, drunkenness declined, but more people died of tainted moonshine.[211] Most nebulously, what about the health consequences of economic recession? Would "deaths of despair" outstrip those of coronavirus?[212] Or would this recession, like past ones, reduce mortality (thanks to less driving, fewer accidents, less drinking, more walking), even as it increased suicides and mental health problems?[213]

The question was how to weigh the wealth shrinkage due to lockdown – insofar as that could be separated from the pandemic's effects – compared with what prevention saved. Future poverty meant lives lost and stunted: accidents on roads unrepaired, deaths outside of hospitals unbuilt, hunger thanks to fields never planted, diseases caused by sewage lines still in the planning stage, a world shortchanged by children's educations cut short, a globe possibly plunged into wars and chaos by prosperity derailed. How much suffering would have been inflicted compared with an untamed pandemic?

Conclusion: Public Health and Public Goods

The State in a Post-pandemic World

NOTHING WILL EVER BE THE SAME. WE HAVE SEEN IT all before. Those are the two rocks between which historians pilot their ships. Philosophers, sociologists, and other social scientists often announce their discovery of earth-shattering novelties that will forever change the world and mark the epoch. Historians' instincts are to emphasize the continuities, smoothing over the fissures. Yet, sometimes fundamental changes do occasion tectonic shifts. Some are noisy and evident, like revolutions, wars, and, yes, pandemics. Others seep in, imperceptibly altering the landscape until some alert observer retrospectively notices the shift of the river's bed – the demographic transition, industrialization, globalization.

Some observers have noted how little effect the Spanish flu pandemic of 1918 had. Its mortality was much higher than Covid-19's has been so far.[1] Indeed, so forgotten was the Spanish flu that it took Covid-19 to remind most people it had taken place. Others argued that, in contrast, the current pandemic will rank with seminal events like the outbreak of World War I or the 1929 stock market crash.[2]

To pronounce on whether the coronavirus pandemic will alter the world would be premature. At best, we can nod at some likely changes.[3] Small, everyday novelties are often the ones we notice most. Will handshakes, not to mention hugs and kisses, be gone forever? Will we all now greet each other in the Japanese manner?[4]

What about social distancing more generally? Will we incorporate into our daily lives what the Dutch called the "one-and-a-half-meter society" and Koreans, "everyday life quarantine"?[5]

Who can predict what normality vaccines will restore as they arrive? But fervent handwashing is likely to remain with us since it also helps prevent other diseases. Perhaps less touching each other or sharing food will also become second nature.[6] How will it affect our emotional ties if everyone is regarded as a threat?[7] Cleanliness spread everywhere during this epidemic. Our hands were germ-free, the Great Mosque of Mecca was closed nightly for a scrubbing, the New York subways were spotless.[8] One could get used to this.

Some changes were likely temporary, only until we come out the other end. Lipstick sales were down, a victim of masks.[9] Children moved back in with their parents.[10] Indian weddings slimmed down.[11] Drive-in cinemas were back.[12] Blowing out candles on birthday cakes was verboten.[13] So was the butterfly stroke in public pools, insofar as they remained open at all.[14] Elevator rides became dangerous. We gained weight, drank more, smoked less.[15] Holidays became staycations. Mating habits and customs adjusted to the interposition of digital space. The AIDS epidemic had brought us outercourse as an example of what sexologists called non-intracorporeally emissive sex. Now sex-at-arms-length continued with drive-by matchmaking, sexting, coronalingus, and farplay.[16] Divorces multiplied among couples overdosing on quality time during lockdown – so much that China imposed a cooling-down period.[17]

Other changes may have greater staying power. Contactless infrastructure was likely here to stay – automatic elevators, doors, sinks, and toilets. Architectural and design offices now specialized in low-contact buildings.[18] Bank tellers had long been immured behind plexiglass. They were now joined by most of their colleagues in retail. How long before the West adopts the devices Japanese taxi drivers use to open doors automatically for passengers? Windows are more likely to be openable in new buildings, or at least more attention paid to air filtration.[19]

Cash had long been in decline in some nations. Sweden was set to become the first cashless society – not for its epidemiological advantages, but to give tax authorities more purchase over citizens. Not everyone was falling in line. Credit cards were still viewed suspiciously in Germany, and mobile phone payments were not even on the horizon. Having moved away from cash before the pandemic, some US cities had suffered a backlash from annoyed consumers taking up the cause of the unbanked and unphoned, forcing stores to accept ready money.[20] Covid will probably move us more quickly in a Swedish direction. In 2005, Mike Davis described automatic temperature detectors employed in Singapore's airport during the SARS epidemic two years earlier as "Orwellian."[21] We are now likely to take this, and much more, in our stride.[22]

Virtual versions of formerly in-person activities often turned out to work better than expected. Many had already been seeping in, their trajectory merely accelerated by the pandemic. Virtual dentistry was useless, virtual medicine much less so. Virtual therapy, tutoring, and yoga were competitors to the real thing in a way virtual massage could not be. Distance learning and work from home had arrived long ago. They notched up their presence.

To announce the demise of universities, offices, or metropolitan city cores, however, seems premature. Many will adapt and prove resilient. Take the courts. They rapidly adjusted, going online. By late April, the supreme courts of the US, UK, Brazil, China, India, and Singapore were working remotely.[23] In March, the Norwegian supreme court decided to hear certain criminal cases based only on written submissions.[24] A Nigerian court pronounced a death penalty via Zoom.[25] Historically and etymologically, courts were places. But the same question arose as for lectures, seminars, conferences, and many other interactions: were they a service or a place?[26]

As technology de-spacialized our interactions, the need decreased for us to coincide simultaneously with each other. Physically proximate meetings will likely be scaled back, continuing online instead. Many, we now realize, are expendable. Among a dozen other US states, Maine permitted remote notarization during the pandemic.[27] With the already-existing software for virtual signatures, this laid waste to the face-to-face encounters once required to finalize legal transactions. Our sociability will probably survive that reform.

Some behaviors turned out to be epidemiologically dangerous. At least this time, sex was not specifically singled out. But singing was, along with its pneumatic corollaries, wind instruments and brass.[28] Choral rehearsals became the bathhouses of Covid-19.[29] Karaoke in small ill-ventilated nightclub rooms was bad. So were *noraebang*, the private singing rooms popular in South Korea.[30] But even outdoor yodeling, if vigorous enough, was dangerous.[31] Some tunes were so irresistible that discouraging sing-alongs failed, and they had to be purged from jukeboxes. Neil Diamond's *Sweet Caroline* was among the offenders.[32] Even better, noise proved to be an epidemiological risk. Elevated sound levels meant raised voices, heavier breathing, and more expectoration. Loud talking was simply dangerous.[33] When they were allowed to reopen, nightclubs turned down the volume, restaurants dampened the noise.[34] Roller coasters in Japan banned screaming.[35] With luck, some of this will stick too.

But of course, the pandemic upended things far beyond such simple practicalities. Working from home may become much more popular and widespread. Downtown real estate, sandwich shops, and much else will suffer if that sticks. Many remote workers have sung the praises of skipping the morning commute, but the nasty underbelly of that practice has been less noted. If the same work can be done at a commuting distance over the internet, it can also be done several time zones or even national borders away. Outsourcing work was nothing new. But where it had earlier applied mainly to back-office tasks, now everyone discovered how much normal work might be done remotely too.

Universalizing work at a distance had the advantage of not favoring the in-office crowd, able to catch a quick word with the boss in the hallway. But its main threat (or opportunity) was to outsource the front- and even the corner-office, too. Bay Area high-tech firms, Facebook among them, allowed many more workers to telecommute during the pandemic. Enough fled the area that rents dropped for the first time in years.[36] But the sweet spot of drawing a San Francisco salary while telecommuting from Montana quickly soured. The same firms also announced they would pay wages proportionate to living costs where employees decamped.[37] And once that Rubicon was crossed, why should bosses pay Montana salaries when Bangalore wages were on offer? Improvements in translation software heightened such possibilities.[38] Blue-collar jobs had often been epidemiologically risky and might disappear in a post-pandemic recession. White-collar jobs could equally vanish as companies made broad structural adjustments.

The pandemic also aggravated already-festering social antagonisms. Frontline workers sacrificed so the rest of us could isolate. They paid in high illness and mortality.[39] The poor more generally suffered, too, with dangerous jobs, crowded housing, and inadequate health care. To class came ethnic distinctions that often reduced to poverty, but may also have had other causes. Discrimination followed the pandemic around the world, tagging the nationality of its most recent stopping place with the stigma of vectordom. The Chinese were shunned as travelers early in the epidemic, as were Westerners in India.[40] So were ethnic minorities in many European nations and Africans in China.[41] Inevitably, Jews were blamed, too, though anti-Semites (as always) varied in their views as to why precisely.[42]

Gender imbalances worsened. Women likely did worse from the lockdown than men, working disproportionately in closed sectors, suffering bigger career sacrifices, and carrying a heavier childcare and domestic load.[43] The volume of baking that went on suggested as much. Possibly, however, gains for women might emerge: permanently flexible work schedules and more equal divisions of household responsibilities.[44] Generational antagonisms also emerged from the murk. Workers in the most affected trades skewed young.[45] But the confrontation went deeper. Aggressive partying on the beaches of Florida, Spain, and Britain, the raves of Berlin and Liverpool let off pent-up youthful steam after lockdown. But they also challenged the anxious self-isolation of the parents who had monopolized jobs, mortgages, and pensions far too long.

An anti-lockdown slogan from Wisconsin touched the core: "My rights are greater than your fear."[46] The schoolteachers who resisted reentering classrooms, the professors too anxious to teach, the civil servants shunning their desks emblematized the problem. The epithet "boomer remover" stripped the pandemic's antagonism naked. Negligently spreading the coronavirus endangered the grandparents, while negligently emitting carbon dioxide threatened the grandchildren – was this the revenge?[47] Disarming young wrath, many elderly agreed. Texas's lieutenant governor offered up the lives of the old on the bonfire of the economy. He suggested that they might be "willing to take a chance" on their survival "in exchange for keeping the America that all America loves for [their] children and grandchildren," and that "there are more important things than living."[48] Bioethicists argued that an implicit inter-generational compact meant that the elderly should retreat to the end of the line when ventilator treatments and, eventually, vaccines were distributed.[49] As we have seen, that offer was cashed in willy-nilly when the oldest were triaged out of intensive care.

WHENCE THE PANDEMIC?

The pandemic had both environmental causes and effects, and its impact on nature was ambiguous. Like other recessions, scaling back economic activity gave the globe a breather. The environment was like human health – some aspects gained as activity lessened. Nature seemed to bounce back as humans hid away during this Anthropause – dolphins in the Trieste harbor, jackals in Tel Aviv parks, peacocks on the streets of Dubai.[50] Less car and plane traffic meant fewer animal deaths, not just humans, and also more connectivity among animal populations.[51] But the demise of public eating hurt scavengers – rats and gulls.

Political leaders used the cover of the pandemic to roll back environmental regulation.[52] And as conservationists stopped patrolling wildernesses, poachers attacked endangered species. The decline in food consumption, thanks to restaurant closings, meant more farm wastage and excess pollution.[53] Medical protective kit and food containers used as restaurants shifted to take-out increased plastic pollution.[54] Reusable bags, packaging, and cups – however waste-reducing – suddenly became vectors of transmission.[55]

The final environmental outcome of such contradictory tendencies will have to be calculated later. Fears of zoonotic transmission may have reduced the consumption of some wild animals even as economic pressures upped the culling of others for food.[56] Conservation plans were delayed or abandoned. Yet, other areas may have rewilded through beneficial neglect. The clean energy sector suffered massive job losses.[57] But the decline in electricity use favored renewables and would likely accelerate coal's demise. Coal generation was down 30%, and in the US, wind and solar surpassed it for the first time.[58] More coal plants were finally being shut than built.[59] Still, the price of fossil fuels was also likely to fall, thanks to recession and improvements in extraction, possibly boosting future demand.[60]

That the pandemic, as such, would have an environmentally beneficial effect was unlikely. Much hung on what reforms followed in its wake. Oil use declined and was forecast not to reach pre-pandemic levels until 2022.[61] Greenhouse gas emissions plunged by 17% in April 2020. For the entire year, projections were for a 4% to 7% drop. Declines differed widely among activities. Aviation was down 60%, public buildings and commerce, 21%, personal transport, 36%. But with everyone sheltering at home, residential use was up a smidgen.[62]

That sounded good, but a fractional drop in one year's output promised no major change.[63] The atmosphere's overall greenhouse gas level hit an all-time high amid the pandemic – 417 ppm for CO_2 in May.[64] Worse, the epidemic and its enforced changes of habit gave a concrete sense of how big the cutbacks would need be to affect global warming. In 2019, the UN estimated that to keep temperature increases under 1.5°C, global CO_2 emissions had to start falling 7.6% annually beginning in 2020 – in other words, largely in line with the first-year effect of the worst economic contraction since the Great Depression.[65]

That also suggested that forsaking the bad habits excoriated by the climate change activists was not enough. Abandoning planes, trains, and automobiles during the pandemic produced only a small reduction of carbon emissions.[66] Even if we all lived as virtuously as Greta Thunberg, tinkering with consumer demand within the existing emissions framework was unlikely to achieve the necessary outcomes. And as the lockdown eased up, emissions surged back.[67] Indeed, though aviation remained down, people who otherwise would have taken public transport likely detoured to automobiles, fearing infection. In England, the public was strongly advised to use any means of transportation *other* than public.[68] More people now contemplated buying cars.[69] In all their environmentally dysfunctional splendor, the suburbs were back in favor, compared with city-center living.[70]

The long-term effects depended on what, if any, structural reforms ensued, but more immediately on the nature of the recovery. The more prolonged and worse for the economy the pandemic was, the better for the environment. But without more far-reaching changes to the core of industrial economies, the pandemic's environmental benefits promised to be merely an epiphenomenon of the economic downturn. As such, they were very costly. The expense of emissions reductions bought by economic decline was orders of magnitude higher than their normal market price – $3,000 to $5,000 per ton of CO_2 emissions avoided, not $24 or $27. With an economic slowdown driving down activity faster than energy use, the US economy's carbon intensity – the emissions per dollar income – would likely increase compared with the pandemic never having happened.[71]

This pandemic intertwined public health and the environment in other ways too. Covid-19 and other zoonotic diseases had been sparked by population growth. As humanity pushed further into nature, it rubbed up against wild animals. Such contacts amplified as bushmeat and farmed wild animals were put on the menu – whether for protein, prestige, or medicinal reasons.[72] Three-quarters of new or emerging diseases that infect humans originated in animals. Sixty percent of emerging infectious diseases over the past half-century have been zoonoses, with 70% of these, in turn, springing from wildlife.[73] The CDC's estimates were similar: that 60% of all infectious diseases could have spread from animals and that three-quarters of emerging ones did.[74]

People and wild animals interact more frequently, thanks to humanity's expanding footprint. Worse, the interactions themselves may be becoming more dangerous.[75] In environments degraded by mining, logging, farming, and construction, the animals that survive may carry more viruses than previously, posing greater threats. For millennia, rats have lived symbiotically with humans, parasites on our warm accommodations, food hoards, and draught animal companions. Bats, some of which have adapted to human proximity, are protected by unusually turbo-charged immune systems and present a heightened danger. Gregarious, living densely, and migrating collectively, bats carry organisms that transmit SARS, Nipah, Marburg, Ebola, and other illnesses to humans.

We share the most viruses with domesticated animals. But we also share many disease organisms with the generalist species that have adapted to us. Rodents, bats, and primates are the main reservoirs, accounting for three-quarters of zoonotic viruses. Rodent numbers have increased as humans came to dominate the landscape, raising the danger of zoonotic crossover.[76] Recent studies in Vietnam revealed many coronaviruses in bats and rats destined for restaurant menus.[77] Increased human contact with ticks, mosquitos, and fleas where forests were disturbed or intermediary hosts proliferated has helped spread illnesses such as Lyme disease and West Nile virus. A "dilution effect" may occur in degraded landscapes, with microorganisms spreading more widely among the fewer intermediary animal hosts that remain, ultimately posing a bigger threat to humans.[78]

Human encroachments on nature, such as mining, deforestation, and the spread of arable land, were dangerous. But more immediately, it pointed to another elephant in the room: wildlife markets and the wild animal trade. The jury remains out on the precise location where the coronavirus jumped to humans. Whether it occurred at the Huanan Seafood Wholesale Market in Wuhan or not, the interface between wild animals and their human predators was on display at its rawest here.

Wet markets are much like farmers' markets in the West. The Huanan market was a wet market, but – unlike many – also had a section devoted to wild meats and animals.[79] In response to widespread outrage at open trafficking in wild animals, the Chinese government shut the Huanan market. It also passed measures early in 2020 to ban the breeding, trading, hunting, transporting, rearing for food, and eating of terrestrial wild animals, whether captive-bred or wild-caught.[80] A national plan to buy out wild-animal breeders was announced. The ban left large loopholes, however, by excluding breeding for fur, medicine, or sale as pets.[81] Eating pangolins was illegal, but using their scales in traditional Chinese medicine remained okay.[82]

Asia's wet markets were only one instance of the widespread wild-animal habit. Perhaps distinctions must be drawn between eating prompted by hunger and consumption for prestige or medical use. African wild-meat markets feed people who have few other sources of protein. One study revealed that bushmeat supplied Liberians with three-quarters of their protein needs.[83] Others suggested that bushmeat often competed in quantity with domesticated animals as a source of protein.[84] But the Africans who brought suitcases of bushmeat through Heathrow were clearly not hungry.[85] Nor were the well-off men in Congo's Brazzaville, who fed their pregnant wives gorilla meat, hoping for strong boy babies.[86]

In cities like Kumasi, Ghana's second-biggest, bushmeat commanded a premium, costlier than beef or mutton.[87] Eaters in the Congo described it as tastier, fresher, more local, and healthier than frozen farmed meats.[88] Whether the Chinese ban will be effective remains to be seen, as also the WHO's aspirational call for a clamp-down on the wildlife trade. Markets were important food sources in the developing world, it announced in April, but when they reopened after the pandemic, they should follow stringent food safety and hygiene standards. The sale and trade in wildlife for food should be rigorously banned.[89]

While the unregulated trade and eating of wildlife was an immediate danger in the less-developed world, bigger issues also loomed. We have touched on the rampant misuse of human antibiotics in the first world's agriculture and animal rearing. That, in turn, reflected larger economic and demographic shifts. As Asia and Africa urbanized and became wealthier, the demand for animal protein spurred the voracious growth of intensive factory farming there too. Meat production had doubled in the last two decades of the twentieth century and was set to repeat that in the following two.[90] That added to the threat posed by the megacities of the global South as spreading grounds for zoonoses.

THE STATE IS DEAD, LONG LIVE THE STATE

As in most disasters, no actor played a bigger role in the pandemic than the state. Where the coronavirus was poorly handled, the defunding of public health programs was often to blame. But in those nations where public health authorities failed to squelch the disease at source, other branches of government had to take up the slack. If a country could not manage a test and trace scheme, then normal activities ceased, and locked-down economies were hooked up to the life support of government stimulus.

Governments intervened across the board, not just mandating public health interventions, propping up businesses, and helping out the unemployed. New economic and labor regulations rose to the challenge. German slaughterhouses – viral hotspots – could no longer subcontract out their nastiest work, which had allowed light-touch temporary employment of foreign workers in bad conditions. Stores rejiggered their layouts to streamline customer throughput, minimizing time spent and contact.[91] Hollywood took a leaf from its cousins in porn who had long relied on strict testing regimens to keep sets VD-free.[92] When and how prostitutes could resume work, where legal, was specified in detail. In Belgium, both parties had to don masks, whatever else they might wear. Greek brothels were to retain customers' contact details for a month. Encounters were limited to fifteen minutes and just two people, who were to "ensure distance," however they managed that.[93]

Just as certain branches happened to profit from the pandemic, others suffered. Some activities were simply more dangerous. Gyms hurt more than golf courses. Anything indoors struggled. Yoga studios, beauty parlors, bowling alleys, bars, and pool halls were bad news. Their movements measured, customers turned out to spend twice as long in electronics stores as gardening centers and more time in used clothing stores than discount emporia. Breakfast restaurants might serve as many customers as a diner but in a narrower time frame. Florists were safer places to be than bookstores.[94]

No one had ever divided the economy into spacing-dependent and -indifferent. It made for odd bedfellows. Some production lines could be strung out, but others seemed crowded by nature – Amazon warehouses and slaughterhouses. Airlines, theaters, and nightclubs found themselves united as epidemiological threats. Construction and manufacturing were much less hit than travel and hospitality.

Beyond the pandemic's ravages, the distribution of government largesse amplified inequities. Subsidies were supposed to help the hardest-hit businesses, though sometimes they went to the best-connected. Germany was the source of half of all government corona-related subsidies in the EU. It was accused of subsidizing its export industries, allowing them to compete unfairly in other European markets.[95] In the US, business complained that government monies went preferentially to construction and manufacturing, more than hospitality, to Republican Texas more than Democratic New York.[96] Companies that had spent vast cash reserves – even borrowing – to buy back shares and drive up their price were now wallowing in the government trough. American Airlines had recently spent $13 billion and Boeing $53 billion to buy their own stocks, yet both were now pleading hardship.[97]

Would subsidies lock in place industries already struggling before the pandemic that should instead be nudged to reform? Many were furious that airlines were bailed out yet again despite good earnings in previous years, extracted from ever more cramped passengers. In a more general sense, mass tourism, however wonderful for those who finally got to experience the world, posed threats to an over-heating globe that needed addressing. How wise was keeping it on life support? Government subsidies went by the billions to businesses of every stripe. The pandemic coincided with a renationalization of railroads in the UK.[98] Government-paid public service ads buoyed the press.[99] Companies demanded liability relief against suits from infected employees before agreeing to reopen.[100]

Commentators attacked bailouts for companies that had not saved up reserves, while still paying executives lavishly, like Booking.com, headquartered in the Netherlands.[101] Much the same could be said for the auto industry. The German economic stimulus program made a bold decision – against the automotive unions – to subsidize electric vehicles, not conventional ones.[102] And what about the cruise ship industry with its scandalous treatment of personnel, unavoidably close-quarters dangers, and liberal use of flags of convenience to avoid taxes and regulation?[103]

Should not higher education, too, be asked to mend its ways as a condition of bailouts – its dependence on a client base of full-freight paying, but now-fickle international students, infla-tion-busting annual tuition hikes, bloated bureaucracy, addic-tion to income-generating sports, legacy preferences, donor leg-ups, and other opaque and at times practically felonious admis-sions practices? Many universities and colleges that had expanded heedlessly in good times were about to find out. But first, they were going to endure a purgatory of squaring the circle between an inherently high-contact business and social distancing regulations.[104]

Economic nationalism was likely to get a hearing once things returned to normal. Globalized supply chains had proven fragile. Few businesses or governments seem to have considered that a worldwide pandemic, affecting everyone simultaneously, would shut down transport and trade right across the globe. Most imme-diately, this hit supplies of protective medical gear. So-called "national stockpiles" turned out to be sheaves of just-in-time con-tracts with Chinese suppliers. Should such materials be manufac-tured closer to home? That assured a steadier supply, but at the cost of inefficient and costly production.

Looking beyond low-tech masks, gowns, and gloves, local pro-duction of medicines was likely to be expensive and inefficient. Pharmaceuticals were a massive, capital-intensive industry, not something nations pursued on a whim. The EU was already a major exporter of medical products, while also importing vast quantities – protective gear from China, pharmaceuticals from the US and Switzerland, generics from India. To produce all that at home at European wages would cost more. This time, the short-ages had been in masks, gowns, gloves, and ventilators. Who knew what the next epidemic would require? Better perhaps to strengthen supply chains and relationships than bring home production.[105] Manufacturing medical kit locally was just the iceberg's tip. Would economic nationalism go further, encouraging further onshoring?[106]

STATE AND CIVIL SOCIETY

Most generally, will the pandemic have changed relations between state and civil society? Those nations which seem to have come through least scathed had the best-functioning states. Regardless of their political complexions, the most competent were the hardiest. Competence, not ideology, determined which nations handled the pandemic best. Competence was not everything, of course. The Swedes picked the wrong direction and competently steered towards it. Among the countries that should have performed better, the US and UK stood out, united in their inability to do much consistently. Johnson's Tory government slalomed its way through a series of hairpin policy U-turns, cherry-picking the scientific offerings that best suited its erratic course.[107] Washington abandoned whatever pretense to leadership it may have entertained. It allowed its vast and diverse continent to splinter apart in various, uncoordinated approaches – a Babel of prevention that left it with the single largest mortality load in the world on or around April 11.[108]

Did the payoff for competence over ideology portend a new and larger role for the state? Would the incompetent ones be able to reform? A large state is not necessarily a capable one. Whatever its shape, whether the state was back, or whether indeed it had ever left, was much discussed – and not just around the pandemic. What baseline of state activity did we measure from? Things looked different if judged from the late nineteenth century, from the 1960s, or from the 1980s with the Reagan and Thatcher administrations' small-state rhetoric. Some argued that the state was shrinking, pointing to neoliberal tendencies that had throttled the state's financing, pared back activities, and privatized functions. Others argued equally plausibly that the state played an ever-increasing role in citizens' lives.[109]

Did the pandemic push states to become bigger players? The story was ambiguous. Laws both tightened up and loosened. Mexico and South Africa banned alcohol sales. But in Italy, drinks were now sold through wine windows, apertures in massive stone walls left over from ancient plague regulations – in effect gloryholes for oenophiles.[110] In the US, rules on public sale and consumption loosened up. Drinks to go, on the European model, were now permitted.[111] Yet overall, the immediate outcome was a massively increased role for the state in everyday life. Global house arrest of billions was among the first effects, along with curbs on travel, residence, schooling, work, assembly, and most other civil rights so fundamental that we never imagined their sacrifice.

Impositions that democratic citizens would earlier have viscerally rejected now became our ticket to freedom. Mass testing, epidemiological surveillance, swarms of contact tracers checking our movements and acquaintances, perhaps someday immunity certificates: no longer police-state policies, these were now means of restoring basic freedoms. One observer confessed that he would gladly permit himself to be scanned and tested and have his prior movements and contacts traced if it meant he could visit his doctor along with his wife.[112]

The left welcomed calls for a stronger state. The pandemic had shown the need for more social programs and solidarity.[113] Though hobbled by a libertarian fringe that rejected masks, lockdowns, and other preventive impositions, conservatives too found much to like. They approved of reforms introduced to streamline bureaucracy, trim regulation, and enhance online activities: notarizing documents, facilitating hospital expansions, easing medical licensing.[114]

The EU enhanced its powers with massive new debt-based economic stimulus packages.[115] Boris Johnson upended Tory orthodoxy by praising FDR's New Deal.[116] The otherwise frugal Germans indulged in deficit spending at home and borrowing at the EU level.[117] Formerly unlikely reforms now caught new wind in their sails. A basic minimum income was instituted in all but name across many Western nations, even the US, during the spring of 2020. Could something like that continue? In America, the dysfunctionalities of a health system that failed to cover all and was channeled via workplaces became painfully evident. Mass unemployment led to millions losing coverage at the very moment when the authorities wanted patients to be tested and treated without worrying about paying the bills. Was health care reform moving closer?[118]

All shades of the political spectrum found virtue in having the government ensure truth, though they differed on whom they considered purveyors of murk and nonsense. When Trump posted misleading comments on social media, liberals were gratified to have them called out, as Twitter began affixing warning labels to his most egregious tweets.[119] Even Facebook eventually began shepherding its content. So, too, Orbán in Hungary introduced draconian punishments for spreading what his government considered untrue or distorted facts about the epidemic.[120] Both China and Taiwan had laws to punish spreading false information.

Privacy was a right put at risk in battles against the pandemic, but also a source of friction that impeded dealing with it. To facilitate telemedicine, especially in rural areas, privacy restrictions were loosened.[121] Data on people's movements and contacts were crucial to squelching transmission. That potentially violated citizens' privacy to protect their health. Which side would prevail? In Asia, where the data was more readily available, privacy raised some concerns. South Korea anonymized phone data tracking clients' movements through gay nightclubs in Seoul.

In the West, the issue was more ticklish. Whether measuring proximity was sufficient on contact tracing phone apps or whether location was also necessary provoked debate over the relative merits of privacy and prevention. Proximity revealed only that you had been near someone infected, location where that had occurred. Arguably, privacy concerns rendered most contact tracing apps ineffective. The WHO's guidelines insisted that the infected's status could be notified to contacts only with their consent, making the system voluntary.[122] The apps developed on the Apple/Google platform entrusted those who proved to be ill with alerting their contacts. Even assuming that they updated their status on the phone, no one knew who or how many were then told, nor whether these contacts then isolated themselves or were tested.[123] Location data was already available to mobile phone operators, credit card companies, banks, mapping app entrepreneurs, private security services, and others who scooped up the digital wake we leave behind. Should it not be put to use by authorities with our best interests in mind?[124]

Of course, misuse of patient data had to be prevented too. Health status should not be used to discriminate, neither for treatment nor for insurance coverage. No argument there. Yet, such concerns were just one part of privacy objections. Existentially, privacy may be a value in itself. Possibly, we cannot exist as humans without shielding our innermost thoughts. If we were completely transparent, unable to keep secrets, if others could entirely grok us and we them, we might psychologically meld. But politically, privacy is more a means than an end. It is a clumsy and imperfect way of protecting people from the consequences of others penalizing them for something they know. In that case, why not cut to the chase and prevent the penalization directly rather than obscure the pertinent knowledge?

Suppose someone is gay, and gays are discriminated against. Are they better served by laws hindering access to their data, thus preserving ignorance of the triggering state, or by forbidding discrimination based on sexual preference? True, privacy and the ability to hide discrimination's triggers do allow individuals to shield against everyday life's constant informal judgments. But as data transparency becomes ever more inevitable, perhaps it makes more sense to cut off the thistle at the root, outlawing discriminatory acts rather than hoping to avoid them by stanching the flow of information. The right not to have to conceal whatever it is that provokes others' prejudice is an important consideration too. Nor, of course, does privacy help those who suffer discrimination against characteristics that cannot be concealed – ethnicity, age, sex, or body size.

As we have seen, the nations that fared best against the pandemic combined deft leadership, effective bureaucracies, and sufficient social trust and compliance to bring civil society along in the difficult tasks demanded. That combination worked well both among nations able to impose targeted quarantines upfront and among those that later shut down more broadly. But immediate public health prevention was only one measure of state capacity and action. Nations that fancied themselves well-prepared and capable proved woefully inadequate – above all, the US and Britain, but most large European countries too. Getting the public health response right was not the only way states and their competences played a role in the pandemic, however. The economic effects also had to be tackled.

Some nations that did not distinguish themselves as public health actors nonetheless responded robustly in economic terms. Both the US and the EU passed trillion-dollar bailouts, subventions, and bank-guarantee packages that dwarfed any earlier reactions to crises short of war. Of course, prevention and bailout traded off. The more effectively nations prevented or moderated the pandemic, the less bailing out was required. As a fraction of GDP, China's stimulus was less than half the American.[125] Fiscal stimulus measures in the Eurozone were proportionately over twice as large as in the thirteen ASEAN+ nations.[126] Prevention trumps post-facto interventions, the proverbial stitch in time. The robust bailers-out had to compensate for their front-end failures.

The scale of the bailout packages and subventions left observers marveling at how government indebtedness that just a year or two earlier, or even faced with the Great Recession in 2008, would have seemed impossible now passed quickly and consensually. Had the basic paradigm of how governments and markets interact shifted?

In a chronically low-inflation environment, could governments fire up the treasury's printing presses? With global cash reserves amply fed by the world's pension plans, ever more billionaires, Asian savers, and massive sovereign wealth funds, and with heightened inequality increasing savings over consumption, liquidity that desperately sought safe harbors stood ready to snap up government bonds. Where the bond markets had once threatened to punish overly profligate governments – James Carville's reincarnation fantasy – now they lined up to buy new product.[127]

Finally came the state's medical response, developing vaccines and cures. Unless the coronavirus decided spontaneously to pack it in, government action would be required not just to prevent and mitigate, but to exit the pandemic altogether. Which systems would prove most competent in this respect? A geopolitical race for vaccines ensued. Russia and China hoped this time to join the ranks of the major biomedical contenders – above all the US and Britain, but not forgetting India or northern Europe, especially Germany, Switzerland, and Sweden. We do not yet know precisely who will deliver the vaccines or medicines that will eventually tame the outbreak. But it is unlikely to be some of the nations that were the most adept public health responders: South Korea, New Zealand, or Australia – all biomedical pygmies.[128]

Worth a mention here too is the geopolitical elephant in the room. Doubtless, the Asian nations dealt more effectively with the pandemic than most Western ones. Their administrative deftness was on display amid broader tectonic shifts among superpowers in other respects, too. Whether this nailed fast the much-ballyhooed slippage of global dominance between the US and China must await the pronouncements of future historians. But let us keep firmly in mind the smarting humiliation that China sought to obscure by pointing to its adroit handling of the pandemic – that of having been its source in the first place, and indeed of several similar recent episodes.

Yes, China dealt well with the coronavirus. But China was also its cause. Better not to have had the problem at all. Global superpowers are not normally the origin of zoonoses springing from sloppy interactions of humans and animals. More precisely, it was the coincidence of China's hypermodernity with pockets of abysmal hygiene that posed the danger. Peasants living in over-proximity to their barnyard animals were normally a threat only to themselves and their neighbors. But with gleaming airports and high-speed rail nearby, it became the world's problem. None of the major powers were likely to emerge from the pandemic with their credentials burnished.[129]

THE ASSUMPTIONS OF TRUST

With the public health interventions that made up the average citizen's immediate encounter with the state, competence was not just a matter of centralized and effective authority taking and enforcing tough decisions. Just as much, it involved citizens willing to have their movements, contacts, and habits closely noted, recorded, and inspected. The pandemic response demanded that citizens accept house arrest by the billions and tolerate being told whom to socialize with. It meant having prescribed whether they could work or go to school, how, when, and where they could shop, what amusements remained available, what protective gear to wear where, and endless other minutely prescribed aspects of lockdown. In other words, whether public health interventions were effective sprang from a pas-de-deux between state and civil society.

Some countries lucked out. For reasons we do not yet understand, bits of the world were simply less hit by the pandemic. Remoteness, customs, habits, and cross-reactive immunity from other sources: all are possible explanations for why the Buddhist triangle in Southeast Asia, or Eastern Europe and parts of the Balkans dodged the bullet's full force, at least during the first wave. Of course, perhaps these nations were simply such effective preventers that they shut the epidemic down. Some populations were younger and healthier than others, therefore less harrowed.

Age structure varied dramatically, as did rates of obesity and diabetes.

But even in the lucky areas and certainly everywhere else, the state and civil society tackled the problem together. The authorities could not force unpopular measures on the citizenry. Citizens acquiesced in what they were persuaded to accept as sensible and resisted measures they disliked or eventually tired of. As we have seen, some governments underestimated their citizens' willingness to comply, Sweden and Britain, above all. Like Modi in India, other leaders overestimated what they could demand, asking the poorest to starve to be safe. Elsewhere, citizens who initially accepted things later grew weary and restive. The least-hit places were often the most resistant. There were limits to what the authorities could demand. Go too far and the social compact frayed. Citizens had to be convinced that their sufferings were worth it. Violating civil rights was tolerated so long as people were persuaded they were safer and better-off for it.

Happy were the nations where rules and norms coincided. People knew what was expected of them and did it. Jacinda Ardern, New Zealand's prime minister, could speak of her "team of five million," but few other leaders were so lucky.[130] In most Western nations, privacy concerns were an almost insurmountable obstacle to effective contact tracing, whether in-person or via phone app. In Taiwan, the average person approached by a tracer named fifteen contacts; in Spain and France, three, in New York City, barely one.[131] Only a fifth of those supposed to self-isolate after symptoms or contact with the infected did so in Britain.[132] The lack of ready testing, much less economic support for those who had to self-isolate, did not help matters.

In most countries, regulations needed enforcement. China locked people up and fined them. Taiwan slapped the non-compliant with eye-watering fines. Sweden assumed that people would obey. Because there were few rules, few violations ensued. The French, Italians, and Spanish handed out fines by the thousands, as did the Americans and British. Yet, the problem was less enforcing and more convincing citizens to adopt rules as norms, doing what was expected. Millions of daily mask violations could not be individually policed. At best, the authorities could set a few examples, *pour encourager les autres.*

How much governments could count on citizens doing the right thing without having to enforce it depended on implicit social and cultural understandings. Thanks in large measure to the nation's many immigrants, and the lack of commonly accepted behavioral norms, authorities in the US had long implemented quite overtly compulsory public health policies.[133] Directly Observed Therapy for tuberculosis, which required patients to take their medicines under supervision, implicitly admitted that informal understandings could not always be relied on.[134] More generally, using the law to mandate conduct of public health relevance betrayed similar assumptions.[135] Following this reasoning, low-trust societies imposed stricter policies than more trusting ones during the pandemic.[136]

The trust the Swedes claimed as the basis of their voluntary approach was one formulation of this logic of relying on informal understandings to achieve specific behavioral outcomes. Trust is one possibility. But shame, obedience, conformity, and fear are other psychological states that also motivate citizens to tack with the prevailing winds. To be free of the state's impositions does not mean being able to do as we please, but to do on our own what otherwise the authorities would have to force from us. We must want to do what the state expects from us. In emergencies, when there can be little wiggle room for individual choice, we must freely select what otherwise would have been an obligation. States could and did compel the necessary behavior. At the extremes, police were summoned and citizens locked up. But overall, the more compliance was voluntary, the more cost-efficient and effective the state's actions were. Since the behaviors required were difficult to compel and better done voluntarily, citizen participation was crucial.

The Asian success story doubtless rested in part on cultural traits that encouraged citizens to comply with authority's demands. Many observers remarked on the Confucian collectivism that allowed deft handling of an inherently communal problem.[137] These nations seem to have drawn on wellsprings of cultural commonalities of trust and reliance in the state – even those that made no bones about enforcing their strictures firmly if necessary. "Trust, but verify" was the Russian proverb that President Reagan adopted when negotiating nuclear disarmament treaties with the Soviets in the 1980s. It served the Asian approach well.

Vietnam has a system of loudspeakers in public places to broadcast the names of scofflaws, debtors, and other miscreants at regular intervals. For enforcement, the nation relied not just on informal standards of compliance but also on its one-party-state propaganda machine and its system of loyal neighborhood party cadres keeping tabs on neighbors.[138] Some observers have attributed South Korea's success to the importance attached to avoiding *minpye* – causing trouble to others.[139] In Thailand, mask-wearing was enforced informally. "If I forget to wear one," one Bangkok resident explained, "the 'aunties' on the streets glare at me intensely, making me run back home in shame to grab a mask."[140] The Japanese wore masks primarily to fit the cultural expectation of doing so.[141]

The Chinese authorities could rely on widespread acceptance of even drastic impositions. "Would you rather get your children and elderly parents infected," a Wuhan public health expert replied when asked about the hardships of isolating the ill apart from their families, "or are you willing to wait and stay away from them for fourteen days? This is a choice between short-term and long-term happiness. I don't think that's hard to understand."[142]

Even so, public goods require public mandates. Not being lemmings, instinctively following the herd, humans have to be socialized into the behavior required of them for life in complex fellowships. The implicit acceptance of the requisite conduct has unsurprisingly been most easily achieved in those nations that could rely on a common upbringing, on the shared assumptions of a dominant culture – what the Germans call a *Leitkultur*. Without a common upbringing and socialization into collective behaviors, how could voluntarist strategies work? High levels of immigration and multiculturalism were likely to undermine a hands-off approach.

Foreign travelers were often blamed for the pandemic's arrival. But a similar logic held for outsiders at home too. Immigrants and ethnic minorities were criticized for not taking the expected precautions and for risky habits and customs at odds with the majority's. Some of the characteristics singled out were merely proxies for poverty. That recent immigrants often worked at exposed frontline jobs and lived in crowded housing naturally left them susceptible. Jobs in Swedish care homes, ill-paid and low-skilled, often went to recent immigrants whose local language skills were lacking. As care home mortality escalated, the question of how infection entered them brought this issue to a boil. Where to assign blame was murky – the authorities who refused to pay the wages required to attract skilled (and native) applicants and regarded such jobs as a means to integrate immigrants? Or the job-takers themselves who posed risks, most of which were outside their control?[143]

The lack of public health information in their native tongues also helped explain why recent immigrants were often afflicted.[144] Who was responsible here? The immigrants who had not sufficiently assimilated or the public health authorities who reached out only sluggishly and belatedly?[145]

Beyond such socio-economic factors, however, it did not take much for the logic that outsiders were different and to blame for their disproportionate affliction to bleed over into cultural traits too. In Germany, Catholic regions had higher infection rates, presumably thanks to public festivals held in February, but no consequences were drawn from this correlation.[146] Elsewhere, however, overtly prejudiced connections were tied, as when a Republican state senator from Ohio wondered whether Blacks were especially hard hit because they did not wash their hands often.[147] Other times, the racism was more covert.

Somalis in Scandinavia, who were unusually hard hit even among poor immigrants, found their habits and customs closely scrutinized. Was it because they insisted on visiting ill family members in large groups?[148] Or the way they plied closer physical contacts than customary among ethnic Nordics?[149] Was it their tendency to socialize despite isolation rules? Social distancing "is alien to us," said one Somali in London.[150] Or their preference for oral over written communication that blinded them to government information?[151]

Somalis themselves at times conceded that they were perhaps not the most compliant ruler-followers.[152] After flare-ups in Aarhus, Denmark's second city, the nativist, far-right Danish People's Party argued that Somalis bore much of the responsibility for not following regulations and holding large gatherings. It wanted masking rules targeted at their neighborhoods, with more stringent prescriptions.[153]

The Danish prime minister then pursued this line of thought, speculating what cultural traits – beyond the practicalities of crowded apartments and dangerous jobs – might account for why so many more "non-Westerners" than natives were afflicted. Apparently, some measure of incompliance was involved. Minorities, she admonished, "always have a responsibility to the larger community and everyone has to take responsibility for listening to what the Danish authorities say."[154]

The Scandinavians were hardly alone in singling out cultural outsiders and minorities as epidemiological flashpoints. The tangihanga, three-day Maori ceremonies in New Zealand, raised some of the same problems as large Muslim funerals in the North of England.[155] Singapore did well in getting its citizens to comply but overlooked the large reservoir of immigrant labor required to keep its sleek social system running. Their crowded dormitories became the source of epidemic flare-up in May.[156]

Of course, the poorest were hit hardest, but at least lockdowns had the virtue of treating everyone formally the same and spelling out the regulations that applied to them. It was in Sweden's voluntarist approach that distinctions between in- and outsiders emerged most starkly. Sweden assumed that everyone would have internalized the standards that they were to comply with. But was that true? A hands-off strategy rested on shared cultural assumptions that all immigrants were not necessarily or yet party to.

Of course, even an ethnically homogeneous society disagrees on much. But the epidemiologically relevant behavior at stake here was often the kind that is shared unconsciously by those who have been lifelong members. Whether to form a line at the bus stop or post office and at what distance to space it; how loudly to speak in public; how much physical contact everyday greetings demand: such are the visceral, unconscious habits taught from birth. Voluntary methods of disease prevention naïvely assumed that everyone agreed on the right course. They presumed a common mindset and sufficiently similar circumstances for all people to agree that, say, distancing and self-isolation were the right approach even if not mandated. When this did not happen, the search for culprits who were in some sense "others" began.

In every nation, the middle classes were in a better position to self-isolate and keep their distance. Sweden was not distinct in that sense, except that ethnic foreignness and lower-class status over-lapped consistently. Ethnic outsiders and the poorest were the same people, living in distinct, ghettoized neighborhoods with multigenerational families crowded into small apartments, high unemployment, and manual work the norm. Even with no travel restrictions or lockdown, the epidemic concentrated in Stockholm and, within the city, in certain segregated postcodes, home to recent immigrants. The voluntary strategy was tailored to the native Swedish middle classes, those trained from birth and well-positioned to implement it.[157] It made the fewest demands of those who could, in any case, cope best, allowing them to shop, eat, and drink in public.

A voluntary strategy, like the Swedish, was not a carte blanche, allowing citizens to do as they pleased. That was the fundamental misunderstanding among libertarians globally, who hailed Sweden's approach as somehow freer. Swedes assumed that the state did not need to mandate the requisite behavior, which they would undertake under their own steam. The necessary conduct had to be achieved one way or the other. The compulsion remained, exerted internally or from without. For those socialized into Swedishness, such behavioral norms may have come easily and naturally. For others, less so. The Swedish strategy rested on a curiously, perhaps even willfully, naïve assumption of cultural homogeneity that most nations – least of all Sweden itself – could take for granted any longer. How odd that a country that prided itself on its tolerance, openness, and worldliness should choose a strategy that rested in effect on a narrow ethno-nationalist prioritizing of its own dominant culture. In this case, much like universal military service, a more compulsory approach, requiring all to follow the same rules, would have been more democratic and inclusive. It would also have saved many thousands of lives.

ONLY THE STATE DELIVERS PUBLIC GOODS

The Covid-19 pandemic was like a visitor from a forgotten and neglected past. Mistakenly, developed nations thought that biomedicine had extracted them from the world where humans were the prey of microorganisms, mere means to other species' ambitions. Syphilis, tuberculosis, smallpox, polio, malaria, and cholera had become sporadic or were confined to developing nations and the margins of the first world. We had suffered other epidemics since the Spanish flu. Other than AIDS, these, too, had been successfully confined to underdeveloped nations, impinging only tangentially on the industrialized world.

Covid-19 changed that. It laid bare our epidemiological interdependence. An immediately and indiscriminately transmissible disease was everyone's problem. True, not everyone was equally vulnerable. The Spanish flu had preferentially killed the young, Covid-19, the old. But add in the predisposing conditions that increased the ranks of potential victims and easily half the population was susceptible. Forty percent of Americans in their twenties were obese. An irascible disease, Covid-19 unpredictably struck some victims harder than others, adding to its danger. Such "long haulers" were often young and often women.[158] Few of us could afford to be insouciant. Those who did not succumb or die were nonetheless threatened. Even if they were not medically affected, no one – however arbitrarily favored – could ignore the pandemic's social and economic effects. The kids partying on the beach still could not go back to their classes or jobs. They were victims of the epidemic, if not of the disease.

Ultimately, the pandemic's main lesson concerned public goods. Public goods are ones where everyone benefits, but to avoid free riders, they cannot be achieved without compulsion. We all enjoy being defended against enemies, but if we are not obliged to pay taxes to keep the military ready, not everyone will pitch in. In theory, the Swedes might have been correct: with enough informal cultural pressure to conform – call it trust if you like – the same outcome could have been achieved without formal coercion. Though they had long histories of exerting formidable cultural pressure, the Asian nations did not give up the stick. Maybe the Swedes will turn out to have shown a new direction. Yet, even if they did manage to achieve the quasi-oxymoron of voluntary compliance, that still left the problem of ignorance – of the asymptomatic carriers who could not comply because they did not realize they ought to. Nor did it solve the timing issue. In a pandemic spreading exponentially, every day's delay mattered. Early decisions had to be mandatory ones. To wait for public opinion to realize the stakes and mobilize itself voluntarily was futile.

Since pandemics make everyone a potential threat to all others, they have to be tackled collectively. Even an apparently individualized solution, like a vaccine, ultimately works best if a critical mass of all participates. In theory, with an effective cure, everyone could suffer the illness and come out the other end, but this solution's inefficiencies are readily apparent. With only the venerable tools of population management to hand, there was no individualized solution other than a permanently worn hazmat suit, or perhaps a remote and well-stocked mountain hut. Compulsion was unavoidable. Those who posed threats to others could not be counted on voluntarily to impose costs on themselves. The mildly ill, who hankered for a walk in the park, and even more so the asymptomatic, could be dissuaded only by enforceable sanctions.

Public goods' collective solutions also imply that all benefit and no one can be ignored. Everyone had to accept the possibility of being quarantined for the collective weal. But until the disease was eradicated everywhere and for all, there was no end of things for anyone. A reserve of infection in one neighborhood, among one set of citizens, or in one part of the world, spelled danger for the rest. We are only as safe as the sickest member of our community. So long as a critical mass has not been vaccinated, there will be no real security. The solution has to be global or not at all.

Acknowledgments

Writing this book spared me climbing the walls during the first lockdown in East Sussex, from March through July. It is a testament to the miracle of the internet that it could be done remotely while everything, not least libraries, was closed.

Lockdown gave me the unexpected and unprecedented blessing of six uninterrupted months with my wife, Lisbet Rausing. Besides domestic bliss, that allowed me to rope her in for endless proofreading and turgid-prose-simplification.

Many thanks to those newspapers – some much more generous than others – that opened much of their coronavirus reportage as a public service. And what a boon the increasingly open-access availability of scientific research is – driven along by preprint dissemination.

Thank you, once again, to Michael Kellogg, who tirelessly helped extract useful information from an avalanche of material. I'm indebted to a series of steadfast informants who passed along pertinent information, articles, and war stories: Annie Maccoby, Marty Peretz, Peter Mandler, Susan Pedersen, George Morris, Tim Smith, Chien-Ling Liu, Teresa Kulawik, Jonathan Cooper, Dominic Lawson, and Jonny Hughes. Gifford Combs shared articles, blogs, and newspaper access, and had the patience to read through an earlier version of the manuscript – for all of which I am very grateful. Åse Clausen invited me to share access via her subscriptions to Swedish newspapers, a huge help.

Christopher Clark first got me thinking by reminding me that I had written two books about past epidemics and inviting me on to his *History of Now* podcast to discuss the current one. Erik Berglöf kindly invited me to participate in a panel at the LSE on the Swedish exception. Another participant was my friend Lars Trägårdh, doubtless in disagreement with everything I have to say about Sweden. Anjana Shrivastava facilitated my first stab in print at understanding the Swedish situation in the pages of the *Berliner Zeitung*. Michael Watson of Cambridge University Press made this happen much more quickly than I ever imagined a university press could act.

Curiously, it is almost impossible to find publicly available information about air traffic – until recently, one of the cornerstones of modern life. OAG Aviation, "the leading supplier of aviation data and insights," very kindly supplied me with what I needed.

Notes

1 SCIENCE, POLITICS, AND HISTORY

1. *Spirit of the Laws*, vi 9.
2. Immanuel Kant, *The Philosophy of Law*, trans. W. Hastie (Edinburgh 1887) 197; Peter J. Steinberger, "Hegel on Crime and Punishment," *American Political Science Review*, 77, 4 (1983) 860.
3. Tom R. Tyler, *Why People Obey the Law* (Princeton 2006).
4. Nathan Stoltzfus, *Hitler's Compromises: Coercion and Consensus in Nazi Germany* (New Haven 2016); Christian Gerlach and Nicolas Werth, "State Violence – Violent Societies," in Michael Geyer and Sheila Fitzpatrick, eds., *Beyond Totalitarianism: Stalinism and Nazism Compared* (Cambridge 2009) 139–51.
5. Yoo Li, *Playing by the Informal Rules: Why the Chinese Regime Remains Stable Despite Rising Protests* (Cambridge 2019).
6. Owen Gingerich, "The Galileo Affair," *Scientific American*, 247, 2 (1982) 143.
7. 50 U.S. Code § 3811.
8. Giorgio Agamben, *State of Exception* (Chicago 2004). Jumping the gun already in February before the true horrors of the pandemic became apparent the following month in northern Italy (but ignoring the sufferings of Wuhan), Agamben pronounced the government's attempts to halt it an illegitimate use of emergency powers. Giorgio Agamben, "The State of Exception Provoked by an Unmotivated Emergency," *Positions Politics*, 26 February 2020. A few weeks later, unrepentant, he repeated the claim, adding for good measure that his fellow Italians now seemed to care for nothing but mere survival, "bare life," regardless of how spiritually or emotionally impoverished that left them. Agamben, "Clarifications," *An und für sich*, 17 March 2020, https://itself .blog/2020/03/17/giorgio-agamben-clarifications/.
9. Naomi Klein, *The Shock Doctrine: The Rise of Disaster Capitalism* (New York 2007).
10. Laylon Wayne Jordan, "The American Image of Mussolini: Public Opinion and the Press in Italian–American Relations, 1922–1930," MA Thesis, College of William and Mary (1967) 56, 111, 153, 228, doi:10.21220/s2-nz0k-v883; Charles F. Delzell, "Remembering Mussolini," *Wilson Quarterly*, 12, 2 (1988) 124.
11. Nicolas Berggruen and Nathan Gardels, *Intelligent Governance for the Twenty-First Century: A Middle Way between West and East* (Cambridge 2013) 44.
12. Andrej Zwitter, "The Rule of Law in Times of Crisis," *Archiv für Rechts- und Sozialphilosophie*, 98, 1 (2012) 100.
13. Mark Scott, "Chinese Diplomacy Ramps Up Social Media Offensive in COVID-19 Info War," *Politico*, 29 April 2020.

14. The State Council Information Office of the People's Republic of China, "Fighting Covid-19: China in Action," June 2020, III, 4, http://english.www.gov.cn/news/top news/202006/07/content_WS5edc559ac6d066592a449030.html.
15. Mohammed Alsherebi, "Saudi Arabia's Clear Response to the Coronavirus Outbreak Is in Stark Contrast to the West," *Euronews*, 3 April 2020.
16. "Democracies Contain Epidemics Most Effectively," *Economist*, 6 June 2020.
17. Nicholas Kristof, "What the Pandemic Reveals about the Male Ego," *New York Times*, 13 June 2020.
18. Hilary Brueck, et al., "China Took at Least 12 Strict Measures to Control the Coronavirus. They Could Work for the US, but Would Likely Be Impossible to Implement," *Business Insider*, 24 March 2020.
19. Ishaan Tharoor, "Trump Aligns with the World's 'Ostrich' Leaders," *Washington Post*, 19 April 2020; "Jair Bolsonaro Isolates Himself, in the Wrong Way," *Economist*, 11 April 2020.
20. Aimee Ortiz, "Iceland's 'Test Everyone' Goal Has Skeptics, but It May Be Working," *New York Times*, 9 April 2020.
21. Griff Witte, "South Dakota's Governor Resisted Ordering People to Stay Home. Now It Has One of the Nation's Largest Coronavirus Hot Spots," *Washington Post*, 13 April 2020.
22. Friedrich Alexander Simon, Jr., *Die indische Brechruhr oder Cholera morbus* (Hamburg 1831) vii; Karl Julius Le Viseur, *Praktische Mittheilungen zur Diagnose, Prognose und Cur der epidemischen Cholera, nach eigenen Beobachtungen* (Bromberg 1832) iii.
23. Avinash Dixit, "R_0 for Covid-19 Research: An Early Estimate and Policy Implications," www.princeton.edu/~dixitak/home/R0ForCovidRes.pdf?fbclid=IwAR1cBP2HB66Btnfy WUgwlBQRd1dZGis2OOhJDk9qWIe0sS9G4LEgANaYD2Q.
24. Michael A. Johansson, et al.,"Preprints: An Underutilized Mechanism to Accelerate Outbreak Science," *PLoS Medicine*, 15, 4 (2018).
25. ArXiv.org; Matthew Hutson, "Boycott Highlights AI's Publishing Rebellion," *Science*, 360, 6390 (18 May 2018) 699.
26. "Scientific Research on the Coronavirus Is Being Released in a Torrent," *Economist*, 7 May 2020.
27. For example, at www.gisaid.org/epiflu-applications/phylodynamics/.
28. www.biorxiv.org; www.medrxiv.org.
29. Roni Caryn Rabin and Ellen Gabler, "Two Huge Covid-19 Studies Are Retracted after Scientists Sound Alarms," *New York Times*, 4 June 2020; Michael Hiltzik, "How a Retracted Research Paper Contaminated Global Coronavirus Research," *Los Angeles Times*, 8 June 2020; "Speeding Up Science during the Pandemic," *Economist*, 9 May 2020.
30. Diana Kwon, "How Swamped Preprint Servers Are Blocking Bad Coronavirus Research," *Nature*, 7 May 2020; Kelsey Lane Warmbrod, et al., "In Response: Yan et al Preprint Examinations of the Origin of SARS-CoV-2," *The Johns Hopkins Center for Health Security*, 20 September 2020.
31. Michael B. Eisen and Robert Tibshirani, "How to Identify Flawed Research Before It Becomes Dangerous," *New York Times*, 20 July 2020.
32. N. Howard-Jones, "Gelsenkirchen Typhoid Epidemic of 1901, Robert Koch, and the Dead Hand of Max von Pettenkofer," *British Medical Journal*, 1 (1973) 103.
33. Peter Baldwin, *Disease and Democracy: The Industrialized World Faces AIDS* (Berkeley 2005) 20–23.
34. Gayle S. Rubin, "Elegy for the Valley of the Kings: AIDS and the Leather Community in San Francisco, 1981–1996," in Martin P. Levine, et al., eds., *In Changing Times: Gay Men and Lesbians Encounter HIV/AIDS* (Chicago 1997) 110–11.
35. Samanth Subramanian, "In Europe, They're Burning Witches Again," *Politico*, 18 May 2020.
36. Hiren Mansukhani, "With Turmeric Milk and Sanitiser Dispensers, Indian Businesses Are Trying to Cash in on Covid-19," *Quartz India*, 14 June 2020. Chinese manufacturers

of traditional medicines hawked their products abroad as immune boosting: Zheng Yiran and Wu Yong, "Herbal Remedies Growing in Popularity Globally," *China Daily*, 23 April 2020.

37. "Give Your Immune System a Boost Now," Vivamayr brochure, printed after March 2020.

38. "Desperate Iranians Are Getting Bad Medical Advice," *Economist*, 18 April 2020; "Some African Politicians Risk Spreading Covid through Quackery," *Economist*, 30 April 2020.

39. Elyse Samuels and Meg Kelly, "How False Hope Spread about Hydroxychloroquine to Treat Covid-19 – and the Consequences That Followed," *Washington Post*, 13 April 2020.

40. Pascal Riché, "Qui est Didier Raoult, le médecin qui veut imposer la chloroquine pour combattre le Covid-19?," *L'Obs*, 23 March 2020; Lara Marlowe, "Coronavirus: France Hoping Unorthodox Virologist Can Save World," *Irish Times*, 23 March 2020.

41. Ben Dooley, "This Drug May Cause Birth Defects. Japan's Pushing It for Coronavirus," *New York Times*, 5 May 2020; Rocky Swift, "After Early Hype, Japan's Homegrown COVID-19 Drug Hope Avigan Faces Rocky Future," *Reuters*, 28 July 2020.

42. John Cook, et al., "Coronavirus, 'Plandemic' and the Seven Traits of Conspiratorial Thinking," *The Conversation*, 15 May 2020; Katie Shepherd, "Who Is Judy Mikovits in 'Plandemic,' The Coronavirus Conspiracy Video Just Banned from Social Media?," *Washington Post*, 8 May 2020.

43. Sarah Mitroff, "11 Coronavirus Health Myths, Fact Checked," *C-Net*, 29 June 2020.

44. "Sun-Shy Indonesians Are Suddenly Soaking Up the Rays," *Economist*, 9 May 2020.

45. Maria Silvia Trigo, et al., "With Officials' Backing, Dubious Virus Remedies Surge in Latin America," *New York Times*, 23 July 2020; "Patient, Don't Heal Thyself," *Economist*, 3 October 2020.

46. Tom Collins, "Tanzania Risks Pariah Status in Covid-19 Response," *African Business*, 27 May 2020.

47. David Pilling, "'The Pandemic Is Gaining Momentum': Africa Prepares for Surge in Infections," *Financial Times*, 19 July 2020; "Impenetrable Doa: Health Minister Says Prayer, Not Face Masks, Is Why Indonesia Remains Coronavirus-Free," *MSN*, 17 February 2020.

48. Dasl Yoon and Timothy W. Martin "Why a South Korean Church Was the Perfect Petri Dish for Coronavirus," *Wall Street Journal*, 2 March 2020.

49. Elizabeth Williamson, "Falwell Focuses on Critics as Coronavirus Cases Near His University Grow," *New York Times*, 16 April 2020.

50. Matthew Ormseth, "Defying State Coronavirus Order, a Thousand Pastors Plan to Hold In-Person Services for Pentecost," *Los Angeles Times*, 20 May 2020.

51. Alexandra Meeks, "With a Worsening Pandemic, California Bans Singing in Places of Worship," *CNN*, 3 July 2020; Kate Conger, et al., "Churches Were Eager to Reopen. Now They Are a Major Source of Coronavirus Cases," *New York Times*, 8 July 2020.

52. Sharon LaFraniere, et al., "Trump Pressed for Plasma Therapy. Officials Worry, Is an Unvetted Vaccine Next?," *New York Times*, 11 September 2020; Dan Diamond, "Trump Officials Interfered with CDC Reports on Covid-19," *Politico*, 11 September 2020.

53. www.gov.uk/government/organisations/scientific-advisory-group-for-emergencies.

54. www.independentsage.org.

55. Christina Gallardo, "UK Scientists Split over Coronavirus Advice to Government," *Politico*, 5 May 2020.

56. "Swedish Ministers Defend Resisting Coronavirus Lockdown," *Financial Times*, 16 April 2020; Göran Eriksson, "Folkhälsonationalism ligger bakom det Svenska undantaget," *Dagens Nyheter*, 28 March 2020; Göran Eriksson, et al., "'Förbered er på det värsta' – spelet bakom coronastrategin," *Svenska Dagbladet*, 4 July 2020.

57. Maud Cordenius, "I Live in Sweden: I'm Not Panicking," *New York Times*, 15 May 2020; Clas Svahn, "Johan Carlson: Smittan kom in från länder som gick under vår radar,"

Dagens Nyheter, 10 June 2020; Johan Norberg, "Coronavirus: L'étonnante politique de la Suède," *Contrepoints*, 28 April 2020.

58. Katarina Lagerwall and Clas Svahn, "Förra statsepidemiologen: 'Långsam spridning kan bygga upp immunitet,'" *Dagens Nyheter*, 14 March 2020; Lasse Skou Andersen, et al., "Mens Danmark lukker ned, fortsætter hverdagen i Sverige: Hvorfor reagerer de to lande så forskelligt?," *Information*, 14 March 2020.

59. Twenty-two medical experts wrote an article demanding that the politicians take back the decision-making from the experts and impose lockdown. "Folkhälsomyndigheten har misslyckats – nu måste politikerna gripa in," *Dagens Nyheter*, 14 April 2020; "Flockimmunitet är en farlig och orealistisk coronastrategi," *Dagens Nyheter*, 14 May 2020.

60. Though whether that holds for the European Central Bank any longer has been questioned during the coronavirus epidemic. Adam Tooze, "The Death of the Central Bank Myth," *Foreign Policy*, 13 May 2020.

61. Helmut Heiber, *The Weimar Republic* (Oxford 1993) ch. 9.

62. James Mackenzie and Barry Moody, "Italy Gets New Technocrat Government," *Reuters*, 16 November 2011; Jonathan Hopkin, "Technocrats Have Taken Over Governments in Southern Europe: This Is a Challenge to Democracy," LSE, *European Politics and Policy*.

63. John Johnson, "Thérèse Coffey Says Ministers Will Have Made Coronavirus Mistakes 'If Advice Was Wrong' from Scientists," *Politics at Home*, 19 May 2020.

64. Mark Landler and Stephen Castle, "For Boris Johnson's Science Advisers, Pressure, Anxieties and 'Pastoral Support,'" *New York Times*, 26 June 2020; David D. Kirkpatrick, et al., "Europe Said It Was Pandemic Ready. Pride Was Its Downfall," *New York Times*, 20 July 2020.

65. Dennis Campbell and Peter Walker, "Ministers Shifting Blame to Public Health England for Covid-19 Errors, Say Experts," *Guardian*, 1 July 2020; Christopher Hope, "Hancock Axes 'Failing' Public Health England," *Telegraph*, 15 August 2020.

66. Ben Hall, "Sweden Launches Inquiry into Coronavirus Handling," *Financial Times*, 30 June 2020; Jean-Baptiste Jacquin, et al., "L'exécutif face à la menace de suites judiciaires," *Le Monde*, 25 March 2020; Lydia Wålsten, "Utkräv ansvar innan corona-kommissionen 2022," *Svenska Dagbladet*, 27 June 2020.

67. Alberto García-Basteiro, et al., "The Need for an Independent Evaluation of the COVID-19 Response in Spain," *Lancet*, 6 August 2020; Martin McKee, et al., "Public Inquiry into UK's Response to Covid-19," *British Medical Journal*, 22 May 2020; George Parker, et al., "Inside Westminster's Coronavirus Blame Game," *Financial Times*, 15 July 2020.

68. Emilio Casalicchio, "UK Civil Service Braces for Coronavirus Inquiry," *Politico*, 7 August 2020.

69. Chris Stokel-Walker, "Cummings Tried to Rewrite History: The Internet Had Other Ideas," *Wired*, 27 May 2020.

70. Jeppe Findalen, "Mail afslører: Brostrøm advarede om skadelige konsekvenser ved at lukke Danmark," *Extra Bladet*, 25 May 2020.

71. Jakob Sorgenfri Kjær and Lars Igum Rasmussen, "Tidslinje: Epidemiens hektiske første dage," *Politiken*, 29 May 2020; Peter Pagh-Schlegel. "Søren Brostrøm om grænselukning: Det er en politisk beslutning," *Altinget*, 14 March 2020.

72. Jakob Sorgenfri Kjær, et al., "Mette Frederiksen var uenig med Søren Brostrøm og tog magten fra ham," *Politiken*, 29 May 2020.

73. "Mette Frederiksens tale ved pressemøde om coronavirus 2020 (transskription)," *Danske Taler*, www.regeringen.dk/nyheder/2020/statsminister-mette-frederiksens-indledning-paa-pressemoede-i-statsministeriet-om-corona-virus-den-11-marts-2020/.

74. "Her er de otte hovedpunkter i den hastelov, regeringen vil have vedtaget i dag," *Politiken*, 12 March 2020; Sofie Bak Thorup, "Ny hastelov giver mulighed for at tvangs-behandle: Lægeforeningen bakker op," *Politiken*, 12 March 2020.

75. Stephen Grey and Andrew MacAskill, "Special Report: Johnson Listened to His Scientists about Coronavirus – But They Were Slow to Sound the Alarm," *Reuters*, 7 April 2020.

76. "UK PM Johnson Warns Public to Prepare to Lose Loved Ones to Coronavirus," *ABC Mundial*, 12 March 2020.

77. George Parker, et al., "UK's Chief Scientific Adviser Defends 'Herd Immunity' Strategy for Coronavirus," *Financial Times*, 13 March 2020. A good overview of the government's muddling is presented in Ed Yong, "The U.K.'s Coronavirus 'Herd Immunity' Debacle," *Atlantic*, 16 March 2020.

78. "Public Request to Take Stronger Measures of Social Distancing across the UK with Immediate Effect," 14 March 2020, http://maths.qmul.ac.uk/~vnicosia/UK_scientists_statement_on_coronavirus_measures.pdf.

79. Heather Stewart, et al., "Johnson: Many More People Will Lose Loved Ones to Coronavirus," *Guardian*, 12 March 2020.

80. "Fifteenth SAGE Meeting on Wuhan Coronavirus (Covid-19)," 13 March 2020, https://assets.publishing.service.gov.uk/government/uploads/system/uploads/attachment_data/file/888783/S0383_Fifteenth_SAGE_meeting_on_Wuhan_Coronavirus__Covid-19__.pdf. Ferguson's own work on the 1918 epidemic also suggested that too firm a suppression of the initial wave might have left some US cities more exposed to a second bout of infection. Martin C. J. Bootsma and Neil M. Ferguson, "The Effect of Public Health Measures on the 1918 Influenza Pandemic in U.S. Cities," *Proceedings of the National Academy of Sciences*, 1 May 2007.

81. Imperial College COVID-19 Response Team, "Report 9: Impact of Non-pharmaceutical Interventions (NPIs) to Reduce COVID-19 Mortality and Healthcare Demand," 16 March 2020, www.imperial.ac.uk/media/imperial-college/medicine/sph/ide/gida-fellowships/Imperial-College-COVID19-NPI-modelling-16-03-2020.pdf.

82. Chloé Hecketsweiler and Cédric Pietralunga, "Les simulations alarmantes des épidémiologistes pour la France," *Le Monde*, 15 March 2020.

83. "Macron Threatens UK Entry Ban in Lieu of More Stringent Measures," *Euractiv*, 22 March 2020.

84. Christina Gallardo, "Herd Immunity Was Never UK's Corona Strategy, Chief Scientific Adviser Says," *Politico*, 5 May 2020; Anya van Wagtendonk, "The UK Backs Away from 'Herd Immunity' Coronavirus Proposal amid Blowback," *VOX*, 15 March 2020.

85. Cabinet Office, "Staying at Home and Away from Others (Social Distancing)," 23 March 2020, www.gov.uk/government/publications/full-guidance-on-staying-at-home-and-away-from-others/full-guidance-on-staying-at-home-and-away-from-others.

86. Mark Landler and Stephen Castle, "Behind the Virus Report That Jarred the U.S. and the U.K. to Action," *New York Times*, 17 March 2020; Nick Paton Walsh, "US, UK Coronavirus Strategies Shifted Following UK Epidemiologists' Ominous Report," *CNN*, 17 March 2020; William Booth, "A Chilling Scientific Paper Helped Upend U.S. and U.K. Coronavirus Strategies," *Washington Post*, 17 March 2020.

87. *PanCAP Adapted US Government COVID-19 Response Plan*, 13 March 2020, https://int.nyt.com/data/documenthelper/6819-covid-19-response-plan/d367f758bec47cad361f/optimized/full.pdf#page=1.

88. "Seruminstitut nedtonede alvor få dage inden nedlukning: Coronavirus var blot en 'alvorlig influenza,'" *Berlingske*, 3 June 2020.

89. "Swedish Ministers Defend Resisting Coronavirus Lockdown," *Financial Times*, 16 April 2020.

90. Hannah Roberts, "Italian Government Defied Scientists to Impose Strict Coronavirus Lockdown," *Politico*, 6 August 2020.

91. "Iran Lifts Tehran's Lockdown, Despite Warnings from Health Officials," *New York Times*, 18 April 2020.

92. Meryl Kornfield, "Florida County's Medical Examiner Begged Officials to Close Beaches, Internal Emails Reveal," *Washington Post*, 3 May 2020.
93. "Coronavirus: Risk in UK Lockdown Easing Too Soon, Warn Scientists," *BBC News*, 30 May 2020.
94. Oliver Wright, et al., "Priti Patel Stands by Coronavirus Quarantine Plan Despite Conservative Rebellion," *Times* (London), 3 June 2020.
95. Uwe Parpart, "Global Virus Lockdown Was 'Madness,'" *Asia Times*, 4 May 2020.
96. David Leonhardt and Lauren Leatherby, "Where the Virus Is Growing Most: Countries With 'Illiberal Populist' Leaders," *New York Times*, 2 June 2020.
97. www.worldometers.info/coronavirus/. Not counting San Marino or Andorra as independent states in epidemiological terms.
98. Jihan Abdalla, "What Is Next for Brazil in Its Coronavirus Fight?," *Aljazeera*, 2 June 2020.
99. Chloé Hecketsweiler, et al., "Coronavirus: Comment Emmanuel Macron s'appuie sur les experts pour gouverner en temps de crise sanitaire," *Le Monde*, 26 March 2020.
100. Robert Mackey, "Trump's Ridiculous Behavior at Pandemic Briefings Baffles a Watching World," *Intercept*, 10 April 2020.
101. John Falkirk, "Sverigebilden förändras – mest intresse för Tegnell," *Svenska Dagbladet*, 12 May 2020.
102. Richard Orange, "Will Sweden's Herd Immunity Experiment Pay Off?," *Prospect*, 1 May 2020.
103. Lars Calmfors, "Partierna går i samma fälla som när de tystnade i invandringsdebatten," *Dagens Nyheter*, 5 May 2020.
104. "Tegnell-hajpen: Ett tecken på svenskars tillit till makten," *SVT Nyheter*, 27 April 2020.
105. John Falkirk, "7 av 10 har förtroende för Tegnell i undersökning," *Svenska Dagbladet*, 2 May 2020.
106. Jens Liljestrand, "Anders Tegnell är den svenska nationalsjälen förkroppsligad," *Expressen*, 15 April 2020.
107. "As Pandemic Wrecks Budgets, States Cut and Borrow to Balance Books," *New York Times*, 14 May 2020.
108. Lawrence K. Altman, "Public Health Fears Cause New York Officials to Detain Foreign Tourist," *New York Times*, 28 April 2009; P. Shenon, "US Approves Force in Detaining Possible SARS Carriers," *New York Times*, 7 May 2003; N. Kristof, "Civil Liberties? If They're Really Sick, Lock 'Em Up," *International Herald Tribune*, 3–4 May 2004.
109. Ronald Bayer and Cheryl Healton, "Controlling AIDS in Cuba," *New England Journal of Medicine*, 320, 15 (1989) 1022–3; Olga Mesa Castillo, et al., "La législation cubaine face au SIDA," in Jacques Foyer and Lucette Khaïat, eds., *Droit et Sida: Comparaison internationale* (Paris 1994) 133–5; Jennifer L. Manlowe, "Gender, Freedom and Safety: Does the US Have Anything to Learn from Cuban AIDS Policy?," in Nancy Goldstein and Jennifer L. Manlowe, eds., *The Gender Politics of HIV/AIDS in Women* (New York 1997) 385–99; Paul Farmer, *The Uses of Haiti* (Monroe 1994) 264–66, 286–87; Marvin Leiner, *Sexual Politics in Cuba: Machismo, Homosexuality, and AIDS* (Boulder 1994) ch. 5.
110. *International Digest of Health Legislation*, 40, 4 (1989) 830; 46, 3 (1995) 316–17.
111. WHO, *Legislative Responses to AIDS* (Dordrecht 1989) 38, 97, 103, 191, 194; Jean-Pierre Cabestan, "SIDA et droit en Chine populaire," in Foyer and Khaïat, *Droit et Sida*, 100; S. S. Fluss and D. K. Latto, "The Coercive Element in Legislation for the Control of AIDS and HIV Infection: Some Recent Developments," *AIDS and Public Policy Journal*, 2, 3 (1987) 15; Christopher Williams, *AIDS in Post-communist Russia and Its Succsssor States* (Aldershot 1995) 59, 73–4, 160–1; *International Digest of Health Legislation*, 38, 4 (1987) 769–71; 41, 3 (1990) 431–32; 42, 1 (1991) 21–25.
112. Baldwin, *Disease and Democracy*, ch. 7.

113. Rowena Mason, "Boris Johnson Boasted of Shaking Hands on Day Sage Warned Not To," *Guardian*, 5 May 2020.

2 NEW DOGS, OLD TRICKS

1. Deuteronomy 23:12–13.
2. Leviticus 13: 1–59; Numbers 5:1–3.
3. Leviticus 15:1–33.
4. Gerhard F. Hasel, "Health and Healing in the Old Testament," *Andrews University Seminary Studies*, 21, 3 (1983) 196; E. W. G. Masterman, "Hygiene and Disease in Palestine in Modern and in Biblical Times," *Palestine Exploration Quarterly*, 50, 4 (1918) 158.
5. Mike Davis, *The Monster at Our Door: The Global Threat of Avian Flu* (New York 2005) 77–79.
6. Roweena Mason, "Boris Johnson Leaves Hospital as He Continues Recovery from Coronavirus," *Guardian*, 12 April 2020.
7. Eugene Scott, "Trump's Fearlessness of Coronavirus Is Powered by the Type of Health Care Only He Gets," *Washington Post*, 6 October 2020.
8. Natalie B. Compton, "People Are Wearing Hazmat Suits on Planes. But Should They?," *Washington Post*, 25 May 2020.
9. www.vyzrtech.com/products/bio-vyzr. See also https://microclimate.com/.
10. John Snow, "Further Remarks on the Mode of Communication of Cholera; Including Some Comments on the Recent Reports on Cholera by the General Board of Health," *Medical Times and Gazette*, 11 (1855) 84.
11. James F. Johnston, *The Chemistry of Common Life*, 10th ed. (New York NY 1863) ii, 266, quoted in Andrew Gordon, "Historical Context for COVID 19 Policies in Japan and Asia (1)," *Tokyo College*, 5 July 2020, https://www.tc.u-tokyo.ac.jp/en/weblog/1896/.
12. Peter Baldwin, "Can There Be a Democratic Public Health? Fighting AIDS in the Industrialized World," in Susan Gross Solomon, et al., eds., *Shifting Boundaries of Public Health: Europe in the Twentieth Century* (Rochester 2008) 36–38.
13. Robyn Dixon, "In a Siberian Village, the Lockdown Is Extreme. Trenches Have Sealed It Off," *Washington Post*, 17 July 2020.
14. "Jair Bolsonaro Isolates Himself, in the Wrong Way," *Economist*, 11 April 2020. That was also the recommendation of Johan Giesecke, senior Swedish epidemiologist. Freddie Sayers, "Swedish Expert: Why Lockdowns Are the Wrong Policy," *UnHerd*, 17 April 2020.
15. "What Turkey Got Right about the Pandemic," *Economist*, 4 June 2020.
16. Republic of Panama, Ministry of Health, "COMUNICADO No. 35 Gobierno Nacional aplica nuevas reglas de movilidad para disminuir contagios por COVID-19," www.minsa.gob.pa/noticia/comunicado-no35-gobierno-nacional-aplica-nuevas-reglas-de-movilidad-para-disminuir-contagios.
17. Solène Cordier, "Les parents séparés peuvent continuer à organiser l'alternance de la garde des enfants," *Le Monde*, 17 March 2020.
18. " Cargo Ship Crews Are Stuck at Sea," *Economist*, 20 June 2020.
19. Erin McCormick and Patrick Greenfield, "Revealed: 100,000 Crew Never Made It off Cruise Ships amid Coronavirus Crisis," *Guardian*, 30 April 2020.
20. Michael T. Osterholm and Neel Kashkari, "Here's How to Crush the Virus until Vaccines Arrive," *New York Times*, 7 August 2020.
21. Miriam Jordan, "Farmworkers, Mostly Undocumented, Become 'Essential' during Pandemic," *New York Times*, 2 April 2020.

22. Peter Ganong, et al., "US Unemployment Insurance Replacement Rates during the Pandemic," Becker Friedman Institute, University of Chicago, Working Paper 2020–62, May 2020.

23. "How Post-Brexit Immigration Rules Will Exclude Key Workers," *Economist*, 16 May 2020.

24. Ofcom, *Online Nation: 2020 Summary Report*, 6, www.ofcom.org.uk/__data/assets/pdf_file/0028/196408/online-nation-2020-summary.pdf.

25. Jean-Marc Vittori, "France and the Art of Getting Back to Work," *Globalist*, 24 June 2020.

26. Supreme Court of Norway, "Remote Hearings in the Supreme Court," www.domstol.no/en/Enkelt-domstol/supremecourt/arkiv/2020/remote-hearings-in-the-supreme-court/.

27. Eugen Weber, *Peasants into Frenchmen: The Modernization of Rural France, 1870–1914* (Stanford 1976) is the classic study.

28. Peter Baldwin, *Contagion and the State in Europe, 1830–1930* (Cambridge 1999) ch. 4.

29. Evelyn Waugh, *Remote People* (London 1985) 167.

30. Gesetz zur Neuordnung seuchenrechtlicher Vorschriften, 20 July 2000, §20(6).

31. Bernal Díaz, *The Conquest of New Spain*, trans. J. M. Cohen (London 1963) 233.

32. Peter N. Stearns, *Battleground of Desire: The Struggle for Self-Control in Modern America* (New York NY 1999) 14

33. Katie Engelhart, "The Powerful History of Potty Training," *Atlantic*, 20 June 2014.

34. Stephanie Juliano, "Superheroes, Bandits, and Cyber-nerds: Exploring the History and Contemporary Development of the Vigilante," *Journal of International Commercial Law and Technology*, 7, 1 (2012) 58.

35. Allan Mitchell, *The Divided Path: The German Influence on Social Reform in France after 1870* (Chapel Hill 1991) 270–71; Allan Mitchell, "Obsessive Questions and Faint Answers: The French Response to Tuberculosis in the Belle Epoque," *Bulletin of the History of Medicine*, 62, 2 (1988) 223–25.

36. John M. Barry, *The Great Influenza: The Story of the Deadliest Pandemic in History* (London 2005) 221; Nancy K. Bristow, *American Pandemic: The Lost Worlds of the 1918 Influenza Epidemic* (New York 2012) 107.

37. Ross Coomber, et al., "Public Spitting in 'Developing' Nations of the Global South: Harmless Embedded Practice or Disgusting, Harmful and Deviant?," in Kerry Carrington, et al., eds., *The Palgrave Handbook of Criminology and the Global South* (Cham 2018) 509–10.

38. Bérangère Barret, "La ville de Marcq-en-Barœul interdit de cracher et de jeter gants et masques dans la rue," *La Voix du Nord*, 6 April 2020.

39. Samuel K. Cohn Jr., *Epidemics: Hate and Compassion from the Plague of Athens to AIDS* (Oxford 2018) 435.

40. Rae Ellen Bichel, "The Plague Is Back, This Time in New Mexico," *NPR*, 29 June 2017; Frank M. Snowden, *Epidemics and Society: From the Black Death to the Present* (New Haven 2019) 39.

41. Two of the best studies: Mariana Valverde, *Diseases of the Will: Alcohol and the Dilemmas of Freedom* (Cambridge 1998); Allan M. Brandt, *The Cigarette Century: The Rise, Fall, and Deadly Persistence of the Product That Defined America* (New York 2007) pt. 4.

42. Laura Reiley, "Latin America's War on Obesity Could Be a Model for U.S.," *Washington Post*, 16 July 2019; Lawrence O. Gostin, et al., "The Legal Determinants of Health: Harnessing the Power of Law for Global Health and Sustainable Development," *Lancet*, 4 May 2019, 1888.

43. Phillippa Lally and Benjamin Gardner, "Promoting Habit Formation," *Health Psychology Review*, 7, suppl. 1 (2013).

44. João Mauricio Castaldelli-Maia, et al., "Tobacco Smoking: From 'Glamour' to 'Stigma': A Comprehensive Review," *Psychiatry and Clinical Neurosciences*, 70 (2016);

Nadira Mallick, et al., "Eating Behaviours and Body Weight Concerns among Adolescent Girls," *Advances in Public Health* (2014).

45. Uri Gneezy, et al., "When and Why Incentives (Don't) Work to Modify Behavior," *Journal of Economic Perspectives*, 2, 4 (2011) 192.

46. Baldwin, *Contagion and the State*, 408–13; Roger Davidson, *Dangerous Liaisons: A Social History of Venereal Disease in Twentieth-Century Scotland* (Amsterdam 2000) 8.

47. L. Duncan Bulkley, *Syphilis in the Innocent* (New York 1894) 143.

48. Charles J. Macalister, *Inaugural Address on the Dangers of the Venereal Diseases* (Edinburgh 1914) 31; Gustave Metzger and Charles Muller, *La coupe de communion et les maladies contagieuses*, 2nd ed. (Geneva 1905) 13–14; *Betænkning angående Forandringer i Reglerne for Uddelingen af Nadverens Sakramente, afgiven af den af Ministeriet for Kirke- og Undervisningsvæsenet den 18. September 1903 nedsatte Kommission* (Copenhagen 1904).

49. House of Commons, 1986–87, Social Services Committee, *Problems Associated with AIDS* (13 May 1987) iii, 337; Margaret Brazier and Maureen Mulholland, "Droit et Sida: Le Royaume-uni," in Jacques Foyer and Lucette Khaïat, eds., *Droit et Sida: Comparaison internationale* (Paris 1994) 364.

50. A. Ravogli, *Syphilis in Its Medical, Medico-Legal, and Sociological Aspects* (New York 1907) 441; *La prophylaxie antivénérienne*, 1, 1 (1929) 589–93; Elizabeth Fee, "Sin versus Science: Venereal Disease in Twentieth-Century Baltimore," in Elizabeth Fee and Daniel M. Fox, eds., *AIDS: The Burdens of History* (Berkeley 1988) 122; Abram S. Benenson, ed., *Control of Communicable Diseases in Man*, 15th ed. (Washington DC 1990) 426.

51. Gunther E. Rothenberg, "The Austrian Sanitary Cordon and the Control of the Bubonic Plague: 1710–1871," *Journal of the History of Medicine*, 28, 1 (1973).

52. Jason S. Jia, et al., "Population Flow Drives Spatio-temporal Distribution of COVID-19 in China," *Nature*, 582 (29 April 2020).

53. *PanCAP Adapted US Government COVID-19 Response Plan*, 13 March 2020, https://int .nyt.com/data/documenthelper/6819-covid-19-response-plan/d367f758bec47 cad361f/optimized/full.pdf#page=1.

54. Nsikan Akpan, "How to Measure Your Nation's Response to Coronavirus," *National Geographic*, 1 May 2020.

55. Hilary Brueck, et al., "China Took at Least 12 Strict Measures to Control the Coronavirus: They Could Work for the US, but Would Likely Be Impossible to Implement," *Business Insider*, 24 March 2020; "Jilin Railway Station Closed amid Local COVID-19 Outbreak," *Jilin China*, 13 May 2020.

56. "Governor Cuomo, Governor Murphy and Governor Lamont Announce Joint Incoming Travel Advisory That All Individuals Traveling from States with Significant Community Spread of COVID-19 Quarantine for 14 Days," 24 June 2020, www.gov ernor.ny.gov/news/governor-cuomo-governor-murphy-and-governor-lamont-announ ce-joint-incoming-travel-advisory-all.

57. Bill Chappell, "N.Y., N.J., Connecticut Now Say Travelers from 31 Hot Spot States Must Quarantine," *NPR*, 21 July 2020.

58. Melanie Kaidan, "Merkel Panic: Germany's Strict New Lockdown Measures amid Coronavirus Second Wave," *Express*, 29 June 2020; "Australia's Internal Travel Restrictions Are Tested in Court," *Economist*, 8 August 2020.

59. Baldwin, *Contagion and the State*, 140, 207, 228–36.

60. "Saudi Arabia Bans Prayers at Mosques over Coronavirus Fears," *Aljazeera*, 20 March 2020; Martin Chulov, "Saudi Arabia Closes Two Holiest Shrines to Foreigners as Coronavirus Fears Grow," *Guardian*, 27 February 2020.

61. "Saudi Arabia to Hold 'Very Limited' Hajj Due to Coronavirus," *Aljazeera*, 22 June 2020.

62. Philippe Gautret, et al., "The 2020 Grand Magal of Touba, Senegal in the Time of the COVID-19 Pandemic," *Travel Medicine and Infectious Disease*, 17 September 2020.

63. Monica Jha, "Eyes in the Sky," *Rest of World*, 23 June 2020.
64. Liam Stack, "2,500 Mourners Jam a Hasidic Funeral, Creating a Flash Point for de Blasio," *New York Times*, 29 April 2020; Oren Liebermann, "Some Ultra-orthodox Jews Are Ignoring Israel's Coronavirus Rules, Despite a Warning to 'Wake Up!,'" *CNN*, 31 March 2020; Lahav Harkov, "Belgian Jews Concerned about Large Haredi Population and Coronavirus," *Jerusalem Post*, 6 April 2020.
65. Mehul Srivastava, "Israel in a 'Dangerous Place' as Virus Infections Surge," *Financial Times*, 7 July 2020.
66. Daniel Burke, "Police Arrest Florida Pastor for Holding Church Services Despite Stay-at -Home Order," *CNN*, 31 March 2020.
67. Tim Waytt, "Coronavirus: More than 100,000 Defy Lockdown and Gather for Funeral in Bangladesh," *Independent*, 20 April 2020.
68. "Churches Turn to the Internet to Reach Their Flocks," *Economist*, 11 April 2020.
69. The Health Protection (Coronavirus, Restrictions) (England) Regulations 2020, 5(6), www.legislation.gov.uk/uksi/2020/350#commentary-c24044061.
70. "The Coronavirus Pandemic Has Exposed Fissures within Religions," *Economist*, 11 April 2020.
71. Alan Cross, "What Churches Really Think about Opening Up," *New York Times*, 14 May 2020.
72. Abdur Rahman Alfa Shaban, "Rwanda COVID-19: Places of Worship Reopen amid Targeted Lockdowns," *Africa News*, 16 July 2020.
73. Javier C. Hernández and Su-Hyun Lee, "No More Jenga, No More 'Amen' as Cities Learn to Live with Coronavirus," *New York Times*, 2 May 2020.
74. Joshua J. McElwee, "Vatican Makes Clear: General Absolution Allowed during Coronavirus Contagion," *National Catholic Reporter*, 20 March 2020.
75. Baldwin, *Contagion and the State*, 51.
76. Michael Stolberg, *Die Cholera im Großherzogtum Toskana* (Landsberg 1995) 27.
77. Ron Synovitz, "Coronavirus vs. the Church: Orthodox Traditionalists Stand behind the Holy Spoon," *Radio Free Europe*, 17 March 2020.
78. Alice Su, "Woman Who Flew from U.S. to China for Coronavirus Test Faces Criminal Charges," *Los Angeles Times*, 18 March 2020.
79. Baldwin, *Contagion and the State*, 41–45.
80. Tara Parker-Pope, "Is the Virus on My Clothes? My Shoes? My Hair? My Newspaper?," *New York Times*, 17 April 2020.
81. Baldwin, *Contagion and the State*, 186, 88.
82. The State Council Information Office of the People's Republic of China, "Fighting Covid-19: China in Action," June 2020, II, 2, http://english.www.gov.cn/news/top news/202006/07/content_WS5edc559ac6d066592a449030.html.
83. Fang Fang, *Wuhan Diary* (New York 2020).
84. "How the Pandemic Has Clogged the Global Economy with Paper Currency," *Blog of JP Konig*, 31 July 2020, http://jpkoning.blogspot.com/2020/07/how-pandemic-has-clogged-global-economy.html.
85. Pete Schroeder and Anna Irrera, "Fed Quarantines U.S. Dollars Repatriated from Asia on Coronavirus Caution," *Reuters*, 6 March 2020.
86. Shaban, "Rwanda COVID-19: Places of Worship Reopen amid Targeted Lockdowns."
87. "Merkel in Berliner Supermarkt: Die Kanzlerin zahlt mit Karte," *Bild*, 13 May 2020.
88. Baldwin, *Contagion and the State*, 49.
89. Baldwin, *Contagion and the State*, 50–51.
90. Public Health England, "Advice for Home Isolation," 28 February 2020, www.gov.uk/ government/publications/wuhan-novel-coronavirus-self-isolation-for-patients-under going-testing/advice-sheet-home-isolation; "Stay at Home: Guidance for Households with Possible Coronavirus (COVID-19) Infection," 28 April 2020, www.gov.uk/govern

ment/publications/covid-19-stay-at-home-guidance/stay-at-home-guidance-for-house holds-with-possible-coronavirus-covid-19-infection.

91. Gemeinde Möhnesee, Öffentliche Bekanntmachung: Allgemeinverfügung zum Zwecke der Verhütung und Bekämpfung der Übertragung von SARS-CoV-2 (Corona-Virus) – Reiserückkehrer aus Risikogebieten – Anordnung häusliche Quarantäne, 19 March 2020, www.gemeinde-moehnesee.de/oeffentliche-bekanntmachung-allge meinverfuegung-zum-zwecke-der-verhuetung-und-bekaempfung-der-uebertragung-v on-sars-cov-2-corona-virus-reiserueckkehrer-aus-risikogebieten-anordnung-haeus liche-q/.

92. Public Health England, "Stay at Home: What To Do If You or Someone You Share Your Home with Has Signs of Coronavirus," March 2020, www.adur-worthing.gov.uk/ media/Media,156906,smxx.pdf.

93. Robert Koch Institut, "Für Patienten und Angehörige: Häusliche Isolierung bei bestätigter COVID-19-Erkrankung," 24 March 2020, www.main-tauber-kreis.de/Landr atsamt/Themen-und-Projekte/Coronavirus.

94. Friedrich Hempel, *Kurzer Bericht über die öffentlichen und privaten Schutz-Maassregeln, welche in den Jahren 1812–1814 in der Türkei und in Russland gegen Ansteckung durch die Orientalische Pest mit unzweifelhaftem Erfolge angewendet worden sind, in Rücksicht auf die Hemmung der Cholera zum Besten der Hospitäler zu Danzig* (Hamburg 1831) 5.

95. The Health Protection (Coronavirus, Restrictions) (England) Regulations 2020, 5(6), www.legislation.gov.uk/uksi/2020/350#commentary-c24044061.

96. Emmy Griffiths, "Piers Morgan's Son Rejects His Dad's Clever Way They Can See Each Other during Lockdown," *Hello!*, 12 May 2020.

97. Allgemeinverfügung des Landratsamtes Main-Tauber-Kreis über die häusliche Absonderung von Personen, die mit dem neuartigen Corona-Virus (SARS-CoV-2) infiziert sind und deren Kontaktpersonen zur Eindämmung und zum Schutz vor der Verbreitung der Atemwegserkrankung COVID-19 vom 23. März 2020, I 2b-c, www.main -tauber-kreis.de/Landratsamt/Themen-und-Projekte/Coronavirus.

98. Baldwin, *Contagion and the State*, 141, 151–55.

3 THE POLITICS OF PREVENTION

1. Jimmie Åkesson, "Tegnell måste ta ansvar för misstagen och avgå," *Dagens Nyheter*, 6 June 2020. Similar point in Gideon Rachman, "A Very Swedish Sort of Failure," *Financial Times*, 15 June 2020.

2. "Covid-19 in the Netherlands: A Timeline," *Actiegroep Containment Nu*, https://www .containmentnu.nl/articles/timeline?lang=en.

3. Thomas Wieder, et al., "Les mille nuances de gris du confinement à l'européenne," *Le Monde*, 19 March 2020.

4. Paul Hockenos, "Germany Found a Strongman for Its Coronavirus Crisis," *Foreign Policy*, 16 April 2020.

5. Stephen Alexander, "COVID-19 Fatalities in Europe's Care Homes Far Higher Than Official Counts," *World Socialist Web Site*, 1 June 2020.

6. Alfonso Flores Bermúdez and Frances Robles, "Coronavirus: Nicaragua's Midnight Burials Tell of a Hidden Crisis," *Irish Times*, 1 June 2020.

7. Lauren Feiner, "Elon Musk Says Orders to Stay Home Are 'Fascist' in Expletive-Laced Rant during Tesla Earnings Call," *CNBC*, 29 April 2020.

8. Johar Bendjelloul and Jonas Lindvist, "Det är klart att det kan kännas lite skrämmande," *Dagens Nyheter*, 6 April 2020.

9. Alexandra Ossola, "Closing Schools for Covid-19 Hurts Students' Financial Future," *Quartz*, 10 September 2020.

10. By some measures, depression may have tripled. But so far the evidence has not identified a spike in suicide: Catherine K. Ettman, et al., "Prevalence of Depression Symptoms in US Adults before and during the COVID-19 Pandemic," *JAMA Network Open*, 2 September 2020; David Gunnell, et al., "Suicide Risk and Prevention during the COVID-19 Pandemic," *Lancet*, 21 April 2020; Ann John, et al., "The Impact of the COVID-19 Pandemic on Self-Harm and Suicidal Behaviour: Protocol for a Living Systematic Review," *F1000 Research*, 29 July 2020. But three times as many South Africans went hungry as before the pandemic: Chijioke O. Nwosu and Adeola Oyenubi, "Income-related Health Inequalities Associated with COVID-19 in South Africa," NIDS-CRAM Wave 1, 15 July 2020, 3, https://cramsurvey.org/wp-content/up loads/2020/07/Nwosu-Estimating-income-related-health-inequalities-associated-with-COVID-19.pdf.

11. Sandeep Jauhar, "People Have Stopped Going to the Doctor. Most Seem Just Fine," *New York Times*, 22 June 2020. That this is wildly optimistic is suggested in the results of serious studies now emerging: Richard Ro, et al., "Characteristics and Outcomes of Patients Deferred for Transcatheter Aortic Valve Replacement Because of COVID-19," *JAMA Network Open*, 30 September 2020.

12. David L. Schriger, "Learning from the Decrease in US Emergency Department Visits in Response to the Coronavirus Disease 2019 Pandemic," *JAMA Internal Medicine*, 3 August 2020.

13. "India's Lockdown Has Brought Unexpected Benefits," *Economist*, 23 April 2020.

14. Andrew Harding, "South Africa Coronavirus Lockdown: Is the Alcohol Ban Working?," *BBC*, 22 April 2020.

15. Tom Schuba, et al., "18 Murders in 24 hours: Inside the Most Violent Day in 60 Years in Chicago," *Chicago Sun Times*, 8 June 2020.

16. Ashley Southall and Neil MacFarquhar, "Gun Violence Spikes in N.Y.C., Intensifying Debate over Policing," *New York Times*, 23 June 2020.

17. "Fears That America Is Experiencing a Serious Crime Wave Are Overblown," *Economist*, 1 August 2020.

18. "The Pandemic Is Creating Fresh Opportunities for Organised Crime," *Economist*, 16 March 2020.

19. Amanda Taub and Jane Bradley, "As Domestic Abuse Rises, U.K. Failings Leave Victims in Peril," *New York Times*, 2 July 2020.

20. Melissa Klein, "Safer Sex in the City: STD Cases Plummet amid Coronavirus Pandemic," *New York Post*, 25 April 2020; Hilary Brueck, "STD Rates Appear to Be Quietly Skyrocketing across the US, As Fewer People Get Tested and Treated during the Pandemic," *Business Insider*, 18 May 2020.

21. Cédric Pietralunga, et al., "Emmanuel Macron face aux enjeux sanitaires et économiques du confinement," *Le Monde*, 24 March 2020.

22. Michael Breen, "What's Fueling Korea's Coronavirus Success – and Relapse," *Politico*, 15 May 2020; Chi-Mai Chen, et al., "Containing COVID-19 among 627,386 Persons in Contact with the Diamond Princess Cruise Ship Passengers Who Disembarked in Taiwan," *Journal of Medical Internet Research*, 22, 5 (2020); Sangchul Park, et al., "Information Technology-Based Tracing Strategy in Response to COVID-19 in South Korea – Privacy Controversies," *Journal of the American Medical Association*, 2 June 2020.

23. Christian Bjørnskov and Stefan Voigt, "This Time is Different? – On the Use of Emergency Measures during the Corona Pandemic," University of Hamburg, Institute of Law and Economics, Working Paper 2020, 36, June 2020.

24. International Covenant on Civil and Political Rights, art 4, www.ohchr.org/en/profes sionalinterest/pages/ccpr.aspx.

25. American Association for the International Commission of Jurists, "Siracusa Principles on the Limitation and Derogation Provisions in the International Covenant on Civil

and Political Rights," www.icj.org/wp-content/uploads/1984/07/Siracusa-principles-ICCPR-legal-submission-1985-eng.pdf. A history of their emergence is in Sara Abiola, "The Siracusa Principles on the Limitation and Derogation Provisions in the International Covenant for Civil and Political Rights (ICCPR): History and Interpretation in Public Health Context," Open Society Institute, Public Health Program Law and Health Initiative, 28 January 2011, http://health-rights.org/index .php/cop/item/memo-the-siracusa-principles-on-the-limitation-and-derogation-provi sions-in-the-international-covenant-for-civil-and-political-rights-iccpr-history-and-inter pretation-in-public-health-context.

26. UN, "COVID-19: States Should Not Abuse Emergency Measures to Suppress Human Rights – UN Experts," 16 March 2020, www.ohchr.org/EN/NewsEvents/Pages/Displ ayNews.aspx?NewsID=25722&LangID=E; UN, "Emergency Measures and COVID-19: Guidance," 27 April 2020, www.ohchr.org/Documents/Events/EmergencyMeasures_ COVID19.pdf.

27. Roojin Habibi, et al., "Do Not Violate the International Health Regulations during the COVID-19 Outbreak," *Lancet*, 29 February 2020.

28. WHO, "International Health Regulations (2005)," art. 31, 32, https://apps.who.int/i ris/bitstream/handle/10665/246107/9789241580496-eng.pdf;jsessionid=374E13D00 F7CB828ACAC787BC306FD89?sequence=1.

29. Lili Bayer, "Hungary's Viktor Orbán Wins Vote to Rule by Decree," *Politico*, 30 March 2020.

30. Lily Bayer, "Hungary Replaces Rule by Decree with 'State of Medical Crisis,'" *Politico*, 18 June 2020.

31. Adina Ponta, "Human Rights Law in the Time of the Coronavirus," *American Society of International Law Insights*, 24, 5 (20 April 2020).

32. *Pace* Tom McTague, "Our Democracy Will Survive This Pandemic," *Atlantic*, 14 May 2020.

33. Francis Fukuyama, "The Thing That Determines a Country's Resistance to the Coronavirus," *Atlantic*, 30 March 2020.

34. Public Health Service Act (42 U.S. Code §264) sect. 361.

35. "Order for Quarantine under Section 361 of the Public Health Service Act 42 Code of Federal Regulations Part 70 (Interstate) and Part 71 (Foreign)," www.cdc.gov/quaran tine/pdf/Public-Health-Order_Generic_FINAL_02-13-2020-p.pdf.

36. CDC, "Legal Authorities for Isolation and Quarantine," www.cdc.gov/quarantine/ab outlawsregulationsquarantineisolation.html.

37. Edgar Walters, "What Can Texas Do If a Coronavirus Outbreak Hits?," *Texas Tribune*, 5 March 2020.

38. "Order by the Mayor of the City of Austin," 14 March 2020, www.austintexas.gov/edi ms/document.cfm?id=337524.

39. Simon Romero, "New Mexico Invokes Riot Law to Control Virus Near Navajo Nation," *New York Times*, 4 May 2020.

40. Deutscher Bundestag, "Zur Frage der Gesetzgebungskompetenz des Bundes für den Öffentlichen Gesundheitsdienst," WD 9-3000-043/19, 31 July 2019, 5, www .bundestag.de/resource/blob/657236/c82ba2db1cd763e2f46439828d73c4e0/WD-9-043-19-pdf-data.pdf.

41. Gesetz zur Neuordnung seuchenrechtlicher Vorschriften, 20 July 2000, §§ 16, 17, https://www.bgbl.de/xaver/bgbl/start.xav?startbk=Bundesanzeiger_BGBl&bk=Bund esanzeiger_BGBl&start=//*%5B@attr_id=%27bgbl100s1045.pdf%27%5D#__bgbl__ %2F%2F%5B%40attr_id%3D%27bgbl100s1045.pdf%27%5D__1606774850230.

42. Allgemeinverfügung des Landratsamtes Main-Tauber-Kreis über die häusliche Absonderung von Personen, die mit dem neuartigen Corona-Virus (SARS-CoV-2) infiziert sind und deren Kontaktpersonen zur Eindämmung und zum Schutz vor der Verbreitung der Atemwegserkrankung COVID-19 vom 23. März 2020, VII2, www.main-

tauber-kreis.de/Landratsamt/Themen-und-Projekte/Coronavirus; "Coronavirus in Deutschland: Diese Grundrechte könnten eingeschränkt werden – Ministerium zeichnet Krisen-Szenario," *Merkur*, 27 February 2020.

43. Gesetz zur Neuordnung seuchenrechtlicher Vorschriften, §26.
44. Landratsamt Rosenheim, Allgemeinverfügung zur Anordnung der Absonderung in häuslicher Quarantäne für Kontaktpersonen der Kategorie I (höheres Infektionsrisiko) zu bestätigten SARS-CoV-2 Fällen, 24 March 2020, www.kolbermoor.de/Allgemeinverf%C3%BCgung%20LRA%20Rosenheim%20zur%20Anordnung%20der%20Absonderung%20in%20h%C3%A4uslicher%20Quarant%C3%A4ne%20f%C3%BCr%20Kontaktpersonen%20der%20Kategorie%20I%2025.03.2020.pdf.
45. Gesetz zur Neuordnung seuchenrechtlicher Vorschriften, §28, 30.
46. Erik Angner and Gustaf Arrhenius, "The Swedish Exception?," *Behavioural Public Policy-Blog*, 23 April 2020.
47. Regeringskansliet, "How Sweden Is Governed," www.regeringen.se/other-languages/english—how-sweden-is-governed/.
48. Nils Karlson, et al., "The Underpinnings of Sweden's Permissive COVID Regime," *VOX: CEPR Policy Portal*, 20 April 2020; Mark Klamberg, "Between Normalcy and State of Emergency: The Legal Framework for Sweden's Coronavirus Strategy," *The Local*, 9 April 2020; Lars Jonung, "Sweden's Constitution Decides Its Exceptional COVID-19 Policy," *VOX^{EU}/CEPR*, 18 June 2020.
49. Ernst-Wolfgang Böckenförde, "The Repressed State of Emergency: The Exercise of State Authority in Extraordinary Circumstances," in Ernst-Wolfgang Böckenförde, *Constitutional and Political Theory* (Oxford 2017) 128.
50. Kungörelse (1974:152) om beslutad ny regeringsform, www.riksdagen.se/sv/dokument-lagar/dokument/svensk-forfattningssamling/kungorelse-1974152-om-beslutad-ny-regeringsform_sfs-1974-152.
51. Anna Jonsson Cornell and Janne Salminen, "Emergency Laws in Comparative Constitutional Law: The Case of Sweden and Finland," *German Law Journal*, 19, 2 (2018) 228–30.
52. Catherine Edwards, "What Sweden's Coronavirus Crisis Law Means (and Doesn't Mean)," *The Local*, 8 April 2020.
53. Smittskyddslag (2004:168), www.riksdagen.se/sv/dokument-lagar/dokument/svensk-forfattningssamling/smittskyddslag-2004168_sfs-2004-168.
54. Ordningslag (1993:1617), www.riksdagen.se/sv/dokument-lagar/dokument/svensk-forfattningssamling/ordningslag-19931617_sfs-1993-1617.
55. Scott Gleason, "Belarus President Plays Hockey, Says Global Coronavirus Measures Are Result of 'Psychosis,'" *USA Today*, 31 March 2020.
56. Wilfredo Miranda, "Nicaragua's 'Express Burials' Raise Fears Ortega Is Hiding True Scale of Pandemic," *Guardian*, 19 May 2020; Ismael Lopez, "Packed Hospital Wards Cast Doubt on Nicaragua's Low Coronavirus Count, Doctors Say," *Reuters*, 11 May 2020.
57. Flores Bermúdez and Robles, "Coronavirus: Nicaragua's Midnight Burials."
58. "Is Pakistan Really Handling the Pandemic Better Than India?," *Economist*, 30 September 2020.
59. Flores Bermúdez and Robles, "Coronavirus: Nicaragua's Midnight Burials."
60. "India's Economy Has Suffered Even More Than Most," *Economist*, 23 May 2020.
61. "Emerging Countries Lift Lockdowns Despite Covid-19 Cases Surge," *Financial Times*, 21 May 2020.
62. Alexis Duval, et al., "Coronavirus: Au jour 1 du confinement, 'on ne verbalise que ceux qui nous prennent pour des cons,'" *Le Monde*, 18 March 2020.
63. Michelle Goldberg, "The Phony Coronavirus Class War," *New York Times*, 18 May 2020.

64. "US Medical Workers Stand Up to Anti-lockdown Protesters," *Aljazeera*, 20 April 2020.
65. Nathan Gardels, "The Other Viral Contagion in China," *WorldPost Archive*, 8 May 2020.
66. Katherine Dunn, "To Tackle Coronavirus, Brits Are Appealing to the Age-Old Rallying Cry: 'Blitz Spirit,'" *Fortune*, 6 March 2020.
67. On misuse of the Blitz analogies: Richard Overy, "Why the Cruel Myth of the 'Blitz Spirit' Is No Model for How to Fight Coronavirus," *Guardian*, 19 March 2020; Steven Fielding, "The Spirit of the Blitz Isn't Back, It's Bunk," *Financial Times*, 19 March 2020; Mary Dejevsky, "Coronavirus and the 'Myth of the Blitz Spirit,'" *Spectator*, 21 March 2020; David Edgerton, "Why the Coronavirus Crisis Should Not Be Compared to the Second World War," *New Statesman*, 3 April 2020.
68. Stephen Grey and Andrew MacAskill, "Johnson Listened to His Scientists about Coronavirus – But They Were Slow to Sound the Alarm," *Reuters*, 7 April 2020.
69. "Covid-19 in the Netherlands: A Timeline," *Actiegroep Containment Nu*, https://www.containmentnu.nl/articles/timeline?lang=en.
70. Erik Angner and Gustaf Arrhenius, "The Swedish Exception?," *Behavioural Public Policy Blog*, 23 April 2020; Christian Stichler, "Die Welt steht still. Nur Schweden nicht," *ZeitOnline*, 24 March 2020.
71. "Swedish Ministers Defend Resisting Coronavirus Lockdown," *Financial Times*, 16 April 2020.
72. Göran Eriksson, "Folkhälsonationalism ligger bakom det Svenska undantaget," *Dagens Nyheter*, 28 March 2020.
73. Lars Trägårdh and Umut Özkırımlı, "Coronavirus Is a Stress Test for Societies …," unpublished ms., a version of which was published as "Why Might Sweden's Covid-19 Policy Work? Trust between Citizens and State," *Guardian*, 21 April 2020.
74. Tim Lister and Sebastian Shukla, "Sweden Challenges Trump – and Scientific Mainstream – by Refusing to Lock Down," *CNN*, 10 April 2020.
75. Lionel Laurent, "No, Sweden Isn't a Miracle Coronavirus Model," *Bloomberg Opinion*, 30 April 2020.
76. Jonas Hinnfors, "Experterna ska inte styra i en demokrati," *Svenska Dagbladet*, 22 March 2020; Lars Calmfors, "Partierna går i samma fälla som när de tystnade i invandringsdebatten," *Dagens Nyheter*, 5 May 2020. A critique in Bengt Jacobsson, "Experter och politisk styrning i coronatider," *Blyerts och blad*, 23 March 2020, https://bengtjacobsson.com/2020/03/23/experter-och-politisk-styrning-i-coronatider/.
77. Richard Orange, "Sweden 'Wrong' Not to Shut Down, Says Former State Epidemiologist," *Guardian*, 24 May 2020.
78. Therese Larsson Hultin, "Bildt: Tegnell ska inte sätta sig på höga hästar," *Svenska Dagbladet*, 9 May 2020.
79. Clas Svahn, "Annika Linde: En månads stängning hade gett oss tid," *Dagens Nyheter*, 19 May 2020.
80. https://vetcov19.se/en/.
81. Erik Wengström, "Coronavirus: Survey Reveals What Swedish People Really Think of Country's Relaxed Approach," *The Conversation*, 29 April 2020.
82. Richard H. Thaler and Cass R. Sunstein, *Nudge: Improving Decisions about Health, Wealth, and Happiness* (New York 2008).
83. David Halpern, *Inside the Nudge Unit: How Small Changes Can Make a Big Difference* (London 2015).
84. Dominic Lawson, "Forget Trendy 'Nudge' Theorists: It's the Queen Who Best Understands Our Lockdown Mood," *Daily Mail*, 13 April 2020.
85. Elisabeth Mahase, "Was the Decision to Delay the UK's Lockdown over Fears of 'Behavioural Fatigue' Based on Evidence?," *British Medical Journal*, 7 August 2020.
86. Susan Michie and Robert West, "Behavioural, Environmental, Social, and Systems Interventions against Covid-19," *British Medical Journal*, 28 July 2020.

87. "Fifteenth SAGE Meeting on Wuhan Coronavirus (Covid-19)," 13 March 2020, www.gov.uk/government/publications/sage-minutes-coronavirus-covid-19-response-13-march-2020.
88. Sarah Boseley, "Herd Immunity: Will the UK's Coronavirus Strategy Work?," *Guardian*, 13 March 2020; Nafeez Ahmed, "Behavioural Scientists Told Government to Use 'Herd Immunity' to Justify Business-as-Usual," *Byline Times*, 23 March 2020.
89. Heather Steward and Mattha Busby, "Coronavirus: Science Chief Defends UK Plan from Criticism," *Guardian*,13 March 2020.
90. "Open Letter to the UK Government Regarding COVID-19," 16 March 2020, https://sites.google.com/view/covidopenletter/home.
91. Marta Paterlini, "'Closing Borders Is Ridiculous': The Epidemiologist behind Sweden's Controversial Coronavirus Strategy," *Nature*, 21 April 2020.
92. Lena Einhorn, "Hur kunde vi släppa in smittan på Stockholms äldreboenden?," *Dagens Nyheter*, 9 April 2020; Stichler, "Die Welt steht still."
93. Christian Stichler, "Schwedens Sonderweg geht langsam zu Ende," *ZeitOnline*, 2 April 2020.
94. "Folkhälsomyndighetens föreskrifter och allmänna råd om allas ansvar att förhindra smitta av covid-19 m.m.," HSLF-FS 2020:12, 1 April 2020, www.folkhalsomyndigheten.se/contentassets/a1350246356042fb9ff3c515129e8baf/hslf-fs-2020-12-allmanna-rad-om-allas-ansvar-covid-19-tf.pdf.
95. Elisabeth Åsbrink, "Coronakrisen visar att Sverige är ett fredsskadat land," *Dagens Nyheter*, 30 March 2020.
96. Göran Eriksson, "Folkhälsonationalism ligger bakom det Svenska undantaget," *Dagens Nyheter*, 28 March 2020.
97. Paterlini, "'Closing Borders Is Ridiculous'"; "Schwedisher Staats-Epidemiologe Tegnell: Sich nur auf Masken zu verlassen, ist sehr gefährlich!," *Bild*, 8 August 2020.
98. Nora Lorek, "Sweden Still Hasn't Locked Down; But Normal Life Is a Luxury for Only a Few," *National Geographic*, 5 May 2020.
99. Another country that had gone from firm to relaxed policies was Japan: Andrew Gordon, "Historical Context for COVID 19 Policies in Japan and Asia (2)," *Tokyo College*, 11 July 2020, www.tc.u-tokyo.ac.jp/en/weblog/1847/.
100. "Kongl. Maj:ts Nådiga Quarantains-Förordning," *Kongl. Förordningar*, 1806; "Kongl. Maj:ts Nådiga Reglemente för Quarantains-Inrättningen på Känsö," *Kongl. Förordningar*, 1807; Baldwin, *Contagion and the State*, 90–91.
101. Baldwin, *Contagion and the State*, 310–11.
102. Baldwin, *Contagion and the State*, ch. 5.
103. Baldwin, *Disease and Democracy*.
104. Smittskyddslag 2004:168, http://rkrattsbaser.gov.se/sfst?bet=2004:168.
105. Marquis Childs, *Sweden: The Middle Way* (New Haven 1936).
106. Lena Martinsson, et al., eds., *Challenging the Myth of Gender Equality in Sweden* (Bristol 2016); Greg Simons and Andrey Manoilo, "Sweden's Self-Perceived Global Role: Promises and Contradictions," *Research in Globalization*, 1 (2019); Jens Rydgren and Sara van der Meiden, "The Radical Right and the End of Swedish Exceptionalism," *European Political Science*, 18 (2019); Richard Milne, "Sweden: Why the 'Moral Superpower' Dissented over Covid-19," *Financial Times*, 15 October 2020.
107. Sigurd Bergmann, et al., "Sweden Hoped Herd Immunity Would Curb COVID-19," *USA Today*, 21 July 2020.
108. David J. Michael, "Nordic Sibling Rivalry: How Norwegian Oil Wealth and Swedish Migrant Work Have Reversed the Centuries-Old Scandinavian Power Dynamic," *Slate*, 11 December 2012; Ivar Ekman, "Young Swedes Flock to Newly Rich Norway for Work," *New York Times*, 30 December 2007.

109. "Sweden's Weak Currency Puts Its Booming Flat White Economy at Risk," *Centre for Economics and Business Research*, 1 July 2019.
110. Rory Carroll, et al., "'Confused, Dangerous, Flippant': Rest of World Pans PM's Handling of Coronavirus," *Guardian*, 24 March 2020; Otto English, "Cruel Britannia: Coronavirus Lays Waste to British Exceptionalism," *Politico*, 5 May 2020.
111. Rajeev Syal, "Abandoned NHS IT System Has Cost £10bn So Far," *Guardian*, 18 September 2013.
112. "Isle of Wight Contact-Tracing App Trial – A Mixed Verdict So Far," *BBC*, 18 May 2020; Catherine Lai, "British Flip-flop on the Tracing App," *Web24News*, 19 June 2020.
113. Daniel Boffey and Robert Booth, "UK Missed Three Chances to Join EU Scheme to Bulk-Buy PPE," *Guardian*, 13 April 2020.
114. Göran Eriksson, "Folkhälsonationalism ligger bakom det Svenska undantaget," *Dagens Nyheter*, 28 March 2020; Gina Gustavsson, "Has Sweden's Coronavirus Strategy Played into the Hands of Nationalists?," *Guardian*, 1 May 2020.
115. Maddy Savage, "Coronavirus: Has Sweden Got Its Science Right?," *BBC News*, 25 April 2020.
116. Göran Eriksson, "Så har coronaviruset gjort Sverige stort igen," *Svenska Dagbladet*, 23 April 2020.
117. Lionel Laurent, "No, Sweden Isn't a Miracle Coronavirus Model," *Bloomberg Opinion*, 30 April 2020.
118. Hela Habib, "'I've Never Written So Many Death Certificates': Is Sweden Having Second Thoughts on Lockdown?," *Independent*, 13 April 2020.
119. Some preliminary thoughts on this in Peter Baldwin, "Umgang mit Corona: Schweden wählt den entspannten Weg," *Berliner Zeitung*, 10 April 2020.
120. Jette Elbæk Maressa, "I Sverige er der ikke mange forbud efter corona, men Malmø kører på lavt blus," *Jyllands Posten*, 26 March 2020.
121. www.youtube.com/watch?v=B4aiiu5hrRM.
122. Dominik Reintjes, "Es braucht in Schweden keine Verbote – anders als in Deutschland," *Wirtschaftswoche*, 7 April 2020.
123. Peter Alestig, "Tegnell: 'Mycket av det vi har sett är inte hållbart,'" *Svenska Dagbladet*, 3 May 2020.
124. Jesper Sundén, "Ambassadören: 'Jag får höra att Sverige gör rätt,'" *Svenska Dagbladet*, 22 May 2020.
125. Tigran Feiler, "Sverige används som skräckexempel i Argentina," *SVT Nyheter*, 10 May 2020.
126. Staffan Dickson, "Mystiske tysken: 'Sverige anses naivt och blint,'" *Omni*, 1 April 2020; "Tyske journalistens frustration: 'Måste förklara för tyskarna,'" *Expressen*, 14 April 2020; Lina Lund, "Vem är tysken som staller Anders Tegnell mot väggen?," *Dagens Nyheter*, 2 April 2020.
127. Griff Witte, "South Dakota's Governor Resisted Ordering People to Stay Home," *Washington Post*, 13 April 2020; Amelia Janaskie, "South Dakota: America's Sweden," *American Institute for Economic Research*, 17 September 2020.
128. "How Uruguay Has Coped with Covid-19," *Economist*, 20 June 2020.
129. Tina Nguyen, "Conservative Americans See Coronavirus Hope in Progressive Sweden," *Politico*, 30 April 2020; Oliver Moody, "Swedes Hailed in the US for Keeping Their Economy Alive during Coronavirus Onslaught," *Times* (London), 23 April 2020.
130. Martin Kulldorff, "Delaying Herd Immunity Is Costing Lives," *American Institute for Economic Research*, 31 August 2020.
131. John Fund and Joel Hay, "Has Sweden Found the Right Solution to the Coronavirus?," *National Review*, 6 April 2020; Paula Neuding, "Sweden Has Resisted Lockdown: But That Doesn't Make it a Bastion of Liberty," *Quillette*, 12 May 2020.

132. Tyler Durden, "Sweden: The One Chart That Matters," *Zero Hedge*, 28 July 2020.
133. Karin Grundberg Wolodarski, "Giesecke: 'Alla andra länder gör fel,'" *Dagens Industri*, 3 April 2020.
134. Nicholas Aylott, referred to in Gideon Rachman, "A Very Swedish Sort of Failure," *Financial Times*, 15 June 2020.
135. David Crouch, "Sweden Slams Shut Its Open-Door Policy towards Refugees," *Guardian*, 24 November 2015.
136. Tore Ellingsen and Jesper Roine, "Sweden and the Virus," in *Sweden through the Crisis* (Stockholm, forthcoming), 15, www.hhs.se/contentassets/421dc1e74c54466a8 d3a88a78c775522/a02.pdf.
137. Lise M. Helsingen, et al., "Trust, Threats, and Consequences of the COVID-19 Pandemic in Norway and Sweden – A Comparative Survey," *MedRxiv*, 20 May 2020.
138. Ronald Inglehart and Christian Welzel, *Modernization, Cultural Change, and Democracy: The Human Development Sequence* (Cambridge 2005) ch. 6.
139. Lars Trägårdh, "Statist Individualism: On the Culturality of the Nordic Welfare State," in Øystein Sørensen and Bo Stråth, eds., *The Cultural Construction of Norden* (Oslo 1997) 253–82. A more elaborate version in Henrik Berggren and Lars Trägårdh, *Är svensken människa? Gemenskap och oberoende i det moderna Sverige* (Stockholm 2015).
140. *Private Eye*, 1531, 6.
141. Gina Gustavsson, "Sverige vill vara pandemins Pippi – och WHO är Prussiluskan," *Dagens Nyheter*, 22 May 2020.
142. Sam Bowman and Pedro Serodio, "Live Free and Die: Sweden's Coronavirus Experience," *Critic*, 26 May 2020.
143. "Låga dödstal hos nordiska grannar," *SVT Nyheter*, 28 May 2020.
144. "Dödstalen i Sverige är katastrofalt höga," *Aftonbladet*, 20 May 2020.
145. Anders W. Jonsson, "Regeringen måste ändra svenska coronastrategin," *Dagens Nyheter*, 28 May 2020.
146. "Hör finländare om att ta emot svenska turister i sommar," *SVT Nyheter*, 28 May 2020; "Coronavirus: Denmark and Norway Exclude Sweden from Tourism," *BBC*, 29 May 2020.
147. Anne Grete Storvik, "Smittevernforsker: Bør betrakte Sverige som utenfor Norden," *Dagens Medisin*, 14 March 2020.
148. Nick Cohen, "Sweden's Covid-19 Policy Is a Model for the Right: It's Also a Deadly Folly," *Guardian*, 23 May 2020.
149. "Do Low-Trust Societies Do Better in a Pandemic?," *Economist*, 2 May 2020.
150. Frederik Bombosch, "Schweden ist mit seiner Corona-Politik gescheitert," *Berliner Zeitung*, 3 June 2020.
151. Thomas Erdbrink, "Sweden Tries Out a New Status: Pariah State," *New York Times*, 22 June 2020.
152. "Tegnell: Fler åtgärder hade behövts," *Sveriges Radio*, 2 June 2020.
153. Clas Svahn, "Tegnell: Det finns saker vi hade kunnat göra bättre," *Dagens Nyheter*, 3 June 2020.
154. Amanda Dahl, "Anders Tegnell: I höst kan vi få se vilka som lyckats," *Dagens Nyheter*, 1 June 2020; Charlie Duxbury, "Sweden's Dr. No-Lockdown Denies 'Tactical Retreat,'" *Politico*, 3 June 2020.
155. Henri P. Kluge, "Statement – Digital Health Is about Empowering People," WHO, 25 June 2020, www.euro.who.int/en/health-topics/health-emergencies/coronavirus-covid-19/statements/statement-digital-health-is-about-empowering-people.
156. "Tegnell: Det är en total feltolkning av data," *Svenska Dagbladet*, 25 June 2020.
157. Paige Winfield Cunningham, "The Health 202: Trump Claims an Increase in Coronavirus Cases Is Due to More Testing," *Washington Post*, 23 June 2020.
158. "Coronautbrott på Vrångö – nu masstestas öborna," *SVT Nyheter*, 11 June 2020.

159. Carla K. Johnson, "Mount Vernon Choir Outbreak Was 'Superspreader Event,' Says CDC Report on How Easily Virus Spreads," *Seattle Times*, 12 May 2020.

160. "Tegnell är modig nog att erkänna misstag – det borde regeringen också göra," *Dagens Nyheter*, 5 June 2020.

161. "Borgfreden er slut: Löfven under kraftig kritik forsvarer svensk coronastrategi," *Politiken*, 7 June 2020; "Centerpartiet: Regeringen måste ändra den svenska coronas-trategin," *SVT Nyheter*, 28 May 2020; Niclas Rolander, "Sweden's PM Rebuked as Covid Deaths Ignite Political Anger," *Bloomberg*, 7 June 2020; Charlie Duxbury, "Swedes Round on Sweden's Corona Approach," *Politico*, 10 June 2020.

162. Rafaela Lindeberg and Niclas Rolander, "Swedish Faith in Covid Strategy Plunges after Errors Revealed," *Bloomberg*, 3 June 2020.

4 WHAT WAS DONE? ACT ONE OF THE PANDEMIC

1. "Lifting Lockdowns: The When, Why and How," *Economist*, 23 May 2020.

2. James Kynge, et al., "Coronavirus: The Cost of China's Public Health Cover-up," *Financial Times*, 6 February 2020.

3. Fred Deveaux, "Democracy Perception Index – 2020," *Dalia*, 15 June 2020. Similar figures for Europeans in Ivan Krastev and Mark Leonard, "Europe's Pandemic Politics: How the Virus Has Changed the Public's Worldview," European Council on Foreign Relations, 24 June 2020, https://ecfr.eu/archive/page/-/europes_pandemic_politic s_how_the_virus_has_changed_the_publics_worldview.pdf.

4. *Global Health and Security Index 2019*, www.ghsindex.org/wp-content/uploads/2020/0 4/2019-Global-Health-Security-Index.pdf.

5. David Willman, "CDC Coronavirus Test Kits Were Likely Contaminated, Federal Review Confirms," *Washington Post*, 20 June 2020.

6. George Packer, "We Are Living in a Failed State," *Atlantic*, June 2020. As one example of the inadequacies of the family connections: Katherine Eban, "How Jared Kushner's Secret Testing Plan 'Went Poof into Thin Air,'" *Vanity Fair*, 30 July 2020.

7. "How the World's Most Powerful Country Is Handling Covid-19," *Economist*, 28 May 2020.

8. Nic Robertson, "The Pandemic Could Reshape the World Order: Trump's Chaotic Strategy Is Accelerating US Losses," *CNN*, 23 May 2020; Tom McTague, "America's Uniquely Humiliating Moment," *Atlantic*, 23 June 2020.

9. Janine Aron and John Muellbauer, "The US Excess Mortality Rate from COVID-19 Is Substantially Worse Than Europe's," *VoxEU*, 29 September 2020.

10. David McKenzie and Brent Swails, "South Africa's HIV Failures Cost More Than 300,000 Lives. Now This Painful Past Is Helping in Covid-19 Fight," *CNN*, 29 April 2020; "What South Africa Learned from AIDS," *Economist*, 16 April 2020; Amy Fallon, "How Fighting HIV Put South Africa on the Front Foot against Covid-19," *Positive.News*, 18 June 2020.

11. Jennifer Bouey, "Strengthening China's Public Health Response System: From SARS to COVID-19," *American Journal of Public Health*, 110, 7 (2020) 939; Chia-ju Lin, "A Textual Analysis of the Coverage of SARS and the Image of China: A Comparative Analysis," *Asian Social Science*, 8, 3 (2012) 54.

12. Joan C. Henderson, "Managing a Health-Related Crisis: SARS in Singapore," *Journal of Vacation Marketing*, 10, 1 (2003) 69–70.

13. Mark A. Rothstein, et al., *Quaranine and Isolation: Lessons Learned from SARS*, Institute for Bioethics, Health Policy and Law, University of Louisville School of Medicine, November 2003, 111.

14. Daniel Duane, "San Francisco Was Uniquely Prepared for Covid-19," *Wired*, 11 August 2020.

15. Richard J. Hatchett, et al., "Public Health Interventions and Epidemic Intensity during the 1918 Influenza Epidemic," *Proceedings of the National Academy of Sciences*, 104, 18 (2007).

16. A readable account in Sebastian G. B. Amyes, *Magic Bullets, Lost Horizons: The Rise and Fall of Antibiotics* (London 2001).

17. Macfarlane Burnet and David O. White, *Natural History of Infectious Disease*, 4th ed. (Cambridge 1972) 263.

18. University of Toronto Joint Centre for Bioethics, "Stand on Guard for Thee: Ethical Considerations in Preparedness Planning for Pandemic Influenza," November 2005, 11.

19. Howard Markel, et al., "Nonpharmaceutical Interventions Implemented by US Cities during the 1918–1919 Influenza Pandemic," *Journal of the American Medical Association*, 298, 6 (2007) 644.

20. Dan Balz, "Crisis Exposes How America Has Hollowed Out Its Government," *Washington Post*, 16 May 2020.

21. Kat Eschner, "The Long Shadow of the 1976 Swine Flu Vaccine 'Fiasco,'" *Smithsonian Magazine*, 6 February 2017; George Dehner, "WHO Knows Best? National and International Responses to Pandemic Threats and the 'Lessons' of 1976," *Journal of the History of Medicine and Allied Sciences*, 65, 4 (2010) 479–80.

22. David Coady and Kenichiro Kashiwase, "Public Health Care Spending: Past Trends," in Benedict Clements, et al., eds., *The Economics of Public Health Care Reform in Advanced and Emerging Economies* (Washington DC 2012).

23. David U. Himmelstein and Steffie Woolhandler, "Public Health's Falling Share of US Health Spending," *American Journal of Public Health*, 106, 1 (2016) 56.

24. Katherine Tully-McManus, "Congress Makes History and Approves Proxy and Virtual Voting," *Governing*, 18 May 2020; Lisa Mascaro, "Senate Reopens Despite Risks as House Preps More Virus Aid," *AP News*, 4 May 2020.

25. Ariane de Vogue, "Supreme Embarrassment: The Flush Heard around the Country," *CNN*, 6 May 2020.

26. "Speaker Outlines New Voting Measures," 1 June 2020, www.parliament.uk/business/news/2020/june/speaker-outlines-new-voting-measures/.

27. Michael Holden and Kylie MacLellan, "UK's Plan B If 'Team Johnson' Is Incapacitated? Answer Is Unclear," *Reuters*, 5 April 2020.

28. Rick Pearson, et al., "Southern Illinois Judge Temporarily Blocks Gov. J. B. Pritzker's Stay-at-Home Order from Applying to Republican State Lawmaker Who Sued," *Chicago Tribune*, 28 April 2020; Wisconsin Court System, "Oral Argument in Wisconsin Legislature v. Palm to Be Livestreamed May 5," www.wicourts.gov/news/view.jsp?id=1234.

29. Adam Liptak, "Supreme Court, in 5–4 Decision, Rejects Church's Challenge to Shutdown Order," *New York Times*, 30 May 2020.

30. Rosalind English, "South African Lockdown Rules Declared Unlawful," *UK Human Rights Blog*, 4 June 2020.

31. "Brazil Resumes Publishing Covid-19 Data after Court Ruling," *BBC*, 9 June 2020.

32. Daniel Bischof, "Was die VfGH-Entscheidung zu Corona bedeutet," *Wiener Zeitung*, 22 July 2020.

33. Daniel McLaughlin, "Court Ruling on Coronavirus Spurs Romanians to Leave Quarantine," *Irish Times*, 10 July 2020; "Romania Passes Law to Stop Virus Patients from Leaving Hospitals," *Daily Sabah*, 21 July 2020.

34. Dan Diamond and Sarah Wheaton, "How the US and Italy Traded Places on Coronavirus," *Politico*, 22 June 2020.

35. Demetri Sevastopulo, "Anxiety Rises ahead of Donald Trump's Tulsa Rally," *Financial Times*, 19 June 2020; Allyson Chiu, "Trump's Tulsa Rally, Protests 'More Than Likely' Linked to Coronavirus Surge, Health Official Says," *Washington Post*, 9 July 2020;

Dhruv Khullar, "How the Protests Have Changed the Pandemic," *New Yorker*, 4 June 2020.

36. Bouey, "Strengthening China's Public Health Response System," 939

37. The State Council Information Office of the People's Republic of China, "Fighting Covid-19: China in Action," June 2020, III 3, http://english.www.gov.cn/news/topnews/202006/07/content_WS5edc559ac6d066592a449030.html; "Senior Chinese Officials 'Removed' as Death Toll Hits 1,000," *BBC*, 11 February 2020.

38. Javier Leira, "Latin American Coronavirus Deaths Overtake North American Fatalities," *Reuters*, 13 July 2020; Zamira Rahim, "Coronavirus Hits Latin America's Political Class," *CNN*, 14 July 2020; Diana Enriquez, et al., "Latin America's COVID-19 Nightmare," *Foreign Affairs*, 1 September 2020.

39. Sarah Santana, et al., "Human Immunodeficiency Virus in Cuba: The Public Health Response of a Third World Country," in Nancy Krieger and Glen Margo, eds., *AIDS: The Politics of Survival* (Amityville 1994) 169.

40. Ruth Maclean, "Coronavirus Accelerates across Africa," *New York Times*, 16 June 2020.

41. Emily Goodin, "Donald Trump Ignores Compulsory Masks Sign as He Tours MASK Factory (But Wears Goggles) Then Praises Workers for Their Efforts – All of Whom Have Their Faces Covered," *Daily Mail*, 5 May 2020; Matthew Choi, "Trump, in Full Reversal, Urges Americans to Wear Masks," *Politico*, 15 July 2020.

42. "Brazil's Jair Bolsonaro Ordered to Wear Mask in Public," *BBC*, 23 June 2020.

43. Silvia Sfregola, "Zingaretti contagiato dal Coronavirus. Il 27 febbraio era a Milano per l'aperitivo anti-panico," *Il Tempo*, 8 March 2020.

44. Anton Troianovski, "Russians Were Urged to Return to Normal Life. Except for Putin," *New York Times*, 30 September 2020.

45. Cheryl Peebles, "No Severance Payment for Dr Catherine Calderwood after Fife Second Home Visit during Coronavirus Lockdown," *Courier*, 10 April 2020.

46. "Romania: Ministers Flout Protective Measures," *Eurotopics*, 2 June 2020.

47. "'Sperrstunden-Wirbel' um Bundespräsident in Lokal," *Kronen Zeitung*, 24 May 2020; "Kurz zu Kleinwalsertal: 'Gewisse Dinge kann man nicht planen,'" *ORF*, 14 May 2020.

48. Eddy Wax, "Phil Hogan's Golfgate Downfall: What Happened, Swing by Swing," *Politico*, 27 August 2020.

49. Margot Molina, "El príncipe Joaquín de Bélgica, multado con 10.400 euros por saltarse el confinamiento," *El País*, 10 June 2020; Jakob Hanke Vela, "Belgian Prince Tests Positive for Virus after Party in Spain," *Politico*, 31 May 2020; Laurenz Gehrke and Aitor Hernández-Morales, "Europe's Elite Skewered for Lockdown Double Standards," *Politico*, 25 May 2020.

50. Emmanuel Igunza, "Kenyan Senator to Be Charged with Flouting Covid-19 Curfew," *BBC*, no date, www.bbc.co.uk/news/live/world-africa-47639452.

51. Toby Helm, et al., "In Private, Tories Were Dismayed, in Public, They Rallied to Save Dominic Cummings," *Guardian*, 23 May 2020.

52. Eric Lipton, et al., "The C.D.C. Waited 'Its Entire Existence for This Moment.' What Went Wrong?," *New York Times*, 3 June 2020.

53. It certainly let the Chinese turn Director-General Tedros Adhanom Ghebreyesus's visit in late January into an exercise in laudatory remarks, praising both China's work on behalf of the world and President Xi's "great leadership capability." "China Focus: Xi Voices Full Confidence in Winning Battle against Novel Coronavirus," *XinhuaNet*, 28 January 2020. And its initial inclusion on its website of traditional Chinese medicine as ineffective against Covid-19 was quickly watered down. Henlen Tilley, "How to Make Sense of 'Traditional (Chinese) Medicine' in a Time of Covid-19," *Somatosphere*, 25 May 2020.

54. Frank Vogl, "March 23, 2020: The Day the US Economy Did Not Crash," *Globalist*, 14 May 2020; "The Fed Has Been Supporting Markets: Now It Must Find Ways to Boost Growth," *Economist*, 20 June 2020.

55. "The Successes of the Fed's Dollar-Swap Lines," *Economist*, 20 June 2020.
56. Resolution Foundation, "Summer Statement," 8 July 2020, 9, www.resolutionfounda tion.org/app/uploads/2020/07/RF_SEU_slidepack.pdf.
57. Takaya Yamaguchi and Tetsushi Kajimoto, "Japan Approves Fresh $1.1 Trillion Stimulus to Combat Pandemic Pain," *Reuters*, 26 May 2020; William Sposato, "Japan Is Testing the Limits of Pandemic Economics," *Foreign Policy*, 10 April 2020.
58. Jeehon Han, et al., "Income and Poverty in the COVID-19 Pandemic," Brookings Papers on Economic Activity, Post-Conference Draft, 6 August 2020.
59. Zachary Parolin, et al., "Monthly Poverty Rates in the United States during the COVID-19 Pandemic," Poverty and Social Policy Working Paper, 15 October 2020, https://st atic1.squarespace.com/static/5743308460b5e922a25a6dc7/t/5f87c59e4cd0011 fabd38973/1602733471158/COVID-Projecting-Poverty-Monthly-CPSP-2020.pdf.
60. "Europe's €750bn Rescue Package Sets a Welcome Precedent," *Economist*, 25 July 2020.
61. Independent SAGE, "COVID-19: What Are the Options for the UK?," 12 May 2020, 16.
62. Adam Vaughan, "How It All Went Wrong in the UK," *New Scientist*, 6 June 2020; Sarah Neville, "Covid-19 Unmasks Weaknesses of English Public Health Agency," *Financial Times*, 22 July 2020.
63. "How Centralisation Impeded Britain's Covid-19 Response," *Economist*, 18 July 2020.
64. John Burn-Murdoch, et al., "Lack of Local Covid-19 Testing Data Hinders UK's Outbreak Response," *Financial Times*, 30 June 2020; Mike Gill, et al., "Lessons from Leicester: A Covid-19 Testing System That's Not Fit for Purpose," *British Medical Journal*, 7 July 2020.
65. "America's Covid-19 Experience Is Tragic but Not That Exceptional," *Economist*, 28 May 2020.
66. Anne-Marie Boxall, "What the US Could Learn from Australia's COVID-19 Response," *Milbank Memorial Fund*, 14 April 2020.
67. "African Union Mobilizes Continent-Wide Response to COVID-19 Outbreak," African Union, 24 February 2020, https://au.int/en/pressreleases/20200224/african-union-mobilizes-continent-wide-response-covid-19-outbreak.
68. Adam Tooze, "'Shockwave," *London Review of Books*, 42, 8 (2020).
69. The State Council Information Office of the People's Republic of China, "Fighting Covid-19: China in Action," June 2020, II, 1, http://english.www.gov.cn/news/top news/202006/07/content_WS5edc559ac6d066592a449030.html.
70. Solomon Hsiang, et al., "The Effect of Large-Scale Anti-contagion Policies on the COVID-19 Epidemic," *MedRxiv*, 21 May 2020, Supplementary Table 1.
71. Farnaz Fassihi, "Power Struggle Hampers Iran's Coronavirus Response," *New York Times*, 17 March 2020.
72. Linda Givetash, "Coronavirus: Trump Says Some Governors 'Have Gone too Far' on Lockdown Measures," *NBC News*, 20 April 2020.
73. Apoorva Mandavilli and Catie Edmondson, "'This Is Not the Hunger Games': National Testing Strategy Draws Concerns," *New York Times*, 25 May 2020; Mike DeBonis, et al., "White House Issues Coronavirus Testing Guidance That Leaves States in Charge," *Washington Post*, 27 April 2020.
74. Alexis C. Madrigal and Robinson Meyer, "How Virginia Juked Its COVID-19 Data," *Atlantic*, 13 May 2020.
75. Dan Balz, "As Washington Stumbled, Governors Stepped to the Forefront," *Washington Post*, 3 May 2020.
76. Jeanne Whalen, et al., "Scramble for Medical Equipment Descends into Chaos as U.S. States and Hospitals Compete for Rare Supplies," *Washington Post*, 24 March 2020.
77. "America's Covid-19 Experience," *Economist*. It later turned out Larry Hogan had overpaid for his Korean tests. Steve Thompson, "Maryland's Governor Touts His

Purchase of Tests from South Korea. Emails Show a U.S. Company Offered Tests at a Lower Price," *Washington Post*, 17 July 2020.

78. Andrew Beaton, "A Million N95 Masks Are Coming from China – on Board the New England Patriots' Plane," *Wall Street Journal*, 2 April 2020; "Many Face Masks Distributed by Massachusetts Found Deficient," *NBCBoston*, 30 April 2020.

79. Seth Masket "Democratic and GOP Governors Enacted Stay-at-Home Orders on the Same Timeline: But All Holdouts Are Republicans," *FiveThirtyEight*, 9 April 2020.

80. www.youtube.com/watch?v=2Kydr2a7Uy4.

81. Kim Barker and Amy Julia Harris, "'Playing Russian Roulette': Nursing Homes Told to Take the Infected," *New York Times*, 24 April 2020.

82. Alexandra Sternlicht, "Cuomo and de Blasio Spar over School Closures in Ongoing Power Struggle," *Forbes*, 12 April 2020.

83. William K. Rashbaum, et al., "He Saw 'No Proof' Closures Would Curb Virus. Now He Has de Blasio's Trust," *New York Times*, 14 May 2020.

84. Jeffery C. Mays and Joseph Goldstein, "Mayor Resisted Drastic Steps on Virus: Then Came a Backlash from His Aides," *New York Times*, 16 March 2020; David Freedlander, "When New York Needed Him Most, Bill de Blasio Had His Worst Week as Mayor," *New York Magazine*, 26 March 2020.

85. Renuka Rayasam, "Why Texas Is So Far behind Other States on Virus Response," *Politico*, 18 March 2020.

86. Paul J. Weber and Jim Vertun, "Political Tensions Rise in Texas as COVID-19 Cases Climb amid Reopening," *Time*, 15 May 2020.

87. J. David Goodman, "In West Texas, Lingering Distrust in Public Health Measures as Virus Spreads," *New York Times*, 4 July 2020.

88. "Georgia Governor Sues Atlanta over Face Mask Rules," *BBC*, 17 July 2020.

89. "The Growing Importance of Latin America's Mayors," *Economist*, 3 October 2020.

90. Gary P. Pisano, et al., "Lessons from Italy's Response to Coronavirus," *Harvard Business Review*, 27 March 2020.

91. "Great Cities after the Pandemic," *Economist*, 11 June 2020.

92. Tim Craig, et al., "Governors Confront Political Furor as They Plot a Cautious Course for Reopening," *Washington Post*, 15 April 2020; Katherine Shaver, "Smartphone Data Shows Out-of-State Visitors Flocked to Georgia as Restaurants and Other Businesses Reopened," *Washington Post*, 7 May 2020.

93. "Rhode Island Begins Door to Door Checks for New Yorkers Fleeing Coronavirus," *New York Post*, 29 March 2020.

94. Simon Romero, "Checkpoints, Curfews, Airlifts: Virus Rips through Navajo Nation," *New York Times*, 9 April 2020.

95. "Amid Lack of Federal Direction, Governor Cuomo, Governor Murphy and Governor Lamont Announce Regional Approach to Combatting COVID-19," New York State, 16 March 2020, www.governor.ny.gov/news/amid-lack-federal-direction-governor-cuomo-governor-murphy-and-governor-lamont-announce.

96. Mark Landler, "In Tackling Coronavirus, Scotland Asserts Its Separateness from England," *New York Times*, 10 July 2020.

97. Anna Lewis, "Welsh Government Tells People in England Not to Travel to Wales for Exercise," *WalesOnline*, 10 May 2020; Elle Duffy, "Coronavirus in Scotland: SNP MP Angus MacNeil Calls for Police to Patrol Scottish Border If Lockdown Is Eased Down South," *Herald*, 10 May 2020.

98. Robert Shrimsley, et al., "Will Coronavirus Break the UK?," *Financial Times*, 20 October 2020.

99. Jens Bostrup, "Vrede i Malmø oven på dagens melding: Danskerne er hykleriske," *Politiken*, 29 May 2020.

100. Richard Milne, "Nordic Co-operation Crumbles at the Norway–Sweden Border," *Financial Times*, 18 June 2020. The same problem reemerged later for Norwegian owners of weekend houses in Sweden. Richard Milne, "Norwegian Owners of Cabins in Sweden Threaten to Sue Their Government," *Financial Times*, 28 August 2020.
101. Hannah Roberts, "Italy Welcomes Tourists (But the Feeling's Not Mutual)," *Politico*, 2 June 2020.
102. Eline Schaart and Hanne Cokelaere, "Belgian Towns Turn Coronavirus Anger on the Dutch," *Politico*, 24 March 2020.
103. Hanne Cokelaere, "Belgium Bursts the Benelux Bubble," *Politico*, 28 May 2020.
104. Anna Fifield, "With Virus under Control, Australia and New Zealand May Form a Travel 'Bubble,'" *Washington Post*, 4 May 2020; "Baltic States Open a Pandemic 'Travel Bubble,'" *BBC*, 15 May 2020; "Danska partier vill inte släppa in svenskar," *Svenska Dagbladet*, 14 May 2020.
105. Florian Eder, et al., "America Out, China In as EU Looks to Reopen External Borders," *Politico*, 23 June 2020.
106. J. Edward Moreno, "Mexico Closes Border in Arizona as Coronavirus Cases in Both Countries Surge," *The Hill*, 3 July 2020.
107. Hsiang, et al., "The Effect of Large-Scale Anti-contagion Policies."
108. Edward Wong, et al., "Local Officials in China Hid Coronavirus Dangers from Beijing, U.S. Agencies Find," *New York Times*, 19 August 2020.
109. "China Didn't Warn Public of Likely Pandemic for 6 Key Days," *AP*, 14 April 2020.
110. "Britain Has the Wrong Government for the Covid Crisis," *Economist*, 18 June 2020.
111. Rachel Donadio, "France: After Lockdown, the Street," *New York Review of Books*, 23 July 2020.
112. Tore Ellingsen and Jesper Roine, "Sweden and the Virus," in *Sweden through the Crisis* (Stockholm, forthcoming), www.hhs.se/contentassets/421dc1e74c54466a8d3a88a78c775522/a02.pdf.
113. D. T. Max, "The Chinese Workers Who Assemble Designer Bags in Tuscany," *New Yorker*, 9 April 2018; Peter S. Goodman and Emma Bubola, "The Chinese Roots of Italy's Far-Right Rage," *New York Times*, 5 December 2019; Sally Ho, "Is There a Connection between Luxury Fashion Brands' Dirty Underground Secret and Italy's Coronavirus Crisis?," *Green Queen*, 26 March 2020.
114. Hannah Kuchler and Andrew Edgecliffe-Johnson, "How New York's Missteps Let Covid-19 Overwhelm the US," *Financial Times*, 21 October 2020.
115. Rachelle N. Binny, et al., "Effect of Alert Level 4 on R_{eff}: Review of International COVID-19 Cases," *Te Pūnaha Matatini*, 22 April 2020, Table 1.
116. Thomas Pueyo, "Coronavirus: Learning How to Dance," *Medium*, 20 April 2020.
117. Cornelius Hirsch, "Europe's Coronavirus Lockdown Measures Compared," *Politico*, 31 March 2020.
118. Thomas Pueyo, "Coronavirus: Should We Aim for Herd Immunity Like Sweden?," *Medium*, 9 June 2020.
119. Göran Eriksson, et al., "'Förbered er på det värsta' – spelet bakom coronastrategin," *Svenska Dagbladet*, 4 July 2020.
120. "How Speedy Lockdowns Save Lives," *Economist*, 4 July 2020.
121. Hsiang, et al., "The Effect of Large-Scale Anti-contagion Policies," 10.
122. Greg Miller and Ellen Nakashima, "President's Intelligence Briefing Book Repeatedly Cited Virus Threat," *Washington Post*, 27 April 2020.
123. Clas Svahn, "Annika Linde: En månads stängning hade gett oss tid," *Dagens Nyheter*, 19 May 2020; "22 Days: How Three Weeks of Dither and Delay at No 10 Cost Thousands of British Lives," *Sunday Times*, 24 May 2020; Bill Chappell, "U.S. Could Have Saved 36,000 Lives If Social Distancing Started 1 Week Earlier," *NPR*, 21 May 2020.

124. Charlie Cooper, "Lockdown One Week Earlier 'Could Have Halved UK Death Toll,'" *Politico*, 10 June 2020.
125. "Twenty-seventh SAGE meeting on Covid-19," 21 April 2020, https://assets .publishing.service.gov.uk/government/uploads/system/uploads/attachment_ data/file/888799/S0396_Twenty-seventh_SAGE_meeting_on_Covid-19.pdf.
126. Adam Vaughan, "How It All Went Wrong in the UK," *New Scientist*, 6 June 2020.
127. *Global Health and Security Index 2019*, www.ghsindex.org/wp-content/uploads/2020/ 04/2019-Global-Health-Security-Index.pdf.
128. Pisano, et al., "Lessons from Italy's Response."
129. Cindy Sui, "What Taiwan Can Teach the World on Fighting the Coronavirus," *ABC News*, 10 March 2020; Nils Gilman and Steven Weber, "The Long Shadow of the Future," *Noēma*, 10 June 2020.
130. Pueyo, "Coronavirus: Learning How to Dance."
131. Chi-Mai Chen, et al., "Containing COVID-19 among 627,386 Persons in Contact with the Diamond Princess Cruise Ship Passengers Who Disembarked in Taiwan," *Journal of Medical Internet Research*, 22, 5 (2020).
132. Antonia Noori Farzan and Miriam Berger, "Taiwan Celebrates Record 200 Days with No Confirmed Local Coronavirus Transmission," *Washington Post*, 29 October 2020.
133. Tom Mitchell, et al., "China and Covid-19: What Went Wrong in Wuhan?," *Financial Times*, 17 October 2020.
134. "China Plans to Crush New Covid Outbreaks with Tough Measures," *Economist*, 30 April 2020.
135. The State Council Information Office of the People's Republic of China, "Fighting Covid-19: China in Action," June 2020, II, 2, http://english.www.gov.cn/news/top news/202006/07/content_WS5edc559ac6d066592a449030.html.
136. Donald G. McNeil Jr., "The Coronavirus in America: The Year Ahead," *New York Times*, 18 April 2020.
137. Lily Kuo, "How Did China Get to Grips with Its Coronavirus Outbreak?," *Guardian*, 9 March 2020.
138. David Brennan, "Fines, Jail Time, and Sackings: What Happens When People Break Coronavirus Quarantines around the World," *Newsweek*, 18 March 2020.
139. Simiao Chen, et al., "Fangcang Shelter Hospitals: A Novel Concept for Responding to Public Health Emergencies," *Lancet*, 2 April 2020.
140. "China Plans to Crush New Covid Outbreaks with Tough Measures," *Economist*, 30 April 2020. A similar situation in Germany, with all residents of a housing complex quarantined, led to clashes and police action. "Germany Coronavirus: Extra Police Enforce German Tower Block Quarantine," *BBC*, 21 June 2020.
141. Sui-Lee Wee and Vivian Wang, "Here's How Wuhan Tested 6.5 Million for Coronavirus in Days," *New York Times*, 26 May 2020.
142. "A Chinese City Will Test All 9.5 Million of Its Residents," *New York Times*, 12 October 2020.
143. Pueyo, "Coronavirus: Learning How to Dance."
144. Alexander Klimburg, et al., "Pandemic Mitigation in the Digital Age: Digital Epidemiological Measures to Combat the Coronavirus Pandemic," *Austrian Institute for European and Security Policy Studies*, 12 (March 2020) 23, www.aies.at/download/2 020/AIES-Studies-2020-12.pdf.
145. Cindy Sui, "In Taiwan, the Coronavirus Pandemic Is Playing Out Very Differently," *ABC News*, 23 April 2020.
146. Sheng-Chia Chung, et al., "A Rapid Systematic Review and Case Study on Test, Contact Tracing, Testing, and Isolation Policies for Covid-19 Prevention and Control," *MedRxiv*, 17 June 2020; Wen-Yee Lee, et al., "Taiwan Used Police Surveillance,

Government Tracking, and $33,000 Fines to Contain Its Coronavirus Outbreak," *Business Insider*, 4 June 2020.

147. Mary Hui, "How Taiwan Is Tracking 55,000 People under Home Quarantine in Real Time," *Quartz*, 31 March 2020.

148. Jonathan Chen on Facebook, 20 March 2020, www.facebook.com/jonathan .chen.1213/posts/10158178965295127. In South Korea, the isolated were paid about $375 a month. Nemo Kim, "South Koreans Keep Calm and Carry On Testing," *Guardian*, 18 March 2020.

149. "Korea Implements Special Entry Procedure," *About Korea*, 26 March 2020, https:// english.visitkorea.or.kr/enu/AKR/FU_EN_15.jsp?cid=2650414.

150. The State Council Information Office of the People's Republic of China, "Fighting Covid-19: China in Action," June 2020, II, 2, http://english.www.gov.cn/news/top news/202006/07/content_WS5edc559ac6d066592a449030.html.

151. National Health Commission of the People's Republic of China, "Protocol for Prevention and Control of COVID-19 (Edition Six)," *Chinese Center for Disease Control and Prevention Weekly*, 20 March 2020, 4.

152. Kai Kupferschmidt and Jon Cohen, "China's Aggressive Measures Have Slowed the Coronavirus," *Science*, 2 March 2020.

153. Mario Cavolo, "If You Still Don't Understand How China Succeeded Stopping the Virus, Read This and Be Forever Enlightened," *Linkedin*, 4 April 2020, www.linkedin .com/content-guest/article/you-still-dont-understand-how-china-succeeded-stop ping-mario-cavolo/?fbclid=IwAR1BpwQq-flDsO_Um2P50tVmgHYMUwITwt0GTw-a7IjxB_OvBLqNBD6refE.

154. Lily Kuo, "'The New Normal': China's Excessive Coronavirus Public Monitoring Could Be Here to Stay," *Guardian*, 9 March 2020.

155. C. Jason Wang, et al., "Response to COVID-19 in Taiwan: Big Data Analytics, New Technology, and Proactive Testing," *Journal of the American Medical Association*, 3 March 2020.

156. Linda Givetash, et al., "Tracking Apps and Thermal Scanners: Life in Post-lockdown South Korea," *NBC News*, 6 May 2020.

157. Jung Won Sonn, "South Korea's Success in Controlling Disease Is Due to Its Acceptance of Surveillance," *Conversation*, 19 March 2020.

158. Pueyo, "Coronavirus: Learning How to Dance."

159. Lee Sung-Eun and Baek Min-Jeong, "Itaewon Cluster under Control but Officials Warn of Silent Transmission," *Korea JoongAng Daily*, 18 May 2020; Cho Ryok Kang, et al., "Coronavirus Disease Exposure and Spread from Nightclubs, South Korea," *Emerging Infectious Diseases*, 26, 10 (October 2020).

160. Oliver Moody, "Germany's Corona Detectives Led Way Out of Lockdown," *Times* (London), 26 May 2020; "Germany's Contact Tracers Try to Block a Second Covid-19 Wave," *Economist*, 28 May 2020.

161. Katrin Bennhold, "Giving Your Number to Strangers? It's Not Flirting; It's a Rule," *New York Times*, 7 June 2020. But apparently this was honored as much in the breach. Eater Staff, "One Day in June," *Eater*, 9 June 2020.

162. "Germany Helps Sex Workers Idled by Covid-19," *Economist*, 4 June 2020.

163. Anna Fifield, "New Zealand Edges Back to Normal after Quashing Coronavirus in 49 Days," *Washington Post*, 16 May 2020.

164. Chloé Hecketsweiler and Cédric Pietralunga, "Les simulations alarmantes des épidémiologistes pour la France," *Le Monde*, 15 March 2020.

165. "Suspension of Entry as Immigrants and Nonimmigrants of Certain Additional Persons Who Pose a Risk of Transmitting 2019 Novel Coronavirus," *Federal Register*, 29 February 2020, https://www.federalregister.gov/documents/2020/03/04/2020-04595/

suspension-of-entry-as-immigrants-and-nonimmigrants-of-certain-additional-persons-who-pose-a-risk-of.

166. Greg Miller, et al., "One Final Viral Infusion: Trump's Move to Block Travel from Europe Triggered Chaos and a Surge of Passengers from the Outbreak's Center," *Washington Post*, 23 May 2020.

167. Angela Giuffrida and Lorenzo Tondo, "Leaked Coronavirus Plan to Quarantine 16m Sparks Chaos in Italy," *Guardian*, 8 March 2020.

168. Cécile Bouanchaud, "Avant le confinement, ils fuient à la campagne: 'On savait qu'il fallait faire vite,'" *Le Monde*, 16 March 2020.

169. Something quite close to this is in "Handling Crises," *Understanding the Civil Service*, www.civilservant.org.uk/skills-crises.html.

170. Laura Hughes and Mure Dickie, "Scotland and Wales Overruled London on Quarantine Deadline," *Financial Times*, 14 August 2020.

171. Tom Payne, "It's an Utter Shambles," *Daily Mail*, 8 June 2020.

172. Tim Shipman, "Jobs Bloodbath Triggers Swifter Lockdown Easing," *Sunday Times*, 7 June 2020.

173. Department for Transport, "Coronavirus (COVID-19): Travel Corridors," 3 July 2020, www.gov.uk/guidance/coronavirus-covid-19-travel-corridors.

174. Sanya Khetani-Shah, "UK Reintroduces Quarantine for Travelers from Spain," *Politico*, 25 July 2020; "Transport Secretary Grant Shapps Caught Up in Spain Rule Change," *BBC*, 26 July 2020.

175. Jack Ewing, "Flying Was Once Routine: During the Pandemic, It's a Feat," *New York Times*, 9 June 2020.

176. "Nearly 200 People Arrested in Hawaii for Violating Travel Quarantine," *KITV4*, 17 July 2020; Jennifer Sinco Kelleher, "Coronavirus: Hawaii Arrests Rogue Tourists to Curb Outbreak," *Mercury News*, 7 May 2020.

177. "Compared with China, U.S. Stay-at-Home Has Been 'Giant Garden Party,' Journalist Says," *NPR*, 29 April 2020.

178. Isabella Kaminska, "Making Sense of Nonsensical COVID-19 Strategy," *Financial Times*, 2 June 2020.

179. "Coronavirus: Ce qui est permis et ce qui est interdit pendant le confinement en France," *Le Monde*, 17 March 2020.

180. Mathilde Damgé, et al., "Combien de fois puis-je sortir de chez moi? Combien de temps cela va durer? Nos réponses à vos questions sur le confinement," *Le Monde*, 18 March 2020.

181. "Forms or Text Message Required to Leave House after Virus Lockdown," *Ekathimerini.com*, 23 March 2020; "Full Lockdown in Effect from Monday to Curb Coronavirus," *Ekathimerini.com*, 22 March 2020.

182. "Coronavirus: Les arrêtés se multiplient pour interdire les accès aux plages, parcs, forêts, montagnes . . .," *Le Monde*, 20 March 2020.

183. "Do Low-Trust Societies Do Better in a Pandemic?," *Economist*, 2 May 2020.

184. Damgé, et al., "Combien de fois puis-je sortir de chez moi?"

185. "The Curious Etiquette of Jogging in Paris," *Economist*, 23 April 2020.

186. Christina Gallardo, "Lockdown Rules Baffle Europeans," *Politico*, 27 March 2020.

187. Shipman, "Jobs Bloodbath Triggers Swifter Lockdown Easing."

188. Sonny Bunch, "Want to Know How Badly We've Botched the Pandemic? Consider the Plight of Movie Theaters," *Washington Post*, 9 July 2020.

189. Denis Cosnard, "Déconfinement: L'État refuse d'ouvrir les parcs dans les villes de la 'zone rouge,'" *Le Monde*, 13 May 2020.

190. Michael Warren, et al., "With Lobbying Push, Gyms Get on Phase One of Trump's Reopening Plan," *CNN*, 24 April 2020.

191. Harry Cole, "No Mancy Panky. Baffling New Northern Lockdown Rules Mean Couples Who Don't Live Together Can Have Sex in a Hotel But Not in Their Homes," *Sun*, 5 August 2020.

192. "Confusion over Sandwich Shop Mask Use after Gove Seen without Face Covering," *Express & Star*, 16 July 2020.

193. Francesca Gillett, "Coronavirus Lockdown: Why Can't Some Businesses Reopen in England Yet?," *BBC*, 27 June 2020.

194. Ministry of Housing, Communities, and Local Government, "COVID-19: Guidance for Small Marriages and Civil Partnerships," 4 July 2020, www.gov.uk/government/publi cations/covid-19-guidance-for-small-marriages-and-civil-partnerships/covid-19-guid ance-for-small-marriages-and-civil-partnerships.

195. "Bryllupper og fødselsdage får lov til at vare til efter midnat," *Jyllands Posten*, 11 June 2020.

196. Steve Hendrix, "Why Israel Is Seeing a Coronavirus Spike after Initially Crushing the Outbreak," *Washington Post*, 7 July 2020.

197. Donald G. McNeil Jr., "The Coronavirus in America: The Year Ahead," *New York Times*, 18 April 2020.

198. Selena Simmons-Duffin, "As States Reopen, Do They Have the Workforce They Need to Stop Coronavirus Outbreaks?," *NPR*, 18 June 2020; Lois Parshley, "The Magnitude of America's Contact Tracing Crisis Is Hard to Overstate," *National Geographic*, 1 September 2020.

199. Sharon Otterman, "N.Y.C. Hired 3,000 Workers for Contact Tracing. It's Off to a Slow Start," *New York Times*, 21 June 2020.

200. Drew Karedes, "More Than 60 Percent of Mass. Contact Tracing Calls Answered," *Boston 25 News*, 4 May 2020; Sam Karlin, "Louisiana Struggles to Get Contact Tracer Calls Answered," *Governing*, 11 June 2020.

201. Independent SAGE, "COVID-19: What Are the Options for the UK?," 12 May 2020, 17.

202. "Eighth SAGE Meeting on Wuhan Coronavirus (Covid-19)," 18 February 2020, https:// assets.publishing.service.gov.uk/government/uploads/system/uploads/attachment_ data/file/888776/S0376_Eighth_SAGE_meeting_on_Wuhan_Coronavirus__Covid-19 __.pdf.

203. Ed Conway and Rowland Manthorpe, "The Inside Story of How UK's 'Chaotic' Testing Regime 'Broke All the Rules,'" *Sky News*, 9 July 2020.

204. "England Leaves Lockdown," *Economist*, 27 June 2020.

205. Shaun Lintern, "Government's Test and Trace System Failing in Areas Battling Major Outbreaks, Leaked Analysis Reveals," *Independent*, 19 July 2020; Josh Halliday, "Test and Trace Failing to Contact Thousands in England's Worst-Hit Areas," *Guardian*, 22 July 2020.

206. Mario Stäuble, "Die Clubs sollen schliessen und nachbessern," *Tagesanzeiger*, 30 June 2020.

207. Rory Cellan-Jones, "England's Test and Trace Programme 'Breaks GDPR Data Law,'" *BBC*, 20 July 2020.

208. Elise Thomas and Cooper Gatewood, "Contact Tracing under Siege: Conspiracy Theories and Violent Threats Seek to Undermine America's Safe Return to Normality," Institute for Strategic Dialogue, 5 June 2020, www.isdglobal.org/wp-content/uploads/2020/06/Contact-Briefing-Under-Siege.pdf.

209. OECD Data, Elderly Population, 2018 or latest available, https://data.oecd.org/pop/ elderly-population.htm.

210. "Why the New Coronavirus May Kill More Men than Women," *Advisory Board*, 25 February 2020.

211. "Smokers Seem Less Likely Than Non-smokers to Fall Ill with Covid-19," *Economist*, 2 May 2020; Shivani Mathur Gaiha, et al., "Association between Youth Smoking,

Electronic Cigarette Use, and Coronavirus Disease 2019," *Journal of Adolescent Health*, 11 August 2020.

212. Takehiro Takahashi, et al., "Sex Differences in Immune Responses That Underlie COVID-19 Disease Outcomes," *Nature*, 26 August 2020.

213. Andy Goren, et al., "A Preliminary Observation: Male Pattern Hair Loss among Hospitalized COVID-19 Patients in Spain: A Potential Clue to the Role of Androgens in COVID-19 Severity," *Journal of Cosmetic Dermatology*, 16 April 2020.

214. CDC, "Evidence Used to Update the List of Underlying Medical Conditions That Increase a Person's Risk of Severe Illness from COVID-19," viewed 27 June 2020, www .cdc.gov/coronavirus/2019-ncov/need-extra-precautions/evidence-table.html.

215. Kamlesh Khunti, et al., "Is Ethnicity Linked to Incidence or Outcomes of Covid-19?," *British Medical Journal*, 20 April 2020; Lucinda Platt and Ross Warwick, "Are Some Ethnic Groups More Vulnerable to COVID-19 Than Others?," Institute for Fiscal Studies, May 2020; OpenSafely Collaborative, "OpenSAFELY: Factors Associated with COVID-19-Related Hospital Death in the Linked Electronic Health Records of 17 Million Adult NHS Patients," *MedRxiv*, 7 May 2020.

216. Archie Bland and Denis Campbell, "Some Leicester Factories Stayed Open and Forced Staff to Come In, Report Warns," *Guardian*, 30 June 2020; Robert Wright and Patricia Nilsson, "How Boohoo Came to Rule the Roost in Leicester's Underground Textile Trade," *Financial Times*, 10 July 2020.

217. The connection between air pollution and Covid-19 was revealed in studies: Xiao Wu, et al., "Air Pollution and COVID-19 Mortality in the United States: Strengths and Limitations of an Ecological Regression Analysis," 26 October 2020, https://projects .iq.harvard.edu/covid-pm; Matthew A. Cole, et al., "Air Pollution Exposure and COVID-19," IZA Institute of Labor Economics, Discussion Paper 13367, June 2020; Edoardo Conticini, et al., "Can Atmospheric Pollution Be Considered a Co-factor in Extremely High Level of SARS-CoV-2 Lethality in Northern Italy?," *Elsevier Public Health Emergency Collection*, 4 April 2020.

218. Public Health England, "Beyond the Data: Understanding the Impact of COVID-19 on BAME Groups," June 2020, 21, https://assets.publishing.service.gov.uk/govern ment/uploads/system/uploads/attachment_data/file/892376/COVID_stakeholde r_engagement_synthesis_beyond_the_data.pdf.

219. Andrew Clark, et al., "Global, Regional, and National Estimates of the Population at Increased Risk of Severe COVID-19 Due to Underlying Health Conditions in 2020," *Lancet*, 15 June 2020.

220. Gov.uk, "Plans to Ease Guidance for Over 2 Million Shielding," 22 June 2020, www .gov.uk/government/news/plans-to-ease-guidance-for-over-2-million-shielding.

221. "The Risk of Severe Covid-19 Is Not Uniform," *Economist*, 21 May 2020. Other studies estimated between 20% and 30%: Amitava Banerjee, et al., "Estimating Excess 1-Year Mortality Associated with the COVID-19 Pandemic According to Underlying Conditions and Age," *Lancet*, 12 May 2020; Andrew Clark, et al., "Global, Regional, and National Estimates of the Population at Increased Risk of Severe COVID-19 Due to Underlying Health Conditions in 2020," *Lancet*, 15 June 2020.

222. "Avis n°6 du Conseil scientifique COVID-19," 20 April 2020, 23, https://solidarites- sante.gouv.fr/IMG/pdf/avis_conseil_scientifique_20_avril_2020.pdf.

223. Mary L. Adams, et al., "Population-Based Estimates of Chronic Conditions Affecting Risk for Complications from Coronavirus Disease, United States," *Emerging Infective Diseases Journal*, 26, 8 (August 2020).

224. Talha Burki, "England and Wales See 20,000 Excess Deaths in Care Homes," *Lancet*, 23 May 2020.

225. Adelina Comas-Herrera, et al., "Mortality Associated with COVID-19 Outbreaks in Care Homes: Early International Evidence," *International Long Term Care Policy Network*,

21 May 2020, https://ltccovid.org/wp-content/uploads/2020/06/Mortality-associated-with-COVID-21-May-1.pdf. Similar figures in European Centre for Disease Prevention and Control, "Surveillance of COVID-19 at Long-Term Care Facilities in the EU/EE," 19 May 2020, www.ecdc.europa.eu/sites/default/files/documents/cov id-19-long-term-care-facilities-surveillance-guidance.pdf.

226. Karen Yourish, et al., "One-Third of All U.S. Coronavirus Deaths Are Nursing Home Residents or Workers," *New York Times*, 11 May 2020.

227. Dan Bilefsky, "31 Deaths: Toll at Quebec Nursing Home in Pandemic Reflects Global Phenomenon," *New York Times*, 16 April 2020.

228. Sophie Borland, "Three in Four Care Homes Say GPs Won't Visit Residents with Coronavirus and Only a Third of Nursing Centres Are Accepting Infected Patients from Hospital as the Full Horrifying Scandal Blighting the Nation's Elderly Is Revealed," *Daily Mail*, 13 May 2020.

229. Office of Governor Gretchen Whitmer, "Executive Order 2020-42 (COVID-19), www .michigan.gov/whitmer/0,9309,7-387-90499_90705-525182-,00.html.

230. "The Risk of Severe Covid-19 Is Not Uniform," *Economist*, 21 May 2020.

231. Mattias Carlsson and Mikael Delin, "Statens hjälp till äldreboenden dröjde en månad," *Dagens Nyheter*, 19 April 2020.

232. Ann-Charlotte Marteus, "Timvikarier vågar inte säga nej – det är väl poängen?," *Expressen*, 5 May 2020.

233. "Swedish Ministers Defend Resisting Coronavirus Lockdown," *Financial Times*, 16 April 2020.

234. Comas-Herrera, et al., "Mortality Associated with COVID-19 Outbreaks in Care Homes."

235. Christian Molnár, et al., "Närmare två tredjedelar av covid-sjuka på SÄBO överlever," *Läkartidningen*, 26 June 2020.

236. "SVT avslöjar: Kommunernas intresseorganisation fick myndigheter att tona ned munskyddskrav," *SVT Nyheter*, 26 April 2020.

237. Fredrik Mellgren, "Lagstiftningen var inte anpassad för situationen," *Svenska Dagbladet*, 16 June 2020.

238. Christian Stichler, "Schwedens Sonderweg geht langsam zu Ende," *ZeitOnline*, 2 April 2020.

239. Mikael Delin, et al., "Så spräckte coronapandemin Sveriges krisberedskap," *Dagens Nyheter*, 12 June 2020.

240. "Coronavirus: What's Going Wrong in Sweden's Care Homes?," *BBC*, 19 May 2020.

241. Benjamin Mueller, "On a Scottish Isle, Nursing Home Deaths Expose a Covid-19 Scandal," *New York Times*, 25 May 2020.

242. Department of Health and Social Care, "Coronavirus: Stay at Home, Protect the NHS, Save Lives," www.gov.uk/government/publications/coronavirus-covid-19-inform ation-leaflet/coronavirus-stay-at-home-protect-the-nhs-save-lives-web-version.

243. For a defense of these tactics from the front line: David Oliver, "Heresy Warning: Re Care Home Covid Deaths," Twitter, 19 May 2020, https://twitter.com/mancunianme dic/status/1262982297357365253.

244. National Audit Office, Department of Health and Social Care, *Readying the NHS and Adult Social Care in England for COVID-19*, 12 June 2020, 11, www.nao.org.uk/wp-content/uploads/2020/06/Readying-the-NHS-and-adult-social-care-in-England-for-COVID-19.pdf.

245. Piers Morgan, "Spare Me Your Hypocritical Claps for the NHS, Prime Minister," *Daily Mail*, 20 May 2020.

246. Robert Booth, "Government Rejected Radical Lockdown of England's Care Homes," *Guardian*, 28 May 2020.

247. Stephen Grey and Andrew Macaskill, "In Shielding Its Hospitals from COVID-19, Britain Left Many of the Weakest Exposed," *Reuters*, 5 May 2020.
248. Devi Sridhar and Yasmin Rafiei, "The Problem with 'Shielding' People from Coronavirus? It's Almost Impossible," *Guardian*, 29 May 2020.
249. Though in South Korea, it was 34%. Comas-Herrera, et al., "Mortality Associated with COVID-19 Outbreaks in Care Homes," Table 1; Christina Gallardo, "London Playbook PM," *Politico*, 19 May 2020, www.politico.eu/newsletter/london-playbook/politico-london-playbook-pm-lend-a-hand-foreign-lessons-app-ing-the-ante/.
250. Maria Eriksdotter, et al., "Tryck tillbaka smittan – då skyddar vi äldre bäst," *Svensksa Dagbladet*, 2 July 2020.

5 WHY THE PREVENTIVE PLAYING FIELD WAS NOT LEVEL

1. Fernand Braudel, *The Mediterranean and the Mediterranean World in the Age of Philip II* (New York 1972–73).
2. David Pilling, "'The Pandemic Is Gaining Momentum': Africa Prepares for Surge in Infections," *Financial Times*, 19 July 2020.
3. Richard J. Hatchett, et al., "Public Health Interventions and Epidemic Intensity during the 1918 Influenza Epidemic," *Proceedings of the National Academy of Sciences*, 104, 18 (2007).
4. Peter Baldwin, *Contagion and the State in Europe, 1830–1930* (Cambridge 1999), 211–26.
5. "Reported Cases and Deaths by Country, Territory, or Conveyance," Worldometer, data from 30 June 2020, www.worldometers.info/coronavirus/.
6. Maria Sacchetti, "Vermont Borders States with Major Covid-19 Outbreaks, But You Won't Find That Here," *Washington Post*, 18 June 2020.
7. Numbers kindly supplied by OAG Aviation, figures for 2019.
8. "Is Pakistan Really Handling the Pandemic Better Than India?," *Economist*, 30 September 2020.
9. Simon Calder, "Thailand Is Top Destination for Travellers from Wuhan," *Independent*, 22 Januay 2020.
10. "Why Has the Pandemic Spared the Buddhist Parts of South-East Asia?," *Economist*, 11 July 2020.
11. Hannah Beech, "No One Knows What Thailand Is Doing Right, but So Far It's Working," *New York Times*, 16 July 2020.
12. Chayanon Phucharoen, et al., "The Characteristics of COVID-19 Transmission from Case to High-Risk Contact," *Eclinical Medicine*, 21 September 2020.
13. "The Hunt for the Origins of SARS-CoV-2 Will Look beyond China," *Economist*, 22 July 2020. Similar arguments were advanced for the low Japanese rates too: Rupert Wingfield-Hayes, "Japan's Mysteriously Low Virus Death Rate," *BBC*, 4 July 2020. Though that left open the question of how such viruses would have remained contained to this area.
14. Bithika Chatterjee, et al., "The Mortality Due to COVID-19 in Different Nations Is Associated with the Demographic Character of Nations and the Prevalence of Autoimmunity," *MedRxiv*, 19 October 2020; Parveen Kumar and Bal Chander, "COVID 19 Mortality: Probable Role of Microbiome to Explain Disparity," *Medical Hypotheses*, 24 August 2020.
15. John M. Barry, *The Great Influenza: The Story of the Deadliest Pandemic in History* (London 2005) 376.
16. Simon Romero and Patricia Mazzei, "New Virus Hot Spots: U.S. Islands from Hawaii to Puerto Rico," *New York Times*, 25 August 2020.
17. Jon Kelly, "A Cluster of Islands: How Shetland Locked Down Early and Stopped the Virus in Its Tracks," *BBC*, 1 June 2020; Abdur Rahman Alfa Shaban, "Virus-Free Mauritius Says COVID-19 Battle Won, But War Still On," *Africa News*, 14 May 2020; Ronan Folgoas and Vincent Gautronneau, "Gilles Simeoni explique son projet de

'green pass' pour la Corse," *Le Parisien*, 8 May 2020; "The Pandemic's Indirect Hit on the Caribbean," *Economist*, 22 August 2020.

18. "Standoffish North Korea Discovers the Limits of Self-reliance," *Economist*, 28 May 2020.

19. Adam Rasgon and Iyad Abuheweila, "Coronavirus Spares Gaza, but Travel Restrictions Do Not," *New York Times*, 8 August 2020; Adam Rasgon and Iyad Abuheweila, "Gaza under Lockdown after First Local Cases of Virus," *New York Times*, 25 August 2020.

20. Owen Amos, "Ten Countries Kept Out Covid. But Did They Win?," *BBC*, 24 August 2020.

21. Georgina Kekea, "Solomon Islands Records First Positive COVID-19 Case," *Solomon Times*, 3 October 2020.

22. Mark Honigsbaum, *Living with Enza: The Forgotten Story of Britain and the Great Flu Pandemic of 1918* (London 2009) 121–22; Alfred W. Crosby, *America's Forgotten Pandemic: The Influenza of 1918*, 2nd ed. (Cambridge 2003) 232–40.

23. Indra Singh, "PM Announces New COVID-19 Measures, Including Ban on Cruise Ships," *FBC News*, 16 March 2020; Edwin Nand, "Fiji Airways Suspends Flights, Implements Leave without Pay," *FBC News*, 21 March 2020.

24. Tomas J. Philipson and Richard A. Posner, *Private Choices and Public Health: The AIDS Epidemic in an Economic Perspective* (Cambridge MA 1993) 152; Sarah Santana, et al., "Human Immunodeficiency Virus in Cuba: The Public Health Response of a Third World Country," in Nancy Krieger and Glen Margo, eds., *AIDS: The Politics of Survival* (Amityville 1994) 168; Julie Margot Feinsilver, *Healing the Masses: Cuban Health Politics at Home and Abroad* (Berkeley 1993) 82–84.

25. Patrick Oppmann, "Cuba Goes a Week without a Single Coronavirus Death," *CNN*, 20 May 2020.

26. Ed Augustin, "Cuba Sets Example with Successful Programme to Contain Coronavirus," *Guardian*, 7 June 2020.

27. *New Scientist*, 18 April 2020, 10.

28. Jamie Smyth, "Frustrated Australians Liken Travel Bans to North Korean Diktats," *Financial Times*, 22 August 2020.

29. Tomas Augustsson, "Island öppnar – efter omfattande testning," *Svenska Dagbladet*, 4 May 2020. New Zealand tested about 4% of Its population, Canada 6%. Anna Fifield, "New Zealand Edges Back to Normal after Quashing Coronavirus in 49 Days," *Washington Post*, 16 May 2020; Paul Waldie, "With Novel Testing Program, Iceland's COVID-19 Battle a Model for the World," *Globe and Mail*, 24 June 2020.

30. "South Dakota Sioux Refuse to Take Down 'Illegal' Checkpoints," *BBC*, 11 May 2020; Letter, US Dept. of Interior, 8 April 2020, https://bloximages.chicago2.vip.townnews .com/rapidcityjournal.com/content/tncms/assets/v3/editorial/f/39/f3916ae9-2096 -57b4-a372-23350cd2245f/5eb61803b538e.pdf.pdf.

31. "NSW Border with Victoria to Close from Wednesday as Daniel Andrews Announces 127 New Coronavirus Cases in the State," *ABC News*, 5 July 2020.

32. Laura Spinney, "Fears of Catastrophe as Greece Puts Migrant Camps into Lockdown," *Guardian*, 21 March 2020.

33. Fiona Hamilton and John Simpson, "Police Will Turn Back Drivers Fleeing Leicester's Coronovirus Lockdown," *Times* (London), 1 July 2020.

34. Feargus O'Sullivan, "Why Norway Is Banning Its Residents from Their Own Vacation Homes," *Citylab*, 17 March 2020; Antonia Noori Farzan, "'Stay on the Mainland': Tensions Grow as Affluent City Dwellers Fearing Coronavirus Retreat to Second Homes," *Washington Post*, 24 March 2020; "Cornwall Leaders Urge Tourists to Stay Away to Save Lives," *CornwallLive*, 21 March 2020; Barbara Krief, "Les Parisiens se réfugient à Belle-Ile-en-Mer: 'Personne n'a pensé qu'ils seraient aussi cons,'" *L'Obs*, 18 March 2020.

35. "Don't Come Back, Italy's South Tells Emigres in Virus-Hit North," *Reuters*, 8 March 2020.
36. "America's Covid-19 Experience Is Tragic but Not That Exceptional," *Economist*, 28 May 2020.
37. "Geografiska skillnader i hur covid-19 drabbat Sverige," *SVT Nyheter*, figures from 21 June 2020.
38. Samuel Laurent, "Le Grand-Est, 'région pilote' de l'épidémie," *Le Monde*, 12 March 2020.
39. "A Fraction of European Regions Account for a Majority of COVID-19 Deaths," *European Data Journalism Network*, 24 June 2020.
40. Michael H. Keller, et al., "A Striking Disconnect on the Virus: Economic Pain with Little Illness," *New York Times*, 6 June 2020.
41. "New Zealand Claims No Community Cases as Lockdown Eases," *BBC*, 27 April 2020.
42. Office for National Statistics, "Comparisons of All-Cause Mortality between European Countries and Regions: January to June 2020," 30 July 2020, www.ons.gov.uk/people populationandcommunity/birthsdeathsandmarriages/deaths/articles/comparisonso fallcausemortalitybetweeneuropeancountriesandregions/januarytojune2020.
43. "Saudi Arabia Declares Cease-Fire in Yemen, Citing Fears of Coronavirus," *New York Times*, 15 April 2020. For perspective, there are 15,000 members of the House of Saud, of whom about 2,000 enjoy some power.
44. Amanda Dahl, "Anders Tegnell: Vi har misslyckats med att skydda våra äldre," *Dagens Nyheter*, 14 April 2020; Karin Thurfjell, "Högst dödlighet i Sverige: 'Komplicerat att jämföra,'" *Svenska Dagbladet*, 19 May 2020.
45. Freddie Sayers, "Why We Aren't Wearing Masks in Sweden," *UnHerd*, 24 July 2020.
46. OECD, "Foreign-Born Population," 10 August 2020, https://data.oecd.org/migra tion/foreign-born-population.htm.
47. Calculated from Table 4, *Demographia World Urban Areas*, 16th ed. (June 2020), Table 4, http://demographia.com/db-worldua.pdf.
48. Thomas Pueyo, "Coronavirus: Should We Aim for Herd Immunity Like Sweden?," *Medium*, 9 June 2020.
49. Swedavia Airports, Statistik, Utförlig Trafikstatistik, Passagerare, Per Flygplats, 2017, www.swedavia.se/om-swedavia/statistik/?_ga=2.258539277.60718265.1592567385-1 665526551.1592567385; Airports Council International, Data Centre, Annual Traffic Data, Passenger Traffic 2017 Final (Annual), https://aci.aero/data-centre/annual-traffic-data/passengers/2017-passenger-summary-annual-traffic-data/.
50. 2019 figures from OAG Aviation.
51. Ana S. Gonzalez-Reiche, et al., "Introductions and Early Spread of SARS-CoV-2 in the New York City Area," *Science*, 17 July 2020.
52. Sayers, "Why We Aren't Wearing Masks in Sweden."
53. Email, 15 March 2020, quoted in Emanuel Karlsten, "Tegnell-mejlen: Så fick flockimmuniteten fäste hos Folkhälsomyndigheten," 12 August 2020, https://emanuelkarl sten.se/tegnell-mejlen-sa-fick-flockimmuniteten-faste-hos-folkhalsomyndigheten/.
54. Daniel B. Klein, et al., "16 Possible Factors for Sweden's High COVID Death Rate among the Nordics," George Mason Economics Department, Working Paper 20–27, 26 August 2020, 13–14.
55. "Numbers of People Who Ski in Europe as of 2018, by Country," *Statista*, www .statista.com/statistics/660546/europe-number-of-people-skiing-by-country/.
56. Gabriel Felbermayr, et al., "Après-ski: The Spread of Coronavirus from Ischgl through Germany," Institut für Weltwirtschaft Kiel, 24 May 2020.
57. Derek Scally, "'Ibiza of the Alps' Ski Resort Blamed for Spread of Coronavirus," *Irish Times*, 19 March 2020.

58. Devon O'Neil, "Skiing and the Pandemic: Lifts in Sweden Will Spin until April 6," *Powder*, 3 April 2020.
59. "Tegnell om WHO:s råd om munskydd: Inget för Sverige," *Svenska Dagbladet*, 5 June 2020; Johanna Cederblad, "Tegnell: 'Ute efter enkla lösningar,'" *Svenska Dagbladet*, 7 June 2020.
60. Shina C. L. Kamerlin and Peter M. Kasson, "Managing COVID-19 Spread with Voluntary Public-Health Measures: Sweden as a Case Study for Pandemic Control," *Clinical Infectious Diseases*, 1 July 2020.
61. That was also the implicit argument of the Belgian public health minister defending her country's mortality figures: Maggie de Block, "In Defense of Belgium's Coronavirus Response," *Politico*, 9 July 2020.
62. Baldwin, *Contagion and the State*, 225.
63. World Shipping Council, "Top 50 World Container Ports," 2018 figures, www.worldshipping.org/about-the-industry/global-trade/top-50-world-container-ports. On the other hand, Antwerp is the next biggest, and the Belgians shut down.
64. Matina Stevis-Gridneff, "E.U. Plans to Bar Most U.S. Travelers When Bloc Reopens," *New York Times*, 26 June 2020.
65. Baldwin, *Contagion and the State*, 151–53.
66. "'Shoot Them Dead': Duterte Warns against Violating Lockdown," *Aljazeera*, 1 April 2020.
67. Jason Burke, "South African Police Fire Rubber Bullets at Shoppers amid Lockdown," *Guardian*, 28 March 2020; Dickens Olewe, "Coronavirus in Africa: Whipping, Shooting and Snooping," *BBC*, 9 April 2020.
68. P. Pavan, "Telangana CM K Chandrasekhar Rao: Will Issue Shoot-at-Sight Orders If People Won't Cooperate for Lockdown," *Mumbai Mirror*, 24 March 2020.
69. Elizabeth Gibney, "Whose Coronavirus Strategy Worked Best?," *Nature*, 581 (7 May 2020) 16.
70. Thomas Hale, et al., "Variation in Government Responses to COVID-19," Version 6.0. *Blavatnik School of Government Working Paper*, May 25, 2020, Figure 2.
71. Karishma Mehrotra, "India Enforced One of the Strongest Lockdowns, Here's How It Stacks Up against Other Countries," *Indian Express*, 10 August 2020.
72. "How Did Vietnam Become Biggest Nation without Coronavirus Deaths?," *VOA News*, 21 June 2020.
73. Maurizio Trevisan, et al., "The COVID-19 Pandemic: A View from Vietnam," *American Journal of Public Health*, 8 July 2020.
74. Anna Jones, "Coronavirus: How 'Overreaction' Made Vietnam a Virus Success," *BBC*, 15 May 2020.
75. Ryan Fahey, "Vietnam Eases Coronavirus Restrictions after Reporting Zero Deaths and Just 268 Cases Following Successful Mass Quarantines, despite Bordering China," *Daily Mail*, 23 April 2020; Xuan Quynh Nguyen and Nguyen Dieu Tu Uyen, "Vietnam Orders 15-Day Nationwide Isolation from April 1," *Bloomberg*, 31 March 2020.
76. "Peru Is Heading towards a Dangerous New Populism," *Economist*, 23 July 2020.
77. Eyder Peralta, "Why Forecasters Can't Make Up Their Mind about Africa and the Coronavirus," *NPR*, 10 June 2020.
78. "Coronavirus in South Africa: Lockdown Extension Condemned," *BBC*, 10 April 2020.
79. "South Africa Sets Out Penalty for Not Wearing Masks in Public," *CGTN Africa*, 14 July 2020.
80. Bamba Gaye, et al., "Socio-demographic and Epidemiological Consideration of Africa's COVID-19 Response," *Nature Medicine*, 11 June 2020.
81. Gregory Gondwe and Farai Mutsaka, "Manhunts after Hundreds Flee Quarantine in Zimbabwe, Malawi," *AP*, 28 May 2020; Rabson Kondowe, "A Country with No

Coronavirus Cases Has Declared a National Disaster and Shut Schools, Large Gatherings," *Quartz*, 24 March 2020.

82. Marguerite Massinga Loembé, et al., "COVID-19 in Africa: The Spread and Response," *Nature Medicine*, 11 June 2020.

83. Soutik Biswas, "How Asia's Biggest Slum Contained the Coronavirus," *BBC*, 23 June 2020; Niha Masih, "How a Packed Slum in Mumbai Beat Back the Coronavirus, as India's Cases Continue to Soar," *Washington Post*, 31 July 2020.

84. Rachel Jones, "In This Sprawling City within a City, Fighting Coronavirus Requires Solidarity," *National Geographic*, 9 June 2020.

85. Abdur Rahman Alfa Shaban, "Rwanda COVID-19: Places of Worship Reopen amid Targeted Lockdowns," *Africa News*, 16 July 2020; Jason Beaubien, "A COVID-19 Success Story in Rwanda: Free Testing, Robot Caregivers," *NPR*, 15 July 2020.

86. Lavie Mutanganshuro, "Govt Commends Rusizi Residents for Collaboration in COVID-19 Fight," *New Times*, 16 July 2020.

87. Gaye, et al., "Socio-demographic and Epidemiological Consideration of Africa's COVID-19 Response."

88. Ruth Maclean, "Coronavirus Accelerates across Africa," *New York Times*, 16 June 2020.

89. *Demographia World Urban Areas*, 16th ed., Table 4.

90. Jason Horowitz and Emma Bubola, "Isolating the Sick at Home, Italy Stores Up Family Tragedies," *New York Times*, 24 April 2020; "The Risk of Severe Covid-19 Is Not Uniform," *Economist*, 21 May 2020.

91. Andrea Vogt, "Third of Italian Adults Live with Their Parents, Report Finds," *Guardian*, 19 September 2012.

92. United Nations, *Household Size and Composition around the World 2017*, 10–11.

93. Joël Mossong, et al., "Social Contacts and Mixing Patterns Relevant to the Spread of Infectious Diseases," *PLoS Medicine*, 25 March 2008.

94. Thomas Steinfeld, "Nu påminns vi om kramandets hyckleri," *Svenska Dagbladet*, 28 April 2020.

95. Lisa Du and Grace Huang, "Japan May Have Beaten Coronavirus without Lockdowns or Mass Testing. But How?," *Time*, 25 May 2020; Andrew Gordon, "Historical Context for COVID 19 Policies in Japan and Asia (2)," *Tokyo College*, 11 July 2020, www.tc.u-tokyo.ac.jp/en/weblog/1847.

96. Matt Bell, "The Cheapest Solution to COVID-19 Is Right in Front of Our Face," *Medium*, 17 April 2020.

97. "Japanese Offices Struggle to Adapt to Social Distancing," *Economist*, 9 May 2020.

98. Ben Dooley and Makiko Inoue, "Japan Needs to Telework. Its Paper-Pushing Offices Make That Hard," *New York Times*, 14 April 2020.

99. United Nations Conference on Trade and Development, *UNCTAD B2C Commerce Index 2019*, Table 6, https://unctad.org/en/PublicationsLibrary/tn_unctad_ict4d14_en.pdf.

100. Adam Satariano and Emma Bubola, "Pasta, Wine, and Inflatable Pools: How Amazon Conquered Italy in the Pandemic," *New York Times*, 26 September 2020.

101. "Handwashing Only 'Soap Tabs' Could Help Halt Spread of COVID-19 in Developing World," London School of Hygiene and Tropical Medicine, 5 May 2020, www.lshtm.ac.uk/newsevents/news/2020/handwashing-only-soap-tabs-could-help-halt-spread-covid-19-developing-world.

102. Frances Stead Sellers, "Americans Are Told to Wash Hands to Fight Coronavirus: But Some Don't Trust the Tap," *Washington Post*, 5 May 2020.

103. Grace Baek, "Navajo Nation Residents Face Coronavirus without Running Water," *CBS News*, 8 May 2020.

104. Central European University, Center for Policy Studies, "Roma Civil Society: Substandard Conditions in Estonia Means No Running Water for Some Roma,"

23 March 2020, https://cps.ceu.edu/article/2020-03-23/roma-civil-society-substandard-conditions-estonia-means-no-running-water-some; Patrick Strickland and Sorin Furcoi, "Slovakia's Roma: Living on the Margins," *Aljazeera*, 24 May 2017.

105. American Society for Microbiology, "As Many as 30 Percent of Travelers Don't Wash Hands after Using Public Restrooms at Airports," *ScienceDaily*, 16 September 2003.

106. International Labour Office, *Women and Men in the Informal Economy*, 3rd ed. (Geneva 2018) 13–14.

107. "Italy's Informal Workers Fall Back on Charity," *Economist*, 6 June 2020.

108. "Brazil's Losing Battle against Covid-19," *Economist*, 28 May 2020.

109. Peter S. Goodman, et al., "European Workers Draw Paychecks. American Workers Scrounge for Food," *New York Times*, 3 July 2020.

110. And the labor market was so tight that employment barely declined during the epidemic. Ben Dooley and Hisako Ueno, "Why Japan's Jobless Rate Is Just 2.6% While the U.S.'s Has Soared," *New York Times*, 20 June 2020. Though oddly, in surveys, the Japanese were most concerned about losing their jobs: Kekst CNC, *COVID-19 Opinion Tracker*, 2nd ed. (27 April–1 May 2020), www.kekstcnc.com/media/2590/ke kst-cnc_research-report_covid-19-opinion-tracker_wave-2_final-1.pdf.

111. Jonathan Cohn, "How COVID-19 Overwhelmed the American State," *Huffington Post*, 18 May 2020.

112. Peter Ganong, et al., "US Unemployment Insurance Replacement Rates during the Pandemic," Becker Friedman Institute, University of Chicago, Working Paper 2020–62, May 2020.

113. Ho Ee Khor and Rolf Strauch, "Why Asia and Europe Are Responding to the Same Crisis Differently," *Project Syndicate*, 7 August 2020.

114. Jose Maria Barrero, et al., "COVID-19 Is Also a Reallocation Shock," NBER Working Paper No. 27137, May 2020.

115. Steven Erlanger, "Who Will Recover Faster from the Virus? Europe or the U.S.?," *New York Times*, 1 July 2020.

116. Jason Groves and Josh White, "Let Teachers Teach! Education Secretary Gavin Williamson Demands Unions 'Do Their Duty' and Let Children Start Returning to the Classroom – But NASUWT Threatens to Sue If Staff Are Put at Risk," *Daily Mail*, 14 May 2020.

117. Lionel Laurent, "The French Are in No Hurry to Return to Work," *Washington Post*, 22 June 2020.

118. Paula Gardner, "Some in Michigan Make More from Unemployment Than Work during Coronavirus," *Bridge*, 26 April 2020.

119. Anna Menin, "Key Worker List: These UK Staff Can Still Send Their Children to School amid Coronavirus Crisis," *CityAM*, 20 March 2020.

120. Emmanuel Macron, "Addresse aux Français," 12 March 2020, Élysée, www.elysee.fr/emmanuel-macron/2020/03/12/adresse-aux-francais.

121. Government of the Netherlands, "COVID-19: Childcare for Children of People Working in Crucial Sectors," 20 March 2020, www.government.nl/documents/publi cations/2020/03/20/childcare-for-children-of-people-working-in-crucial-sectors.

122. Leslie Hook and Hannah Kuchler, "How Coronavirus Broke America's Healthcare System," *Financial Times Magazine*, 30 April 2020.

123. Robert Hughes, "How Did Spending on Health Care Plunge during a Pandemic?," *American Institute for Economic Research*, 31 July 2020.

124. Ian Austen, "Two Medical Systems, Two Pandemic Responses," *New York Times*, 1 May 2020.

125. Hilary Brueck, et al., "China Took at Least 12 Strict Measures to Control the Coronavirus: They Could Work for the US, But Would Likely Be Impossible to

Implement," *Business Insider*, 24 March 2020; The State Council Information Office of the People's Republic of China, "Fighting Covid-19: China in Action," June 2020, II, 2, http://english.www.gov.cn/news/topnews/202006/07/content_WS5edc559ac6 d066592a449030.html.

126. Jessica Silver-Greenberg and Amy Julia Harris, "'They Just Dumped Him Like Trash': Nursing Homes Evict Vulnerable Residents," *New York Times*, 21 June 2020.

6 WHERE AND WHY SCIENCE MATTERED

1. Emmanuel Macron, "Addresse aux Français," 12 March 2020, Élysée, www.elysee.fr/ emmanuel-macron/2020/03/12/adresse-aux-francais.

2. Daniel F. Gudbjartsson, et al., "Spread of SARS-CoV-2 in the Icelandic Population," *New England Journal of Medicine*, 14 April 2020; Enrico Lavezzo, et al., "Suppression of COVID-19 Outbreak in the Municipality of Vo, Italy," *MedRxiv*, 18 April 2020.

3. Young Joon Park, et al., "Contact Tracing during Coronavirus Disease Outbreak, South Korea, 2020," *Emerging Infectious Diseases*, 26, 10 (October 2020). Similarly: Mi Seon Han, et al., "Clinical Characteristics and Viral RNA Detection in Children with Coronavirus Disease 2019 in the Republic of Korea," *JAMA Pediatrics*, 28 August 2020. Broadly similar results in Russell M. Viner, et al., "Susceptibility to SARS-CoV-2 Infection among Children and Adolescents Compared with Adults," *JAMA Pediatrics*, 25 September 2020; Rebecca T. Leeb, et al., "COVID-19 Trends among School-Aged Children – United States, March 1– September 19, 2020," *Morbidity and Mortality Weekly Report*, 28 September 2020.

4. Taylor Heald-Sargent, et al., "Age-Related Differences in Nasopharyngeal Severe Acute Respiratory Syndrome Coronavirus 2 (SARS-CoV-2) Levels in Patients with Mild to Moderate Coronavirus Disease 2019 (COVID-19)," *JAMA Pediatrics*, 30 July 2020; Terry C. Jones, et al.," An analysis of SARS-CoV-2 Viral Load by Patient Age," *MedRxiv*, 9 June 2020; Julie Poline, et al., "Systematic SARS-CoV-2 Screening at Hospital Admission in Children: A French Prospective Multicenter Study," *Clinical Infectious Diseases*, 25 July 2020.

5. Adriana S. Lopez, et al., "Transmission Dynamics of COVID-19 Outbreaks Associated with Child Care Facilities – Salt Lake City, Utah, April–July 2020," *Morbidity and Mortality Weekly Report*, 11 September 2020; Magdalena Okarska-Napierała, et al., "SARS-CoV-2 Cluster in Nursery, Poland," *Emerging Infectious Diseases*, 27, 1 (2021).

6. "South Korea Closes Schools Again after Biggest Spike in Weeks," *BBC*, 29 May 2020; Lee Crawfurd, et al., "Back to School: An Update on COVID Cases as Schools Reopen," Center for Global Development, 12 June 2020, www.cgdev.org/blog/back-school-update-covid-cases-schools-reopen.

7. Apoorva Mandavilli, "Schoolchildren Seem Unlikely to Fuel Coronavirus Surges, Scientists Say," *New York Times*, 22 October 2020.

8. The State Council Information Office of the People's Republic of China, "Fighting Covid-19: China in Action," June 2020, II, 2, http://english.www.gov.cn/news/top news/202006/07/content_WS5edc559ac6d066592a449030.html.

9. Alan Levinovitz, "Chairman Mao Invented Traditional Chinese Medicine," *Slate*, 22 October 2013.

10. "China Is Ramping Up Its Promotion of Its Ancient Medical Arts," *Economist*, 31 August 2017.

11. Marta E. Hanson, "Conceptual Blind Spots, Media Blindfolds: The Case of SARS and Traditional Chinese Medicine," in Angela Ki Che Leung and Charlotte Furth, eds., *Health and Hygiene in Chinese East Asia* (Durham NC 2010) 228.

12. "China Issues Guideline for Promoting Traditional Chinese Medicine," *XinhuaNet*, 26 October 2019.

13. Wang Xiaodong, "Bigger Role for TCM Urged in Disease Control," *China Daily*, 28 May 2020.
14. Zhou Wenting, "TCM Leaves Its Mark in COVID-19 Recovery," *China Daily*, 29 May 2020.
15. Wang Xiaoyu, "Experts Urge More Research into TCM Use," *China Daily*, 18 April 2020.
16. Zhao Xinying, "Traditional Chinese Medicine Proves Effective against COVID-19," *China Daily*, 17 April 2020.
17. Zhao Yimeng, "Practitioners Call for Wider Recognition of Age-Old Skill," *China Daily*, 9 April 2020.
18. Henlen Tilley, "How to Make Sense of 'Traditional (Chinese) Medicine' in a Time of Covid-19," *Somatosphere*, 25 May 2020.
19. Zheng Yiran and Wu Yong, "TCM Builds Credibility in Global Fight," *China Daily*, 1 May 2020.
20. National Health Commission & State Administration of Traditional Chinese Medicine, "Diagnosis and Treatment Protocol for Novel Coronavirus Pneumonia," Trial Version 7, 3 March 2020, http://covid-19.chinadaily.com.cn/a/202003/27/WS5e7c25ba a310128217282337.html.
21. The State Council Information Office of the People's Republic of China, "Fighting Covid-19: China in Action."
22. National Health Commission, "Diagnosis and Treatment Protocol."
23. Hui Luo, et al., "Can Chinese Medicine Be Used for Prevention of Corona Virus Disease 2019 (COVID-19)? A Review of Historical Classics, Research Evidence, and Current Prevention Programs," *Chinese Journal of Integrative Medicine*, 26, 17 February 2020.
24. Renyi Wu, et al., "An Update on Current Therapeutic Drugs Treating COVID-19," *Current Pharmacology Reports*, 6, 11 May 2020.
25. Mike Davis, *The Monster at Our Door: The Global Threat of Avian Flu* (New York 2005) 75.
26. "Dossier: Herd Immunity in the Netherlands," *Actiegroep Containment Nu*, https://www.containmentnu.nl/articles/dossier-herd-immunity-in-the-netherlands?lang=en.
27. Yasmeen Abutaleb and Josh Dawsey, "New Trump Pandemic Adviser Pushes Controversial 'Herd Immunity' Strategy, Worrying Public Health Officials," *Washington Post*, 31 August 2020; Scott Gottleib, "Sweden Shouldn't Be America's Pandemic Model," *Wall Street Journal*, 30 August 2020.
28. Scott W. Atlas, "Reentry after the Panic: Paying the Health Price of Extreme Isolation," *The Hill*, 13 April 2020; Mallory Moench, "Meet Trump's New Coronavirus Adviser: Stanford Expert Scott Atlas Wants to Reopen Now, 'Safely,'" *San Francisco Chronicle*, 15 August 2020; Ashley Collman, "Meet Trump's New Coronavirus Adviser Dr. Scott Atlas, a Stanford Physician Who Frequently Criticized Lockdown Measures and Believes in the Full Reopening of Schools," *Business Insider*, 13 August 2020.
29. Aaron Blake, "Fauci Finally Loses His Patience with Rand Paul," *Washington Post*, 23 September 2020.
30. Jullien Gaer, "In Defence of a 'Herd Immunity' Strategy," *Telegraph*, 2 September 2020; Sarah Boseley, "Covid UK: Scientists at Loggerheads over Approach to New Restrictions," *Guardian*, 22 September 2020; "A Deliberate 'Population Immunity' Strategy before a Vaccine: Why It Wouldn't Work and Why It Shouldn't Be Tried," Independent SAGE Report 16, 25 September 2020, https://www.independentsage.org/a-deliberate-population-immunity-strategy-before-a-vaccine-why-it-wouldnt-work-and-why-it-shouldnt-be-tried/.
31. "Great Barrinton Declaration," https://gbdeclaration.org/.
32. Sarah Owermohle and David Lim, "Trump Advisers Consult Scientists Pushing Disputed Herd Immunity Strategy," *Politico*, 6 October 2020.
33. Sheryl Gay Stolberg, "White House Embraces a Declaration from Scientists That Opposes Lockdowns and Relies on 'Herd Immunity,'" *New York Times*, 13 October 2020.
34. Rupert Beale, "How to Block Spike," *London Review of Books*, 42, 10 (2020).

35. Patience K. Kiyuka, et al., "Human Coronavirus NL63 Molecular Epidemiology and Evolutionary Patterns in Rural Coastal Kenya," *Journal of Infectious Diseases*, 217, 11 (2018).
36. Robert J. Barro, "Non-pharmaceutical Interventions and Mortality in US Cities during the Great Influenza Pandemic, 1918–1919," NBER Working Paper 27049, July 2020.
37. Tomas Pueyo, "Coronavirus: The Hammer and the Dance," *Medium*, 19 March 2020.
38. Calla Wahlquist and Margaret Simons, "Melbourne's 'Hard Lockdown' Orders Residents of Nine Public Housing Towers to Stay Home as Coronavirus Cases Surge," *Guardian*, 4 July 2020.
39. "Leicester Lockdown Tightened as Cases Rise," *BBC*, 30 June 2020; Caitlin Oprysko, "Texas, Florida Governors Order Bars Closed, Impose New Restrictions as Cases Surge," *Politico*, 26 June 2020.
40. Harry Cockburn, "Catalonian Regional Government Orders 'Indefinite' Lockdown of Spain's Segria Region Due to Covid-19," *Independent*, 4 July 2020; "Spain Imposes Local Lockdown in Galicia," *BBC*, 5 July 2020.
41. Mehul Srivastava, "Israel in a 'Dangerous Place' as Virus Infections Surge," *Financial Times*, 7 July 2020; "Binyamin Netanyahu Boasted Too Soon of Defeating the Coronavirus," *Economist*, 23 July 2020.
42. Tim Shipman, "Our Future after Coronavirus Lockdown Begins to Take Shape: A Marathon Game of Whack-a-Mole," *Times* (London), 3 May 2020.
43. Martin Kulldorff, "'Hög dödlighet i dag kan ge färre döda på sikt," *Dagens Nyheter*, 4 May 2020.
44. Clas Svahn, "Giesecke: Om ett år är övriga Norden i kapp Sveriges dödstal," *Dagens Nyheter*, 10 May 2020; Johan Giesecke, "The Invisible Pandemic," *Lancet*, 5 May 2020; Emanuel Karlsten, "Tegnell-mejlen: Berättelsen om Johan Giesecke och Folkhälsomyndigheten," 11 August 2020, https://emanuelkarlsten.se/tegnell-mejlen-berattelsen-om-johan-giesecke-och-folkhalsomyndigheten/.
45. Chris Pleasance, "Swedish Covid-19 Expert Says Other Scandinavian Countries Will Be Hit Just as Badly When They Lift Restrictions and New Zealand Faces DECADES of Quarantining Foreigners If They Wipe Virus Out," *Daily Mail*, 8 May 2020.
46. Vienna International Airport, "Coronavirust PCR Tests Now Possible at Vienna Airport," www.viennaairport.com/pcrtest; "Coronavirus: Travellers Charged €190 at Vienna Airport to Avoid 14-day COVID-19 Quarantine," *Euronews*, 6 May 2020.
47. Elizabeth Kolbert, "How Iceland Beat the Coronavirus," *New Yorker*, 8 and 5 June 2020; Paul Waldie, "With Novel Testing Program, Iceland's COVID-19 Battle a Model for the World," *Globe and Mail*, 24 June 2020. The problem with this was that the rate of false negatives in the early days of an infection were very high, so testing would not catch all of the infected.
48. Twenty-one to Sweden's 4,029 on 25 May 2020 for a population about half the size, www.worldometers.info/coronavirus/#countries.
49. An analysis of their adoption of the strategy is in Emanuel Karlsten, "Tegnell-mejlen: Så fick flockimmuniteten fäste hos Folkhälsomyndigheten," 12 August 2020, https://emanuelkarlsten.se/tegnell-mejlen-sa-fick-flockimmuniteten-faste-hos-folkhalsomyndigheten/.
50. Tim Lister and Sebastian Shukla, "Sweden Challenges Trump – and Scientific Mainstream – by Refusing to Lock Down," *CNN*, 10 April 2020; Derek Robertson, "'They Are Leading Us to Catastrophe': Sweden's Coronavirus Stoicism Begins to Jar," *Guardian*, 30 March 2020; Jonas Grönvik, "Problem när länder inte har rätt bild av Sverige," *Svenska Dagbladet*, 20 May 2020.
51. Thibault Larger, "Sweden Didn't Seek Herd Immunity to the Coronavirus, Top Diplomat Says," *Politico*, 4 October 2020.

52. Petter J. Larsson, "Anders Tegnell hyllar brittisk tanke kring flockimmunitet: 'Dit vi behöver komma,'" *Aftonbladet*, 16 March 2020.

53. Kim Hjelmgaard, "Swedish Official Anders Tegnell Says 'Herd Immunity' in Sweden Might Be a Few Weeks Away," *USA Today*, 28 April 2020.

54. That herd immunity is the goal is assumed in Olle Häggström, et al., "Alternativ coronastrategi för Sverige kan rädda liv," *Dagens Nyheter*, 29 April 2020.

55. Tore Ellingsen and Jesper Roine, "Sweden and the Virus," in *Sweden through the Crisis* (Stockholm, forthcoming), www.hhs.se/contentassets/421dc1e74c54466a8d3a88a78c 775522/a02.pdf. That is also the conclusion of Johan Anderberg, *Flocken* (Stockholm, 2021).

56. George Martin, "Coronavirus: Stockholm Could Have 'Herd Immunity' by Next Month, Swedish Health Chief Claims," *Yahoo News UK*, 19 April 2020.

57. Marta Paterlini, "'Closing Borders Is Ridiculous': The Epidemiologist behind Sweden's Controversial Coronavirus Strategy," *Nature*, 21 April 2020.

58. Tia Ghose, "Way More People May Have Gotten Coronavirus Than We Thought, Small Antibody Study Suggests," *LiveScience*, 18 April 2020; Natalie E. Dean and Caitlin Rivers, "Antibody Tests Show We're Nowhere Near Herd Immunity," *Washington Post*, 29 April 2020.

59. Noah Higgins-Dunn, et al., "New York Antibody Study Estimates 13.9% of Residents Have Had the Coronavirus, Gov. Cuomo Says," *CNBC*, 23 April 2020.

60. "Los primeros resultados del ENECovid19 muestran que el 5% de la población ha desarrollado anticuerpos frente a la enfermedad," https://www.ciencia.gob.es/portal/ site/MICINN/menuitem.edc7f2029a2be27d7010721001432ea0/?vgnextoid=54fbe2c a61f02710VgnVCM1000001d04140aRCRD&vgnextchannel=4346846085f90210VgnV CM1000001034e20aRCRD.

61. Henrik Salje, et al., "Estimating the Burden of SARS-CoV-2 in France," *Science*, 13 May 2020; Nadja Popovich and Margot Sanger-Katz, "The World Is Still Far from Herd Immunity for Coronavirus," *New York Times*, 28 May 2020; Shuchi Anand, et al., "Prevalence of SARS-CoV-2 Antibodies in a Large Nationwide Sample of Patients on Dialysis in the USA," *Lancet*, 25 September 2020.

62. Patrick Eickemeier, "Fast die Hälfte der getesteten Bürger in Ischgl waren infiziert," *Tagesspiegel*, 25 June 2020.

63. "Politics This Week," *Economist*, 23 July 2020; "India's Economy Shrinks by a Quarter as Covid-19 Gathers Pace," *Economist*, 3 September 2020.

64. "Experten om antalet smittade i Spanien: 'Inte bra för Sverige,'" *SVT Nyheter*, 13 May 2020.

65. Aarti Nagarkar, et al., "Epidemiological and Serological Surveillance of COVID-19 in Pune City," 16 August 2020, www.iiserpune.ac.in/userfiles/files/Pune_Serosurvey_ Technical_report-16_08_2020.pdf.

66. Joseph Goldstein, "68% Have Antibodies in This Clinic. Can Neighborhood Beat a Next Wave?," *New York Times*, 9 July 2020.

67. Lewis F. Buss, "COVID-19 Herd Immunity in the Brazilian Amazon," *MedRxiv*, 21 September 2020; Andrew Jeremijenko, et al., "Evidence for and Level of Herd Immunity against SARS-CoV-2 Infection," *MedRxiv*, 28 September 2020.

68. Lindsay Isaac and Jay Croft, "WHO Says No Evidence Shows That Having Coronavirus Prevents a Second Infection," *CNN*, 25 April 2020.

69. Hilary Brueck, "The WHO Made a Thinly Veiled Dig at Sweden's Loose Coronavirus Lockdown, Saying 'Humans Are Not Herds' and Old People Are Not Disposable," *Business Insider*, 11 May 2020; "WHO: Herd Immunity for the Coronavirus Is a 'Dangerous Concept,'" *Telegraph*, 12 May 2020.

70. Akiko Iwasaki and Ruslan Medzhitov, "Scared That Covid-19 Immunity Won't Last? Don't Be," *New York Times*, 31 July 2020.

71. Jeffrey Seow, et al., "Longitudinal Evaluation and Decline of Antibody Responses in SARS-CoV-2 Infection," *MedRxiv*, 11 July 2020.
72. "If Memory Serves," *New Scientist*, 3289, 4 July 2020.
73. Haley E. Randolph and Luis B. Barreiro, "Herd Immunity: Understanding COVID-19," *Immunity*, 20 May 2020.
74. "Herd immunity, an 'Unethical' COVID-19 Strategy, Tedros Warns Policymakers," *UN News*, 12 October 2020.
75. Ivar Arpi, "Kalla det Johan Giesecke-syndromet," *Svenska Dagbladet*, 22 April 2020.
76. "Allvarliga fel om smittade – rapport dras tilbaka," *Svenska Dagbladet*, 22 April 2020.
77. Emanuel Karlsten, "Folkhälsomyndigheten om siffrorna: 'Det blev alldeles galet,'" 21 April 2020, https://emanuelkarlsten.se/04/folkhalsomyndigheten-om-siffrorna-det-blev-alldeles-galet/. This was not to be the last time the Swedish public health authorities turned out to be making arithmetic mistakes: "Folkhälsomyndigheten räknade fel – två gånger," *SVT Nyheter*, 21 July 2020.
78. Folkhälsomyndigheten, "Skattning av peakdag och antal infekterade i covid-19-utbrottet i Stockholms län februari–april 2020," 24 April 2020, www.folkhalsomyndigh eten.se/publicerat-material/publikationsarkiv/s/skattning-av-peakdag-och-antal-infe kterade-i-covid-19-utbrottet-i-stockholms-lan-februari-april-2020/.
79. Folkhälsomyndigheten, "Uppdaterad modellering av spridningen av covid-19 i Stockholms län," 23 April 2020, www.folkhalsomyndigheten.se/nyheter-och-press/n yhetsarkiv/2020/april/uppdaterad-modellering-av-spridningen-av-covid-19-i-stock holms-lan/.
80. Folkhälsomyndigheten, "Första resultaten från pågående undersökning av antikroppar för covid-19-virus," 20 May 2020, www.folkhalsomyndigheten.se/nyheter-och-press/ny hetsarkiv/2020/maj/forsta-resultaten-fran-pagaende-undersokning-av-antikroppar-for-covid-19-virus/.
81. Mathias Ståhle, "Karolinska: 17,2 procent har antikroppar," *Svenska Dagbladet*, 24 June 2020.
82. Eric J. W. Orlowski and David J. A. Goldsmith, "Four Months into the COVID-19 Pandemic, Sweden's Prized Herd Immunity Is Nowhere in Sight," *Journal of the Royal Society of Medicine*, 11 August 2020.
83. Thomas Erdbrink, "Sweden Tries Out a New Status: Pariah State," *New York Times*, 22 June 2020.
84. Hannah Frejdeman, "Expert: Norge har lyckats bäst – om vaccin kommer," *Svenska Dagbladet*, 24 July 2020.
85. "Tegnell: Nu bærer Sveriges omstridte coronastrategi frugt," *Politiken*, 16 September 2020.
86. Lars Dahlager, "Tog vi fejl om flokimmunitet? De meget lave svenske smittetal tyder på det," *Politiken*, 17 September 2020; Ivan Cherberko, "Anti-re-quarantine Medicine," *Vedomosti*, 21 September 2020.
87. Hanna Törnquist, "Tegnell: Viktigt nu att vi inte tappar kontrollen," *Svenska Dagbladet*, 22 September 2020.
88. "'Avoid Contact with All but Your Family': Uppsala Becomes First Swedish Region to Get Local Coronavirus Measures," *The Local*, 20 October 2020.
89. "Ökad smitta i Stockholm – hemisolering infört," *Svenska Dagbladet*, 12 October 2020; Richard Orange, "Sweden Considers 'Local Lockdowns' in Shift in Coronavirus Strategy," *Telegraph*, 17 October 2020; Johan Carlström, "Regeringen vill införa ny pandemilag – M kritiska," *Svenska Dagbladet*, 19 October 2020.
90. Fredrik Mellgren, "Belgisk professor i SVT: Flockimmunitet dröjer," *Svenska Dagbladet*, 17 May 2020.
91. "FHM:s antikroppstester avviker från prognoserna – matematikern 'ser två förklaringar,'" *SVT Nyheter*, 20 May 2020.
92. "Läkaren om antikroppstesterna: 'Antikroppar inte detsamma som immunitet,'" *SVT Nyheter*, 20 May 2020.

93. Hugo Ewald and Amanda Dahl, "Tester: 7,3 procent bär på antikroppar i Stockholm," *Dagens Nyheter*, 20 May 2020.
94. The evidence against this position is marshaled in Thomas Pueyo, "Coronavirus: Should We Aim for Herd Immunity Like Sweden?," *Medium*, 9 June 2020.
95. Freddie Sayers, "Nobel Prize-Winning Scientist: The Covid-19 Epidemic Was Never Exponential," *UnHerd*, 2 May 2020.
96. Toby Young, "Nobel Laureate Skewers Member of Imperial College Modelling Team," *Lockdown Skeptics*, 30 May 2020.
97. Freddie Sayers, "Sunetra Gupta: Covid-19 Is on the Way Out," *UnHerd*, 21 May 2020; "We May Already Have Herd Immunity: An Interview with Professor Sunetra Gupta," *Reaction*, 21 July 2020; José Lourenço, et al., "Fundamental Principles of Epidemic Spread Highlight the Immediate Need for Large-Scale Serological Surveys to Assess the Stage of the SARS-CoV-2 Epidemic," *MedRxiv*, 26 March 2020. Other arguments for herd immunity included Raj S. Bhopal, "COVID-19 Zugzwang: Potential Public Health Moves towards Population (Herd) Immunity," *Public Health in Practice*, 15 July 2020.
98. Clas Svahn, "Giesecke: Om ett år är övriga Norden i kapp Sveriges dödstal," *Dagens Nyheter*, 10 May 2020. His protégé, Tegnell, knew better than to fall for such nonsense. He dismissed the idea that one could stop the epidemic in its tracks via herd immunity and in late May suddenly began insisting that vaccination would also be necessary. Hugo Ewald and Amanda Dahl, "Tester: 7,3 procent bär på antikroppar i Stockholm," *Dagens Nyheter*, 20 May 2020.
99. Apoorva Mandavilli, "You May Have Antibodies after Coronavirus Infection: But Not for Long," *New York Times*, 18 June 2020.
100. Daniel M. Altmann and Rosemary J. Boyton, "SARS-CoV-2 T Cell Immunity: Specificity, Function, Durability, and Role in Protection," *Science Immunology*, 17 July 2020.
101. Andrew Joseph, "Immunity to the Coronavirus Remains a Mystery," *Stat*, 11 June 2020.
102. Alba Grifoni, et al., "Targets of T Cell Responses to SARS-CoV-2 Coronavirus in Humans with COVID-19 Disease and Unexposed Individuals," *Cell*, 181 (2020); Julian Brown, et al., "Presence of SARS-CoV-2 Reactive T Cells in COVID-19 Patients and Healthy Donors," *MedRxiv*, 22 April 2020; Alessandro Sette and Shane Crotty, "Pre-existing Immunity to SARS-CoV-2: The Knowns and Unknowns," *Nature Reviews Immunology*, 7 July 2020; Julian Braun, et al., "SARS-CoV-2-Reactive T Cells in Healthy Donors and Patients with COVID-19," *Nature*, 29 July 2020; Jose Mateus, et al., "Selective and Cross-Reactive SARS-CoV-2 T Cell Epitopes in Unexposed Humans," *Science*, 4 August 2020; Annika Nelde, et al., "SARS-CoV-2-Derived Peptides Define Heterologous and COVID-19-Induced T Cell Recognition," *Nature Immunology*, 30 September 2020.
103. Nina Le Bert, et al., "SARS-CoV-2-Specific T Cell Immunity in Cases of COVID-19 and SARS, and Uninfected Controls," *Nature*, 15 July 2020.
104. Daniel P. Oran and and Eric J. Topol, "Prevalence of Asymptomatic SARS-CoV-2 Infection," *Annals of Internal Medicine*, 3 June 2020.
105. José Lourenço, et al., "The Impact of Host Resistance on Cumulative Mortality and the Threshold of Herd Immunity for SARS-CoV," *MedRxiv*, 16 July 2020.
106. Takuya Sekine, et al., "Robust T Cell Immunity in Convalescent Individuals with Asymptomatic or Mild COVID-19," *BioRxiv*, 29 June 2020.
107. Ollie Bengtsson, "FHM: Stockholm kan ha 40 procents immunitet," *Dagens Nyheter*, 17 July 2020; Charlie Duxbury, "Sweden Split on Coronavirus Immunity," *Politico*, 23 July 2020.
108. Per Kudo, "Smittan ökar kraftigt i Stockholms innerstad," *Svenska Dagbladet*, 9 October 2020.

109. Angkana T. Huang, et al., "A Systematic Review of Antibody Mediated Immunity to Coronaviruses: Kinetics, Correlates of Protection, and Association with Severity," *Nature Communications*, 17 September 2020.
110. "Astra Zenecas vaccin mot covid-19 ifrågasätts," *SVT Nyheter*, 11 July 2020; William A. Haseltine, "Did the Oxford Covid Vaccine Work in Monkeys? Not Really," *Forbes*, 16 May 2020; Adam Finn and Richard Malley, "A Vaccine That Stops Covid-19 Won't Be Enough," *New York Times*, 24 August 2020.
111. Rachael Schraer, "Immunity May Be More Widespread Than Tests Suggest," *BBC*, 1 July 2020.
112. John Lauerman and James Paton, "First Coronavirus Vaccines May Not Prevent Infection," *Detroit News*, 15 June 2020.
113. Regieringskansliet, "Strategi med anledning av det nya coronaviruset," 7 April 2020, www.regeringen.se/regeringens-politik/regeringens-arbete-med-anledning-av-nya-coronaviruset/strategi-med-anledning-av-det-nya-coronaviruset/.
114. Peter Baldwin, *Contagion and the State in Europe, 1830–1930* (Cambridge 1999) 171–73.
115. "'Do It at Home' Coronavirus Saliva Test Trialled," *BBC*, 22 June 2020; Laurence J. Kotlikoff and Michael Mina, "A Cheap, Simple Way to Control the Coronavirus," *New York Times*, 3 July 2020; Daniel B. Larremore, et al., "Test Sensitivity Is Secondary to Frequency and Turnaround Time for COVID-19 Surveillance," *MedRxiv*, 27 June 2020.
116. Paul Romer, "Simulating Covid-19: Part Two," https://paulromer.net/covid-sim-part2/; "Romer on Testing," *Grumpy Economist*, 21 September 2020; Julian Peto, "How to Ramp Up Covid-19 Mass Testing Immediately in the UK," *Financial Times*, 31 March 2020. Resting on this premise, of testing rather than lockdown, is also Danielle Allen, et al., "Roadmap to Pandemic Resilience: Massive Scale Testing, Tracing, and Supported Isolation (TTSI) as the Path to Pandemic Reslience for a Free Society," Edmund J. Safra Center for Ethics, 20 April 2020.
117. Joshua Gans, *The Pandemic Information Gap: The Brutal Economics of COVID-19* (Cambridge MA 2020).
118. William Haseltine, "How We Can Contain Covid-19 without a Vaccine," *CNN*, 4 September 2020.
119. "New Saliva Test for Coronavirus Piloted in Southampton," Department of Health and Social Care, 22 June 2020, www.gov.uk/government/news/new-saliva-test-for-coronavirus-piloted-in-southampton.
120. Aitor Hernández-Morales, "Know Your Status: Lessons from AIDS for the Coronavirus Epidemic," *Politico*, 20 April 2020.
121. Leon Mutesa, et al., "A Strategy for Finding People Infected with SARS-CoV–2: Optimizing Pooled Testing at Low Prevalence," *MedRxiv*, 3 August 2020.
122. Ned Augenblick, et al., "Group Testing in a Pandemic: The Role of Frequent Testing, Correlated Risk, and Machine Learning," http://faculty.haas.berkeley.edu/ned/GroupTestingInAPandemic.pdf.
123. Dimitrios Gouglas, et al., "Estimating the Cost of Vaccine Development against Epidemic Infectious Diseases: A Cost Minimisation Study," *Lancet*, 17 October 2018.
124. Annalisa Merelli, "Tracking the $5.1 Billion the US Has Spent on Covid-19 Medical Research," *Quartz*, 9 July 2020; Helen Branswell, et al., "Operation Warp Speed Promised to Do the Impossible. How Far Has It Come?," *Stat*, 8 September 2020.
125. Pierre Azoulay and Benjamin Jones, "Beat COVID-19 through Innovation," *Science*, 8 May 2020.
126. "The World Is Spending Nowhere Near Enough on a Coronavirus Vaccine," *Economist*, 8 August 2020.
127. Matt Appuzo, et al., "How the World Missed COVID-19's Silent Spread," *New York Times*, 27 June 2020.

128. Rongrong Yang, et al., "Comparison of Clinical Characteristics of Patients with Asymptomatic vs Symptomatic Coronavirus Disease 2019 in Wuhan, China," *JAMA Network Open*, 27 May 2020; Daniel P. Oran and and Eric J. Topol, "Prevalence of Asymptomatic SARS-CoV-2 Infection," *Annals of Internal Medicine*, 3 June 2020.

129. Jacqueline Howard, "WHO Clarifies Comments on Asymptomatic Spread of Coronavirus," *CNN*, 10 June 2020.

130. Luca Ferretti, "Quantifying SARS-CoV-2 Transmission Suggests Epidemic Control with Digital Contact Tracing," *Science*, 368, 6491 (8 May 2020); Tapiwa Ganyani, et al., "Estimating the Generation Interval for Coronavirus Disease (COVID-19) Based on Symptom Onset Data, March 2020," *Eurosurveillance*, 25, 17 (April 2020); Xi He, et al., "Temporal Dynamics in Viral Shedding and Transmissibility of COVID-19," *Nature Medicine*, 15 April 2020.

131. Seungjae Lee, et al., "Clinical Course and Molecular Viral Shedding among Asymptomatic and Symptomatic Patients with SARS-CoV-2 Infection in a Community Treatment Center in the Republic of Korea," *JAMA Internal Medicine*, 6 August 2020.

132. Seyed M. Moghadas, et al., "The Implications of Silent Transmission for the Control of COVID-19 Outbreaks," *Proceedings of the National Academy of Sciences*, 6 July 2020.

133. Ferretti, "Quantifying SARS-CoV-2 Transmission."

134. The State Council Information Office of the People's Republic of China, "Fighting Covid-19: China in Action."

135. National Health Commission of the People's Republic of China, "Protocol for Prevention and Control of COVID-19 (Edition Six)," *Chinese Center for Disease Control and Prevention Weekly*, 20 March 2020, 4, http://covid-19.chinadaily.com.cn/a/20200 3/27/WS5e7c2586a310128217282335.html.

136. "Adresse aux français du Président de la République Emmanuel Macron," 16 March 2020, www.elysee.fr/front/pdf/elysee-module-15345-fr.pdf.

137. Lena Einhorn, "Hur kunde vi släppa in smittan på Stockholms äldreboenden?," *Dagens Nyheter*, 9 April 2020; Christian Stichler, "Die Welt steht still. Nur Schweden nicht," *ZeitOnline*, 24 March 2020.

138. Marta Paterlini, "'Closing Borders Is Ridiculous': The Epidemiologist Behind Sweden's Controversial Coronavirus Strategy," *Nature*, 21 April 2020.

139. Allgemeinverfügung des Landratsamtes Main-Tauber-Kreis über die häusliche Absonderung von Personen, die mit dem neuartigen Corona-Virus (SARS-CoV-2) infiziert sind und deren Kontaktpersonen zur Eindämmung und zum Schutz vor der Verbreitung der Atemwegserkrankung COVID-19 vom 23. März 2020, I1e, www .main-tauber-kreis.de/Landratsamt/Themen-und-Projekte/Coronavirus.

140. Nicoletta Lanese, "'Superspreader' in South Korea Infects Nearly 40 People with Coronavirus," *LiveScience*, 23 February 2020; Lea Hammer, et al., "High SARS-CoV-2 Attack Rate Following Exposure at a Choir Practice – Skagit County, Washington, March 2020," *Morbidity and Mortality Weekly Report*, 69, 19, 15 May 2020; Tangi Salaün, "Five Days of Worship That Set a Virus Time Bomb in France," *Reuters*, 30 March 2020.

141. Timothy Williams and Danielle Ivory, "Chicago's Jail Is Top U.S. Hot Spot as Virus Spreads behind Bars," *New York Times*, 8 April 2020; Laura Hawks, et al., "COVID-19 in Prisons and Jails in the United States," *JAMA Internal Medicine*, 28 April 2020.

142. Gabriel Felbermayr, et al., "Après-ski: The Spread of Coronavirus from Ischgl through Germany," Institut für Weltwirtschaft Kiel, 24 May 2020; Julia Bernewasser, "Ischgl war der 'Ground Zero' für Deutschland," *Tagesspiegel*, 27 May 2020.

143. Elizabeth McGraw, "A Few Superspreaders Transmit the Majority of Coronavirus Cases," *Conversation*, 5 June 2020.

144. Carl Zimmer, "Most People with Coronavirus Won't Spread It. Why Do a Few Infect Many?," *New York Times*, 30 June 2020.

145. Isaac Ghinai, et al., "Community Transmission of SARS-CoV-2 at Two Family Gatherings – Chicago, Illinois, February–March 2020," *Morbidity and Mortality Weekly Report*, 69, 15, 17 April 2020.

146. Ashish Goyal, et al., "Wrong Person, Place and Time: Viral Load and Contact Network Structure Predict SARS-CoV-2 Transmission and Super-spreading Events," *MedRxiv*, 7 August 2020.

147. Donald G. McNeil, Jr., "Bacteria Study Offers Clues to Typhoid Mary Mystery," *New York Times*, 26 August 2013.

148. Gary Wong, et al., "MERS, SARS, and Ebola: The Role of Super-spreaders in Infectious Disease," *Cell Host and Microbe*, 18, 4 (2015).

149. Gabriel Rotello, *Sexual Ecology: AIDS and the Destiny of Gay Men* (New York 1997) 9, 40–42, 51, 86; Ilan H. Meyer and Laura Dean, "Patterns of Sexual Behavior and Risk Taking among Young New York City Gay Men," *AIDS Education and Prevention* 7, suppl. 13–23 (1995) 17, 19, 21–22; World Bank, *Confronting AIDS: Public Priorities in a Global Epidemic* (Oxford 1997) 68, 139–56.

150. Kai Kupferschmidt, "Case Clustering Emerges as Key Pandemic Puzzle," *Science*, 22 May 2020.

151. Dillon Adam, et al., "Clustering and Superspreading Potential of Severe Acute Respiratory Syndrome Coronavirus 2 (SARS-CoV-2) Infections in Hong Kong," *Research Square*, 21 May 2020; Dillon C. Adam and Benjamin C. Cowling, "Just Stop the Superspreading," *New York Times*, 2 June 2020.

152. Richard A. Stein, "Super-spreaders in Infectious Diseases," *International Journal of Infectious Diseases*, 15, 8 (2011).

153. Max S. Y. Lau, et al., "Characterizing Super-spreading Events and Age-Specific Infectivity of COVID-19 Transmission in Georgia, USA," *MedRxiv*, 22 June 2020.

154. Ramanan Laxminarayan, et al., "Epidemiology and Transmission Dynamics of COVID-19 in Two Indian States," *Science*, 30 September 2020.

155. J. O. Lloyd-Smith, et al., "Superspreading and the Effect of Individual Variation on Disease Emergence," *Nature*, 17 November 2005.

156. David Shaywitz, "Black Swans, Networks, and COVID-19," *AEI*, 10 March 2020; Akira Endo, et al., "Estimating the Overdispersion in COVID-19 Transmission Using Outbreak Sizes outside China," *Wellcome Open Research*, 9 April 2020.

157. Christos Nicolaides, et al., "Hand-Hygiene Mitigation Strategies against Global Disease Spreading through the Air Transportation Network," *Risk Analysis*, 40, 4 (2020).

158. Paul Fine, et al., "'Herd Immunity': A Rough Guide," *Clinical Infectious Diseases*, 52, 7 (2011).

159. Lourenço, et al., "The Impact of Host Resistance on Cumulative Mortality and the Threshold of Herd Immunity for SARS-CoV"; M. Gabriela M. Gomes, et al., "Individual Variation in Susceptibility or Exposure to SARS-CoV-2 Lowers the Herd Immunity Threshold," *MedRxiv*, 21 May 2020; Tom Britton, et al., "A Mathematical Model Reveals the Influence of Population Heterogeneity on Herd Immunity to SARS-CoV-2," *Science*, 23 June 2020; James Hamblin, "A New Understanding of Herd Immunity," *Atlantic*, 13 July 2020.

160. Alexei T. Tkachenko, et al., "Persistent Heterogeneity Not Short-Term Overdispersion Determines Herd Immunity to COVID-19," *MedRxiv*, 11 August 2020; Ricardo Aguas, et al., "Herd Immunity Thresholds for SARS-CoV-2 Estimated from Unfolding Epidemics," *MedRxiv*, 24 July 2020.

161. Richard Coker, "'Harvesting' Is a Terrible Word – But It's What Has Happened in Britain's Care Homes," *Guardian*, 8 May 2020.

162. Andrew Gordon, "Historical Context for COVID 19 Policies in Japan and Asia (1)," *Tokyo College*, 5 July 2020, www.tc.u-tokyo.ac.jp/en/weblog/1896/#_ftn4.

163. Kim Ho, "Thais Most Likely to Wear Facemasks in ASEAN," *YouGov*, 19 May 2020.
164. Matt Bell, "The Cheapest Solution to COVID-19 Is Right in Front of Our Face," *Medium*, 17 April 2020.
165. Richard C. Paddock, "In Indonesia, False Virus Cures Pushed by Those Who Should Know Better," *New York Times*, 31 July 2020.
166. Alfred W. Crosby, *America's Forgotten Pandemic: The Influenza of 1918*, 2nd ed. (Cambridge 2003) 103.
167. WHO, "Advice on the Use of Masks in the Context of COVID-19," 6 April 2020, https://apps.who.int/iris/handle/10665/331693; Johanna Cederblad, "Tegnell: 'Ute efter enkla lösningar,'" *Svenska Dagbladet*, 7 June 2020.
168. Alberto Giubilini and Julian Savulescu, "Vaccination, Risks, and Freedom: The Seat Belt Analogy," *Public Health Ethics*, 12, 3 (2019).
169. Mathilde Damgé, et al., "Combien de fois puis-je sortir de chez moi? Combien de temps cela va durer? Nos réponses à vos questions sur le confinement," *Le Monde*, 18 March 2020.
170. Olivier Faye, "Port du masque: Le gouvernement amorce un virage à 180 degrés," *Le Monde*, 6 April 2020; Rachel Donadio, "France: After Lockdown, the Street," *New York Review of Books*, 23 July 2020.
171. Richard O. J. H. Stutt, et al., "A Modelling Framework to Assess the Likely Effectiveness of Facemasks in Combination with 'Lock-down' in Managing the COVID-19 Pandemic," *Proceedings of the Royal Society A*, 476, 2238 (10 June 2020); Jeremy Howard, et al., "Face Masks against COVID-19: An Evidence Review," *Preprints*, 12 May 2020; Wei Lyu and George L. Wehby, "Community Use of Face Masks and COVID-19: Evidence from a Natural Experiment of State Mandates in the US," *Health Affairs*, 16 June 2020; Derek K. Chu, et al., "Physical Distancing, Face Masks, and Eye Protection to Prevent Person-to-Person Transmission of SARS-CoV-2 and COVID-19," *Lancet*, 27 June 2020.
172. Renyi Zhang, et al. "Identifying Airborne Transmission as the Dominant Route for the Spread of COVID-19," *Proceedings of the National Academy of Science*, 30 June 2020. Similar study in Timo Mitze, et al., "Face Masks Considerably Reduce COVID-19 Cases in Germany," IZA Institute of Labor Economics, *Discussion Paper Series*, 13319, June 2020.
173. Apoorva Mandavilli, "W.H.O. Finally Endorses Masks to Prevent Coronavirus Transmission," *New York Times*, 5 June 2020.
174. Apoorva Mandavilli, "239 Experts with One Big Claim: The Coronavirus Is Airborne," *New York Times*, 4 July 2020.
175. Julia Marcus, "The Dudes Who Won't Wear Masks," *Atlantic*, 23 June 2020.
176. "Brazil's Bolsonaro Waters Down Law Requiring Face Masks," *BBC*, 3 July 2020; Liam Stack and Joseph Goldstein, "New York Threatens Orthodox Jewish Areas with Lockdown over Virus," *New York Times*, 25 September 2020.
177. Laurenz Gehrke and Ashley Furlong, "Timelime: How Europe Embraced the Coronavirus Face Mask," *Politico*, 16 July 2020.
178. Erica Treijs, "Över 130 länder kräver munskydd – men inte Sverige," *Svenska Dagbladet*, 31 July 2020.
179. Emilio Casalicchio, "How Masks Became a Fault Line in Britain's Culture War," *Politico*, 16 July 2020.
180. Amitai Etzioni, "Wearing a Face Mask Is Patriotic," *National Interest*, 19 May 2020.
181. Peter Glick, "Masks and Emasculation," *Scientific American*, August 2020.
182. Erin Blakemore, "How to Make Masks That Everyone Will Want to Wear," *National Geographic*, 10 July 2020.
183. Alicia Cohn, "Woman Browbeats Reporter for Wearing a Mask at Ohio Lockdown Protest," *The Hill*, 1 May 2020.

184. Chase Biefeldt, "As Boise Hands Out Face Masks for Mayor McLean's Health Order, Protesters Say It Encroaches on Their Freedom," *KTVB7*, 3 July 2020.

185. Tim Elfrink and Felicia Sonmez, "Pelosi Asks House Committees to Require Masks, Setting Up Clash with GOP Holdouts," *Washington Post*, 17 June 2020.

186. Leah Asmelash and Hollie Silverman, "City's Proclamation Requiring Face Masks in Stores and Restaurants Is Amended after Threats of Violence," *CNN*, 3 May 2020; Meagan Flynn, "Georgia Gov. Brian Kemp Forbids Cities, Counties from Requiring Masks as Coronavirus Surges in the State," *Washington Post*, 16 July 2020.

187. Ruth Igielnik, "Most Americans Say They Regularly Wore a Mask in Stores in the Past Month; Fewer See Others Doing It," *Pew Research Center*, 23 June 2020.

188. Julie Bosman, "Amid Virus Surge, Republicans Abruptly Urge Masks Despite Trump's Resistance," *New York Times*, 1 July 2020; Aamer Madhani and Laurie Kellman, "Republicans, with Exception of Trump, Now Push Mask-Wearing," *AP News*, 30 June 2020.

189. Luis Ferré-Sadurni and Maria Cramer, "New York Orders Residents to Wear Masks in Public," *New York Times*, 15 April 2020.

190. California Department of Public Health, "Guidance for the Use of Face Coverings," 18 June 2020, https://www.madera.courts.ca.gov/Images/CA%20Dept%20of%20 Public%20Health%20-%20Guidance-for-Face-Coverings_06-18-2020.pdf.

191. Alan Kim, et al., "These Are the States Requiring People to Wear Masks When Out in Public," *CNN*, https://www.cnn.com/2020/06/19/us/states-face-mask-coronavirus-t rnd/index.html; "What U.S. States Require Masks in Public?," https://masks4all.co /what-states-require-masks/. Viewed 20 July 2020.

192. Robert Tait, "Czechs Get to Work Making Masks after Government Decree," *Guardian*, 30 March 2020.

193. Katrin Bennhold, "Giving Your Number to Strangers? It's not Flirting; It's a Rule," *New York Times*, 7 June 2020.

194. Kate Connolly, "Germans Could Be Fined Up to €10,000 as Face Mask Rules Brought In," *Guardian*, 27 April 2020. Meanwhile, whether masks worked in banks, which normally frowned on customers wearing them, was discussed. Renae Merle, "Banks Face a Unique Coronavirus Problem: Now Everyone Is Wearing a Mask, *Washington Post*, 22 July 2020.

195. "Coronavirus: 'We Do Not Recommend Face Masks for General Wearing,'" *BBC*, 3 April 2020; Rebecca Miller, "Grant Shapps Lists Four Reasons Why Sadiq Khan's Face Mask Demands Are 'Counterproductive,'" *Express*, 17 April 2020.

196. "Twenty-sixth SAGE meeting on Covid-19," 16 April 2020, https://assets .publishing.service.gov.uk/government/uploads/system/uploads/attachment_ data/file/888798/S0394_Twenty-sixth_SAGE_meeting_on_Covid-19_.pdf.

197. "SPI-B Return to SAGE on the Use of Facemasks in a Community Setting," 20 April 2020, https://assets.publishing.service.gov.uk/government/uploads/sys tem/uploads/attachment_data/file/888572/4c._200420_SPI- B_return_to_SAGE_CMO_on_facemasks_FINAL_S0208.pdf.

198. "Twenty-seventh SAGE meeting on Covid-19," 21 April 2020, https://assets .publishing.service.gov.uk/government/uploads/system/uploads/attachment_ data/file/888799/S0396_Twenty-seventh_SAGE_meeting_on_Covid-19.pdf.

199. Rowena Mason, "Face Coverings to Be Made Compulsory on Public Transport in England," *Guardian*, 4 June 2020; James Robinson, "So Much for the New Rules! TfL Hands Out 30,000 Free Masks as One in Five Bus and Tube Passengers Try to Ride without Face-Covering Risking a £100 Fine Today," *Daily Mail*, 15 June 2020.

200. Sarah Dean, "Britain Is the Worst-Hit Country outside of the US and Brazil. But It Still Won't Wear Masks," *CNN*, 12 July 2020.

201. James Gant and Luke May, "'I Will Not Be Masked, Tested, Tracked or Poisoned': Hundreds of Anti-mask Activists March on London's Hyde Park to Protest the Mandatory Use of Face Coverings in Shops from Thursday," *Daily Mail*, 19 July 2020; "With Face-Masks, Britain Imported an American Culture War," *Economist*, 8 August 2020.

202. Public Health Agency of Sweden, "FAQ about COVID-19," www.folkhalsomyndigh eten.se/the-public-health-agency-of-sweden/communicable-disease-control/covid-19/.

203. Clas Svahn, "Johan Carlson: Smittan kom in från länder som gick under vår radar," *Dagens Nyheter*, 10 June 2020; Cederblad, "Tegnell: 'Ute efter enkla lösningar.'"

204. Anette Holmqvist and Jonathan Jeppsson, "Stefan Löfvens svar på läsarnas frågor," *Aftonbladet*, 7 May 2020.

205. Gretchen Vogel, "'It's Been So, So Surreal.' Critics of Sweden's Lax Pandemic Policies Face Fierce Backlash," *Science*, 6 October 2020. This is an excellent account of the Swedish approach more generally.

206. Imperial College London and YouGov, "Covid-19: Insights on Face Mask Use: Global Review," 14 May to 4 June 2020, www.imperial.ac.uk/media/imperial-college/insti tute-of-global-health-innovation/ICL-YouGov-Covid-19-Behaviour-Tracker_Global_ FaceMask_20200609_VF.pdf?referringSource=articleShare.

207. Anette Holmqvist and Jonathan Jeppsson, "Stefan Löfvens svar på läsarnas frågor," *Aftonbladet*, 7 May 2020.

208. WHO, "Advice on the Use of Masks in the Context of COVID-19," 6 April 2020, https://apps.who.int/iris/handle/10665/331693.

209. WHO, "Advice on the Use of Masks in the Context of COVID-19," 5 June 2020, www .who.int/publications/i/item/advice-on-the-use-of-masks-in-the-community-during-home-care-and-in-healthcare-settings-in-the-context-of-the-novel-coronavirus-(2019-n cov)-outbreak.

210. Cederblad, "Tegnell: 'Ute efter enkla lösningar,'" TT, "Tegnell: Munskydd passar inte i coronastrategi," *Aftonbladet*, 5 June 2020.

211. Cederblad, "Tegnell: 'Ute efter enkla lösningar.'"

212. Wolfgang Hansson, "När blir det tvång på munskydd i Sverige?," *Aftonbladet*, 3 April 2020.

213. Leif Bjermer, et al., "Varför vägrar du införa munskydd, Tegnell?," *Aftonbladet*, 12 June 2020.

214. Louise Schou Drivsholm, "Der skal være tunge argumenter for at indføre maskepåbud i Danmark. Det er der ikke i dag," *Information*, 22 July 2020. One might be tempted to correlate mask resistance with those nations that had also introduced laws against headcoverings, but the French threw a wrench into that argument.

215. "What Countries Require Masks in Public or Recommend Masks?," https://masks4all .co/what-countries-require-masks-in-public/.

216. Cecilie Lund Kristiansen and Johan Blem Larsen, "Regeringen indfører krav om mundbind i offentlig transport i Aarhus," *Politiken*, 7 August 2020.

217. Kirsten Nilsson, et al., "Sundhedsstyrelsen vil ændre ulogiske retningslinjer: Hjemmehjælpere skal også bære mundbind," *Politiken*, 15 August 2020.

218. Hasse Svens, "Finland uppmanar nu till munskydd," *SVT Nyheter*, 13 August 2020.

219. Ole Petter Ottersen, "Safe and Responsible Return to Campus," President's Blog, 12 August 2020, https://blog.ki.se/rektor/2020/08/12/safe-and-responsible-return-to-campus/.

220. "Besked om munskydd dröjer – nu tar företagen egna beslut," *SVT*, 23 August 2020.

221. Tom Britton, "Sveriges coronastrategi behöver ändras inför hösten," *Dagens Nyheter*, 9 August 2020.

222. "Schwedisher Staats-Epidemiologe Tegnell: Sich nur auf Masken zu verlassen, ist sehr gefährlich!," *Bild*, 8 August 2020.

223. Doree Lewak, "Hipsters Are Coughing Up $300 for Bespoke Coronavirus Face Masks," *New York Post*, 22 May 2020; Sarah Spellings, "Cloth Masks to Shop Now," *Vogue*, 28 July 2020.

224. Lisa W. Foderaro and Ken Belson, "In the Spotlight, the Politics of Buckling Up," *New York Times*, 14 April 2007.

225. OECD, International Transport Forum, *Road Safety Annual Report* 2018, 54.

7 FROM STATE TO CITIZEN

1. Of 1.3 billion Chinese, the 2010 census lists only 1,448 as naturalized citizens. "The Upper Han," *Economist*, 19 November 2016. In other words, about as many as the Chinese who are statistically likely to be struck by lightning each year.

2. The State Council Information Office of the People's Republic of China, "Fighting Covid-19: China in Action," June 2020, http://english.www.gov.cn/news/topnews/20 2006/07/content_WS5edc559ac6d066592a449030.html.

3. "Fem krogar i Stockholm stängs av smittskyddsskäl," *Dagens Nyheter*, 27 April 2020.

4. Quoted in Tore Ellingsen and Jesper Roine, "Sweden and the Virus," in *Sweden through the Crisis* (Stockholm, forthcoming), 10, www.hhs.se/contentassets/421dc1e74 c54466a8d3a88a78c775522/a02.pdf.

5. *The Week*, 12 June 2020, 8.

6. Marina Lopes, "Brazil's Favelas, Neglected by the Government, Organize Their Own Coronavirus Fight," *Washington Post*, 10 June 2020.

7. "Waving Slippers at the 'Cockroach' President of Belarus," *Economist*, 20 June 2020.

8. Patrick Wintour, "Revolutionary Guards to Enforce Coronavirus Controls in Iran," *Guardian*, 13 March 2020.

9. Richard Milne, "Swedish Ministers Defend Resisting Coronavirus Lockdown," *Financial Times*, 15 April 2020.

10. Clas Svahn, "Johan Carlson: Smittan kom in från länder som gick under vår radar," *Dagens Nyheter*, 10 June 2020.

11. Johar Bendjelloul and Jonas Lindvist, "Det är klart att det kan kännas lite skrämmande," *Dagens Nyheter*, 6 April 2020.

12. Smittskyddslag 2004:168, ch. 2, §1, http://rkrattsbaser.gov.se/sfst?bet=2004:168.

13. Olof Petersson, ""Sverige valde coronastrategi med 2004 års smittskyddslag," *Dagens Nyheter*, 8 June 2020.

14. John Snow, "Further Remarks on the Mode of Communication of Cholera; Including Some Comments on the Recent Reports on Cholera by the General Board of Health," *Medical Times and Gazette*, 11 (1855) 84.

15. Per Svensson, "Här föddes Sveriges märkliga coronastrategi," *Dagens Nyheter*, 17 June 2020.

16. Susan Sontag, *Illnesss as Metaphor* (New York 1978); Holly Allen, "Bad Mothers and Monstrous Sons: Autistic Adults, Lifelong Dependency, and Sensationalized Narratives of Care," *Journal of Medical Humanities*, 38 (2017); Dennis Mahoney and Terence Chorba, "Romanticism, Mycobacterium, and the Myth of the Muse," *Emerging Infectious Diseases*, 25, 3 (2019).

17. William Macmichael, *A Brief Sketch of the Progress of Opinion upon the Subject of Contagion* (London 1825) 5–7, 28–31.

18. [Carl Trafvenfelt], *Sammandrag af Läkares åsigter och erfarenhet af den Epidemiska Choleran uti Asien och Europa* (Stockholm 1832) ii, 24–34.

19. Elizabeth Fee, *Disease and Discovery: A History of the Johns Hopkins School of Hygiene and Public Health, 1916–1939* (Baltimore 1987) 20–21; Barron H. Lerner, *Contagion and Confinement: Controlling Tuberculosis along the Skid Road* (Baltimore 1998) 170;

Judith Walzer Leavitt, *Typhoid Mary: Captive to the Public's Health* (Boston 1996) 23–25.

20. John Duffy, *The Sanitarians: A History of American Public Health* (Urbana 1990) 195.

21. Margaret Humphreys, *Yellow Fever and the South* (New Brunswick 1992) 122.

22. The debate is carried out in Richard Wilkinson and Kate Pickett, *The Spirit Level: Why Equality Is Better for Everyone* (London 2010); Christopher Snowdon, *The Spirit Level Delusion: Fact Checking the Left's New Theory of Everything* (London 2010); Angus Deaton, *The Great Escape: Health, Wealth and the Origins of Inequality* (Princeton 2013); Harry G. Frankfurt, *On Inequality* (Princeton 2015).

23. Lion Murard and Patrick Zylberman, *L'hygiène dans la république: La santé publique en France, ou l'utopie contrariée (1870–1918)* (Paris 1996); Anthony S. Wohl, *Endangered Lives: Public Health in Victorian Britain* (London 1983).

24. Dora B. Weiner, *The Citizen-Patient in Revolutionary and Imperial Paris* (Baltimore 1993).

25. Daniel Schiff, *Abortion in Judaism* (Cambridge 2002) 16.

26. *R v. Brown* [1993] 2 All ER 75, 4, 37, www.bailii.org/uk/cases/UKHL/1993/19.html; Robert H. Lowie, *The Origin of the State* (New York 1927) 93; Trevor J. Saunders, *Plato's Penal Code: Tradition, Controversy, and Reform in Greek Penology* (Oxford 1991) 263.

27. John Baker, *An Introduction to English Legal History*, 5th ed. (Oxford 2019) 571.

28. Paul Starr, *The Social Transformation of American Medicine* (New York 1982) 189–94.

29. Michael Burleigh and Wolfgang Wippermann, *The Racial State: Germany 1933–1945* (Cambridge 1991) 290.

30. Paul Julian Weindling, *Epidemics and Genocide in Eastern Europe, 1890–1945* (Oxford 2000).

31. Gunnar Broberg and Mattias Tydén, *Oönskade i folkhemmet: Rashygien och sterilisering i Sverige* (Stockholm 1991); Maija Runcis, *Steriliseringar i folkhemmet* (Stockholm 1998); Maciej Zaremba, *De rena och de andra: Om tvångssteriliseringar, rashygien och arvsynd* (n.p. 1999); Gunnar Broberg and Nils Roll-Hansen, eds., *Eugenics and the Welfare State* (East Lansing 1996); Stefan Kuhl, *The Nazi Connection: Eugenics, American Racism, and German National Socialism* (Oxford 1994); Patrick Zylberman, "Les damnés de la démocratie puritaine: Stérilisations en Scandinavie, 1929–1977," *Le Mouvement Social* 187 (1999) 99–125. In a more general sense, similar parallels are drawn in James Q. Whitman, *Hitler's American Model: The United States and the Making of Nazi Race Law* (Princeton 2017).

32. Joshua Gamson, "Rubber Wars: Struggles over the Condom in the United States," *Journal of the History of Sexuality*, 1, 2 (1990) 271–74. More recent sales figures in Credit Suisse, "The Global Condom Market," 13 September 2016.

33. Andrzej Kulczycki, "The Acceptability of the Female and Male Condom: A Randomized Crossover Trial," *Perspectives on Sexual and Reproductive Health*, 36, 3 (2004).

34. Paula A. Treichler, "How to Use a Condom: Lessons from the AIDS Epidemic," in Joshua Oppenheimer and Helena Reckitt, eds., *Acting on AIDS: Sex, Drugs, and Politics* (London 1997) 53–54; Steven D. Pinkerton and Paul R. Abramson, "The Joys of Diversification: Vaccines, Condoms, and AIDS Prevention," *AIDS and Public Policy Journal* 10, 3 (1995) 152; Grand View Research, "Condom Market Size, Share and Trends Analysis Report," July 2019, www.grandviewresearch.com/industry-analysis/condom-market.

35. "The Global Adult Toys Market Was Worth $23.7Bn in 2017 and Is Projected to Reach $35.5Bn by 2023," *Business Wire*, 2 October 2018; "Global $52.7Bn Sex Toys Market Outlook, 2026," *Cision*, 11 December 2019, www.prnewswire.com/news-releases/global-52-7bn-sex-toys-market-outlook-2026—rising-presence-of-online-retailers-drives-the-industry-300973202.html.

36. Anna Iovine, "Sex Toy Sales Are Skyrocketing Because of Social Distancing," *MashableUK*, 25 March 2020, https://mashable.com/article/sex-toy-sales-coronavirus

/?europe=true; Tanya Basu, "How Coronavirus Is Transforming Online Dating and Sex," *MIT Technology Review*, 26 March 2020.

37. John-Manuel Andriote, *Victory Deferred: How AIDS Changed Gay Life in America* (Chicago 1999) 23; Gayle S. Rubin, "Elegy for the Valley of the Kings: AIDS and the Leather Community in San Francisco, 1981–1996," in Martin P. Levine, et al., eds., *In Changing Times: Gay Men and Lesbians Encounter HIV/AIDS* (Chicago 1997) 103, 111.

38. Amanda Sealy, "How Japan's Music-Playing, Water-Spraying TOTO Toilets Took Over the World," *CNN*, 9 December 2018; Peter Baldwin "The Return of the Coercive State: Behavioral Control in Multicultural Society," in T. V. Paul, et al., ed., *The Nation-State in Question* (Princeton 2003) 108–9.

39. Guy Hocquenghem, *Homosexual Desire* (Durham NC 1993) ch. 4; Daniel Mendelsohn, *The Elusive Embrace: Desire and the Riddle of Identity* (New York 1999) 73–74; Peter M. Davies, et al., *Sex, Gay Men, and AIDS* (London 1993) 127–29; Mario Mieli, *Homosexuality and Liberation: Elements of a Gay Critique* (London 1980) 148–49.

40. Michael Warner, *The Trouble with Normal: Sex, Politics, and the Ethics of Queer Life* (New York 1999) 38.

41. H. von Druten, et al., "Homosexual Role Behavior and the Spread of HIV," in D. Friedrich and W. Ceckmann, eds., *AIDS in Europe: The Behavioural Aspect* (Berlin 1995) v 4, 259; Mirko D. Grmek, *History of AIDS* (Princeton 1990) 168–69; Gabriel Rotello, *Sexual Ecology: AIDS and the Destiny of Gay Men* (New York 1997) 77–78.

42. Institute of Tropical Medicine Antwerp. "New Disease among HIV-Infected Gay Men," *ScienceDaily*, 30 November 2009; Laura Escolà-Vergé, et al., "Outbreak of Intestinal Amoebiasis among Men Who Have Sex with Men, Barcelona (Spain), October 2016 and January 2017," *Eurosurveillance*, 22, 30 (2017).

43. Peter Baldwin, *Disease and Democracy: The Industrialized World Faces AIDS* (Berkeley 2005) ch. 6.

44. Norbert Elias, *The Civilizing Process* (London 2000).

45. Alex Chase-Levenson, *The Yellow Flag: Quarantine and the British Mediterranean World, 1780–1860* (Cambridge 2020) 172–73

46. Andrew Franta, "Godwin's Handshake," *Publications of the Modern Language Association*, 122, 3 (2007) 698–99; Evan Andrews, "The History of the Handshake," *History*, www.history.com/news/what-is-the-origin-of-the-handshake.

47. "Don't Shake Hands with the Captain!," *We Travel 2U Cruise*, 6 August 2015, https://wetravel2ucruise.blogspot.com/2015/08/dont-shake-hands-with-captain.html.

48. Centers for Disease Control, "Zoonotic Diseases," www.cdc.gov/onehealth/basics/zoonotic-diseases.html.

49. Thomas Almeroth-Williams, *City of Beasts: How Animals Shaped Georgian London* (Manchester 2019).

50. Malcolm Anderson, *In Thrall to Political Change: Police and Gendarmerie in France* (Oxford 2011) 152.

51. Adolph Knigge, *Practical Philosophy of Social Life*, trans. P. Will (Troy 1805) 13, 123.

52. Friedrich Weinbrenner, *Wie schützt man sich vor Ansteckung?* (Bonn 1908) 7–9.

53. *Our Sexual Future with Robots*, https://responsiblerobotics.org/2017/07/05/frr-report-our-sexual-future-with-robots/, 27–28. The literature on automaton sex is growing: Kate Devlin, *Turned On: Science, Sex, and Robots* (London 2018); David Levy, *Love and Sex with Robots: The Evolution of Human–Robot Relationships* (New York 2008); John Danaher and Neil McArthur, eds., *Robot Sex: Social and Ethical Implications* (Cambridge MA 2018); Kathleen Richardson, *Sex Robots: The End of Love* (Cambridge 2019).

54. Laura Bradley, "TV Shows Are Now Using Mannequins for Sex Scenes Thanks to COVID-19," *Daily Beast*, 13 July 2020; Henry Goldblatt, "How to Shoot a Sex Scene in a Pandemic: Cue the Mannequins," *New York Times*, 13 July 2020.
55. New York City Health, "Safer Sex and COVID-19," https://www1.nyc.gov/assets/doh/downloads/pdf/imm/covid-sex-guidance.pdf.
56. Joseph Henrich, et al., "The Puzzle of Monogamous Marriage," *Philosophical Transactions of the Royal Society: Biological Sciences*, 367 (2012) 657.
57. Nancy Tomes, *The Gospel of Germs: Men, Women, and the Microbe in American Life* (Cambridge MA 1998) ch. 7.
58. Slavoj Žižek, *Pandemic! COVID-19 Shakes the World* (New York 2020) 55.
59. "What Next for Countries That Are Nearly Covid-Free?," *Economist*, 23 April 2020.
60. James Pasley, "People in China Are Making 3 Billion Trips to Celebrate the Lunar New Year, and It's Not Going to Help the Wuhan Coronavirus Outbreak," *Business Insider*, 22 January 2020.
61. S. F. Bloomfield, et al., "Too Clean, or Not Too Clean: The Hygiene Hypothesis and Home Hygiene," *Clinical and Experimental Allergy*, 36, 4 (2006).
62. Josef Neu and Jona Rushing, "Cesarean versus Vaginal Delivery: Long-Term Infant Outcomes and the Hygiene Hypothesis," *Clinics in Perinatology*, 38, 2 (2011).
63. Rosmund Hutt, "These Are the World's Five Biggest Slums," *World Economic Forum*, 19 October 2016.
64. Olanike O. Kehinde and Babatunde E. Ogunnowo, "The Pattern of Antibiotic Use in an Urban Slum in Lagos State, Nigeria," *West African Journal of Pharmacy*, 24, 1 (2013); Sylvia Omulo, et al., "Evidence of Superficial Knowledge Regarding Antibiotics and Their Use: Results of Two Cross-Sectional Surveys in an Urban Informal Settlement in Kenya," *PLoS One*, 2 October 2017.
65. Sunicha Chanvatik, et al., "Antibiotic Use in Mandarin Production (*Citrus reticulata* Blanco) in Major Mandarin-Producing Areas in Thailand," *PLoS One*, 13 November 2019.
66. Chris Dall, "Lawmakers Urge EPA to Rethink Use of Antibiotics on Citrus Trees," CIDRAP, 29 August 2019, www.cidrap.umn.edu/news-perspective/2019/08/lawmakers-urge-epa-to-rethink-use-antibiotics-citrus-trees; Maryn McKenna, "Should Citrus Farmers Use Antibiotics to Combat Greening Disease?," *National Geographic*, 1 March 2016.
67. R. Monina Klevens, "Invasive Methicillin-Resistant *Staphylococcus aureus* Infections in the United States," *Journal of the American Medical Association*, 298, 15 (2007) 1763; Athena P. Kourtis, et al., "Vital Signs: Epidemiology and Recent Trends in Methicillin-Resistant and in Methicillin-Susceptible *Staphylococcus aureus* Bloodstream Infections – United States," *Morbidity and Mortality Weekly Report*, 68, 9 (2019).
68. CDC, National Center for Health Statistics, Infectious or Immune Diseases, www.cdc.gov/nchs/fastats/infectious-immune.htm.
69. Mike Davis, *The Monster at Our Door: The Global Threat of Avian Flu* (New York 2005) 91.
70. Gregory L. Armstrong, et al., "Trends in Infectious Disease Mortality in the United States during the 20th Century," *Journal of the American Medical Association*, 281, 1 (1999).
71. "Total Disease Burden by Cause, World, 1990–2017," *Our World in Data*, https://ourworldindata.org/grapher/total-disease-burden-by-cause?stackMode=relative.
72. Robert N. Proctor, *Racial Hygiene: Medicine under the Nazis* (Cambridge MA 1988) 235–37.
73. John M. Barry, *The Great Influenza: The Story of the Deadliest Pandemic in History* (London 2005) 347.
74. Peter Baldwin, "Can There Be a Democratic Public Health? Fighting AIDS in the Industrialized World," in Susan Gross Solomon, et al., eds., *Shifting Boundaries of Public Health: Europe in the Twentieth Century* (Rochester 2008) 27–28.

75. Stephen Davies, *The Historical Origins of Health Fascism* (London 1991); Bryan S. Turner, *The Body and Society: Explorations in Social Theory* (London 1996) 210.
76. Shauneen M. Garrahan and Andrew W. Eichner, "Tipping the Scale: A Place for Childhood Obesity in the Evolving Legal Framework of Child Abuse and Neglect," *Yale Journal of Health Policy, Law, and Ethics*, 12, 2 (2012) 356–64; Todd Varness, et al., "Childhood Obesity and Medical Neglect," *Pediatrics*, 123, 1 (2009); Lindsey Murtagh and David S. Ludwig, "State Intervention in Life-Threatening Childhood Obesity," *Journal of the American Medical Association*, 306, 2 (2011).
77. Darla Harms, *No Fat Chicks: Overcoming Body Shame and Living in Authenticity* (Kindle ed., 24 April 2020); Lisa Cassidy, "Body Shaming in the Era of Social Media," in Cecilea Mun, ed., *Interdisciplinary Perspectives on Shame* (Lanham 2019).

8 WHO IS RESPONSIBLE FOR OUR HEALTH?

1. Marc Santora, "Overhaul Urged for Laws on AIDS Tests and Data," *New York Times*, 2 February 2006.
2. Jan Hatzius, et al., "Measuring the Impact of Lockdowns and Social Distancing on Global GDP," Goldman Sachs Economic Research, 26 April 2020, Exhibit 2, www .gspublishing.com/content/research/en/reports/2020/04/27/3a0089c7-c1d1-4243-8dbd-da6141a501be.html.
3. Asli Demirgüç-Kunt, et al., "The Sooner the Better: The Early Economic Impact of Non-pharmaceutical Interventions during the COVID-19 Pandemic," World Bank Group, Policy Research Working Paper 9257, May 2020, 14.
4. "The 90% Economy That Lockdowns Will Leave Behind," *Economist*, 30 April 2020.
5. European Parliament, *Uncertainty/EU/Hope: Public Opinion in Times of Covid-19*, June 2020, 7, www.europarl.europa.eu/at-your-service/files/be-heard/eurobarometer/202 0/public_opinion_in_the_eu_in_time_of_coronavirus_crisis/report/en-covid19-sur vey-report.pdf.
6. Oskar Forsberg, "Förtroendet för Tegnell och Löfven ökar," *Aftonbladet*, 19 April 2020.
7. "What Next for Countries That Are Nearly Covid-Free?," *Economist*, 23 April 2020.
8. "2020 Edelman Trust Barometer Spring Update," 5 May 2020, www.edelman.com/res earch/trust-2020-spring-update.
9. Mark É. Czeisler, et al., "Public Attitudes, Behaviors, and Beliefs Related to COVID-19, Stay-at-Home Orders, Nonessential Business Closures, and Public Health Guidance – United States, New York City, and Los Angeles, May 5–12, 2020," *Morbidity and Mortality Weekly Report*, 12 June 2020.
10. Henry Olsen, "The Coronavirus Polling Bump Is Real. But Trump's Is Abnormally Small," *Washington Post*, 31 March 2020; Daniel Odin Shaw, "The Coronavirus 'Rally 'round the Flag' Bump and Trump's 2020 Campaign," *International Scholar*, 22 April 2020.
11. John Lichfield, "Coronavirus: France's 'Strange Defeat,'" *Politico*, 8 May 2020; Adam Nossiter, "As Paris Tiptoes toward Normalcy, Infections Are Sharply Down," *New York Times*, 20 May 2020.
12. Rachel Donadio, "France: After Lockdown, the Street," *New York Review of Books*, 23 July 2020.
13. "Japan Is Not Rallying around Its Prime Minister," *Economist*, 23 May 2020.
14. "Avis du Conseil scientifique COVID-19," 12 March 2020, https://solidarites-sante.go uv.fr/IMG/pdf/avis_conseil_scientifique_12_mars_2020.pdf; Chloé Hecketsweiler and Cédric Pietralunga, "Les simulations alarmantes des épidémiologistes pour la France," *Le Monde*, 15 March 2020.

15. Emmanuel Macron, "Addresse aux Français," 12 March 2020, Élysée, www.elysee.fr/emmanuel-macron/2020/03/12/adresse-aux-francais. The background is in Ali Ghanchi, "Adaptation of the National Plan for the Prevention and Fight against Pandemic Influenza to the 2020 COVID-19 Epidemic in France," *Disaster Medicine and Public Health Preparedness,* 7 April 2020.

16. "Avis du Conseil scientifique COVID-19," 14 March 2020, https://solidarites-sante.gouv.fr/IMG/pdf/avis_conseil_scientifique_14_mars_2020.pdf.

17. "Coronavirus: Edouard Philippe annonce la fermeture de tous les lieux publics 'non indispensables,'" *Le Monde,* 14 March 2020.

18. "Avis du Conseil scientifique COVID-19," 16 March 2020, https://solidarites-sante.gouv.fr/IMG/pdf/avis_conseil_scientifique_16_mars_2020.pdf.

19. Cédric Pietralunga et Alexandre Lemarié, "Coronavirus: L'exécutif réfléchit au confinement des Français," *Le Monde,* 16 March 2020.

20. "Adresse aux français du Président de la République Emmanuel Macron," 16 March 2020, www.elysee.fr/front/pdf/elysee-module-15345-fr.pdf.

21. Nicolas Chapuis, "Coronavirus: Les forces de l'ordre en première ligne pour faire respecter le confinement," *Le Monde,* 17 March 2020.

22. "Non, un décret n'a pas déjà préparé le déploiement de l'armée pour imposer un couvre-feu en France," *Le Monde,* 16 March 2020.

23. "Do Low-Trust Societies Do Better in a Pandemic?," *Economist,* 2 May 2020. The figure given for the first week was 92,000 tickets. "Avis du Conseil scientifique," 23 March 2020, https://solidarites-sante.gouv.fr/IMG/pdf/avis_conseil_scientifique_23_mars_2020–2.pdf.

24. "Coronavirus: Plus d'un million d'amendes distribuées pendant le confinement," *Les Echos,* 12 May 2020.

25. "Coronavirus: Bavaria Leads the Way as Germany Mulls Nationwide Lockdown," *Straits Times,* 20 March 2020.

26. "An Overview of the Updated Restrictions on Public Life in Germany," *Spiegel International,* 23 March 2020.

27. "Governments Are Starting to Ease Restrictions," *Economist,* 16 April 2020.

28. "Do Low-Trust Societies Do Better in a Pandemic?"

29. Mark Quinlivan, "Coronavirus: Worst Districts for Lockdown Breaches Revealed by Police," *Newshub,* 28 April 2020.

30. Alexis Duval, et al., "Coronavirus: Au jour 1 du confinement, 'on ne verbalise que ceux qui nous prennent pour des cons,'" *Le Monde,* 18 March 2020.

31. Ashley Southall, "Scrutiny of Social-Distance Policing as 35 of 40 Arrested Are Black," *New York Times,* 7 May 2020; Kim Bellware, "Violent Arrest in New York Raises Questions about Police Enforcement of Social Distancing Orders," *Washington Post,* 5 May 2020.

32. Lily Kuo, "'The New Normal': China's Excessive Coronavirus Public Monitoring Could Be Here to Stay," *Guardian,* 9 March 2020.

33. Helen Pidd and Vikram Dodd, "UK Police Use Drones and Roadblocks to Enforce Lockdown," *Guardian,* 26 March 2020; Michelle Toh, "Singapore Deploys Robot 'Dog' to Encourage Social Distancing," *CNN,* 8 May 2020.

34. Jon Henley, "Swedish City to Dump Tonne of Chicken Manure in Park to Deter Visitors," *Guardian,* 29 April 2020.

35. Lloyd Bent, "Police Dye the Water in Buxton 'Blue Lagoon' to Deter Swimmers during Coronavirus Lockdown," *Derbyshire Times,* 1 April 2020.

36. Kuo, "'The New Normal.'"

37. Johnny Diaz, "KFC Birthday Party Costs $18,000 in Covid-19 Fines in Australia," *New York Times,* 11 July 2020.

38. Concepción de León, "Maryland Man Sentenced to a Year in Jail for Violating Ban on Large Parties," *New York Times,* 28 September 2020.

39. Falah Gulzar, "China: Watch What Happens If a Coronavirus Patient Refuses to Cooperate at a Checkpoint," *Gulf News*, 27 February 2020.
40. Alice Su, "Woman Who Flew from U.S. to China for Coronavirus Test Faces Criminal Charges," *Los Angeles Times*, 18 March 2020.
41. "Guidelines for Investigation and Management of Close Contacts of COVID-19 Cases," *Chinese Center for Disease Control and Prevention Weekly*, 12 March 2020, www .chinadaily.com.cn/pdf/2020/Guidelines.for.Investigation.and.Management.of .Close.Contacts.of.COVID-19.Cases.pdf.
42. Oliver Moody, "Germans Were Meticulous in Tracking Those Who Had Made Contact," *Times* (London), 23 April 2020.
43. Cabinet Office, "Coronavirus Outbreak FAQs: What You Can and Can't Do," 8.1, 11 May 2020, www.gov.uk/guidance/local-covid-alert-levels-what-you-need-to-know.
44. The Health Protection (Coronavirus, Restrictions) (England) Regulations 2020, 8, www.legislation.gov.uk/uksi/2020/350#commentary-c24044061.
45. "Hancock: Follow Covid Rules or They Will Get Tougher," *BBC*, 20 September 2020.
46. Sarantis Michalopoulos, "Greece Tightens Measures, All New Arrivals Will Be Quarantined," EURACTIV.com, 16 March 2020, www.euractiv.com/section/corona virus/news/greece-on-total-lockdown-all-new-arrivals-will-be-quarantined; "An Overview of the Updated Restrictions on Public Life in Germany," *Spiegel International*, 23 March 2020.
47. Snigdha Poonam, "Is It the Housework?," *The Ballot*, 11 June 2020; Topher Gauk-Roger and Scottie Andrew, "Los Angeles Can Cut Off Power and Water at Properties Hosting Parties during the Pandemic," *CNN*, 6 August 2020.
48. Gareth Davies, "'Overzealous' Police Use Coronavirus Powers to Charge Shoppers for Buying 'Non-essential Items,'" *Telegraph*, 30 March 2020.
49. "Folkhälsomyndigheten har misslyckats – nu måste politikerna gripa in," *Dagens Nyheter*, 14 April 2020; Paula Neuding, "Sweden Has Resisted Lockdown: But That Doesn't Make It a Bastion of Liberty," *Quillette*, 12 May 2020.
50. Erica Oden, "How Social Distancing Fines Are Working, or Not Working, across America," *CNN*, 11 April 2020.
51. Mallika Kallingal, "Ankle Monitors Ordered for Louisville, Kentucky Residents Exposed to Covid-19 Who Refuse to Stay Home," *CNN*, 3 April 2020.
52. Moriah Balingit, "Armed Militia Helped a Michigan Barbershop Open, a Coronavirus Defiance That Puts Republican Lawmakers in a Bind," *Washington Post*, 12 May 2020.
53. Ivan Pereira, "Cops Arrest Armed Men, Texas Bar Owner Who Violated Order to Close," *ABC News*, 5 May 2020.
54. Jennifer Kendall and Elizabeth Evans, "TABC Suspends Seven Bars, Two in Central Texas, for Not Complying with Abbott's Order to Close Bars," *Fox7 Austin*, 30 June 2020.
55. Ed Shanahan, "Party Guests Won't Talk after 9 Test Positive. Now They Face Subpoenas," *New York Times*, 1 July 2020.
56. Kuo, "'The New Normal.'"
57. Amelia Wade, "Covid-19 Coronavirus: Kiwis File 4200 Reports to Police of People Flouting Lockdown," *New Zealand Herald*, 30 March 2020.
58. Jenni Russell, "Lockdown Is Turning Us into a Nation of Spies," *Times* (London), 13 May 2020.
59. "True British Spirit Brought Out by Time of Crisis," *Private Eye*, 1519 (3–23 April 2020) 34.
60. Anna Mikhailova, et al., "How Neil Ferguson, the Architect of Lockdown, Was Brought Down by Failing to Obey His Own Rules," *Telegraph*, 5 May 2020.
61. Vivek Chaudhary, et al., "Who Sunk Neil Ferguson?," *Daily Mail*, 9 May 2020.
62. Glen Owen, et al., "Who Knifed Dominic Cummings?," *Mail on Sunday*, 23 May 2020.

63. Madeline Holcombe, "New York Tourist Is Arrested in Hawaii after Posting Beach Pictures on Instagram," *CNN*, 16 May 2020.
64. Nazia Parveen, "Stephen Kinnock Targeted by Police for Visiting Father, Neil," *Guardian*, 29 March 2020.
65. Regieringskansliet, "Strategi med anledning av det nya coronaviruset," 7 April 2020, www.regeringen.se/regeringens-politik/regeringens-arbete-med-anledning-av-nya-coronaviruset/strategi-med-anledning-av-det-nya-coronaviruset/.
66. US Department of Justice, Civil Rights Division, "COVID-19 Alert: Fraudulent Face Mask Flyers," www.ada.gov/covid-19_flyer_alert.html; "The Department of Justice Warns of Inaccurate Flyers and Postings Regarding the Use of Face Masks and the Americans with Disabilities Act," 30 June 2020, www.justice.gov/opa/pr/department-justice-warns-inaccurate-flyers-and-postings-regarding-use-face-masks-and.
67. Denis Cosnard and Sofia Fischer, "Imposer le masque dans la rue, une gageure pour les maires," *Le Monde*, 13 May 2020.
68. Tim Elfrink, "'This Is No Longer a Debate': Florida Sheriff Bans Deputies, Visitors from Wearing Masks," *Washington Post*, 11 August 2020.
69. Eesha Pendharkar, "Coastal Maine Businesses Will Have to Enforce Face Covering Requirement," *Bangor Daily News*, 1 July 2020.
70. Valeria Olivares, "As Face Mask Requirements Pop Back Up across Texas, Gov. Greg Abbott Faces Criticism from Local Leaders and Fellow Republicans," *Texas Tribune*, 20 June 2020.
71. Abha Bhattarai, "Retail Workers Are Being Pulled into the Latest Culture War: Getting Customers to Wear Masks," *Washington Post*, 8 July 2020.
72. Austin Horn, "Starbucks Says Customers Must Wear Masks at Its Cafes," *NPR*, 9 July 2020; Hannah Denham and Taylor Telford, "Walmart Will Require Face Masks at All U.S. Stores," *Washington Post*, 15 July 2020. While Southern chains, like Winn-Dixie went in the opposite direction: Laura Reiley, "Deep South Supermarket Winn-Dixie Takes a Stand: No Masks Required," *Washington Post*, 20 July 2020.
73. Nathaniel Meyersohn, "Walmart and Others Will Still Serve Customers Who Refuse to Wear Masks, Despite New Rules," *CNN*, 26 July 2020.
74. "Limiting Workplace Violence Associated with COVID-19 Prevention Policies in Retail and Services Businesses," CDC, 24 August 2020, www.cdc.gov/coronavirus/2019-ncov/community/organizations/business-employers/limit-workplace-violence.html.
75. Meryl Kornfield, "Three People Charged in Killing of Family Dollar Security Guard Over Mask Policy," *Washington Post*, 5 May 2020.
76. "French Bus Driver Dies Following Attack by Passengers Who Refused to Wear Masks," *Guardian*, 10 July 2020.
77. Dan Bloom, "Government Confirms New Face Mask Rules – Where You Will and Won't Have to Wear Them," *Daily Mirror*, 23 July 2020.
78. Rong-Gong Lin II and Sandhya Kambhampati, "Some Shun Wearing Masks Even Though They're Essential Coronavirus Protection," *Los Angeles Times*, 12 June 2020.
79. Luke Money and Stephanie Lai, "Not Wearing a Mask Could Cost You Hundreds in Westside as Officials Pledge Enforcement," *Los Angeles Times*, 2 July 2020.
80. Patrick Svitek, "Gov. Greg Abbott Orders Texans in Most Counties to Wear Masks in Public," *Texas Tribune*, 2 July 2020.
81. County of Hildago, Texas, "County Order 20–011 Related to the COVID-19 Public Health Emergency," 20 July 2020, www.hidalgocounty.us/DocumentCenter/View/39796/07202020-Hidalgo-County-Emergency-Order-20-011; https://publish.twitter.com/?query=https%3A%2F%2Ftwitter.com%2FHidalgoCounty%2Fstatus%2F1285579864494538753&widget=Tweet.
82. Joshua Bote, "Eight People in Indonesia Who Refused to Wear Face Masks Ordered to Dig Graves for COVID-19 Victims as Punishment," *USA Today*, 15 September 2020.

83. Janine Hosp, "Unser Verlangen nach starker Führung," *Tagesanzeiger*, 29 April 2020.

84. Google, COVID-19 Community Mobility Report, Sweden, 11 April 2020, www .gstatic.com/covid19/mobility/2020-04-11_SE_Mobility_Report_en.pdf.

85. Asger Lau Andersen, et al., "Pandemic, Shutdown and Consumer Spending: Lessons from Scandinavian Policy Responses to COVID-19," 12 May 2020, https://arxiv.org/pdf/2005.04630.pdf.

86. Ryan Bourne, "A View So Radical That Some Simply Won't See It. The Driver of Our Problems Isn't Lockdown. It's the Virus," *Conservative Home*, 13 May 2020.

87. Tom Chivers, "How Much Difference Would an Earlier Shutdown Have Made?," *UnHerd*, 21 May 2020.

88. Dominic Lawson, "Forget Trendy 'Nudge' Theorists: It's the Queen Who Best Understands Our Lockdown Mood," *Daily Mail*, 13 April 2020.

89. Sally Weale, "Low Attendance at Scaled-Down Schools Sparks Fears for Vulnerable Pupils," *Guardian*, 23 March 2020; James Kirkup, "Why the English Sacrificed Liberty for Lockdown," *UnHerd*, 23 April 2020.

90. "Why the Czechs Are Sticking to Their Masks," *Eurotopics*, 26 May 2020.

91. "Change in Average Mobility (Based on Distance Travelled)," *Unacast*, www .unacast.com/covid19/social-distancing-scoreboard?view=state&fips=09.

92. Executive Order 2020-42 (COVID-19), www.michigan.gov/whitmer/0,9309,7-387-90 499_90705-525182-,00.html.

93. Dhrumil Mehta, "Most Americans Like How Their Governor Is Handling the Coronavirus Outbreak," *FiveThirtyEight*, 10 April 2020.

94. Hillary Hoffower, "Meet Ron DeSantis, the Florida Governor Who Just Issued a Stay-at-Home Order for His State and Was Heavily Criticized for Leaving Beaches Open to Spring Breakers in March," *Business Insider*, 1 April 2020.

95. William Davies, "Coronavirus and the Rise of Rule-Breakers," *New Statesman*, 8 July 2020.

96. Werner Bartens, "Die Kurve der Dummheit abflachen," *Süddeutsche Zeitung*, 14 May 2020.

97. Dana Goldstein and Eliza Shapiro, "'I Don't Want to Go Back': Many Teachers Are Fearful and Angry over Pressure to Return," *New York Times*, 11 July 2020; Anemona Hartocollis, "Colleges Face Rising Revolt by Professors," *New York Times*, 3 July 2020.

98. Josh Halliday and Sally Weale, "Thousands of Primary Schools in England Snub Call to Restart Classes," *Guardian*, 3 June 2020.

99. Sean Coughlan, "Plan Dropped for All Primary Pupils Back in School," *BBC*, 9 June 2020.

100. UTLA, "The Same Storm, but Different Boats: The Safe and Equitable Conditions for Starting LAUSD in 2020–21," July 2020, www.utla.net/sites/default/files/samestorm diffboats_final.pdf. Teachers unions around the world had similarly fraught relations with the authorities: Miriam Berger, "Teachers Unions around the World Clash with Governments over Coronavirus and School Reopening Plans," *Washington Post*, 12 September 2020.

101. Barbara Moens, "How the Pandemic Will Shake Up the University Landscape," *Politico*, 16 June 2020.

102. Elaine Drayton and Ben Waltmann, "Will Universities Need a Bailout to Survive the COVID-19 Crisis?," Institute for Fiscal Studies, Briefing Note BN300, July 2020, www .ifs.org.uk/uploads/BN300-Will-universities-need-bailout-survive-COVID-19-crisis-1 .pdf.

103. Stephen Beard, "UK Universities Stand to Lose Billions If the Pandemic Keeps Foreign Students Away," *Marketplace*, 12 May 2020; Jyoti Madhusoodanan,

"'Disturbing and Cruel.' Universities Blast New Visa Rule for International Students," *Science*, 8 July 2020.

104. A. David Paltiel, et al., "Assessment of SARS-CoV-2 Screening Strategies to Permit the Safe Reopening of College Campuses in the United States," *JAMA Network Open*, 31 July 2020.

105. "Yale Updates Fall COVID-19 Testing Protocols for Students," *Yale News*, 29 July 2020; Martha E. Pollack and Michael I. Kotlikoff, "We Run Cornell. Here's How We've Kept Low Covid-19 Rates on Campus," *Washington Post*, 30 September 2020; Shawn Hubler, "Colleges Learn How to Suppress Coronavirus: Extensive Testing," *New York Times*, 2 October 2020.

106. "The Big Ten Conference Adopts Stringent Medical Protocols; Football Season to Resume October 23–24, 2020," *BigTen*, 16 September 2020; Amy Hollyfield, "United to Launch COVID-19 Testing Program for SFO Passengers Traveling to Hawaii," *ABC7News*, 24 September 2020; Antonia Noori Farzan, "Lufthansa to Roll Out Rapid Coronavirus Testing, a Move That Could Change Pandemic Air Travel," *Washington Post*, 23 September 2020.

107. "Thousands of Homeless 'Back on Streets by July,'" *BBC*, 4 June 2020; Amelia Gentleman, "Treasury Announces £85m for Rough Sleeper Accommodation," *Guardian*, 24 June 2020.

108. Britta Kramsjö, "Låg smittspridning bland Stockholms hemlösa," *Svenska Dagbladet*, 9 July 2020; James Deutsch, "A Street-Wise Philosopher Explains What It Means to Be Homeless amid the Pandemic," *Smithsonian Magazine*, 24 August 2020.

109. "France Is Leaving Lockdown. Now the Trouble Begins," *Economist*, 14 May 2020.

110. Lydia Wålsten, "När Europa öppnar gränser ligger Sverige dåligt till," *Svenska Dagbladet*, 17 May 2020.

111. Fred Deveaux, "Democracy Perception Index – 2020," *Dalia*, 15 June 2020.

112. Dan Balz and Emily Guskin, "Americans Widely Oppose Reopening Most Businesses, Despite Easing of Restrictions in Some States, Post–U. Md. Poll Finds," *Washington Post*, 5 May 2020; Robert Griffin and Mayesha Quasem, "What's Driving the Shutdown Protests? It's Not Economic Pain," *Washington Post*, 19 May 2020.

113. Scott Clement and Dan Balz, "Despite Widespread Economic Toll, Most Americans Still Favor Controlling Outbreak over Restarting Economy, Post–ABC Poll Finds," *Washington Post*, 1 June 2020.

114. Jean-Marc Vittori, "France and the Art of Getting Back to Work," *Globalist*, 24 June 2020.

115. Matthew Smith, "Brits Split on Changes to Coronavirus Lockdown Measures," *YouGov*, 11 May 2020.

116. Toby Helm, et al., "Fearful Britons Remain Strongly Opposed to Lifting Coronavirus Lockdown," *Guardian*, 3 May 2020.

117. James Johnson, "Boris Johnson Risks Dragging Brits Out of Lockdown against Their Will," *Politico*, 12 May 2020.

118. Harry Cole and Matt Dathan, "'Like the Mary Celeste.' Just One in 20 Civil Servants Have Returned to Their Desks Sparking Fury from Cabinet Ministers," *Sun*, 3 March 2020.

119. Fintan O'Toole, "Coronavirus Has Exposed the Myth of British Exceptionalism," *Guardian*, 11 April 2020.

120. "British People Turn Out Not to Have a Fierce Love of Liberty after All," *Private Eye*, 1519 (3–23 April 2020) 34.

121. "Britain Has the Wrong Government for the Covid Crisis," *Economist*, 18 June 2020.

122. Alexa Lardieri, "Poll: Democrats, Independents, GOP All Turning on Trump amid Coronavirus, Protests," *USNews*, 10 June 2020.

123. Jacey Fortin and Johnny Diaz, "After Crowding at Lake of the Ozarks, Missouri Officials Urge Quarantine," *New York Times*, 26 May 2020.

124. Isobel van Hagen and Matteo Moschella, "Arrests as Revelers Defy Distancing Rules after Pubs Reopen in England," *NBC News*, 5 July 2020; "Police to Review Response to 'Nuisance' Rave and Party," *BBC*, 21 June 2020.

125. John Dingwall, "Beer Gardens Hailed 'Resounding Success' after Thousands of Scots Get the Pints In," *Daily Record*, 6 July 2020.

126. "Nigeria's Lagos Risks New Lockdown If Distancing Flouted," *Barron's*, 9 May 2020.

127. Eleanor Barlow and Tara Fitzpatrick, "Riot Police Clash with Liverpool Fans as Supporters Defy Lockdown Rules for Title Party," *Daily Record*, 27 June 2020; Sam Elliott and Hayley Parker, "Moment Mass Brawl Erupts in Staffordshire Beer Garden as Pubs Reopen," *Stoke Sentinel*, 5 July 2020.

128. Silvana Paternostro, "Covid-19 Brings Out the Dark Side of a Caribbean Carnival City," *Financial Times*, 5 July 2020.

129. Derek Hawkins, et al., "As Coronavirus Infections Surge Nationwide, 21 States See Increase in Average Daily New Cases," *Washington Post*, 13 June 2020; Hans Henri P. Kluge, "Statement – Preparing for the Autumn Is a Priority Now at the WHO Regional Office for Europe," WHO, 18 June 2020, www.euro.who.int/en/about-us/regional-director/statements-and-speeches/2020/statement-preparing-for-the-autumn-is-a-priority-now-at-the-who-regional-office-for-europe.

130. Marc Ambinder, "'Reopen' Protest Movement Created, Boosted by Fake Grassroots Tactics," *The Conversation*, 24 April 2020; "Armed Protesters Enter Michigan Statehouse," *BBC*, 1 May 2020.

131. Diana Daly, "What Are the 'Reopen' Protesters Really Saying?," *The Conversation*, 1 May 2020.

132. Keena Lipsitz and Grigore Pop-Eleches, "Where Are People Less Likely to Obey Coronavirus Restrictions? Republican Counties," *Washington Post*, 14 May 2020.

133. Valeria Olivares, "Several Texas Cities Worry Hospitals May Run Out of Beds in Two Weeks or Sooner," *Texas Tribune*, 5 July 2020; Antonia Noori Farzan, et al., "Dozens of Fla. Hospitals Run Out of ICU Beds as U.S. Approaches 3 Million Coronavirus Cases," *Washington Post*, 8 July 2020.

134. Duval, et al., "Coronavirus: Au jour 1 du confinement, 'on ne verbalise que ceux qui nous prennent pour des cons.'"

135. Bernard-Henri Lévy, *The Virus in the Age of Madness* (New Haven 2020) 57–58, 68.

136. "Proteste während der COVID-19-Pandemie in Deutschland," *Wikipedia*.

137. "Germany: Thousands of Protesters Slam Isolation Measures," *DW*, 9 May 2020; "Police Attacked While Enforcing Social Distancing Measures," *DW*, 12 April 2020.

138. Geir Moulson, "Thousands Protest in Berlin against Coronavirus Restrictions," *HuffPost*, 1 August 2020; Matthew Karnitschnig, "German Coronavirus Deniers Test Merkel Government," *Politico*, 4 August 2020; Katrin Bennhold, "Far Right Germans Try to Storm Reichstag as Virus Protests Escalate," *New York Times*, 31 August 2020; Megan Specia, "As Europe's Coronavirus Cases Rise, So Do Voices Crying Hoax," *New York Times*, 28 September 2020.

139. Sarah Rainsford, "Coronavirus Crisis Tests Putin's Grip on Power in Russia," *BBC*, 22 April 2020.

140. Hannah Roberts, "Salvini Occupies Italian Parliament in Lockdown Protest," *Politico*, 30 April 2020.

141. "Belgrade Protesters Storm Serb Parliament over Curfew," *BBC*, 8 July 2020.

142. Clea Skopeliti, "Reform UK: Brexit Party to Rebrand as Anti-lockdown Voice," *Guardian*, 1 November 2020.

143. James Johnson, "If Britons Are the Most Pro-lockdown, It's Probably Because We're the Most Obedient," *Guardian*, 5 May 2020; Nazia Parveen, "Piers Corbyn among 19 Held in Coronavirus Lockdown Protests, *Guardian*, 16 May 2020.

144. "Coronavirus: Van Morrison Lockdown Protest Songs 'Dangerous,'" *BBC*, 18 September 2020.

145. Sarah Schaffer DeRoo, et al., "Planning for a COVID-19 Vaccination Program," *Journal of the American Medical Association*, 18 May 2020.

146. Peter Baldwin, *Contagion and the State in Europe, 1830–1930* (Cambridge 1999) ch. 4.

147. Tyler Pager, "'Monkey, Rat and Pig DNA': How Misinformation Is Driving the Measles Outbreak among Ultra-Orthodox Jews," *New York Times*, 9 April 2019; Azhar Hussain, et al., "The Anti-vaccination Movement: A Regression in Modern Medicine," *Cureus* 3 July 2018.

148. "Russian Orthodox Church Officially Opposes Compulsory Vaccinations of Children," *Russian Faith*, 4 July 2019.

149. WHO, "Ten Threats to Global Health in 2019," https://www.who.int/news-room/spotlight/ten-threats-to-global-health-in-2019.

150. Neil F. Johnson, et al., "The Online Competition between Pro- and Anti-vaccination Views," *Nature*, 13 May 2020.

151. *Wellcome Global Monitor 2018*, 106. Similar figures in Heidi J. Larson, et al., "The State of Vaccine Confidence 2016: Global Insights through a 67-Country Survey," *EBioMedicine*, 13 September 2016; Alexandre de Figueiredo, et al., "Mapping Global Trends in Vaccine Confidence and Investigating Barriers to Vaccine Uptake," *Lancet*, 10 September 2020.

152. Sarah Boseley, "Measles Cases at Highest for 20 Years in Europe, as Anti-vaccine Movement Grows," *Guardian*, 21 December 2018.

153. *Wellcome Global Monitor 2018*, 108.

154. Eve Dubé, et al., "Vaccine Hesitancy, Vaccine Refusal, and the Anti-vaccine Movement," *Expert Review of Vaccines*, 14, 1 (2014) 106.

155. Jeffrey Kluger, "Why the Anti-vaccine Crowd Won't Fade Away," *Time*, 25 September 2014.

156. *Wellcome Global Monitor 2018*, 106.

157. Rebecca Rosman, "Racism Row as French Doctors Suggest Virus Vaccine Test in Africa," *Aljazeera*, 4 April 2020; David Whitehouse, "Ending Europe's Colonial Approach to Medicine in Africa," *Africa Report*, 7 April 2020.

158. Jan Hoffman, "Mistrust of a Coronavirus Vaccine Could Imperil Widespread Immunity," *New York Times*, 18 July 2020; Peter Jamison, "Anti-vaccination Leaders Fuel Black Mistrust of Medical Establishment as Covid-19 Kills People of Color," *Washington Post*, 17 July 2020.

159. John Cohen, "The Line Is Forming for a COVID-19 Vaccine. Who Should Be at the Front?," *Science*, 29 June 2020.

160. COCONEL Group, "A Future Vaccination Campaign against COVID-19 at Risk of Vaccine Hesitancy and Politicization," *Lancet Infectious Diseases*, 20 May 2020.

161. "Expectations for a COVID-19 Vaccine," Associated Press–NORC Center for Public Affairs Research, https://apnorc.org/projects/expectations-for-a-covid-19-vaccine/.

162. Amy Goldstein and Scott Clement, "7 in 10 Americans Would Be Likely to Get a Coronavirus Vaccine, Post–ABC Poll Finds," *Washington Post*, 2 June 2020.

163. Rachel H. Dodd, et al., "Willingness to Vaccinate against COVID-19 in Australia," *Lancet Infectious Diseases*, 30 June 2020.

164. Jon Henley, "Coronavirus Causing Some Anti-vaxxers to Waver, Experts Say," *Guardian*, 21 April 2020.

165. "Donald Trump Is Hoping for a Covid-19 Treatment by November," *Economist*, 18 July 2020.

166. Jeanne M. Santoli, et al., "Effects of the COVID-19 Pandemic on Routine Pediatric Vaccine Ordering and Administration: United States, 2020," *Morbidity and Mortality Weekly Report*, 15 May 2020.
167. Jack Goodman and Flora Carmichael, "Bill Gates 'Microchip' Conspiracy Theory and Other Vaccine Claims Fact-Checked," *BBC*, 30 May 2020.
168. Peter Jamison, "Anti-vaccination Leaders Seize on Coronavirus to Push Resistance to Inoculation," *Washington Post*, 5 May 2020.
169. George Ramsay, "Novak Djokovic Tests Positive for Coronavirus after Adria Tour Event," *CNN*, 24 June 2020.
170. Tom Leonard, "Could This Conspiracy Theory Kill Thousands? Disgraced British Doctor Andrew Wakefield, Who Lost His Licence for Saying the MMR Jab Caused Autism, Is Already at Heart of a Movement That Says the Pandemic Is a Hoax and No One Should Have Vac," *Daily Mail*, 16 July 2020.
171. Paul L. Fidel, Jr. and Mairi C. Noverr, "Could an Unrelated Live Attenuated Vaccine Serve as a Preventive Measure to Dampen Septic Inflammation Associated with COVID-19 Infection?," *mBio*, 19 June 2020; Luis E. Escobar, et al., "BCG Vaccine Protection from Severe Coronavirus Disease 2019 (COVID-19)," *Proceedings of the National Academy of Sciences*, 28 July 2020.
172. "Expectations for a COVID-19 Vaccine," Associated Press–NORC Center for Public Affairs Research.
173. Sharon LaFraniere, et al. "Scientists Worry about Political Influence over Coronavirus Vaccine Project," *New York Times*, 2 August 2020; David Crow and Kiran Stacey, "Why Is the 'Anti-vaxxer' Movement Growing during a Pandemic?," *Financial Times*, 19 August 2020.
174. Olivia Goldhill, "China Is Telling State Employees It's Safe to Use an Experimental Coronavirus Vaccine," *Quartz*, 31 July 2020.
175. Isabelle Khurshudyan and Carolyn Y. Johnson, "Russia Unveils Covid Vaccine 'Sputnik V,' Claiming Breakthrough in Global Race before Final Testing Complete," *Washington Post*, 11 August 2020. Though, stung by criticism, they then rolled out the mass testing retrospectively. "Russia to Begin COVID-19 Vaccine Trials on 40,000 People Next Week," *Reuters*, 20 August 2020.
176. Sui-Lee Wee, "China Gives Unproven Covid-19 Vaccines to Thousands, with Risks Unknown," *New York Times*, 26 September 2020.
177. Working Group on Readying Populations for COVID-19 Vaccine, *The Public's Role in COVID-19 Vaccination: Planning Recommendations Informed by Design Thinking and the Social, Behavioral, and Communication Sciences*, July 2020, www.centerforhealthsecurity.org/our-work/pubs_archive/pubs-pdfs/2020/200709-The-Publics-Role-in-COVID-1 9-Vaccination.pdf.

9 DIFFICULT DECISIONS IN HARD TIMES

1. "Survey: COVID-19 Affecting Patients' Access to Cancer Care," *Cancer Action Network*, 15 April 2020, https://www.fightcancer.org/releases/survey-covid-19-affecting-patients %E2%80%99-access-cancer-care.
2. Sophie Borland, "2.4 Million Patients Are Caught in Coronavirus Cancer Backlog," *Daily Mail*, 31 May 2020.
3. Dalton Conley, "Who You Gonna Call? COVID-19 and the Future of Telemedicine," *Milbank Quarterly*, 15 July 2020; "Telehealth in Physical Therapy in Light of COVID-19," American Physical Therapy Association, 16 March 2020; Brittany Lazur, et al., "Telebehavioral Health: An Effective Alternative to In-Person Care," *Milbank Memorial Fund*, October 2020.
4. "Fler vill träffa läkaren via mobilen," *Svenska Dagbladet*, 13 July 2020.

5. Erin Rhoda, "3 New Ways Mainers Can Access Health Care Remotely," *Bangor Daily News*, 19 March 2020.

6. Sophie Williams, "'I Can Recover at Home': Cosmetic Surgeons See Rise in Patients Amid Pandemic," *BBC*, 10 July 2020.

7. Eliza Shapiro, "Child Vaccinations Plummet 63 Percent, a New Hurdle for N.Y.C. Schools," *New York Times*, 20 May 2020; Bianca Bharti, "As Canada's Child Vaccination Rates Drop Due to Lockdown, Experts Fear Other Infectious Outbreaks," *National Post*, 11 June 2020.

8. Jacques Follorou, "Entre retards de diagnostic et traitements interrompus, les répercussions du Covid-19 inquiètent," *Le Monde*, 2 May 2020.

9. Josh Katz, et al., "In Shadow of Pandemic, U.S. Drug Overdose Deaths Resurge to Record," *New York Times*, 15 July 2020.

10. Will Stone and Elly Yu, "Eerie Emptiness of ERs Worries Doctors as Heart Attack and Stroke Patients Delay Care," *Kaiser Health News*, 7 May 2020; Kathleen P. Hartnett, et al., "Impact of the COVID-19 Pandemic on Emergency Department Visits – United States, January 1, 2019–May 30, 2020," *Morbidity and Mortality Weekly Report*, 12 June 2020; "A Sharp Drop in Accident-and-Emergency Admissions Worries Medics," *Economist*, 8 April 2020; Lenny Bernstein and Frances Stead Sellers, "Patients with Heart Attacks, Strokes and Even Appendicitis Vanish from Hospitals," *Washington Post*, 19 April 2020.

11. Kat Lay, "Australia's Mild Flu Season Good News for Britain," *Times* (London), 29 July 2020; "The Southern Hemisphere Skipped Flu Season in 2020," *Economist*, 12 September 2020.

12. Jasper V. Been, et al., "Impact of COVID-19 Mitigation Measures on the Incidence of Preterm Birth," *Lancet*, 13 October 2020; Gitte Hedermann, et al., "Changes in Premature Birth Rates during the Danish Nationwide COVID-19 Lockdown," *MedRxiv*, 23 May 2020; Roy K. Philip, et al., "Reduction in Preterm Births during the COVID-19 Lockdown in Ireland," *MedRxiv*, 5 June 2020.

13. Eloi Marijon, et al., "Out-of-Hospital Cardiac Arrest during the COVID-19 Pandemic in Paris, France," *Lancet*, 27 May 2020.

14. Enrico Baldi, et al., "Out-of-Hospital Cardiac Arrest during the Covid-19 Outbreak in Italy," *New England Journal of Medicine*, 29 April 2020.

15. "The New Pandemic Threat: People May Die Because They're Not Calling 911," *American College of Cardiology*, 22 April 2020.

16. Figures calculated from those in Office of National Statistics, "Deaths Registered by Place of Occurrence," in "Deaths Registered Weekly in England and Wales, Provisional: Week Ending 17 July 2020," www.ons.gov.uk/peoplepopulationandcommunity/births deathsandmarriages/deaths/bulletins/deathsregisteredweeklyinenglandandwales provisional/latest#deaths-registered-by-place-of-occurrence.

17. Denise Grady, "The Pandemic's Hidden Victims: Sick or Dying, but Not from the Virus," *New York Times*, 20 April 2020.

18. April Dembosky, "Organ Transplants Down as Stay-At-Home Rules Reduce Fatal Traffic Collisions," *NPR*, 20 May 2020.

19. "Lifting Lockdowns: The When, Why and How," *Economist*, 23 May 2020; Marguerite Massinga Loembé, et al., "COVID-19 in Africa: The Spread and Response," *Nature Medicine*, 11 June 2020; Jan Hoffman and Ruth Maclean, "Slowing the Coronavirus Is Speeding the Spread of Other Diseases," *New York Times*, 14 June 2020; Kaja Abbas, et al., "Routine Childhood Immunisation during the COVID-19 Pandemic in Africa: A Benefit–Risk Analysis of Health Benefits versus Excess Risk of SARS-CoV-2 Infection," *Lancet*, 17 July 2020.

20. Timothy Roberton, et al., "Early Estimates of the Indirect Effects of the COVID-19 Pandemic on Maternal and Child Mortality in Low-Income and Middle-Income Countries: A Modelling Study," *Lancet*, 12 May 2020.

21. David L. Schriger, "Learning from the Decrease in US Emergency Department Visits in Response to the Coronavirus Disease 2019 Pandemic," *JAMA Internal Medicine*, 3 August 2020.

22. Molly M. Jeffrey, et al., "Trends in Emergency Department Visits and Hospital Admissions in Health Care Systems in 5 States in the First Months of the COVID-19 Pandemic in the US," *JAMA Internal Medicine*, 3 August 2020.

23. Chih-Wei Sung, et al., "Impact of COVID-19 Pandemic on Emergency Department Services Acuity and Possible Collateral Damage," *Resuscitation*, 29 May 2020.

24. Kristina Hedberg, "Akuterna undrar: Var är alla vanliga patienter?," *Dagens Nyheter*, 17 April 2020; "Färre söker vård för hjärtinfarkt efter corona," *Aftonbladet*, 13 April 2020.

25. Fredrik Mellgren, "Tusentals svenskar har oupptäckt cancer," *Svenska Dagbladet*, 9 August 2020.

26. Cécile Bouanchaud, "Avant le confinement, ils fuient à la campagne," *Le Monde*, 16 March 2020; Thomas Chatterton Williams, "I Didn't Feel Parisian Until I Escaped Paris," *New York Times Magazine*, 11 May 2020.

27. Kevin Quealy, "The Richest Neighborhoods Emptied Out Most as Coronavirus Hit New York City," *New York Times*, 15 May 2020. Leading to long-term problems as the census undercounted the populations of posh neighborhoods: Dana Rubinstein, "Why Rich New Yorkers Are Causing Big Problems for the Census," *New York Times*, 13 July 2020.

28. Azi Paybarah, et al., "Where New Yorkers Moved to Escape Coronavirus," *New York Times*, 17 May 2020.

29. Ollie Williams, "Brits Keep Calm and Flee to the Country over Fears of London Lockdown," *Forbes*, 20 March 2020; Victoria Ward, "Affluent Londoners Flee City for Rural Idylls amid Fears of Lockdown," *Telegraph*, 19 March 2020.

30. "Government Bans Norwegians from Travelling to Cabins amid Coronavirus," *Reuters*, 19 March 2020.

31. Adam Gorlick, "The Productivity Pitfalls of Working from Home in the Age of COVID-19," *Stanford News*, 30 March 2020.

32. Maya Oppenheim, "Women Bearing Burden of Childcare and Homeschooling in Lockdown, Study Finds," *Independent*, 14 May 2020; Thomas Lyttleton, et al., "Gender Differences in Telecommuting and Implications for Inequality at Home and Work," *SocArxiv Papers*, 7 July 2020; Caitlyn Collins, et al., "COVID-19 and the Gender Gap in Work Hours," *Gender, Work, and Organization*, 2 July 2020.

33. "Sourdough Economics: No Need to Knead," *Economist*, 9 July 2020; Geneva Abdul, "Pandemic-Baking Britain Has an 'Obscene' Need for Flour," *New York Times*, 20 May 2020.

34. Jung Won Sonn, "South Korea's Success in Controlling Disease Is Due to Its Acceptance of Surveillance," *Conversation*, 19 March 2020.

35. Anton Friedrich Fischer, *Es wird Tag! Deutschland darf die herrschende Brechruhr (Cholera) nicht als Pest und Contagion betrachten: Ein Wort an die hohen Staatsbeamten Deutschlands und zur Beruhigung des Publikums* (Erfurt 1832) 22.

36. Peter Baldwin, *Contagion and the State in Europe, 1830–1930* (Cambridge 1999) 62–63.

37. Baldwin, *Contagion and the State*, 49, 72.

38. Folkhälsomyndigheten, "Förekomst av covid-19 i olika yrkesgrupper: Bekräftade covid-19 fall i Sverige 13 mars–27 maj 2020," www.folkhalsomyndigheten.se/contentassets/5e248b82cc284971a1c5fd922e7770f8/forekomst-covid-19-olika-yrkesgrupper.pdf.

39. Sarah Collerton and John Harrison, "Meet Britain's Unlikely Key Workers," *BBC*, 1 July 2020.
40. Marissa G. Baker, "Nonrelocatable Occupations at Increased Risk during Pandemics: United States, 2018," *American Journal of Public Health*, 8 July 2020; Jonathan I. Dingel and Brent Neiman, "How Many Jobs Can Be Done at Home?," NBER Working Papers 26948, June 2020.
41. Erik Brynjolfsson, et al., "COVID-19 and Remote Work: An Early Look at US Data," NBER Working Paper Series 27344, June 2020.
42. From 27% to 47%. Office for National Statistics, Coronavirus (COVID-19) roundup; Industries operating under lockdown; Selected measures of employment by industry groups (based on likely state of operations), UK, 2019 and 6 to 19 April 2020; Economy; % employees working remotely 6–19 April 2020; 19 May 2020, www.ons.gov.uk/people populationandcommunity/healthandsocialcare/conditionsanddiseases/articles/coro naviruscovid19roundup/2020-03-26#labourmarket.
43. Eurofound, "Living, Working, and COVID-19," www.eurofound.europa.eu/publica tions/report/2020/living-working-and-covid-19.
44. Ben Dooley and Makiko Inoue, "Japan Needs to Telework. Its Paper-Pushing Offices Make That Hard," *New York Times*, 14 April 2020.
45. Mariya Brussevich, et al., "Who Will Bear the Brunt of Lockdown Policies? Evidence from Tele-workability Measures across Countries," IMF Working Paper WP/20/88, June 2020.
46. Bernard-Henri Lévy, *The Virus in the Age of Madness* (New Haven 2020) xvi.
47. Office for National Statistics, "Coronavirus (COVID-19) Related Deaths by Occupation, England and Wales: Deaths Registered between 9 March and 25 May 2020," 26 June 2020, www.ons.gov.uk/peoplepopulationandcommunity/healthandsocial care/causesofdeath/bulletins/coronaviruscovid19relateddeathsbyoccupationenglan dandwales/deathsregisteredbetween9marchand25may2020#men-and-deaths-involv ing-covid-19-by-occupation.
48. Folkhälsomyndigheten, "Förekomst av covid-19 i olika yrkesgrupper."
49. Remy F. Pasco, et al., "Estimated Association of Construction Work with Risks of COVID-19 Infection and Hospitalization in Texas," *JAMA Network Open*, 29 October 2020.
50. Public Health England, "Disparities in the Risks and Outcomes of COVID-19," June 2020, Table 5.1, https://assets.publishing.service.gov.uk/government/uploads/ system/uploads/attachment_data/file/892085/disparities_review.pdf.
51. Office for National Statistics, "Coronavirus (COVID-19) Related Deaths by Occupation, England and Wales: Deaths Registered between 9 March and 25 May 2020," 26 June 2020.
52. "One in Five Groenlo Abattoir Workers Have Covid-19, Health Board Will Carry Out Spot Checks," *DutchNews.nl*, 25 May 2020; "German Slaughterhouse Outbreak Crosses 1,000," *DW*, 20 June 2020; Lasse Skou Andersen, "Ingen ved helt, hvorfor coronavirus trives så godt på slagterier. Her er tre teorier," *Information*, 3 August 2020.
53. Francis Green, "Schoolwork in Lockdown: New Evidence on the Epidemic of Educational Poverty," Centre for Learning and Life Chances in Knowledge Economies and Societies, Research Paper 67, https://www.llakes.ac.uk/sites/default/ files/LLAKES%20Working%20Paper%2067_0.pdf; Richard Adams, "Gap between Rich and Poor Pupils in England 'Grows by 46% in a Year,'" *Guardian*, 1 September 2020.
54. Caroline Sharp, et al., "The Challenges Facing Schools and Pupils in September 2020," National Foundation for Educational Research, 5, www.nfer.ac.uk/media/4119/scho ols_responses_to_covid_19_the_challenges_facing_schools_and_pupils_in_septem ber_2020.pdf.

55. Alison Andrew, et al., "Learning during the Lockdown: Real-Time Data on Children's Experiences during Home Learning," Institute for Fiscal Studies Briefing Note BN288, https://www.ifs.org.uk/publications/14848.
56. Claire Cain Miller, "In the Same Towns, Private Schools Are Reopening While Public Schools Are Not," *New York Times*, 16 July 2020.
57. Lucia Newman, "Chile Students Struggle with Lack of Internet," *Aljazeera*, 23 June 2020.
58. Mayor's Office of the Chief Technology Officer, "Truth in Broadband: Access and Connectivity in New York City," April 2018, https://tech.cityofnewyork.us/wp-content/uploads/2018/04/NYC-Connected-Broadband-Report-2018.pdf.
59. Lara Fishbane and Adie Tomer, "As Classes Move Online during COVID-19, What Are Disconnected Students to Do?," *Brookings*, 20 March 2020.
60. Department for Business, Energy, and Industrial Strategy, et al., "New Guidance Launched to Help Get Brits Safely Back to Work," 11 May 2020, www.gov.uk/government/news/new-guidance-launched-to-help-get-brits-safely-back-to-work.
61. Folkhälsomyndigheten, "Förekomst av covid-19 i olika yrkesgrupper."
62. Greta Privitera, "Italy's 'Boys' Club' Politics Shuts Women Out of Coronavirus Debate," *Politico*, 18 May 2020.
63. Tiffany Ford, et al., "Race Gaps in COVID-19 Deaths Are Even Bigger Than They Appear," *Brookings*, 16 June 2020.
64. "Technical Details: SARS-CoV2 Serological Survey in Mumbai by NITI-BMC-TIFR," https://www.tifr.res.in/TSN/article/Mumbai-Serosurvey%20Technical%20report-NITI.pdf.
65. Richard A. Oppel, Jr., et al., "The Fullest Look Yet at the Racial Inequity of Coronavirus," *New York Times*, 5 July 2020; Silvia Muñoz-Price, et al., "Racial Disparities in Incidence and Outcomes among Patients with COVID-19," *JAMA Network Open*, 25 September 2020.
66. Ewen M. Harrison, et al., "Ethnicity and Outcomes from COVID-19: The ISARIC CCP-UK Prospective Observational Cohort Study of Hospitalised Patients," *SSRN*, 17 June 2020.
67. Lucinda Platt and Ross Warwick, "Are Some Ethnic Groups More Vulnerable to COVID-19 Than Others?," The Institute for Fiscal Studies Deaton Review, May 2020; Office for National Statistics, "Coronavirus (COVID-19) Related Deaths by Ethnic Group, England and Wales: 2 March 2020 to 10 April 2020," 7 May 2020, www.ons.gov.uk/peoplepopulationandcommunity/birthsdeathsandmarriages/deaths/articles/coronavirusrelateddeathsbyethnicgroupenglandandwales/2march2020to10april2020.
68. Lena Masri, "COVID-19 Takes Unequal Toll on Immigrants in Nordic Region," *Reuters*, 24 April 2020; Clive Cookson and Richard Milne, "Nations Look into Why Coronavirus Hits Ethnic Minorities So Hard," *Financial Times*, 28 April 2020; Folkehelseinstituttet, "COVID-19-Epidemien: Kunnskap, situasjon, prognose, risiko og respons i Norge etter uke 14," 5 April 2020, 8, www.fhi.no/contentassets/c9e459cd7cc24991810a0d28d7803bd0/vedlegg/notat-om-risiko-og-respons-2020-04-05.pdf; "One in Every 100 Norwegian Somalis Has Tested Positive for Coronavirus," *The Local*, 8 April 2020.
69. Shelly Tan, et al., "Amid the Pandemic, Public Transit Is Highlighting Inequalities in Cities," *Washington Post*, 15 May 2020.
70. Frida Sundkvist, "Corona härjar bland fattiga – rika klarar sig," *Expressen*, 28 June 2020.
71. Marta Bivand Erdal, et al., "Migrants and COVID-19 in Norway: Five Reflections on Skewed Impacts," PRIO Blogs, 6 April 2020, https://blogs.prio.org/2020/04/migrants-and-covid-19-in-norway-five-reflections-on-skewed-impacts/.
72. Clyde W. Yancy, "COVID-19 and African Americans," *Journal of the American Medical Association*, 15 April 2020; Allan S. Noonan, et al., "Improving the Health of African Americans in the USA: An Overdue Opportunity for Social Justice," *Public Health Reviews*, 37, 12 (2016); US Department of Health and Human Services, Office of

Minority Health, "Profile: Black/African Americans," https://www.minorityhealth.hhs
.gov/omh/browse.aspx?lvl=3&lvlid=61.

73. Folkhälsomyndigheten, "Hälsa hos personer som är utrikes födda – skillnader i hälsa
utifrån födelseland," 13 June 2019, www.folkhalsomyndigheten.se/publicerat-mater
ial/publikationsarkiv/h/halsa-hos-personer-som-ar-utrikes-fodda–skillnader-i-halsa-ut
ifran-fodelseland/?pub=61466.

74. Rita Hamad, et al., "Association of Neighborhood Disadvantage with Cardiovascular
Risk Factors and Events among Refugees in Denmark," *JAMA Network Open*, 21 August
2020.

75. Krithi Ravi, "Ethnic Disparities in COVID-19 Mortality: Are Comorbidities to Blame?,"
Lancet, 19 June 2020; Jacqui Wise, "Covid-19: Known Risk Factors Fail to Explain the
Increased Risk of Death among People from Ethnic Minorities," *British Medical Journal*,
11 May 2020.

76. Aseem Malhotra, et al., "Poor Metabolic Health Is a Major Issue for Increased COVID-
19 Mortality in BAME Patient Groups," *Physician*, 8 July 2020.

77. Lise G. M. Hanssens, et al., "Access, Treatment, and Outcomes of Care: A Study of
Ethnic Minorities in Europe," *International Journal of Public Health*, 61 (2016).

78. Lena H. Sun and Ben Guarino, "Anti-vaxxers Target Communities Battling Measles,"
Washington Post, 20 May 2019; Ed Silverman, "STAT-Harris Poll: The Share of
Americans Interested in Getting Covid-19 Vaccine as Soon as Possible Is Dropping,"
STAT, 19 October 2020.

79. Alison Andrew, et al., "Educational Gaps Are Growing during Lockdown," Institute
for Fiscal Studies Briefing Note, 18 May 2020, www.ifs.org.uk/publications/14849;
"As Schools Reopen, How Can Pupils Make Up for Lost Time?," *Economist*, 18 July
2020.

80. "Coronavirus: What You Need to Know – Racial Disparities in COVID-19," National
Educational Union, 7 May 2020, https://neu.org.uk/coronavirus-what-you-need-know
-racial-disparities-covid-19.

81. Peter Baldwin, *Command and Persuade: Crime, Law, and the State across History* (Cambridge
MA 2021) ch. 12.

82. Barbara Bleisch, "Maskierte Mündigkeit," *Tagesanzeiger*, 7 July 2020.

83. Alexandra Teslya, et al., "Impact of Self-Imposed Prevention Measures and Short-Term
Government-Imposed Social Distancing on Mitigating and Delaying a COVID-19
Epidemic: A Modelling Study," *PLoS Medicine*, 21 July 2020.

84. Monica Gandhi, et al., "Masks Do More Than Protect Others during COVID-19:
Reducing the Inoculum of SARS-CoV-2," *Journal of General Internal Medicine*, August
2020; Monica Gandhi, "Facial Masking for Covid-19 – Potential for 'Variolation' as We
Await a Vaccine," *New England Journal of Medicine*, 8 September 2020.

85. Atul Gawande, *Being Mortal: Medicine and What Matters in the End* (New York 2014);
Daniel Callahan and Sherwin B. Nuland, "The Quagmire: How American Medicine Is
Destroying Itself," *New Republic*, 18 May 2011.

86. Charles L. Sprung, et al., "Changes in End-of-Life Practices in European Intensive Care
Units from 1999 to 2016," *Journal of the American Medical Association*, 322, 17 (2019).

87. Robert D. Truog, et al., "The Toughest Triage – Allocating Ventilators in a Pandemic,"
New England Journal of Medicine, 21 May 2020.

88. Lisa Rosenbaum, "Trolleyology and the Dengue Vaccine Dilemma," *New England
Journal of Medicine*, 374, 4 (2018).

89. Jean-François Bonnefon, et al., "The Social Dilemma of Autonomous Vehicles," *Science*,
24 June 2016.

90. Ezekiel J. Emanuel, et al., "Fair Allocation of Scarce Medical Resources in the Time of
Covid-19," *New England Journal of Medicine*, 21 May 2020.

91. WHO, "Ethical Considerations in Developing a Public Health Response to Pandemic Influenza," 2007, www.who.int/csr/resources/publications/WHO_CDS_EPR_GIP _2007_2c.pdf?ua=1.
92. E. Lee Daugherty Biddison, et al., "Too Many Patients: A Framework to Guide Statewide Allocation of Scarce Mechanical Ventilation during Disasters," *Contemporary Reviews in Critical Care Medicine*, April 2019.
93. Socialstyrelsen, *Nationella principer för prioritering inom intensivvård under extraordinära förhållanden* (March 2020), www.socialstyrelsen.se/globalassets/sharepoint-dokument/dokument-webb/ovrigt/nationella-prioriteringar-intensivvarden.pdf.
94. Lisa Röstlund and Anna Gustafson, "Dokument visar vilka som inte får intensivvård," *Dagens Nyheter*, 10 April 2020; Olof Svensson, "Dokument visar: De prioriteras bort från intensivvård," *Aftonbladet*, 9 April 2020.
95. Lisa Röstlund and Anna Gustafson, "Läkare: Vi tvingas till hårda prioriteringar," *Dagens Nyheter*, 24 April 2020. Similarly, 21% of patients in Swedish intensive care during the first half of 2020 were over seventy, while in Denmark the figure was over double that. Bojan Pancevski, "Coronavirus Is Taking a High Toll on Sweden's Elderly. Families Blame the Government," *Wall Street Journal*, 18 June 2020.
96. Shina C. L. Kamerlin and Peter M. Kasson, "Managing COVID-19 Spread with Voluntary Public-Health Measures: Sweden as a Case Study for Pandemic Control," *Clinical Infectious Diseases*, 1 July 2020.
97. Maciej Zaremba, "Varför fick de äldre dö utan läkarvård?," *Dagens Nyheter*, 13 October 2020; Anna Gustafsson and Lisa Röstlund, "Forskare: Riktlinjen diskriminerande mot dementa," *Dagens Nyheter*, 4 October 2020; "Äldre nekas sjukhusvård under pandemin," *Ekuriren*, 12 May 2020.
98. Fredrick Mellgren and Henrik Ennart, "Okända kurvan visar hur äldre prioriteras bort," *Svenska Dagbladet*, 29 May 2020. More examples of elderly Covid-19 patients denied intensive care: Lisa Röstlund and Anna Gustafsson, "De valdes bort av vården – fast vårdplatser stod tomma," *Dagens Nyheter*, 9 June 2020.
99. Torbjörn Tännsjö, "Vi bör rädda de unga om vården inte kan klara alla," *Dagens Nyheter*, 25 March 2020. His arguments can be found in English in Torbjörn Tännsjö, *Setting Health-Care Priorities: What Ethical Theories Tell Us* (Oxford 2019) ch. 10.
100. Ingemar Engström, et al., "Principer för prioriteringar av intensivvård ifrågasätts," *Läkartidningen*, 31 March 2020. Norway may have been even more utilitarian in prioritizing the young: "Så ska intensivvården prioritera i coronakrisen," *Expressen*, 4 April 2020.
101. British Medical Association, "COVID-19 – Ethical Issues: A Guidance Note," www .bma.org.uk/media/2226/bma-covid-19-ethics-guidance.pdf.
102. Arbeitsgruppe Ethik der Österreichischen Gesellschaft für Anästhesiologie, Reanimation und Intensivmedizin, "Allokation intensivmedizinischer Ressourcen aus Anlass der Covid 19 Pandemie," 17 March 2020, www.oegari.at/web_files/cms_da ten/covid-19_ressourcenallokation_gari-statement_v1.7_final_2020-03-17.pdf.
103. "COVID-19 Pandemic: Triage for Intensive-Care Treatment under Resource Scarcity," *Swiss Medical Weekly*, 24 March 2020. The Australians' logic on age was similar: Sydney Health Ethics, "An Ethics Framework for Making Resource Allocation Decisions within Clinical Care: Responding to COVID-19," 2 April 2020, www.sydney.edu.au/ content/dam/corporate/documents/faculty-of-medicine-and-health/research/cent res-institutes-groups/she.-clinical-ethics.-resource-allocation-framework.-version-1.-2-april-2020.pdf.
104. New York Task Force on Life and the Law, "Ventilator Allocation Guidelines," November 2015, 45, www.health.ny.gov/regulations/task_force/reports_publica tions/docs/ventilator_guidelines.pdf.

105. Geert Meyfroidt, et al., "Ethical Principles Concerning Proportionality of Critical Care during the 2020 COVID-19 Pandemic in Belgium: Advice by the Belgian Society of Intensive Care Medicine," www.hartcentrumhasselt.be/professioneel/nieuws-profes sioneel/ethical-principles-concerning-proportionality-of-critical-care-during-the-covid -19-pandemic-advice-by-the-belgian-society-of-ic-medicine.
106. Matina Stevis-Gridneff, et al., "When COVID-19 Hit, Many Elderly Were Left to Die," *New York Times*, 8 August 2020.
107. Kollengode Ramanathan, et al., "Planning and Provision of ECMO Services for Severe ARDS during the COVID-19 Pandemic and Other Outbreaks of Emerging Infectious Diseases," *Lancet Respiratory Medicine*, 20 March 2020.
108. Graeme MacLaren, et al., "Preparing for the Most Critically Ill Patients with COVID-19: The Potential Role of Extracorporeal Membrane Oxygenation," *Journal of the American Medical Association*, 7 April 2020.
109. NIH, *Coronavirus Disease 2019 (COVID-19) Treatment Guidelines*, 17 July 2020 edition, 46, www.covid19treatmentguidelines.nih.gov.
110. NHS England, "Clinical Guide for Extra Corporeal Membrance Oxygenation (ECMO) for Respiratory Failure in Adults during the Coronavirus Pandemic," 25 June 2020. The June version has been removed and replaced with a later one now at https://www.nice .org.uk/Media/Default/About/COVID-19/Specialty-guides/Speciality-Guide-Extra-Corporeal-Membrane-Oxygenation-ECMO-Adult.pdf.
111. Lisa Rosenbaum, "Facing Covid-19 in Italy: Ethics, Logistics, and Therapeutics on the Epidemic's Front Line," *New England Journal of Medicine*, 14 May 2020; Greta Privitera, "Italian Doctors on Coronavirus Frontline Face Tough Calls on Whom to Save," *Politico*, 9 March 2020.
112. Marco Vergano, et al., "SIAARTI Clinical Ethics Recommendations for the Allocation of Intensive Care Treatments in Exceptional, Resource-Limited Circumstances," 16 March 2020, www.siaarti.it/SiteAssets/News/COVID19%20-%20documenti%20S IAARTI/SIAARTI%20-%20Covid-19%20-%20Clinical%20Ethics%20Reccomendatio ns.pdf; Silvia Camporesi and Maurizio Mauri, "Ethicists, Doctors and Triage Decisions: Who Should Decide? And on What Basis?," *Journal of Medical Ethics*, 10 July 2020.
113. Frederico Nicoli and Alessandra Gasparetto, "Italy in a Time of Emergency and Scarce Resources," *Journal of Clinical Ethics*, 31, 1 (2020).
114. Lucia Craxì, et al., "Rationing in a Pandemic: Lessons from Italy," *Asian Bioethics Review*, 16 June 2020.
115. Comitato Nazionale per la Bioetica, "Covid-19: Clinical Decision-Making in Conditions of Resource Shortage and the 'Pandemic Emergency Triage' Criterion," 8 April 2020, http://bioetica.governo.it/media/4008/p136_2020_covid-19-clinical-decision-making-in-conditions-of-resource-shortage-and-the-pandemic-emergency-tri age-criterion_en.pdf.
116. Comité consultatif national d'éthique, "COVID-19: Contribution du CCNE: Enjeux éthiques face à une pandémie" (13 March 2020) 4, 9, www.ccne-ethique.fr/sites/def ault/files/reponse_ccne_-_covid-19_def.pdf.
117. Comité consultatif national d'éthique pour les sciences de la vie et de la santé, "Questions éthiques soulevées par une possible pandémie grippale," Avis 106 (5 February 2009) 14, www.ccne-ethique.fr/sites/default/files/publications/avis_106 .pdf.
118. Amitai Etzioni, "Coronavirus Is Creating a Dangerous Ethical Choice for Doctors," *National Interest*, 6 April 2020.
119. Geert Meyfroidt, et al., "Ethical Principles Concerning Proportionality of Critical Care during the 2020 COVID-19 Pandemic in Belgium: Advice by the Belgian Society of Intensive Care Medicine," www.hartcentrumhasselt.be/professioneel/nieuws-

professioneel/ethical-principles-concerning-proportionality-of-critical-care-during-the-covid-19-pandemic-advice-by-the-belgian-society-of-ic-medicine.

120. Swiss Society of Intensive Care Medicine, "Recommendations for the Admission of Patients with COVID-19 to Intensive Care and Intermediate Care Units," *Swiss Medical Weekly*, 24 March 2020. This was, however, contradicted in Nationale Ethikkommission im Bereich der Humanmedizin, *Influenza-Pandemieplan Schweiz* 2006, 186, www.nek-cne.admin.ch/inhalte/Themen/Stellungnahmen/10_ethische_fragen_de.pdf.

121. Commonwealth of Massachusetts, "Crisis Standards of Care: Planning Guidance for the COVID-19 Pandemic," 7 April 2020, https://d279m997dpfwgl.cloudfront.net/wp/2020/04/CSC_April-7_2020.pdf.

122. "Open Letter to Crisis Standards of Care Advisory Committee," https://docs.google.com/document/d/13kGxuxmIIdxbo3X2Kh_i7ruyelSsXBzEiQRL73KK_Vc/edit.

123. Mike Baker, "Whose Life Is Worth Saving? In Washington State, People with Disabilities Are Afraid They Won't Make the Cut," *New York Times*, 23 March 2020.

124. "Annex to ESF 8 of the State of Alabama Emergency Operations Plan," revised 9 April 2010, 8, https://adap.ua.edu/uploads/5/7/8/9/57892141/alabamas_ventilator_rationing_plan.pdf.

125. US Department of Health and Human Services, Office for Civil Rights, "Civil Rights, HIPAA, and the Coronavirus Disease 2019 (COVID-19)," 28 March 2020, www.hhs.gov/sites/default/files/ocr-bulletin-3-28-20.pdf. Similar guidance from the European Disability Forum, "Updated Statement: Ethical Medical Guidelines in COVID-19: Disability Inclusive Response," 24 March 2020, www.edf-feph.org/newsroom/news/updated-statement-ethical-medical-guidelines-covid-19-disability-inclusive-response-0.

126. National Institute for Health and Care Excellence, "COVID-19 Rapid Guideline: Critical Care in Adults," 20 March 2020, www.nice.org.uk/guidance/ng159/resources/covid19-rapid-guideline-critical-care-in-adults-pdf-66141848681413.

127. "NICE Amends COVID-19 Critical Care Guideline after Judicial Review Challenge," Hodge, Jones & Allen, 31 March 2020, www.hja.net/press-releases/nice-amends-covid-19-critical-care-guideline-after-judicial-review-challenge/. Similar backtracking can be found here: Matt Discombe, "'Prejudiced' Hospital Admissions Guidance for the Elderly Dropped by NHSE," *HSJ*, 15 April 2020, www.hsj.co.uk/patient-safety/prejudiced-hospital-admissions-guidance-for-the-elderly-dropped-by-nhse/7027414.article.

128. Deutscher Ethikrat, *Solidarity and Responsibility during the Coronavirus Crisis: Ad Hoc Recommendation* (Berlin 2020) 3–4, https://www.ethikrat.org/fileadmin/Publikationen/Ad-hoc-Empfehlungen/englisch/recommendation-coronavirus-crisis.pdf.

129. Reinhard Merkel, "Beatmung in der Medizin: Eine Frage von Recht und Ethik," *Frankfurter Allgemeine Zeitung*, 4 April 2020.

130. Deutsche Interdisziplinäre Vereinigung für Intensiv- und Notfallmedizin, et al., "Entscheidungen über die Zuteilung von Ressourcen in der Notfall- und der Intensivmedizin im Kontext der COVID-19-Pandemie," 25 March 2020, https://dynamic.faz.net/download/2020/COVID-19_Ethik_Empfehlung_Endfassung_2020-03-25.pdf. Nor do the German guidelines seem to be distinguished from other European nations' : Susanne Joebges and Nikola Biller-Adorno, "Ethics Guidelines on COVID-19 Triage: An Emerging International Consensus," *Critical Care*, 6 May 2020.

131. Almost 40/100,000. https://en.wikipedia.org/wiki/List_of_countries_by_hospital_beds. Slightly different figures here, but still outstanding for Germany: Niall McCarthy, "The Countries with the Most Critical Care Beds Per Capita," *Forbes*, 12 March 2020.

132. Jochen Bittner, "Germany Has More Than Enough Ventilators. It Should Share Them," *New York Times*, 17 March 2020. At 25,000, Germany already had more per

capita than Russia, the country with the highest number in Europe, and more than the US, to judge from the figures here: "The Ventilator Problem," *Meduza*, 20 March 2020.

133. Baldwin, *Contagion and the State*, 72.

134. Peter Singer and Michael Plant, "When Will the Pandemic Cure Be Worse Than the Disease?," *Project Syndicate*, 6 April 2020.

135. https://twitter.com/realdonaldtrump/status/1241935285916782593?lang=en.

136. Nafeez Ahmed, "Behavioural Scientists Told Government to Use 'Herd Immunity' to Justify Business-as-Usual," *Byline Times*, 23 March 2020; Nafeez Ahmed, "Treasury and Downing Street Advisors Intervened to Delay COVID-19 Lockdown," *Byline Times*, 3 July 2020.

137. https://twitter.com/khalafroula/status/1267017318594379776.

138. "Emerging Countries Lift Lockdowns Despite Covid-19 Cases Surge," *Financial Times*, 21 May 2020.

139. Joseph Cotterill, "Johannesburg Covid-19 Crisis: 'The Storm Is upon Us,'" *Financial Times*, 13 July 2020.

140. Niko Le Mieux, "Malawi to Go on Lockdown from Today through May," *Foreign Brief*, 18 April 2020; "Informal Vendors Rally against Coronavirus Lockdown in Malawi," *Aljazeera*, 16 April 2020.

141. "Malawi High Court Blocks Coronavirus Lockdown," *Aljazeera*, 17 April 2020.

142. "Emerging Countries Lift Lockdowns Despite Covid-19 Cases Surge," *Financial Times*.

143. The State Council Information Office of the People's Republic of China, "Fighting Covid-19: China in Action," June 2020, III, 1, http://english.www.gov.cn/news/top news/202006/07/content_WS5edc559ac6d066592a449030.html.

144. "Sustaining Containment of COVID-19 in China," *Lancet*, 16 April 2020.

145. What one observer called disaster Communism: Slavoj Žižek, *Pandemic! COVID-19 Shakes the World* (New York 2020) ch. 10.

146. Kekst CNC, *COVID-19 Opinion Tracker*, 2nd ed. (25 April–1 May 2020), www .kekstcnc.com/media/2590/kekst-cnc_research-report_covid-19-opinion-tracker_wave-2_final-1.pdf.

147. European Parliament, *Uncertainty/EU/Hope: Public Opinion in Times of Covid-19*, June 2020, 17, www.europarl.europa.eu/at-your-service/files/be-heard/eurobarometer/2020/public_opinion_in_the_eu_in_time_of_coronavirus_crisis/report/en-covid19-survey-report.pdf.

148. Solomon Hsiang, et al., "The Effect of Large-Scale Anti-contagion Policies on the COVID-19 Epidemic," *MedRxiv*, 21 May 2020.

149. Seth Flaxman, et al., "Estimating the Effects of Non-pharmaceutical Interventions on COVID-19 in Europe," *Nature*, 8 June 2020. Dissenting from such conclusions: Christian Bjørnskov, "Did Lockdown Work? An Economist's Cross-Country Comparison," *SSRN*, 6 August 2020; Rabail Chaudhry, et al., "A Country Level Analysis Measuring the Impact of Government Actions, Country Preparedness and Socioeconomic Factors on COVID-19 Mortality and Related Health Outcomes," *EClinicalMedicine*, 21 July 2020.

150. Wan Yang, et al., "COVID-19 Transmission Dynamics and Effectiveness of Public Health Interventions in New York City during the 2020 Spring Pandemic Wave," *MedRxiv*, 9 September 2020.

151. Erik Berglöf, "Forskarna har lärt av krisen – men inte beslutsfattarna," *Dagens Nyheter*, 1 June 2020.

152. Valerie Cerra and Sweta Chaman Saxena, "Growth Dynamics: The Myth of Economic Recovery," *American Economic Review*, 98, 1 (2008).

153. Carmen M. Reinhart and Kenneth S. Rogoff, "Recovery from Financial Crises: Evidence from 100 Episodes," National Bureau of Economic Research, Working Paper 19823, January 2014.

154. Philipp Carlsson-Szlezak, et al., "What Coronavirus Could Mean for the Global Economy," *Harvard Business Review*, 3 March 2020.
155. Robert J. Barro, et al., "The Coronavirus and the Great Influenza Pandemic: Lessons from the 'Spanish Flu' for the Coronavirus's Potential Effects on Mortality and Economic Activity," National Bureau of Economic Research, Working Paper 26866, April 2020.
156. Martin Karlsson, et al., "The Impact of the 1918 Spanish Flu Epidemic on Economic Performance in Sweden," *Journal of Health Economics*, 34 (2014).
157. Elizabeth Brainerd and Mark V. Siegler, "The Economic Effects of the 1918 Influenza Epidemic," Centre for Economic Policy Research, Discussion Paper 3791, February 2003; Thomas A. Garrett, "War and Pestilence as Labor Market Shocks: U.S. Manufacturing Wage Growth 1914–1919," Federal Reserve Bank of St. Louis, Working Paper 2006-018C, March 2006.
158. Sergio Correia, et al., "Pandemics Depress the Economy, Public Health Interventions Do Not: Evidence from the 1918 Flu," SSRN, 26 March 2020.
159. Asli Demirgüç-Kunt, et al., "The Sooner the Better: The Early Economic Impact of Non-pharmaceutical Interventions during the COVID-19 Pandemic," World Bank Group, Policy Research Working Paper 9257, May 2020.
160. Sumedha Gupta, et al., "Tracking Public and Private Responses to the COVID-19 Epidemic: Evidence from State and Local Government Actions," NBER Working Paper Series 27027, April 2020.
161. William J. Luther, "Behavioral and Policy Responses to COVID-19: Evidence from Google Mobility Data on State-Level Stay-at-Home Orders," SSRN, 11 May 2020.
162. Demirgüç-Kunt, et al., "The Sooner the Better," 22–23.
163. Austan Goolsbee and Chad Syverson, "Fear, Lockdown, and Diversion: Comparing Drivers of Pandemic Economic Decline 2020," Becker Friedman Institute Working Paper 2020–80, June 2020.
164. David Leonhardt, "'More Severe Than the Great Recession,'" *New York Times*, 17 March 2020.
165. Ryan Bourne, "A View So Radical That Some Simply Won't See It. The Driver of Our Problems Isn't Lockdown. It's the Virus," *Conservative Home*, 13 May 2020.
166. Faiz Siddiqui, "The Bay Area Ordered Millions to Shelter in Place. Elon Musk Had Tesla Employees Report to Work Anyway," *Washington Post*, 19 March 2020; Faiz Siddiqui and Josh Dawsey, "Tesla's Elon Musk Receives Support from Trump as He Reopens Factory in Defiance of County Order," *Washington Post*, 12 May 2020; Rachel Lerman, "Elon Musk Already Restarted Tesla Production. Now the County Says It's Allowed Next Week," *Washington Post*, 13 May 2020; Faiz Siddiqui, "Tesla Defied County Orders So It Could Restart Production. Days Later, Workers Tested Positive for the Coronavirus," *Washington Post*, 9 June 2020.
167. The two sides of the argument are laid out in Mark Harrison, *Contagion: How Commerce Has Spread Disease* (New Haven 2012); Alex Chase-Levenson, *The Yellow Flag: Quarantine and the British Mediterranean World, 1780–1860* (Cambridge 2020) 80–81.
168. Quoted in Paul Kane, "Hard-Hit Industries Clamor for Regulations during Pandemic," *Washington Post*, 4 July 2020.
169. US Chamber of Commerce, "Joint Letter: Business Leaders Call on President, VP, and NGA to Lead on Face Covering Concerns," 2 July 2020, www.uschamber.com/letters-congress/joint-letter-business-leaders-call-president-vp-and-nga-lead-face-covering-concerns.
170. Manny Fernandez and Sarah Mervosh, "Texas Pauses Reopening as Virus Cases Soar across the South and West," *New York Times*, 25 June 2020.
171. Steven Swinford and Andrew Ellson, "Rishi Sunak Targets Two-Metre Rule and Calls For a Spending Spree," *Times* (London), 11 June 2020.

172. "Contribution of Travel and Tourism to GDP as a Share of GDP," Knoema, https://knoema.com/atlas/topics/Tourism/Travel-and-Tourism-Total-Contribution-to-GDP/Contribution-of-travel-and-tourism-to-GDP-percent-of-GDP.

173. Ed Augustin, "Cuba Sets Example with Successful Programme to Contain Coronavirus," *Guardian*, 7 June 2020.

174. Nektaria Stamouli, "Greece's Tourist Reopening Brings More Infections but No Economic Panacea," *Politico*, 20 July 2020.

175. Maria Sacchetti, "Maine's Vacationland Hot Spots Are Ghost Towns as Tourism Struggles amid Coronavirus," *Washington Post*, 2 July 2020.

176. Nick Murray, "Covid Catastrophe: Consequences of Society Shutdowns," Maine Policy Institute, August 2020, https://mainepolicy.org/project/covid-catastrophe-consequences-of-societal-shutdowns/.

177. Bill Trotter, "Maine's Summer Tourist Season Managed to Beat Low Expectations after a Dismal Spring," *Bangor Daily News*, 4 September 2020.

178. Tony Romm, "Myrtle Beach Reopened to Survive the Summer. Now, It's a Coronavirus 'Petri Dish,'" *Washington Post*, 2 July 2020.

179. Stephen Burgen, "Video of Drunken Brits Maskless in Magaluf Appals Spaniards," *Guardian*, 14 July 2020.

180. "Der Ballermann macht die Medien für die Schließung verantwortlich," *Mallorca Zeitung*, 16 July 2020.

181. Johanna Read, "Here's Where Americans Can Travel Now. But Should They?," *National Geographic*, 7 July 2020.

182. "Avatar: James Cameron Returns to New Zealand to Resume Filming," *Stuff*, 2 June 2020; Joel McManus and Tom Hunt, "'Political Favouritism' for Hollywood Film Crews, Says Opposition MP," *Stuff*, 2 June 2020.

183. Charu Suri, "Why Work from Home When You Can Work from Barbados, Bermuda or ... Estonia?," *New York Times*, 19 August 2020.

184. Sangmin Aum, et al., "Inequality of Fear and Self-Quarantine: Is There a Trade-off between GDP and Public Health?," NBER Working Paper No. 27100; Jonathan Rothwell and Hannah Van Drie, "The Effect of COVID-19 and Disease Suppression Policies on Labor Markets," *Brookings*, 27 April 2020.

185. A cross section of figures: Joe Hasell, "Which Countries Have Protected Both Health and the Economy in the Pandemic?," *Our World in Data*, 1 September 2020.

186. "China's World-Beating Growth Rate of ... 3.2%," *Economist*, 18 July 2020; Keith Bradsher, "China's Economy Rebounds from Coronavirus, but Shares Fall," *New York Times*, 15 July 2020; "What Is Fuelling China's Economic Recovery?," *Economist*, 19 September 2020.

187. John Detrixhe, "The Pandemic Barely Dented Taiwan's Economy," *Quartz*, 29 September 2020; Ezekiel J. Emanuel, et al., "Learning from Taiwan about Responding to Covid-19 – and Using Electronic Health Records," *Stat*, 30 June 2020.

188. Johan Norberg, "Coronavirus: L'étonnante politique de la Suède," *Contrepoints*, 28 April 2020.

189. Richard Milne, "Coronavirus 'Medicine' Could Trigger Social Breakdown," *Financial Times*, 25 March 2020.

190. Richard Milne, ""Swedish CEOs Worry Cure Will Be Worse Than Medicine," *Financial Times*, 29 March 2020.

191. Yıldız Akkaya, et al., "GDP Growth in Sweden Relative to Other Countries in the Wake of Covid-19," Sveriges Riksbank, *Economic Commentaries*, 5, 12 June 2020, www.riksbank.se/globalassets/media/rapporter/ekonomiska-kommentarer/engelska/2020/gdp-growth-in-sweden-relative-to-other-countries-in-the-wake-of-covid-19.pdf.

192. Sean Williams, "Have Both Sides Got It Wrong on Sweden's Strategy?," *Mundus*, 18 May 2020.

193. Michael Olsen and Michel Thykier, "Hvem er hårdest ramt? Så mange slag har Danmarks og Sveriges økonomi fået," *Politiken*, 12 June 2020.

194. Joakim Goksör, "Svensk coronastrategi ingen ekonomisk vinnare," *SvD Näringsliv*, 9 June 2020; Olsen and Thykier, "Hvem er hårdest ramt?"

195. OECD, www.oecd.org/economic-outlook/june-2020/. Viewed 2 August 2020; European Commission, *European Economic Forecast: Summer 2020 (Interim)*, July 2020, https://ec.europa.eu/info/sites/info/files/economy-finance/ip132_en.pdf.

196. Eurostat, "GDP and Employment Growth Rates, % Change over the Previous Quarter, 2020Q1," https://ec.europa.eu/eurostat/statistics-explained/index.php?title=File:G DP_and_employment_growth_rates,_%25_change_over_the_previous_quarter,_bas ed_on_seasonally_adjusted_data,_2020Q1.png.

197. Germany's exports of goods and services as a percentage of GDP amounted to 47.4% in 2018, Sweden's, 45.8%. World Bank, "Exports of Goods and Services (% of GDP)," https://data.worldbank.org/indicator/NE.EXP.GNFS.ZS.

198. Eurostat, https://ec.europa.eu/eurostat/documents/2995521/11156775/2-310720 20-BP-EN.pdf/cbe7522c-ebfa-ef08-be60-b1c9d1bd385b.

199. www.investing.com/economic-calendar/swedish-gdp-426.

200. Richard Milne, "Swedish Companies Reap Benefits of Country's Covid-19 Approach," *Financial Times*, 26 July 2020.

201. Richard Milne, "Sweden's Light-Touch Covid-19 Approach Spared Economy, Says SEB Chief," *Financial Times*, 15 July 2020.

202. "Swedish Firms Have Outshone German Ones in the Pandemic," *Economist*, 8 August 2020.

203. Susanna Sundström, "Varumärket Sverige – så har det klarat pandemin," *SvD Näringsliv*, 30 October 2020.

204. "Economic Data, Commodities and Markets," *Economist*, 22 August 2020.

205. Michael Andrews, "Bar Talk: Informal Social Interactions, Alcohol Prohibition, and Invention," *SSRN*, 4 December 2019.

206. Marshall Burke, "COVID-19 Reduces Economic Activity, Which Reduces Pollution, Which Saves Lives," *G-Feed*, 8 March 2020, http://www.g-feed.com/2020/03/covid-19-reduces-economic-activity.html.

207. "India's Lockdown Has Brought Unexpected Benefits," *Economist*, 23 April 2020.

208. Sarah Goodyear, "Cities Are Starting to Report Big Declines in Car Crashes, but Increases in Speeding," *CityMetric*, 16 April 2020; Luz Lazo, "The Coronavirus Pandemic Emptied America's Roadways. Now Speeders Have Taken Over," *Washington Post*, 11 May 2020.

209. IPSOS, "Impact of Coronavirus to New Car Purchase in China," 12 March 2020, www .ipsos.com/sites/default/files/ct/news/documents/2020-03/impact-of-coronavirus-to-new-car-purchase-in-china-ipsos.pdf.

210. Tanya Powley and Claire Bushey, "Wealthy, Virus-Wary Tourists Turn to Private Jets," *Financial Times*, 25/26 July 2020.

211. Kirk Semple, "At Least 70 Dead in Mexico from Drinking Tainted Alcohol," *New York Times*, 13 May 2020.

212. Jonathan Rose, "The Cure May Be Deadlier Than the Disease. Much Deadlier," *History News Network*, 19 April 2020.

213. Nick Drydakis, "The Relationship between Recessions and Health," *IZA World of Labor*, August 2016; Ioannis Laliotis, et al., "Total and Cause-Specific Mortality before and after the Onset of the Greek Economic Crisis," *Lancet Public Health*, 4 November 2016.

CONCLUSION: PUBLIC HEALTH AND PUBLIC GOODS

1. Although in New York City, the absolute excess death rates in the spring of 2020 approached those during the fall of 1918, and the relative rates, compared with normal mortality, were higher – and that despite the advantages of modern medicine. Jeremy Samuel Faust, et al., "Comparison of Estimated Excess Deaths in New York City during the COVID-19 and 1918 Influenza Pandemics," *JAMA Network Open*, 13 August 2020.
2. Lawrence Summers, "Covid-19 Looks Like a Hinge in History," *Financial Times*, 14 May 2020; Wade Davis, "The Unravelling of America," *Rolling Stone*, 6 August 2020.
3. Lists of possible outcomes can be found at Bfinn, "162 Benefits of Coronavirus," Lesswrong, 12 May 2020, www.lesswrong.com/posts/5u5Het5Lkcb2nSWJp/162-benefits-of-coronavirus; "Second Order Effects," Mental Model Club, https://docs.google.com/document/d/17YkH4kc63t7JI7JJZR6i3-iebJd7kfRAzAK_ssl8bt4/edit.
4. Steve Mirsky, "Hand Out," *Scientific American*, August 2020; "Coronavirus: Will We Ever Shake Hands Again?," *BBC*, 6 May 2020.
5. "Covid-19 in the Netherlands: A Timeline," Actiegroep Containment Nu, https://www.containmentnu.nl/articles/timeline?lang=en; Javier C. Hernández and Su-Hyun Lee, "No More Jenga, No More 'Amen' as Cities Learn to Live with Coronavirus," *New York Times*, 2 May 2020.
6. "China Asks: What's the Safest Way to Use Chopsticks?," *Economist*, 23 April 2020; Tanmoy Goswami, "We're Touching Our Smartphones More Than Ever. And It's Changing the Ancient Connection between the Body and the Brain," *The Correspondent*, 8 October 2020.
7. Greta Privitera, "The Emotional Cost of Coronavirus," *Politico*, 19 August 2020; Philip Kiefer, "Will We Ever Trust Crowds Again?," *National Geographic*, 29 September 2020.
8. " Saudi Arabia Closes Grand Mosque, Prophet's Mosque between Night and Morning Prayers," *Arab News*, 5 March 2020.
9. Alexandra Ossola, "It Is Time for the 'Lipstick Index' to Go Away for Good," *Quartz*, 6 August 2020.
10. Dan Kopf, "The Share of Americans in Their 20s Moving Home Is Skyrocketing," *Quartz*, 20 July 2020.
11. Manavi Kapur, "Coronavirus Has Made It Easier for Millennials to Scale Back the Big Fat Indian Wedding," *Quartz India*, 18 September 2020.
12. "Mid-century Modern," *Economist*, 1 August 2020.
13. Caitlin Gibson, "Blowing Out Candles Is Basically Spitting on Your Friends' Cake. Will We Ever Do it Again?," *Washington Post*, 20 July 2020.
14. Kaya Burgess, "Coronavirus: Arrive Dressed for a Swim and Avoid Butterfly Stroke When Pools Reopen," *Times* (London), 16 June 2020.
15. "The Silent Pandemic: How Lockdown Is Affecting Future Health," COVID Symptom Study, 29 July 2020, https://covid.joinzoe.com/post/lockdown-weight-gain?mc_cid=95335863dc&mc_eid=f488a21227; "A Million People Have Stopped Smoking since the COVID Pandemic Hit Britain," Action on Smoking and Health, 15 July 2020, https://ash.org.uk/media-and-news/press-releases-media-and-news/pandemicmillion/; Michael S. Pollard, et al., "Changes in Adult Alcohol Use and Consequences during the COVID-19 Pandemic in the US," *JAMA Network Open*, 29 September 2020.
16. "Pandating: Coronavirus and the Language of Love," *1843*, 15 July 2020.
17. Brigitta Forsberg, "Japanska män vill slippa 'coronaskilsmässa,'" *Svenska Dagbladet*, 16 May 2020; Alice Yan, "New Law Requires 30-Day Cooling-off Period before Chinese Couples Can Divorce," *South China Morning Post*, 31 May 2020.

18. "Ready for Reopening? We Can Help," Gallagher Design, https://gallagherdesign.com /news/ready-for-reopening-we-can-help/.
19. Chris Mooney, et al., "As America Struggles to Reopen Schools and Offices, How to Clean Coronavirus from the Air," *Washington Post*, 26 June 2020.
20. Rebecca Bellan, "As More Cities Ban Cashless Businesses, New York Wants to Follow," *Bloomberg CityLab*, 6 March 2019; Ann Carrns, "Who Gets Hurt When the World Stops Using Cash," *New York Times*, 11 September 2020.
21. Mike Davis, *The Monster at Our Door: The Global Threat of Avian Flu* (New York 2005) 79.
22. Johanna Read, "Will New Travel Technology Invade Your Privacy?," *National Geographic*, 29 September 2020.
23. https://remotecourts.org/.
24. Toril Marie Øie, "The Chief Justice on the Hearing of Cases in the Supreme Court during the Coronavirus Outbreak," Supreme Court of Norway, 8 April 2020, www .domstol.no/en/Enkelt-domstol/supremecourt/arkiv/2020/the-chief-justice-on-the-hearing-of-cases-in-the-supreme-court-during-the-coronavirus-outbreak-8-april/.
25. Bukola Adebayo, "A Man Was Sentenced to Death via Zoom in Nigeria, Sparking Criticism from Rights Groups," *CNN*, 7 May 2020.
26. Richard Susskind, *Online Courts and the Future of Justice* (Oxford 2019) pt. 2.
27. Gabrielle Mannino, "Mills Signs Executive Order to Allow Remote Notarization in Response to Coronavirus, COVID-19," *News Center Maine*, 8 April 2020.
28. Though the offense seems to have been the volume of the activity, not the act itself, so that loud singing and speech were equally dangerous. Lauren Moss, "Singing 'No Riskier Than Talking' for Virus Spread," *BBC*, 20 August 2020. It followed, not surprisingly, that lower-volume singing was safer. Nicola Davis and Charlotte Higgins, "Performers Could Sing or Play Softly to Reduce Covid Risk, Study Shows," *Guardian*, 20 August 2020.
29. "Choral Singing Has Been Hit Hard by the Pandemic," *Economist*, 8 July 2020.
30. Lee Sung-Eun and Baek Min-Jeong, "Itaewon Cluster under Control but Officials Warn of Silent Transmission," *Korea JoongAng Daily*, 18 May 2020.
31. Joseph Gamp, "Yodeling Concert in Switzerland Blamed for Worst COVID-19 Supercluster in Europe," *New York Post*, 19 October 2020.
32. Jack Beresford, "Irish Pub Bans Neil Diamond's 'Sweet Caroline' from Venue amid Coronavirus Fears," *Irish Post*, 2 August 2020.
33. B. Bake, et al., "Exhaled Particles and Small Airways," *Respiratory Research*, 11 January 2019.
34. Preston City Council, "Quick Guide to Covid-19 Infection Control for Pubs, Restaurants, Cafes etc," 9 August 2020, www.preston.gov.uk/media/3088/CoVid-Guide-for-Pubs-Restaurants-Cafes-etc-Intervention-Area-/pdf/CoVid_Guide_for_Pub s_Restaurants_Cafes_etc_Intervention_Area.pdf?m=637325859409070000.
35. River Davis, "Reopened Theme Parks Ban Screaming on Roller Coasters. Riders Are Howling," *Wall Street Journal*, 8 July 2020.
36. Katherine Bindley, "Remote Work Is Reshaping San Francisco, as Tech Workers Flee and Rents Fall," *Wall Street Journal*, 14 August 2020.
37. Janina Conboye, "Will Facebook's Salary-by-Location Move Set Precedent for Tech?," *Financial Times*, 7 July 2020; Kate Conger, "Facebook Starts Planning for Permanent Remote Workers," *New York Times*, 21 May 2020.
38. Andrew Kortina, "Virtualization, Forklifts, Microphones, Shipping Containers, Video Conferencing, Stethoscopes ... Who Wins and Loses as COVID Accelerates," https:// kortina.nyc/essays/virtualization-forklifts-microphones-shipping-containers-video-con ferencing-stethoscopes.

39. Amnesty International, "Exposed, Silenced, Attacked: Failures to Protect Health and Essential Workers during the COVID-19 Pandemic," 13 July 2020, www.amnesty.org/en/documents/pol40/2572/2020/en/.

40. Kunal Purohit and Tunali Mukherjee, "Foreign Tourists Face Hostility in India amid Coronavirus Panic," *Aljazeera*, 24 March 2020.

41. Yasmeen Serhan and Timothy McLaughlin, "The Other Problematic Outbreak: As the Coronavirus Spreads across the Globe, So Does Racism," *Atlantic*, 13 March 2020; Nathan Vanderklippe, "'Stay Away from Here': In China, Foreigners Have Become a Target for Coronavirus Discrimination," *Globe and Mail*, 9 April 2020.

42. Souad Mekhennet, "Far-Right and Radical Islamist Groups Are Exploiting Coronavirus Turmoil," *Washington Post*, 10 April 2020; Walter Russell Mead, "Amid the Pandemic, Anti-Semitism Flares Up," *Wall Street Journal*, 15 April 2020.

43. Angela Cochran, "What Will We Learn about Scholarly Publishing as a Result of COVID-19?," *Scholarly Kitchen*, 28 April 2020; Greta Privitera, "Italy's Problem with Working Women Made Worse by Coronavirus," *Politico*, 6 July 2020; "Downturns Tend to Reduce Gender Inequality. Not under Covid-19," *Economist*, 4 June 2020.

44. Titan Alon, et al., "The Impact of COVID-19 on Gender Equality," NBER Working Paper 26947, April 2020.

45. Robert Joyce and Xiaowei Xu, "Sector Shutdowns during the Coronavirus Crisis: Which Workers Are Most Exposed?," Institute for Fiscal Studies, 6 April 2020.

46. Displayed on a sign in a photo, in Seung Min Kim and Mike DeBonis, "Republicans Grow Nervous about Losing the Senate amid Worries over Trump's Handling of the Pandemic," *Washington Post*, 10 May 2020.

47. Tim Wirth, "Wacht auf, liebe Senioren! Ältere Menschen zu diffamieren, ist falsch. Aber sie müssen umdenken. Jetzt," *Tagesanzeiger*, 7 April 2020.

48. Quoted in Chris Cillizza, "What Texas Lt. Gov. Dan Patrick Misses So, So Badly in His 'Let's Get Back to Work' Pledge," *CNN*, 24 March 2020; Daniel Burke, "The Dangerous Morality behind the 'Open It Up' Movement," *CNN*, 24 April 2020.

49. Larry R. Churchill, "On Being an Elder in a Pandemic," *Hastings Center*, 13 April 2020.

50. Christian Rutz, et al., "COVID-19 Lockdown Allows Researchers to Quantify the Effects of Human Activity on Wildlife," *Nature Ecology and Evolution*, 22 June 2020.

51. Lauren Moore, "Reports of UK Roadkill Down Two-Thirds – but Will Hedgehogs Thrive after Lockdown?," *Conversation*, 12 May 2020; Tricia Nguyen, et al., "Special Report 4: Impact of COVID-19 Mitigation on Wildlife–Vehicle Conflict," Road Ecology Center, UC Davis, 24 June 2020, https://roadecology.ucdavis.edu/files/content/projects/COVID_CHIPs_Impacts_wildlife.pdf.

52. Jeff Tollefson, "Five Ways That Trump Is Undermining Environmental Protections under the Cover of Coronavirus," *Nature*, 28 April 2020.

53. James Fair, "Pump and Dump: Could the Covid-19 Pandemic Create More Pollution?," *Ends Report*, 30 April 2020.

54. Kristin Hughes, "Protector or Polluter? The Impact of COVID-19 on the Movement to End Plastic Waste," World Economic Forum, 6 May 2020.

55. William J. Sutherland, et al., "A Solution Scan of Societal Options to Reduce SARS-CoV-2 Transmission and Spread," *Research Gate*, May 2020.

56. Saket Badola, "Indian Wildlife amidst the COVID-19 Crisis: An Analysis of Status of Poaching and Illegal Wildlife Trade," TRAFFIC, 2020, www.traffic.org/site/assets/files/12885/wildlife-amidst-covid-19-india-web.pdf; Dina Fine Maron, "Poaching Threats Loom as Wildlife Safaris Put on Hold Due to COVID-19," *National Geographic*, 13 April 2020; "Lockdown Allowed Illegal Fishing to Spike in Philippines, Satellite Data Suggest," *Mongabay*, 7 June 2020.

57. Tim McDonnell, "Clean Energy Lost Nearly Half a Million US Jobs in April Alone," *Quartz*, 13 May 2020.

58. Kate Larsen, et al., "Taking Stock 2020: The COVID-19 Edition," Rhodium Group, 9 July 2020, https://rhg.com/wp-content/uploads/2020/07/Taking-Stock-2020-The-COVID-19-Edition.pdf.
59. Michael C. Coren, "The Coal Industry Is Finally Closing More Plants Than It's Building," *Quartz*, 6 August 2020.
60. Dieter Helm, "The Environmental Impacts of the Coronavirus," *Environmental and Resource Economics*, 7 May 2020, 29.
61. International Energy Agency, "Oil Market Report – August 2020," www.iea.org/reports/oil-market-report-august-2020.
62. Corinne Le Quéré, et al, "Temporary Reduction in Daily Global CO2 Emissions during the COVID-19 Forced Confinement," *Nature Climate Change*, 19 May 2020.
63. "Can Covid Help Flatten the Climate Curve?," *Economist*, 21 May 2020.
64. Andrew Freedman and Chris Mooney, "Earth's Carbon Dioxide Levels Hit Record High, Despite Coronavirus-Related Emissions Drop," *Washington Post*, 4 June 2020.
65. UN Environment Programme, *Emissions Gap Report 2019*, xx.
66. "Seize the Moment," *Economist*, 23 May 2020.
67. Brad Plumer and Nadja Popovich, "Emissions Are Surging Back as Countries and States Reopen," *New York Times*, 17 June 2020.
68. Department for Transport, "Coronavirus (COVID-19): Transport and Travel Guidance," 7 April 2020, www.gov.uk/government/collections/coronavirus-covid-19-transport-and-travel-guidance.
69. Jack Stewart, "Pandemic Shifts People's Feelings about Owning a Car," *Marketplace*, 20 July 2020.
70. Aitor Hernández-Morales, et al., "The Death of the City," *Politico*, 27 July 2020; Lisa Prevost, "5 Ways the Coronavirus Has Changed Suburban Real Estate," *New York Times*, 17 July 2020; Sophie Gallagher, "Escape to the Country: Will People Leave Cities Behind Post-pandemic?," *Independent*, 14 August 2020.
71. Larsen, et al., "Taking Stock 2020: The COVID-19 Edition."
72. For those with the time, David Quammen, *Spillover: Animal Infections and the Next Pandemic* (New York 2012) is a writerly account.
73. Kate E. Jones, et al., "Global Trends in Emerging Infectious Diseases," *Nature*, 21 February 2008.
74. "Zoonotic Diseases," CDC, www.cdc.gov/onehealth/basics/zoonotic-diseases.html.
75. John Vidal, "'Tip of the Iceberg': Is Our Destruction of Nature Responsible for Covid-19?," *Guardian*, 18 March 2020.
76. Christine K. Johnson, et al., "Global Shifts in Mammalian Population Trends Reveal Key Predictors of Virus Spillover Risk," *Proceedings of the Royal Society B*, 8 April 2020.
77. Nguyen Quynh Huong, et al., "Coronavirus Testing Indicates Transmission Risk Increases along Wildlife Supply Chains for Human Consumption in Viet Nam, 2013–2014," *BioRxiv*, 17 June 2020.
78. UN Environment Programme, *Preventing the Next Pandemic: Zoonotic Diseases and How to Break the Chain of Transmission* (2020) 29, www.unenvironment.org/resources/report/preventing-future-zoonotic-disease-outbreaks-protecting-environment-animals-and.
79. Sally Ho, "Stop Confusing Wet Markets with Wildlife Markets," *Africa Sustainable Conservation News*, 21 April 2020; Zhenzhong Si, "Is It Fair to Blame Unsanitary Wet Market Conditions in China for the Coronavirus Outbreak?," *LinkedIn*, 7 February 2020, www.linkedin.com/pulse/fair-blame-unsanitary-wet-market-conditions-china-coronavirus-si; Mario Cavolo, "Fact Check on China's 'Wet Markets': Here's the Reality," *LinkedIn*, 3 April 2020, www.linkedin.com/pulse/fact-check-chinas-wet-markets-heres-reality-mario-cavolo.
80. "China's Legislature Adopts Decision on Banning Illegal Trade, Consumption of Wildlife," *XinhuaNet*, 24 February 2020.

81. "Wuhan Bans Eating Wild Animals as Coronavirus Drives a Crackdown in China," *CBS News*," 21 May 2020; Wildlife Conservation Society, "WCS Statement and Analysis: On the Chinese Government's Decision Prohibiting Some Trade and Consumption of Wild Animals," WCS Newsroom, 26 February 2020.
82. "Covid-19 Has Put Pangolins in the Spotlight," *Economist*, 2 May 2020.
83. "The Bushmeat Trade," Parliamentary Office of Science and Technology, Postnote 236, February 2005, www.parliament.uk/globalassets/documents/post/postpn236 .pdf.
84. John E. Fa, et al., "Bushmeat and Food Security in the Congo Basin: Linkages between Wildlife and People's Future," *Environmental Conservation*, 30, 1 (2003).
85. Ben Webster, "Customs Officers Seize One Tonne of Giraffe and Chimpanzee Meat," *Times* (London), 27 August 2019.
86. Theodore Trefon, "Covid-19 and the Culture of Eating Wild Animals in Central Africa," *African Arguments*, 23 March 2020.
87. Yepoka Yeebo, "Inside Ghana's Biggest Bushmeat Market," *Mosaic*, 26 September 2016.
88. Alexandre M. Chausson, et al., "Understanding the Sociocultural Drivers of Urban Bushmeat Consumption for Behavior Change Interventions in Pointe Noire, Republic of Congo," *Human Ecology*, 18 March 2019; Roger Albert Mbete, et al., "Household Bushmeat Consumption in Brazzaville, the Republic of the Congo," *Tropical Conservation Science*, 6 December 2016.
89. WHO, "WHO Director-General's Opening Remarks at the Media Briefing on COVID-19," 17 April 2020, www.who.int/dg/speeches/detail/who-director-general-s-open ing-remarks-at-the-media-briefing-on-covid-19—17-april-2020.
90. Sohel Ahmed, et al., "Does Urbanization Make Emergence of Zoonosis More Likely? Evidence, Myths, and Gaps," *Environment and Urbanization*, 14 September 2019.
91. Abha Bhattarai, "How the Pandemic Is Changing Shopping," *Washington Post*, 21 May 2020.
92. Michele C. Hollow, "Lessons on Coronavirus Testing from the Adult Film Industry," *New York Times*, 18 June 2020.
93. Eline Schaart and Nektaria Stamouli, "Sex Workers at a Coronavirus Crossroads," *Politico*, 20 June 2020.
94. Katherine Baicker, et al., "Is It Safer to Visit a Coffee Shop or a Gym?," *New York Times*, 6 May 2020.
95. Björn Finke, "Vestager sieht Bevorzugung Deutschlands bei Staatshilfen," *Süddeutsche Zeitung*, 17 May 2020.
96. Jim Tankersley, et al., "Small-Business Aid Funds Run Dry as Program Fails to Reach Hardest Hit," *New York Times*, 15 April 2020.
97. Emily Flitter and Peter Eavis, "Some Companies Seeking Bailouts Had Piles of Cash, Then Spent It," *New York Times*, 24 April 2020.
98. Gwyn Topham and Lucy Campbell, "Northern Rail Franchise to Be Renationalized," *Guardian*, 29 January 2020.
99. "Should Governments Prop Up the Media?," *Politico*, 5 May 2020.
100. Jim Tankersley and Charlie Savage, " Businesses Seek Sweeping Shield from Pandemic Liability before They Reopen," *New York Times*, 28 April 2020.
101. "Netherlands: State Aid for Multinationals?," *Politico*, 17 April 2020.
102. Joshua Posaner, "German Coalition Agrees €130B Economic Rescue Package," *Politico*, 4 June 2020; Thomas Kreutzmann, "Die Wut auf die SPD in der Autokrise," *Tagesschau*, 7 June 2020.
103. "Stryg krydstogtskibenes bekvemmelighedsflag," *Jyllands-Posten*, 12 May 2020.
104. Roger C. Schonfeld, "Forecasting the US Higher Education Market: A Primer," *Scholarly Kitchen*, 5 May 2020.

105. Sam Lowe, "Onshoring Is No Panacea for EU Medical Supplies," *Encompass*, June 2020.
106. Philipp Carlsson-Szlezak, et al., "What Coronavirus Could Mean for the Global Economy," *Harvard Businss Review*, 3 March 2020.
107. Andrew McDonald, "8 U-turns in 8 Months from Boris Johnson's Government," *Politico*, 17 August 2020.
108. Michael Finnegan, "COVID-19 Death Toll in the U.S. Surpasses 20,000, Now Highest in the World," *Los Angeles Times*, 11 April 2020.
109. Some of these debates are discussed in Peter Baldwin, *Command and Persuade: Crime, Law, and the State across History* (Cambridge MA 2021).
110. Hannah Sparks, "Medieval 'Wine Windows' Are Reopening, Reviving Italian Plague Tradition," *New York Post*, 6 August 2020.
111. Marianna Brady, "Coronavirus: How the Pandemic Is Relaxing US Drinking Laws," *BBC*, 15 May 2020.
112. Tom McTague, "Our Democracy Will Survive This Pandemic," *Atlantic*, 14 May 2020.
113. Peter Kufner, "Es braucht eine neue Solidarität für Österreich," *Die Presse*, 30 April 2020.
114. Nick Murray, "Covid Catastrophe: Consequences of Society Shutdowns," Maine Policy Institute, August 2020, https://mainepolicy.org/project/covid-catastrophe-consequences-of-societal-shutdowns.
115. Jean-Noël Cuénod, "Europe et plan de relance: À quand la démocratie?," Un plouc chez les bobos, 22 July 2020, https://jncuenod.blog.tdg.ch/archive/2020/07/22/e urope-et-plan-de-relance-a-quand-la-democratie-307710.html. Hence the question of whether this was the EU's Hamilton moment, of federalizing the debt. Sony Kapoor, "This Isn't Europe's 'Hamilton' Moment," *Politico*, 22 May 2020.
116. Oliver Wright, "Boris Johnson Looks Set to Upend Decades of Tory Orthodoxy," *Times* (London), 29 June 2020.
117. Jesper Thobo-Carlsen, "Nu er også borgerlige og nationalister blevet glade for den store, stærke stat," *Politiken*, 20 July 2020; Matthew Karnitschnig, "German Conservatives' Eurobond Awakening," *Politico*, 20 May 2020.
118. Amitai Etzioni, "Donald Trump Is Redefining the Role of 'Big Government' in America," *National Interest*, 17 May 2020.
119. Elizabeth Dwoskin, "Twitter Labels Trump's Tweets with a Fact Check for the First Time," *Washington Post*, 27 May 2020.
120. Lili Bayer, "Hungary's Viktor Orbán Wins Vote to Rule by Decree," *Politico*, 30 March 2020.
121. US Department of Health and Human Services, "Notification of Enforcement Discretion for Telehealth Remote Communications during the COVID-19 Nationwide Public Health Emergency," www.hhs.gov/hipaa/for-professionals/spe cial-topics/emergency-preparedness/notification-enforcement-discretion-telehealth /index.html.
122. WHO, "Ethical Considerations to Guide the Use of Digital Proximity Tracking Technologies for COVID-19 Contact Tracing," 28 May 2020, www.who.int/publica tions/i/item/WHO-2019-nCoV-Ethics_Contact_tracing_apps-2020.1.
123. Rory Cellan-Jones and Leo Kelion, "Coronavirus: The Great Contact-Tracing Apps Mystery," *BBC*, 22 July 2020.
124. An attitude somewhat exasperated with overly insistent privacy concerns is expressed in Nils Gilman and Steven Weber, "The Long Shadow of the Future," *Noēma*, 10 June 2020.
125. "Xi Jinping Is Reinventing State Capitalism. Don't Underestimate It," *Economist*, 13 August 2020.

126. Ho Ee Khor and Rolf Strauch, "Why Asia and Europe Are Responding to the Same Crisis Differently," *Project Syndicate*, 7 August 2020.

127. Eric Levitz, "A Historian of Economic Crisis on the World after COVID-19," *New York*, 7 August 2020, an interview with Adam Tooze.

128. Tyler Cowen, "The U.K.'s Response to Covid-19 Has Been World-Class," *Bloomberg*, 22 July 2020.

129. Kevin Rudd, "The Coming Post-COVID Anarchy," *Foreign Affairs*, 6 May 2020.

130. Noah Smith, "'A Team of Five Million.' How New Zealand Beat Coronavirus," *Direct Relief*, 3 August 2020.

131. Benjamin Mueller, "Contact Tracing, Key to Reining in the Virus, Falls Flat in the West," *New York Times*, 3 October 2020.

132. Louise E. Smith, et al., "Adherence to the Test, Trace and Isolate System," *MedRxiv*, 18 September 2020.

133. Peter Baldwin "The Return of the Coercive State: Behavioral Control in Multicultural Society," in T. V. Paul, et al., eds., *The Nation-State in Question* (Princeton 2003) 121–23.

134. Christopher H. Foreman, *Plagues, Products, and Politics: Emergent Public Health Hazards and National Policymaking* (Washington DC 1994) 63.

135. Edward P. Richards, "The Jurisprudence of Prevention: The Right of Societal Self-Defense against Dangerous Individuals," *Hastings Constitutional Law Quarterly*, 16, 329 (1989).

136. "Do Low-Trust Societies Do Better in a Pandemic?," *Economist*, 2 May 2020.

137. Andrew Salmon, "Why East Beat West on Covid-19," *Asia Times*, 15 May 2020.

138. Anna Jones, "Coronavirus: How 'Overreaction' Made Vietnam a Virus Success," *BBC*, 15 May 2020.

139. Nemo Kim, "South Koreans Keep Calm and Carry On Testing," *Guardian*, 18 March 2020.

140. Sirachai Arunrugstichai and Rachel Hartigan, "A Look inside Thailand, Which Prevented Coronavirus from Gaining a Foothold," *National Geographic*, 18 June 2020.

141. Kazuya Nakayachi, et al., "Why Do Japanese People Use Masks against COVID-19, Even Though Masks Are Unlikely to Offer Protection from Infection?," *Frontiers in Psychology*, 4 August 2020.

142. Quoted in Nathan Vanderklippe, "'Out-of-Home Quarantine' Measures in China Helped Limit Spread of COVID-19, Epidemiologists Say," *Globe and Mail*, 7 April 2020.

143. Ann-Christine From Utterstedt, et al., "Äldreomsorgen är inte en integrationsåtgärd," *Aftonbladet*, 17 April 2020.

144. Erik Angner and Gustaf Arrhenius, "The Swedish Exception?," *Behavioural Public Policy-Blog*, 23 April 2020.

145. Faisa Warsame, et al., "Det offentliges informasjon om korona var ikke godt nok tilpasset ulike språkgrupper," *Vårt Oslo*, 2 April 2020.

146. Gabriel Felbermayr, et al., "Après-ski: The Spread of Coronavirus from Ischgl through Germany," Institut für Weltwirtschaft Kiel, 24 May 2020.

147. Allyson Chiu, "Ohio GOP Lawmaker Fired from ER Job over Remarks about 'Colored Population' and Covid-19," *Washington Post*, 11 June 2020.

148. Marta Bivand Erdal, et al., "Migrants and COVID-19 in Norway: Five Reflections on Skewed Impacts," PRIO Blogs, 6 April 2020, https://blogs.prio.org/2020/04/migra nts-and-covid-19-in-norway-five-reflections-on-skewed-impacts/.

149. Sofie Fraser, et al., "Smittevernoverlege i Oslo bekymret for økning i øst: Mange bor trangt," *VG*, 2 April 2020.

150. Yusuf Sheikh Omar, "Why Is the Somali Diaspora So Badly Hit by COVID-19?," *African Arguments*, 13 May 2020.

151. Nathalie Rotschild, "The Hidden Flaw in Sweden's Anti-lockdown Strategy," *Foreign Policy*, 21 April 2020.

152. Anne Speckhard, et al., "When Religion and Culture Kill: COVID-19 in the Somali Diaspora Communities in Sweden," *Homeland Security Today*, 3 April 2020.

153. Torsten Cordes and Martin Borre, "DF kræver somalisk mindretal maskeret," *Berlingske*, 14 August 2020.

154. "Mette Frederiksen: For mange ikke-etniske danskere er smittet," *Jyllands Posten*, 15 August 2020.

155. Anna Fifield, "New Zealand Edges Back to Normal after Quashing Coronavirus in 49 Days," *Washington Post*, 16 May 2020.

156. Megan K. Stack, "A Sudden Coronavirus Surge Brought Out Singapore's Dark Side," *New York Times*, 20 May 2020.

157. Elsa Kulgelberg, "Den svenska coronastrategin är till för medelklassen," *Dagens Nyheter*, 29 June 2020.

158. Ed Yong, "Long-Haulers Are Redefining COVID-19," *Atlantic*, 19 August 2020.

Index

#MeToo movement, 188

Aarhus, 167, 284
Abe, Shinzo, 17
addiction
  socially determined, 178
aerosol transmission, 138
  masks, 163
  superspreading, 161
AfD, 217
Africa, 92, 131
  comorbidities, 132
  demographic characteristics, 132
AIDS, 15, 16, 27, 28, 33, 34, 43, 44, 84, 89,
      115, 160, 176, 182, 185, 188, 191
  mortality of, 193
  Sweden, 72
  traditional disease prevention tactics, 19,
      86
  treatments, 198
air bridges, 97
air travel
  eastern Europe, 122
  pandemic, 66, 127
airlines, 214, 271
Alabama, 243
Albania, 81, 101
Albert, Jan, 150
alcohol consumption, 43
alcohol regulation, 274
Alcoholic Beverage Commission, 206
amebiasis, 184
American Airlines, 271
American Medical Association, 86
American Samoa, 124
anal sex, 183, 184
animal protein, 269

animal welfare, 192
animals
  consumed, 268
  excrement, 186
  medicinal use of, 141
  public health implications of, 186
  wild, 187
Ansarin, Maulana Jubayer Ahmed, 47
antibiotics
  agricultural use of, 191
  misuse of, 190
anticipatory statutorification, 61
anti-Semitism, 263
anti-smoking, 43
antivaccinationism, 218
  reassurance of, 222
  social incidence of, 220
antivaccinators, 72
Antwerp, 47
Apple/Google contact tracing apps, 75, 276
Ardern, Jacinda, 280
Argentina, 76
Arizona, 97
Arlanda, 127
Armenia, 58, 81
asymptomatic carriers, 36, 70, 153, 287
  approach in Germany, 159
  dangers posed by, 158
  effects of Covid-19 on, 157
  history of concept, 155
  implications for voluntarist strategies,
      158
  incompatibility with certain strategies, 157
  masks, 167
  Swedish approach to, 158
  testing, 156
Atkins, Dr., 195

Atlanta, 127
Atlas, Scott, 142
Austin, 59
Australia, 92, 97, 103, 123
    enforcement, 204
    Spanish flu, 123, 143
Austria, 88
Austrian plague wall, 45
autism, 175
    and vaccination, 219
auto industry, 271
autocracies
    and pandemics, 10
avian flu, 13, 85, 193
aviation, 258, 265
avigan, 17
Azerbaijan, 81

bacteriology, 103, 113, 176, 179, 182
    public health implications of, 189
Baker, Charlie, 94
Bangladesh, 114
Barnes, Tori, 252
Barranquilla, 216
basic minimum income, 275
Bavaria, 28, 29, 53, 202
    AIDS, 29
behavioral fatigue, 69
Behavioural Insights Team, 69
Beijing, 89, 145
Beijing University of Chinese Medicine, 140
Belarus, 14, 25, 122, 144, 172
Belgium, 47, 97
Belgrade, 217
Belts and Roads Initiative, 140
Berlin, 125
Betjeman, John, 179
Bildt, Carl, 67
biomedicine
    solutions to epidemic disease, 86
Blitz, spirit of, 64, 210
Bloomberg, Michael, 43
Bnei Brak, 47
body shaming, 195
Boeing, 271
Bolsonaro, Jair, 36, 62, 64, 67, 246
    experts, 25
    masks, 89
    quack remedies, 17
    vertical distancing, 115
Botswana, 131
Braudel, Fernand, 120

Brazil, 14, 63
    informal sector, 135
    self-help by citizens, 172
bread, whole grain, 194
Brexit, 22, 74
Britain
    compliance, 210
    enforcement, 205
    masks, 208
British Medical Association, 240
Britton, Tom, 151, 168
Brodin, Petter, 151
Brostrøm, Søren, 21
Brüning, Heinrich, 20
Buddhist nations
    infection, 122
Bulgaria, 116
Burundi, 18
bushmeat, 267, 268

California, 38, 95, 133, 145
    mask mandate, 165
    masks, 209
Cambodia, 122
Cameron, David, 69
Cameron, James, 253
Canada
    care home mortality, 116
Canadian Medical Association, 86
cancer, 175
care homes, 162
    Britain, 117
    employees, 283
    mortality in, 115
CARES Act, 91, 93, 136
Caribbean, 123
Carlson, Johan, 173
Carville, James, 278
cash, 261
    as public health threat, 49
Catalonia, 145
Catholic Church, 11
Catholicism and the pandemic, 283
Cato Institute, 251
CDC, 24, 59, 83, 90, 92
    contact tracing, 111
    masks, 208
    zoonoses, 267
Cesarean births, 190
Charlotte, NC, 127
Chicago, 56
childcare, 38, 136, 138

children, as vectors, 139
China
    ability to take decisions, 12
    AIDS, 28
    economy growing again, 254
    enforcement, 203, 204
    firm measures, 64
    lunar new year, 190
    national identity, 170
    political stability, 11
    public relations campaign, 171
    public spitting, 42
    response to pandemic, 82, 102
chloroquine, 17
cholera, 42
    19C epidemics, 71
    20C, 86
    epidemic London 1853, 34
    epidemics of 19C, 14
    etiology, 15
    precautions against in nineteenth
        century, 49, 50
Christian Social Union, Germany, 53
chronic disease, 27, 43, 176, 191, 193
    individual responsibility, 184
churches, 38
    pandemic, 18, 88
    as public health threat, 47
    superspreading venues, 159
cities, flight from, 227
citrus greening, 191
civil society
    role in pandemic, 279
    role in public health, 199, 203
civilizing process, 185
class and the pandemic, 263
Clausewitz, Carl von, 9
cleanliness, 183, see hygiene, personal
Clueless, 188
Colorado, 63
commissions of inquiry, 21
communications technology and
        pandemic, 38
communion
    as public health threat, 47
comorbidities, 233
    effects on pandemic, 132
    susceptibility to Covid-19, 114
compelling behavior, 11
competence, 273
compliance, 62, 281
    state's tools to achieve, 40

with public health mandates, 199
with law, 7
condoms, 33, 35, 182, 195, 235
Connecticut, 46, 96, 211
consensus required by all political systems,
        10
conservatives' view of lockdown, 53, 77
constitution
    Germany, 244
    Sweden, 61
    US, 59, 93
construction industry, 271
contact tracing, 36
    Australia, 107
    Britain, 112
    China, 105
    defining contacts, 204
    Europe, 108
    Germany, 107, 111
    Louisiana, 111
    Massachusetts, 111
    New York, 111
    New Zealand, 107
    number of contacts named, 280
    South Korea, 106
    Taiwan, 102, 106
    Wuhan, 111
contagious disease laws, 28
    Denmark, 21
    Germany, 6, 41, 59
    Sweden, 60, 61, 73, 173
Conte, Giuseppe, 164
Copenhagen, 80, 125, 127
Corsica, 123
Corzine, Jon S., 168
cosmetic surgery, 224
coughing, public, 42
courts, 261
    pandemic regulation, 88
Covid-19
    antibody tests, 148
    etiology of, 16, 19
    quack remedies for, 17
    secondary flare ups, 145
crucial workers, 136
cruise ship industry, 271
cruise ship personnel, 37
cruise ships, 185
Cuba, 89, 123, 253
    AIDS, 28, 124
Cummings, Dominic, 21, 90, 207
Cuomo, Andrew, 94, 96, 108

cybersex, 188
cytokine storms, 141
Czech Republic, 122, 165, 211

Daily Mail, 206
Daily Telegraph, 206
Damme, Pierre van, 150
Davis, Mike, 261
Davos, 191
de Blasio, Bill, 95
  herd immunity, 95
debt slavery, 181
deconfinement, 211, 214
Defense Production Act, 93
Delhi, 205
democracies
  decision-making ability, 12
  led by women, 13
  pandemic mortality, 13
  pandemics, 10
Democrats, 63, 89
demography, effect on pandemic, 132
Deng Xiaoping, 189
dengue fever, 238
Denmark, 19, 24, 74, 99
  compliance, 210
  counterfoil to Sweden, 21
  masks, 167
  weddings, 111
density, urban, 132
Denver, 127
Department of Health, US, 243
Department of Homeland Security, 38
DeSantis, Ron, 94, 211
desertion, 180
DeWine, Mike, 94
Dharavi, 131, 190
diabetes, 175
Diamond Princess, 102
Diamond, Neil, 262
diphtheria, 177
Directly Observed Therapy, 281
disease
  causation, 176
  filth, 42, 176
  social incidence of, 113
disinfection, 48
  in nineteenth century, 50
dispersion factor, 160
distancing
  public health implications of, 183
divorce, 260

Djibouti, 131
Djokovic, Novak, 221
Do Not Resuscitate orders, 237
dressing during the pandemic, 39
drinking, 179
drug use, 43
due process
  pandemic, 88
Duterte, Rodrigo, 130

east coast, US, 133
Ebola, 15, 33, 85, 94, 157
economic effects of pandemic, 249
economic response to pandemic, 91, 135
Economist, 80
Ecuador, 58
Egypt, 121
elderly
  as victims of Covid-19, 112
  in Sweden, 70
  isolation of, 36
  protecting, 118
  susceptibility to Covid-19, 115
Electrolux, 256
emergencies, *see* exception, states of
emergencies, medical, 224
emergency measures, 57
emergency medical treatment
  and pandemic, 55
emergency room visits, 226
  Sweden, 227
  Taipei, 226
emerging illnesses, 193
energy use, decline in, 265
environmental effects, 264
epidemic disease
  history of, 31
epidemiologists
  as politicians, 20
epidemiology
  as determinng public health response, 14
epistocracy, 19
Ericsson, 256
Estonia, 58, 80, 122
eSwatini, 115
Ethics Council, Germany, 244
ethnic implications of pandemic, 263
ethnic minorities, 35
  Covid-19, 113
  susceptibility to Covid-19, 114
etiology of Covid-19, 138, 168
etiquette, 187

Etzioni, Amitai, 242
EU, 75, 90, 92
    borrowing programs, 275
eucharist, 47
    as public health issue, 44
eugenics, 181
Europe, eastern, 121
European Commission, 98, 255
Eurovision song contest, 97
euthanasia
    Nazi, 11, 245
exception, states of, 12
exceptionalism
    Sweden, 74, 75, 127
    US, 74
excess deaths, 225
excretion, public, 41
expertise
    pandemic, 66, 81
        Sweden, 67
    politics, 20
    preventive strategies, 25
    rule by, 19
extracorporeal membrane oxygenation,
    241

Facebook, 263, 275
facial recognition technology, 106
factory farming, 191
Falwell, Jerry, 18
Fangcang shelter hospitals, 104
farmworkers, 134
Fauci, Anthony, 26
Federal Reserve Board, 91
federalism, 91
    Australia, 92
    Germany, 92
felching, 184
Ferguson, Neil, 23, 100, 206
Fiji, 115, 124
Financial Times, 246
Finland, 25, 146
    masks, 167
fisting, 183
Fixx, James, 195
flattening the curve, 144
Flint, Michigan, 208
Florida, 25, 47, 95, 145
    farmers, 191
    masks, 208
Floyd, George, 89, 215
flu, 191

Fontana, Attilio, 53
Fox News, 77
frailty, 243
France
    antibody testing, 147
    change in authorities' approach, 201
    lockdown, 103, 201
    public compliance, 202
Frederiksen, Mette, 21
furloughing, 135

Galicia, 145
Galileo, 11
Gallup, 59
Garcetti, Eric, 209
gay bathhouses, 160
gays, 35
Gaza Strip, 124
gender implications of pandemic,
    263
generational antagonisms, 212, 264
geoepidemiology, 121
Georgia, 95, 161
German–Swedish Chamber of Commerce,
    76
Germany, 99
    enforcement of lockdown, 202
    exporter, 255
    view of Sweden, 76
giardiasis, 184
Giesecke, Johan, 77, 146, 152
gilets jaunes, 164
Global Health Security Index, 83, 101
globalization, 272
Goethe, 41
goods, safety of, 48
Goolsbee, Austan, 251
Gothenburg, 72
government advice on Covid-19, 50
governors, US
    public health role, 211
Great Barrington Declaration, 143
Great Recession, 277
Greece, 26, 80, 133
    enforcement, 205
    low rates of infection, 122
    measures for the elderly, 116
    refugee camps, 125
    reopening, 253
    technocratic government, 20
greenhouse gas emissions, 266
    cost of reducing, 267

greeting, habits of, 123, 187, 194
  styles of, 185
Guam, 123
Guatemala, 58
Guillain-Barré syndrome, 87
Guinea, 17
Gupta, Sunetra, 152

H6N2 influenza, 192
habits
  consequential for public health, 181
  disease, 43
  public health implications of, 175
Haiti, 130
Hajj, 46
Halpern, David, 69
hammer and dance strategy, 143
hand washing, 134
Handelsbanken, 256
handshaking, 185, 194, 259, 260, 284
Hanta, 85
Harbin, 103
Harries, Jenny, 26
harvesting, epidemiological, 162
Hawaii, 109, 123
hazmat suits, 34
health care financing, 137
health fascism, 195
health insurance
  lack of, 137
Hegel, G. F. W., 10
hepatitis, 191
herd immunity, 54, 79, 142
  Britain, 22, 24, 142
  Netherlands, 142
  prevalence, 147
  required for mitigation strategy, 145
  Stockholm, 148
  strategy, 69
  Sweden, 142, 172
  various sources, 143
HEROS Act, 93
Hidalgo County, 209
HIV, see AIDS
Hogan, Larry, 94
Holocaust, 181
homeless, 214
homeschooling, 205
homosexuality
  and tracing, 107
  definition of, 184
Hong Kong, 99, 234

care homes, 118
hospitality industry, 109, 271
hospitals
  Italy, 236
House of Commons, 88
House of Lords, 215
House of Representatives, US, 87
households
  multigenerational, 114, 126, 132, 136
  single-person, 78, 127, 132
Huanan Seafood Wholesale Market, 268
huanglongbing, 191
Hubei, 24, 46, 89, 99, 102, 126
  quarantines, 104
Human Rights Defenders Coalition,
  Malawi, 247
Hungary, 58, 122
hydroxychloroquine, 17, 18
hygiene hypothesis, 190
hygiene, personal, 186, 189, 260
  immunity implications of, 190
  public health implications of, 183

Iceland, 14, 123, 125, 139
illness
  social determinants of, 175
immigration, effect on public health, 283
immunity
  antibodies as measure of, 123, 151
  cross-reactive, 152, 161, 221
  cytokines, 153
  differentially distributed, 161
  disputes over, 150
  from vaccines, 148
  how measured, 150
  natural, 148, 152
  overreactive, 141
  personal hygiene, 186
  T cells, 152, 153
  to pandemic disease, 33
immunity passports, 138
incidence, variability, 126
India, 14, 41, 62, 130, 161
  informal sector, 135
  travel, 122
individual behavior
  and disease control, 27, 28
individual responsibility
  as public health tactic, 176
  public health, 174, 179, 184, 194
individualism, Swedish cult of, 78
Indonesia, 18, 63

infection
 social incidence of, 232
informal sector of the economy, 135
intensive care beds, 238
interactions, physical, 133
international organizations
 pandemic, 90
International Sanitary Conferences, 46
internet commerce, 134
iodine, 33
Iowa, 165
Iran, 18, 25, 46, 93, 99, 126, 147
 self-help, 172
Ireland, 26
Ischgl, 128, 147
 superspreading venue, 159
islands, 130
 able to protect themselves, 123
Isle of Wight, 75
Israel, 145
 weddings, 111
Itaewon, 107
Italy, 93, 96
 informal sector, 135
 lockdown, 14, 22, 29, 37, 39
 technocratic government, 20
Iwasaki, Akiko, 152

Japan, 14, 91
 elderly, 113
 firing workers, 135
 island nation, 123
 masks, 282
 public opinion, 200
 response to pandemic, 133
Jews, ultra-orthodox, 47
Jilin, 46
Johnson, Boris, 21, 24, 26, 74, 274
 hospitalization, 33
 illness, 89
 laggard response, 100
 reopening, 215
 resists lockdown, 22
 travel restrictions, 109
 whack-a-mole strategy, 145
Jyllands Posten, 76

Kalaf, Roula, 246
Känsö, 72
Kant, Immanuel, 10
Karachi, 190
Karolinska, 153, 167, 239

Keelung, 102
Kennedy Jr., Robert, 221
Kentucky, 205
Kenya, 131, 143
Kibera, 131, 190
Kigali, 131
Kinnock, Stephen, 207
Knigge, Adolphe, 187
Koch, Robert, 16, 51, 155, 176
Königsberg, 229
Kumasi, 269
Kumbh Mela, 46
Kyrgyzstan, 81

Lacalle Pou, Luis, 77
Lagos, 216
Lake of the Ozarks, 216
Lancet, 247
Lansing, MI, 211
Laos, 122
Latin America, 96
Latvia, 58, 80
leaders, and pandemic regulations, 89
Leicester, 72, 92, 114, 125, 145, 218, 252
Leitkultur, 283
leprosy, 31, 44
Lesotho, 115
levée en masse, 180
Levitt, Michael, 152
Lévy, Bernard-Henri, 217
libertarians
 herd immunity, 142
 Sweden, 77, 142
lifestyle, and disease, 43
Lind, Annika, 67
Linde, Ann, 65, 146
Liverpool, 216
lockdown
 Africa, 85
 beneficial effects of, 56
 Britain, 24
 business opinion of, 251, 252
 class aspects of, 229
 collateral damage of, 55, 56
 commerce, 252
 compliance with, 209
 costs of, 248
 economic effects of, 254
 enforcement of, 110
 loosening of, 63
 opening up, 79, 110, 211
 first nations to do so, 246

pleasant aspects of for well-off, 228
politicizing of, 216
protests against, 217
public opinion, 63, 214, 232
    China, 64
    Sweden, 65
strict, 130
timing of, 251
universal, 251
variable enforcement of, 109
Lombardy, 46, 53, 96, 99, 108
    intensive care beds, 241
London, 96, 127
    masks, 165
Longstocking, Pippi, 79
Lorenzo, 75
Los Angeles, 147, 205
Lukashenko, Alexander, 62, 144, 172
Lyme disease, 268

Macron, Emmanuel, 23, 26, 57, 136, 200,
        201, 202
    and quack remedies, 17
Madagascar, 17
Madrid, 147
Magh Mela, 46
Maine, 122, 125, 132, 224, 262
    masks, 208
    reopening, 253
Malawi, 131, 246
Maldives, 123
Mallorca, 253
Malmö, 96
Manaus, 148
Manhattan, 227
Mann, Thomas, 191
Mao, 139
Maoris, 284
Marburg, 85
Marcq-en-Barœul, 42
Marseille, 203
Maryland, 94, 204
masks
    aerosol transmission, 164
    Asia, 162
    Britain, 165
    consensus on their usefulness, 163
    controversy over, 162
    enforcement, 207
    geographical prevalence, 164
    mandated, 165, 234
    politicization, 164

recognized as useful, 138
    supply, 163
    Sweden, 128, 166, 207
    Swedish rejection of, 158
    usefulness of, 235
Massachusetts, 94
masturbation, 188
Mauritius, 115, 123
Mbeki, Thabo, 16
McQueen, Steve, 168
Mecca, 46
Medicaid, 137
medical procedures
    postponing, 224
Medicare, 137
Medina, 46
Melbourne, 145
Merkel, Angela, 49, 89
MERS, 33, 85, 157, 160, 193
Mexico, 41, 258
Miami, 147
miasma, 176
Michigan, 205, 211
Mills, Janet, 253
Minneapolis, 127, 215
Minnesota, 38, 116
minorities, ethnic
    infection, 232
Missouri, 216
mitigation strategy, 23, 53, 65, 68,
        144
    herd immunity, 142
    protecting vulnerable, 112
MMR vaccinations, 219
Modi, Narendra, 62, 247, 280
Moldavia, 80
Mongolia, 28
monogamy, 188
Montesquieu, 10
Moore, Michael, 208
moral hazard, 181
Morgan, Piers, 51
Morocco, 121
mortality
    excess, 84
    figures, Brazil, 88
    Sweden, 67, 79
MRSA, 191
Mudanjiang, 105
multiculturalism, effect on public health,
        283
Mumbai, 131, 147, 232

Musk, Elon, 54, 251
  and quack remedies, 17
Myanmar, 122

Nairobi, 17, 131
Nankai University, 140
National Bioethics Committee, Italy, 242
National Institute for Health and Care
    Excellence, *see* NICE
National Institutes of Health, 241
National Review, 77
nationalism, economic, 272
Native Americans, 96, 134
Navajo, 59, 125, 134
Nazis, 181
  public health, 194
needle exchanges, 103, 129, 160
Netflix, 228, 247
Netherlands, 14, 25, 29, 56, 65, 97,
    147
  geoepidemiology of, 129
New Jersey, 46, 96, 168
New Mexico, 59
New Scientist, 148
New South Wales, 125
New York, 27, 46, 96, 133
New York City, 42, 56, 127
  enforcement, 203
  mask requirement, 163
New York Times, 80
New Zealand, 97, 99, 103, 123, 126,
    146
  enforcement, 203, 206
  travel shut down, 190
Newsom, Gavin, 94
NHS, 75, 117
  postponed procedures, 224
  rationing, 237
Nicaragua, 14, 54, 62, 172
NICE, 237, 243
noise
  as public health threat, 262
non-pharmaceutical interventions, 32
norovirus, 185
North Korea, 123
North Macedonia, 81
Northern League, 53, 217
Norway, 19, 25, 74, 78, 96, 116, 128
  compliance, 210
nudge theory, 68, 169
Nudge Unit, 69
Nutter, Michael, 94

Obama, Barack, 94
obesity, 43, 175, 195
OECD, 255
Old Testament, 31
  dietary prescriptions, 32
Operation Warp Speed, 221
oral sex, 183, 184
Orangi Town, 190
Orbán, Viktor, 275
Oslo, 127, 233
outercourse, 188, 260
outsourcing work, 263
oxytetracycline, 191

Pacific archipelago, 124
Pakistan, 18, 62, 135
  travel, 122
palm civets, 142
Pan Leiting, 140
Panama, 36
pandemic, Covid-19
  routes of spread, 98
pandemics
  as political events, 10
pangolins, 187, 268
Paris, 63, 126, 201, 227
Parliament, UK, 87
Pasteur, Louis, 176
Paul, Rand, 142
Payroll Protection Plan, US, 135
Pelosi, Nancy, 164
People's Party, Denmark, 284
Peru, 58, 131
pets, 186
pharmaceuticals, 272
Philadelphia, 42
Philippines, 124, 130, 135, 238
phone apps, 275
  contact tracing, 106, 158
pilgrims
  as public health threat, 46, 105, 126
plague, 31, 42, 176, 185
Poland, 122
police powers
  used in pandemic, 59
polio, 44, 186
politicians
  blaming experts, 20
pollution, 257
polygamy, 188
population density, and pandemic, 125, 132
populism, 181

government funding, 86
pandemic, 25, 67
pornography, 188
Porte d'Aix, 203
postponed treatments
developing world, 226
poverty rate during pandemic, 92
Powis, Stephen, 26
PPE, 75, 116, 272
Africa, 132
precautions, individual, 235
preprints, scientific, 15
Prescott, AZ, 194
presymptomatic transmission, 157
Pritzker, J. B., 94
privacy, 275, 276
hindrance to public health efforts, 280
public health implications, 107, 228
vaccination, 221
Private Eye, 206, 215
prohibition, 257
promiscuity, 188
protective gear, *see* PPE
protests
pandemic, 88
public goods, 287
public health
curtails individual rights, 197
democracy, 180
different approaches, 179
enforcement of, 202
environmentalist, 177
history of, 173
individual responsibility, 182
individual susceptibility, 178
individualization of, 197
sanitation, 178
totalitarian, 181
voluntary compliance with, 173
what citizens owe the state, 181
Public Health England, 21, 92
public health interventions
harshness of, 130
public opinion on government measures,
200
public urination laws, 41
Puerto Rico, 114, 123
Pune, 147
punishment, as tool of governance, 11
punishment for violating public health
regulations, 105
Putin, Vladimir, 90

Qatar, 148
Qinghai, 204
Qom, 46
Quakers, 185
quarantine, 31
China, 104
domestic, 100, 125
exodus from, 109
expense of, 129
household, 51
internal, 46
SARS victims, 27
travelers, 51, 215
targeted, 14, 39, 102
antecedents of, 51
techniques of, 35
quarantine law, 1806, Sweden, 72
quarantinism, neo-, 51
Qingdao, 105

Raoult, Didier, 17
rate of transmission, 97
Reagan, Ronald, 282
recession
economic, 248
public health effects of, 258
regulationist system of sex work, 192
religious leaders and the pandemic, 18
Republicans, 63, 89, 125
response to pandemic
delays to, 98
Rhode Island, 46, 96, 125
Riga, 177
rimming, 184
Roma, 134
Romania, 58
Rotterdam, 129
Ruhr, 125
Rusizi, 131
Russell, George William, 19
Russia, 217
Rutte, Mark, 65
Rwanda, 47, 156
Ryan, Mike, 66

safe sex, 35, 185
SAGE, 19, 23, 69
Independent, 19
masks, 165
sailors, cargo, 37
Saint Peter's cathedral, 47
Samoa, 124

San Francisco, 85, 162
Sandinista Party, 54
sanitation, 134
Santa Clara, 147
Santa Monica, 209
SARS, 13, 27, 33, 85, 89, 157, 193
  decoding of virus, 15
  immunity, 153
  TCM used against, 140
Saudi Arabia, 13, 46, 76, 85, 126
  elderly, 113
  royal family, 126
Scania, 80, 125
Schengen agreement, 97
Schiphol, 129
schools
  kept open, 138
  public vs. private, 231
  reopening, 139, 212
schoolteachers, 212, 264
science
  as basis for prevention, 18
  dictating preventive strategies, 23
Scientific Advisory Group for Emergencies,
    see SAGE
scientific cooperation in face of pandemic,
    14
Scotland, 96
screening, see testing
seatbelts, 163, 168
Seattle, 127
SEB, 256
second wave of pandemic, 80
Segria, 145
self-driving cars, 238
self-employed
  pandemic, 135
Senate, US, 87
Senegal, 131
Seoul, 95, 107, 145, 159
Serbia, 122
Sévigné, Madame de, 183
sex
  and disease, 32
sex dolls, 188
sex prevalence of Covid-19, 113
sex toys, 183
sex workers, 34, 107, 185, 187, 192, 270
  Sweden, 192
sex, distanced, 260
sexually transmitted diseases, 16, 27, 29, 43
  Sweden, 72, 116, 175, 182, 187, 195

Shapps, Grant, 109
Shenzhen, 142
Shetlands, 123
Shuluta, 36
sickness pay programs, 136
Singapore, 27, 85, 99, 145
  care homes, 118
  enforcement, 203
  immigrant labor, 284
singing
  dangerous activity, 18
  public health threat, 47, 81, 111, 262
Sioux, 125
Siracusa Principles, 57
skiing, and pandemic, 127
slaughterhouses
  superspreading venues, 159
Slovakia, 165
Slovenia, 122
slums, and pandemic, 131
smallpox, 176
  Sweden, 72
smoking, 43, 113, 179
sneezing, public, 42
snitching, 206
Snow, John, 34, 174, 185, 234
Social Democratic Party, Sweden, 77, 81
social distancing, 66, 87, 235, 260
  class aspects of, 227
  difficult in developing world, 134
  Finland, 167
  France, 163, 201
  history of, 187
  Hollywood, 188
  informal enforcement, 206
  masks, 163, 165
  protests against, 217
  public health implications of, 185
  reopening, 252
  Somalis, 284
  Sweden, 79, 166, 167
  violations, 89
  voluntary, 172, 210
socialization of behavior, 40, 41, 129, 283
Söder, Markus, 53
Solomon Islands, 124
Somalis, 284
Sonora, 97
South Africa, 56, 88, 109, 121, 130, 131, 246
  enforcement, 203
South Carolina, 253
South Dakota, 77, 125, 165, 211

South Korea, 64, 93, 96, 99, 282
  as island, 123
  privacy, 229
Southampton, 156
Spain, 116, 147
  enforcement, 203
  reopening, 253
Spanish flu, 42, 85, 112, 121, 124, 143, 194
  economic effects of, 249
  masks, 162
speed of response to pandemic, 98
spitting, public, 42
spittoons, 42
sports, professional, 214
Sputnik V vaccine, 222
Sri Lanka, 253
Staffordshire, 216
Starbucks, 208
Starmer, Keith, 88
state of emergency, 57
Stenhouse, John, 34
Stichler, Christian, 76
Stockholm, 76, 125, 127
  closures, 171
streptomycin, 191
subsidies, government, 271
sugar tax, 43
superspreading, 159
  aerosol transmission, 161
  airports, 161
  by individuals, 159
  by professions, 160
  means of combating, 160
suppression strategy, 23, 24, 55, 144
Supreme Court
  Austria, 88
  Romania, 88
  US, 87
Sweden, 14
  AIDS, 28
  alleged lack of powers, 60
  approach to pandemic, 171, 198
  as exemplar, 73
  change in tactics, 29
  compliance, 210
  demographic characteristics, 127
  economic effects of pandemic, 254
  enforcement, 203
  eugenics, 182
  exporter, 255
  hands-off approach, 54
  public health based on expertise, 19

relaxed approach, 286
  traditional approach to contagious
    disease, 71
  use of expertise, 26
  voluntary curtailment of behavior, 198
Sweden Democrat party, 53, 69, 74, 77
swine flu
  mass vaccination against in 1976, 87
Switzerland, 209
symptoms of Covid-19, 100
syphilis, 44, 72, 182, 220
  antibiotic resistant, 184, 191

Taipei, 226
Taiwan, 123, 125
  contact tracing, 106
  economy growing again, 254
  foreign arrivals, 105
  response to pandemic, 101
Tanzania, 18, 41
targeted quarantine, 204
  costs of, 248
  economic effect of, 254
TCM, 139, 268
  part of Chinese culture, 140
  practitioners, 140
  treated as equivalent to Western
    medicine, 140
teachers, 232
teachers' unions, 26
  Britain, 136
technocracy
  government by, 19
technology, and lockdowns, 134
Tegnell, Anders, 19, 65, 71, 75, 76, 80, 81,
    127
  care home mortality, 116
  cult of personality, 26
  denies role of asymptomatics, 158
  herd immunity, 146, 149, 150
  masks, 166, 168
Telangana, 130
telecommuting, 228, 229, 262
  Japan, 134
  who can?, 230
telemedicine, 224, 261, 275
Tesla, 54, 251
test and trace policy, 52, 79
testing, 36, 94
  antigen, 155
  Austria, 146
  China, 104

testing (cont.)
  Iceland, 146
  New York, 104
  PCR, 156
  sample pooling, 156
  South Korea, 107
  universal, 155
Texas, 59, 95, 145, 205
  masks, 208, 209
Thailand, 122, 282
Thunberg, Greta, 266
tobacco use, 43
toilet paper, 183
Tönnies, Ferdinand, 78
totalitarianism, 181
tourism, 271
  lockdown, 252
traditional Chinese medicine, see TCM
transmissible diseases, 43
transmission via objects, 48
transportation, 266
travel
  as dangerous, 189
  infection, 122
  public health implications, 189
travel restrictions, 24, 45, 58, 59, 97, 99
  Australia, 107, 124
  Britain, 109
  China, 103
  Iceland, 125
  New Zealand, 107
  rural areas, 125
  US, 108
  Vietnam, 131
treatments, postponed, 225
triage
  Austria, 240
  Belgium, 241
  Britain, 240, 243
  disabled, 243
  elderly in hospitals, 117
  France, 242
  Germany, 244
  Italy, 241
  Massachusetts, 243
  medical, 236
  New York, 241
  Sweden, 239
  Switzerland, 243
  Washington, 243
trolleyology, 237
Trump, Donald, 64, 67, 74, 81, 83, 93, 246
  expertise, 18, 25, 81
  herd immunity, 142
  hospitalization, 33
  inattentive, 100
  masks, 89
  press conferences, 95
  public opinion, 200, 215
  quack remedies, 17
  social media, 275
  travel restrictions, 108
trust in government, 68, 172, 199, 281
  Sweden, 65, 78, 80
tuberculosis, 175
  drug-resistant, 191
Turkey, 36, 245
Turkmenistan, 14
Tuscany, 47
Tuskegee experiments, 220, 233
typhoid fever, 176
Typhoid Mary, 157, 160

Uganda, 131
Ukraine, 48, 122
Umrah, 46
UN, 58
UN International Covenant on Civil and
      Political Rights, 57
unemployment, 91, 135
unemployment benefits, 135, 256
uniforms, 180
United Teachers Los Angeles, 212
universal testing
  universities, 213
universities, 272
  response to pandemic, 213
urban sanitation, 178
Uruguay, 14
US
  compliance, 211
  eugenics, 182
  response to pandemic, 83
utilitarianism
  triage, 237
  various arguments for, 238

vaccination, 11, 217
  compulsory, 40
  flu, 220
  public acceptance of, 219
  religious objections, 219
  Sweden, 173
vaccination law, 1853, Sweden, 72

vaccine development, 221
  cost of, 138, 156
  global competition, 278
Vallance, Patrick, 22, 26
Van Morrison, 217
vegans, 195
vegetarianism, 187
Veneto, 96
ventilators, 75, 238, 244, 245
Vermont, 109, 122, 132
Victorians, sexual habits, 188
Vietnam, 27, 85, 122, 130
  system of social control, 282
Vrångö, 81
vulnerable, protecting, 112

wage support schemes, 135
Wakefield, Andrew, 221
Wales, 96
Wallenberg, Jacob, 254
Walmart, 208
Wang Wei, 140
Warsaw ghetto, 182
Washington, 95
Waugh, Evelyn, 41
Wayback Machine, 21
Weimar Republic, 20
west coast, US, 133
West Hollywood, 209
West Nile virus, 268
West Virginia, 116
wet markets, 142, 187, 268
white-collar employees, 39
Whitmer, Gretchen, 94, 211
Whitty, Chris, 26
WHO, 13, 66, 80, 82, 83, 90, 226

asymptomatic transmission, 157
guidelines for allocating resources, 239
herd immunity, 148
masks, 163, 166
phone apps, 276
vaccination, 219
wildlife trade, 269
Williamsburg, 47
Wisconsin, 116
women's rights, 192
work from home, *see* telecommuting
workers
  affected by pandemic, 38
  crucial, 37
    children of, 231
  divisions among, 39
Wuhan, 82, 98, 103, 204
  contact tracing, 105, 111
  testing, 104
  travel restrictions, 45
Wyoming, 211

Xining, 204

yellow fever, 42, 72
young, as vectors of transmission,
  138

Zealand, 80, 125
Zika, 15
Zimbabwe, 131
Zingaretti, Nicola, 90
zombie companies, 136
Zoom, 39, 228, 261
zoonoses, 186, 193, 267, 279
Zurich, 112